Chaos,

Complexity,

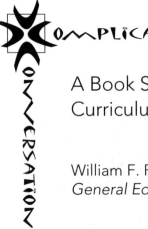

OMPLICATED

CONVERSATION

A Book Series of Curriculum Studies

William F. Pinar
General Editor

VOLUME 6

PETER LANG
New York • Washington, D.C./Baltimore • Bern
Frankfurt am Main • Berlin • Brussels • Vienna • Oxford

Chaos, Complexity, Curriculum, and Culture

A CONVERSATION

EDITED BY William E. Doll, Jr.,
M. Jayne Fleener,
Donna Trueit,
John St. Julien

PETER LANG
New York • Washington, D.C./Baltimore • Bern
Frankfurt am Main • Berlin • Brussels • Vienna • Oxford

Library of Congress Cataloging-in-Publication Data

Chaos, complexity, curriculum, and culture: a conversation /
edited by William E. Doll, Jr., M. Jayne Fleener, Donna Trueit, John St. Julien.
p. cm. — (Complicated conversation; v. 6)
Includes bibliographical references and index.
1. Education—Curricula—Philosophy. 2. Postmodernism and education.
I. Doll, William E. II. Fleener, M. Jayne III. St. Julien, John.
IV. Trueit, Donna. V. Series.
LB1570.C44   375'.001—dc22   2004014127
ISBN 978-0-8204-6780-1
ISSN 1534-2816

Bibliographic information published by **Die Deutsche Bibliothek**.
Die Deutsche Bibliothek lists this publication in the "Deutsche
Nationalbibliografie"; detailed bibliographic data is available
on the Internet at http://dnb.ddb.de/.

Excerpt from "Gifts" by Shu Ting from *A Splintered Mirror:*
Chinese Poetry from the Democracy Movement, translated by Donald Finkel.
Translation copyright 1991 by Donald Finkel. Reprinted by permission of North Point Press,
a division of Farrar, Straus and Giroux, LLC.

The images in Chapter 4 from Brent Davis, Dennis Sumara, and Rebecca Luce-Kapler,
Engaging Minds: Learning and Teaching in a Complex World. Mahwah NJ, 2000.
Reprinted by permission of the publisher. All rights reserved.

Cover art: *Cherry (Fractal 22)* by Mike Fifield (www.cognitivedistortion.com)
Cover concept by Kerri Richardson
Cover design by Lisa Barfield

∞

© 2005, 2008 Peter Lang Publishing, Inc., New York
29 Broadway, 18th Floor, New York, NY 10006
www.peterlang.com

Printed in the United States of America

To those who have led us in the past,
now travel with us in the present,
and will guide us in the future
in our quest to understand
the complexity of Being,
we dedicate this book.

Contents

Fourth Iteration: Aesthetics, Culture, and Learning

Illustrations

Figures

Table

 # Preface

At a New Orleans AERA meeting (1994), Robert Kahn suggested we form an AERA Special Interest Group (AERA SIG), focusing on chaos and complexity theory. During his tenure as president (1995–1998), we became aware that chaos and complexity were two theories, not one. During Jayne Fleener's tenure as our SIG President (1998–2001), she and others suggested we bring forth a book exploring what chaos and complexity were all about. Such a task proved daunting, for even with the strong popularity of these concepts, too few of us could really acquire the grasp we wanted of the concepts or their articulation. Various drafts of the book came forward and many essays were written and rewritten and, again, rewritten.

During Sherrie Reynolds' tenure as SIG president (2001–2004) our recursions were productive and a book began to emerge. William Pinar, friend, colleague, and supporter, encouraged our work and asked us to submit for his Complicated Conversations series with Peter Lang. Chris Myers of Lang (USA) was both supportive and patient as we continued writing and rewriting. To create conversations we wrote small editorial comments, inserted into text boxes, into various essays.

During Jens Rasmussen's tenure as our Chaos and Complexity SIG President (2004–), this book was brought to life. We editors and authors hope readers will benefit from our struggles in understanding and elucidating these New Sciences (and their import for curriculum) as we have.

Our deep gratitude is extended to Peter Lang and its staff, especially to Lisa Dillon, who aided and gently prodded us to completion. Without such perturbation we doubt this book would have emerged. We are also indebted to graduate assistants Sarah Smitherman, Kerri Richardson, and Jie Yu for their time and technological skills.

M. JAYNE FLEENER

Introduction:
Chaos, Complexity,
Curriculum, and Culture
Setting Up the Conversation

Chaos and complexity are perspectives of New Science and postmodern inquiry that may implicate significant changes in how we understand and approach curriculum studies. As parts of a constellation of postmodern conversations, chaos and complexity entail a (Ludwig) Wittgensteinian way of "seeing-as" that has implications for cultural systems of meaning. Chaos and complexity approaches may offer ways of "showing the fly out of the fly bottle" as curricular debates and issues of schooling are explored, perceived, and in some cases dissolved from these potentially postmodern perspectives.

My own introduction to and involvement with chaos and complexity is subsumed under the umbrella of New Sciences emerging over the last thirty years of the twentieth century. I have been involved with New Science now for about fifteen years. My first attraction to New Science was through chaos mathematics and fractal geometry. As a then mathematics teacher, the challenges to traditional deductive systems were exciting for me as well as my students. The beauty of fractal art, the creation of fractal music, and the modeling of nature reconnected mathematics with the Greek notion of the "music of the spheres." Mathematics and the natural world of which we are a part became a dance of creativity and emerging pattern. Through fractal geometry, mathematics seemed infused with creativity, beauty, and relationship. The study of mathematics seemed potentially connected, holistic, and meaningful rather than lost in the fragmentation of modern mathematics.

As a philosopher and curricularist, my explorations into chaos mathematics were also transformative. Having long ago rejected traditional analytic philosophy and moved beyond the self-centeredness and nihilism of existentialism, I found in New Science approaches to meaning, purpose, and systems an understanding that seemed compatible with my postmodern leanings. As a logician, I was able to study the power of recursion and the emergence of a new logic that was relational and evolving rather than analytic and deductive.

I also have found and begun to explore how New Science ideas can transform our thinking about schooling and the curriculum. How can the curriculum reflect and facilitate learning from these emerging perspectives? How do our very ideas of the curriculum, teaching, and learning change when we understand social institutions and relations from a New Science perspective?

I have been fortunate to meet kindred spirits along the way as I have pursued my journey into New Science. Many of those who have contributed to this book are the innovators and companions with whom I have shared this journey, often (re)discovering the very paths they have already traversed. They too will tell their stories of sense-making and New Science. Their differing approaches and understandings will contribute to ongoing conversations as we shift our thinking from modernist ideas about schooling to transitory postmodern perspectives with uncertain yet promising futures.

To provide a beginning for conversation, I offer a perspective of the field of New Science that has helped me make sense of the many different approaches to New Science studies. In particular, I explore the question: What is New Science? I will offer a perspective of postmodernism characterized by the logics of meaning, systems, and relationship that will connect New Science with postmodernism and offer my own interpretive framework for applying New Science to education.

What Is New Science?

There is no consensus, nor should there be, on how to describe or define New Science. Typically, scholarship that refers to "New Science" includes the techniques and explorations of complex adaptive systems theory, the theory of dissipative structures, or chaos theory. Incorporated into the latter are chaos mathematics and dynamical systems theories. The constellation of "New Sciences," however, offers more than new analytic tools. The promise of New Science is in reconnecting us with geometries of relationship, poetry of interconnectedness, dynamic emergence, patterns that connect. Challenging "representational" epistemologies (Osberg and Biesta, 2003), the New Sciences reflect a significant shift away from efforts to model a hidden reality or uncover truths of nature. As Deborah Osberg and Gert Biesta (2003) say:

> Complexity's challenge to representation comes from the idea that models of complex systems appear *not* to be representations in the usual sense of the word. They cannot be understood to "stand for" or depict reality. They don't say something about how the world really is.... For Paul Cilliers, complex systems can't be reduced because of the nonlinear nature of their interconnections which means the information they contain is not in the individual elements making up the system, but *distributed* in their pattern of connections. (5)

In other words, the New Sciences of complexity fundamentally challenge the underlying epistemologies of modern science and disrupt the quest for certainty, truth, and objective knowledge. Reducing processes fundamentally destroys complex relationships and emergent properties of dynamical systems. The clockwork universe no longer is a viable metaphor for the breathing, growing, evolving, complex world in which we live. The New Sciences do not have, as a goal, therefore, to reduce complexity, but to embrace it.

The perspectives of New Science that make sense to me, namely complex adaptive systems, dissipative structures, and chaos dynamics, are different perspectives of complexity. Complex adaptive systems theory offers perspectives of organic growth and biological processes. Autopoiesis as "self-creation" or "self-organization" is an aspect of living systems that challenges the determinism or mechanics of Darwinian evolutionary growth. Extended to social systems, complex adaptive systems theory reconceptualizes ways of thinking about life, living, social organization, and meaning as a social dynamic.

Dissipative structures consider models of dynamic emergence in fluid and quantum interactions. The turbulence of rivers or the dynamics of the atmosphere are aspects of dissipative structures that consider how energy and emergence operate at varying levels of organization and disorganization. Perturbation, organization, and exchanges of energy and matter are features of dissipative structures analyses that are used to explore emergence and dynamic interchange. Playing on the Newtonian notion that energy dissipates to eventually lead to system death, dissipative structures display exactly the opposite kind of behavior. Thus, rather than reaching a stable equilibrium state of maximum entropy, dissipative structures engage with their environments, reaching and utilizing critical points of instability to achieve higher states of organizational stability and complexity.

Chaos dynamics, as another perspective of New Science, considers recurring patterns across layers of complexity. Patterns are explored not for their regularities but for their irregularities, bumpiness, and brokenness. Fractal dimensions, strange attractors, and patterns of organization in randomness are aspects of chaos dynamics that lend themselves to a different kind of meaning—and appreciation for self-similarity and emergence through systems feedback and recursive dynamics.

The New Sciences of Complex Adaptive Systems, dissipative structures, and chaos dynamics challenge the Newtonian assumptions of an orderly universe and an underlying analytic. Like Giambattista Vico's *New Science,* (*NS*) written almost three hundred years ago, the New Sciences are approaches to meaning that go beyond the myopic perspective of Modernism or the techniques of modern science. Vico's own challenges shed light on the new analytic as Vico, himself, objected to the implications of the mechanical and mathematical perspectives arising from the new sciences of the seventeenth century.

Vico's New Science

Vico explored an approach to understanding our traditions and approaches to meaning as early as the first decade of the eighteenth century. These ideas were ultimately represented in his book *New Science*[1] whose title was an ironic twist on the science fervor of the times. His approach was to explore the evolution of culture and society by considering the relationships among language, meaning, creativity, morality, and emotion:

> In this way, my New Science simultaneously offers a *history of the ideas, customs, and deeds of humankind.* From these three topics, we shall derive the principles of the history of human nature, which are the principles of universal history that we previously seemed to lack. (Vico, 1999, 368)[2]

Contrary to the influences at the time, Vico rejected the study of nature, which emphasized categorization, measurement, and prediction, and stressed the study of culture and of human societies. Like Francis Bacon, Vico argued that in order to transform the conditions of one's method and cultural context, study should focus on human endeavors, our own social, evolutionary path. Critical of Bacon and Descartes, however, Vico rejected their emphasis on rational thought and the appropriation of nature. Only when we fail to understand ourselves and our own cultural contexts do we approach nature as something separate from us: "When man is sunk in ignorance, he makes himself the measure of the universe" (120).

The ancient wisdom of poetic logic, according to Vico, was to invent ways of understanding our natural world, not through analysis but through interpretation of our own imagery, stories, myths, and metaphors. Rather than emphasizing quantitative measure, poetic logic encourages relational, social, and human approaches to meaning.

Vico uses the term "logic" in a different way from Aristotle before him and later logicians of the nineteenth and twentieth centuries. He attempts to capture the "middle ground" of "logos." Language itself becomes an interaction among rather than a transmission of meanings. Thus, rather than underlying structure, poetic logic explores emergent and dynamic meanings revealed through human discourse.

Vico discusses three ages of human society in his *New Science*—the first age is predominated by poetic wisdom:

> As the first wisdom of the pagan world, poetic wisdom must have begun with a metaphysics which, unlike the rational and abstract metaphysics of today's scholars, sprang from the senses and imagination of the first people. (375)

The weaker its power of reasoning, the more vigorous the human imagination grows. (185)

The poetic wisdom of the ancients has been lost, according to Vico:

The countless abstract expressions which permeate our languages today have divorced our civilized thought from our senses....The art of writing has greatly refined the nature of our thought; and the use of numbers has intellectualized it....As a result, we are by nature incapable of forming the vast image of that mistress which some call 'Sympathetic Nature.'...We are likewise incapable of entering into the vast imaginative powers of the earliest people. (378)

The second age of human society is characterized, according to Vico, as the Age of Authority or the Age of Heroes. Originally, the authority was of a divine nature, evolving, however, to human authority. Human authority, as an exercise of free will, suppressed primitive urges: "so to control their bodily impulses" (388). Following human authority is the time of the authority of nature. While divine authority places the human context within the natural environment, human authority creates hierarchies of authority and heroes. Hierarchies of authority relationships among humans are created as heroes or rulers are identified.

The third age of human society emphasizes reason. The shift is an indication of a failing rather than an advancement of society:

When people cannot know the truth, they strive to follow what is certain and defined. In this way, even if their intellect cannot be satisfied by abstract knowledge, *scienza*, at least their will may repose in common knowledge, *coscienza*." (137)

The language of science divorces us from the poetic logic of inspiration. As described by Paul Colilli (1997):

The fate of many epistemological modes was sealed by Galileo in the moment when he founded modern natural science. In order to understand the book of the universe, Galileo predicated, we must learn how to read the language in which it is composed, and the basis for interpreting the world of nature consists of "figures, numbers and movements"..."not smell, nor taste, nor sounds." (50)

The emphasis on reason has separated us from the poetic logic of our ancestors. In this age of reason, Vico describes how "thinking is completely divorced from the body" (Colilli, 1997, 4) and meaning is restricted by science. A contemporary of Isaac Newton, Vico rebelled against, while anticipating, the consequences of what has become the modern paradigm with its emphasis on measured reasoning. According to Vico, this third age of human society will collapse back to more primitive, connected, relational, spiritual origins.

Vico struggled with the role of philosophy to re-create a poetic wisdom. The tension between technical reason and poetic logic is most evident as philosophy tries to explore this conflict: "If philosophy is to benefit humankind, it must raise and support us as frail and fallen beings, rather than strip us of our nature or abandon us in our corruption" (Vico, 1999, 129). Speaking

metaphorically, Vico's New Science is an approach to philosophy that cele-
brates the poetic wisdom of our ancestors and moderates rationality with creativity, inspiration, and myth.

> To summarize, I have defined the three principles of my New Science as divine
> providence, the moderation of passions through marriage, and the immortality
> of human souls attested by burial. And I have adopted the criterion that what-
> ever all or most people feel must be the rule of social life. . .These are the bound-
> aries of human reason, and transgressing them means abandoning our humanity.
> (360)

Applied to our current contexts, Colilli (1997) presents a late twentieth
century perspective of Vico's approach based on Vico's notion of poetic
logic:

> Poetic logic as a contemporary theory assumes a well-defined status of relevance
> if we are of the conviction that the solution to any interpretative problem must
> be rooted in the interplay among matter, spirit, and the everyday operations of
> the human imagination. (xv)

The promise of the contemporary version of New Science, for us, is not
a reinvention or rediscovery of the past, or an expansion of the powerful tools
of modern science, but a manifestation of a poetic logic that will allow us to
invent new ways of being in our natural world, new ways of understanding,
and new ways of interacting that celebrate and explore the interplay among
matter and spirit, knowing and meaning, imagination and reality. The story
of the constellation of approaches captured under the umbrella of the New
Sciences of chaos and complexity is the narrative of transmutation as modern
society attempts to reconnect with a way of being that is more holistic, relational, and meaningful without being retroactive as a repeating of the past.
The New Sciences mark a shift, a recursive revisiting of our poetic understandings. Understood from the perspective of Vico's poetic logic as New
Science, tracing the origins of the New Sciences of chaos and complexity is
important for understanding how our own previous scientific inquiry has
served to separate us from our natural environment and ourselves. Likewise
as an exploration, New Science potentially reconnects us with our own natural, mythical, spiritual, and metaphorical ways of knowing by offering an
approach to relationship, meaning, and systems that overcomes the limitations of modernist emphasis on quantification, measurement, and certainty.

Modernism, Quantification, and Certainty

Understanding the science of modernism will offer insight into how we
as a society have created our underlying myths and metaphors of meaning. In
dialectic with modern science, the New Sciences of chaos and complexity

respond to and challenge modern science while reinventing new metaphors and ways of thinking about our world and ourselves. Whatever we consider the origins of modernity, whether, for example, we consider the Reformation, the advent of modern science, the Industrial Revolution, or the French and American Revolutions as the origins of modernism, the scientific method has become the paragon of truth, the ideal for reasoning, and the model of fairness and justice during the modern era. Beliefs in universal truth, objective measures, social progress, and the power of individual rationality are consequences of an emphasis on the scientific method as the paragon of rationality. These beliefs form the cornerstones of modernity that affect all aspects of our social lives including our educational, political, economic, and social institutions.

Scientific methodology includes both empirical/testable measures and abstract/mathematical formalizations of theory. Law-like relationships in nature can be hypothesized and tested by mathematics. Assuming mathematics to be objective and pure, applying mathematical measurement allows for abstraction and confirmation. Mathematics offers the means for predictive calculation and nature becomes quantifiable, predictable, and controllable. As Edmund Husserl (1997/1954) describes:

> By means of pure mathematics and the practical art of measuring, one can produce. . .a completely new kind of inductive prediction; namely, one can "calculate." (33)

We have confused mathematics as a tool for mathematics as the representation of reality or truth. In the process, we have forgotten that mathematics is our own invention or creation. Confusing our tools of mathematics with some hidden, underlying reality, our guiding metaphor of modernism has been that the world and all that is in it behaves like a clock. Clocks are predictable. The inner workings of clocks can be examined piecemeal. Clocks invite measurement and the treatment of time as an absolute. The consequence of this view is that we have ignored spiritual, aesthetic, and relational realities, focusing only on that which can be measured. As Susan Griffin (1980) describes:

> And it is said that nature can be understood only by reduction, that only by reducing her to numbers does she become clear. . . . It is decided that that which cannot be measured and reduced to number is not real. It is questioned whether or not motion is real. It is discovered that motion can be measured by measuring space through which movement moves and the time in which the moving takes place. It is decided motion is real. . . . It is said that God is a mathematician. (11–14)

Galileo hypothesized that we could use mathematics to explore nature; however, this method has become overgeneralized as we, in the modern era, have confused our models for the things they represent. These models have lost their "as if" quality and become not just the way we understand but that which we take as given. As Vico predicted, we have emphasized the rational over the relational, the given over experience, and truth over interpretation and feeling. Because we feel we can know nature better than ourselves by virtue of objective measures and mathematical prediction, we have separated understanding of ourselves from scientific investigation or tried to reduce the humanities to quasi-scientific approaches where the influence of the observer is removed. This imbalance, resulting from emphasizing scientific knowing over other ways of knowing (see e.g., Belenky et al., 1986), has resulted in the hegemony of scientific rationality with an underlying logic of domination.

The logic of domination, according to Karen Warren (1996), is a "structure of argumentation which leads to a justification of subordination" (21) and is intrinsic to the origins of and developments in the modern age. The logic of domination along with value-hierarchical thinking and value dualism, characterize modernism as an "oppressive conceptual framework." The logic of domination is intrinsic to the scientific paradigm and the mathematization of reality. Carolyn Merchant, in *The Death of Nature* (1980), describes how modern science reveals an underlying logic of domination as it emphasizes control over women/nature and the use of women's/nature's resources for the purposes of man:

> These social events (Lancashire witch trials) influenced Bacon's philosophy and literary style. Much of the imagery he used in delineating his new scientific objectives and methods derives from the courtroom, and, because it treats nature as a female to be tortured through mechanical inventions, strongly suggests the interrogations of the witch trials and the mechanical devices used to torture witches. (168)

The emphasis on quantification and underlying logic of domination are challenged by complex adaptive systems, dissipative structures, and chaos dynamics as approaches to inquiry and paragons of the complexity of relationship and pattern. New Science has emerged in the decades of the twentieth century as a form of poetic logic, a way of exploring our world and ourselves that emphasizes experience, understanding, meaning, and spirit. New Science emerged from but has gone far from its origins in general systems thinking.

Systems Thinking and New Science

Bertalanffy (1968, 1975) was among the first to explore general systems theory as an approach to understanding complex phenomenon as they evolve. According to Fritjof Capra (1996) systems thinking rejects the mechanistic and reductionistic thinking of modern science and emphasizes holism, emergence, and patterns of organization. As Capra (1996) says:

> The basic tension is one between the parts and the whole. The emphasis on the parts has been called mechanistic, reductionistic, or atomistic; the emphasis on the whole holistic, organismic, or ecological. In twentieth-century science the holistic perspective has become known as "systemic" and the way of thinking it implies as "systems thinking." (17)

Systems approaches concentrate on relationship, evolution, and structure rather than parts or mechanisms of behavior. An underlying assumption of systems theory is that we cannot understand the complexity of systems by studying their parts. Emergence, dynamical change, and growth are related to organization and relationship rather than static structure. Levels of organization and embedded yet recurring relational characteristics are also important considerations for understanding internal dynamics as well as system-environment relationships. Properties of emergence through generation and self-creative processes are characteristics and indications of levels of organization. Finally, systems, as systems, have historical contexts and relational characteristics that make generalizability and predictability impossible.

New Science has evolved from its origins in general systems theory in several related but distinct domains of inquiry. James Gleick (1987) focuses on chaos theory as quintessential New Science. Others, however, (e.g., Waldrop, 1993) emphasize studies and techniques of complex adaptive systems (CAS) as representing the paradigm shift represented by New Science. Others focus on dissipative structures (Bohm, 1980, for example) as characterizing the shift from explicit to implicit relationships and emergence. These various approaches to New Science represent multiple perspectives while reflecting alternative underlying assumptions and guiding metaphors for inquiry. Postmodern science, as New Science, involves more than techniques or approaches of inquiry but entails an underlying logic of postmodernism. The relationship among CAS, dissipative structures, and chaos theory as aspects of New Science will be described below. The relationship between New Science and postmodern inquiry will be explored in the last section of this chapter.

Nonequilibrium Physics, Dynamical Systems, and Chaos

Ilye Prigogine initiated the field of nonequilibrium physics by creating new paradigms to study the irreversibility of many chemical reactions in thermodynamic interaction. Nonequilibrium physics explores system behavior at far-from-equilibrium states.

While these explorations were occurring in physics, Edward Lorenz, a meteorologist, instigated and developed techniques for studying dynamical studies such as the weather. A focus of dynamical systems studies is on the amplification of small perturbations having disproportionate effects. Nonlinearity and nonequilibrium dynamics are two characteristics of complex systems.

Complex adaptive systems research applies many of the findings of complex systems studies to living systems, exploring how far-from-equilibrium states and nonlinearity may affect living systems. Self-creativity or autopoiesis seems to be the response of living systems to these states. Autopoietic characteristics as the self-generating potential of living systems, together with self-referentiality, and self-similarity, characterize CAS as a New Science perspective exploring nonlinearity and nonequilibrium dynamics.

Independently, chaos mathematics was born as studies of emergent patterns and recursive relationships were explored. Scaling characteristics of complex relationships across levels of complexity became a measure of chaos. Benoit Mandelbrot developed fractal geometry to explore scaling characteristics and patterns of relationship in nonlinear, emergent systems. Fractal dimension as a measure of system relationship provides a way of describing irregularities, breaks, and branching, in recursively generated systems. Many biological systems that exhibit branching structure, such as the cardiovascular system, can be explored using fractal geometry. Fractal dimension explains, for example, how the complex, expansive network of blood vessels can extend over most of the body without taking up much space in the body.

New Science includes these various perspectives and is a constellation of approaches that considers how systems emerge, evolve, and relate both to themselves through time and to their environments. As a constellation and more than a smorgasbord of scientific approaches and techniques, New Science is an interpretive framework for understanding complex and emerging relationships from a systems or holistic perspective. Juxtaposed, the meaning of a constellation is our interpretation of its organizational structure and relationships and cannot be condensed to a single essence or placed in a particular hierarchical order. Each of these differing perspectives of New Science is quintessential New Science, part of a constellation of ways of interpreting complexity.

Reconnecting us with a geometry of relationship, a poetry of interconnectedness, and an emergence of meaning, New Science is an approach to meaning that goes beyond modernism or the techniques of modern science. New Science as a postmodern logic of relationship, meaning, and systems may offer new ways of "seeing-as," or, as Wittgenstein discusses in the *Philosophical Investigations* (1953), an approach to the problems of curriculum as a way of "showing the fly the way out of the fly bottle."

New Science as a Constellation of Postmodern Logics

Postmodernism has been characterized in a variety of ways. As part of the postmodern perspective, it is extremely appropriate that no single definition can be offered since postmodernism itself is a complex social phenomenon that captures a variety of contexts, perspectives, and understandings. Nevertheless, postmodernism can be understood from the perspective of what it is *not*. As a rejection (deconstructive postmodernism) or transformation (constructive postmodernism) of modernism, postmodernism eschews foundations, universality, determinacy, control, uniformity, objectivity, and certainty. In either sense, postmodernism moves beyond modernist notions of control, method, and measurement. As one observer (Thomas Schwandt, 2001) says:

> Postmodernism is an attitude toward the social world, more of a diagnosis than a theory. It opposes four central doctrines that form the core of the Enlightenment tradition: (1) the notion of a rational, autonomous subject; a self that has an essential human nature; (2) the notion of foundationalist epistemology (and foundationalist philosophy in general); (3) the notion of reason as a universal, a priori capacity of individuals; (4) the belief in social and moral progress through the rational application of social scientific theories to the arts and social institutions. . . . Postmodernism is also characterized by its distrust of and incredulity toward all "totalizing" discourses or metanarratives—those large-scale or grand theoretical frameworks that purportedly explain culture, society, human agency, and the like. . . . In place of these metaframeworks, postmodern theory endorses heterogeneity, difference, fragmentation, and indeterminacy. (120)

Through these weavings of heterogeneity, difference, fragmentation, and indeterminacy, New Science emerges as a fabric of poetic logic.

New Science as a postmodern approach to inquiry and a form of poetic logic involves and is driven by a perspective that rejects the logic of domination and piecemeal approaches to knowledge inherent in modernism. Post-epistemological (Rorty, 1980) New Science as postmodern inquiry asks very different questions. Judith Genova (1995) distinguishes postmodern inquiry from inquiry of past epochs in the following way. According to her, the ancients asked "*What* is the world made of?" The medievals were concerned with questions related to "*Who* made the world?" The moderns were driven by "*How* does the world work?" Postmodernism, according to Genova (1995), asks "*Why*?" In order for New Science to be understood as post-modern inquiry, it must be interpreted not from the perspective of techniques but from the perspective of meaning.

Modernism confuses science and its tools by conflating the tools of science for the meaning of science in its tenacious pursuit of exploring how the universe "works." For example, the clock, as a fundamental tool of science in the modern era, became the predominate metaphor for the universe. By confusing the tool, the clock, with meaning structures, understanding how the universe works, science has lost its own meaning and purpose. Postmodernism attempts to reintroduce meaning and purpose into the all-too-human endeavor of science. As described by James Loder and W. Jim Neidhardt (1992):

> A technological perception of science reduces the meaning of science to the manipulation of the material world. Thus, "science and technology" takes on an inflated mythological force, creating a truncated world view in which human control of the systematic relationship between ends and means suppresses issues of purpose and meaning. The only metaphysic that can come from a technological outlook is a closed-system determinism. (4)

Postmodernism recognizes that science, as a meaning system, is more closely aligned with spirituality, relationship, and interdependence than was previously thought. When science becomes and is reduced to its methods, as it has during the modern era, all meaning is lost. When questions of "Why?" are explored, meaning is reintroduced. Underlying postmodern approaches to inquiry are the logics of systems, relationship, and meaning. (See Fleener, 2002, for an elaboration.)

Postmodern Logics

Logic has traditionally been used to explore abstract structure and form. Aristotle's separation of logical form and empirical inquiry were clarified and extended by Immanuel Kant's categories of reasoning. Kant challenged empirical science as an avenue to truth and accepted that science could never achieve certain knowledge about the external world. His agenda was to show how true knowledge could be derived from experience through categories of reasoning. For Kant (see Sabastian Gardner, 1999, for a textual analysis of Kant's *Critique of Pure Reason*), mathematics is *synthetic* knowledge derived through experience, not about reality, as such, but about our ideas of reality, and can lead to certain knowledge. Thus, according to Kant, mathematics and the laws of nature, quantified through mathematics, are not about external reality, per se, but about our ideas of the external world. This perspective is in direct contrast to that taken by the scientific agenda as it has been played out in the last three hundred years. Morris Kline (1982), commenting on that agenda, especially from a Newtonian perspective, says:

> His doctrine that what mathematics asserts is not inherent in the physical world but comes from man's mind should have given pause to all mathematicians. . . . Unlike Kant, mathematicians and physicists still believed in an external world subject to laws independent of human minds. The world was rationally designed and man merely uncovered that design and used it to predict what would happen in the external world. (77)

John Dewey took a different tack and defined logic not as a form of reasoning, separate from experience, but as a mode of inquiry, thus merging logic and science. "In Dewey's view, logical theory should address not just a formal study of linguistic syntax but it should be grounded in a theory of experience" (Burke, 1994, 136). Dewey's logic of inquiry explores, from a process perspective, how sense-making and science are ongoing activities.

Alfred North Whitehead's (1978/1929) process approach further blurs the distinction between experience and reason by emphasizing that all that is, at the most basic levels of being, are "drops of experience":

> "Actual entities"—also termed "actual occasions"—are the final real things of which the world is made up. There is no going behind actual entities [as occasions of experience] to find anything more real. . . . The final facts are, all alike, actual entities; and these actual entities are drops of experience, complex and interdependent. (18)

Ideas of experience, formalized as abstractions, are themselves relationships as well. The significance and subtly of shifting from "things" to "relationships" or, as Whitehead describes, "substances" to "actual entities" [as drops of experience] is to shift from an emphasis on epistemology to ontological interconnectedness. Becoming, as a process, is fundamental reality, according to Whitehead, a "creative advance into novelty" (28).

> It is fundamental to the metaphysical doctrine of the philosophy of organism, that the notion of an actual entity as the unchanging subject of change is completely abandoned. An actual entity is at once the subject of experiencing and the superject of its experiences. (29)

Together with Dewey's logic of inquiry, logic as abstract form is rejected in favor of relationship and experience. The relationships among ontology, hermeneutics, and language were further explored by Ludwig Wittgenstein.

Wittgenstein, in *Culture and Value* (1980), rejected early attempts to understand the logical foundations of mathematics and developed a post-structural theory of meaning, extending the pragmatism of John Dewey, avoiding the idealism of Kant, and focusing on the relationship of meaning. Systems of meaning are revealed through "language-games," according to Wittgenstein, and science, as a social meaning structure, is an intricate "language-game" itself. For Wittgenstein (1953):

> We want to say that there can't be any vagueness in logic. The idea now absorbs us, that the ideal "*must*" be found in reality. Meanwhile we do not as yet see *how* it occurs there, nor do we understand the nature of this "must." We think it must be in reality; for we think we already see it there. . . . Where does this idea come from? It is like a pair of glasses on our nose through which we see whatever we look at. It never occurs to us to take them off. (101–03)

Wittgenstein's logic of meaning, Dewey's logic as inquiry, and Whitehead's logic of relationship offer me a holographic perspective (Fleener,

2002) of New Science that counters the science of modernism and its underlying logic of domination. Especially meaningful to me is Wittgenstein's notion that to change our understandings is like putting on a new pair of glasses. Just as I recall, at ten years of age, all of sudden seeing leaves in trees, blades of grass, and the "man" in the moon with my first pair of glasses, so the New Sciences have provided new metaphors, new ways of seeing, new ways of talking about science and scientific inquiry. "Seeing-as" is important for how we make sense of our world. A "change of aspect," according to Wittgenstein (1953), is necessary in order for us to "see-as" differently and to change how we make sense of (through our language and actions) the world we live in. "Being aspect-blind makes one incapable of seeing shades of meaning and thus incapable of change" (214). New Science from a postmodern perspective, with underlying logics of relationship, meaning, and systems, may offer such a change in aspect, a new lens through which we may see our world.

New Science as a Change in Aspect

As Edmund Husserl (1997/1954) argues, the crisis of modern society has occurred because we have mistaken our mathematics and science, our tools for understanding, for measures and predictors of reality or natural law. We have, at the same time, ignored inspiration, intuition, analogy/metaphor, and other ways of knowing in elevating the status of mathematics and science as the determiners and measures of truth.

> All knowledge of laws could be knowledge only of predictions, grasped as lawful, about occurrences of actual or possible experiential phenomena, predictions which are indicated when experience is broadened through observations and experiments. . . . To be sure, everyday induction grew into induction according to scientific method, but that changes nothing of the essential meaning of the pregiven world as the horizon of all meaningful induction. . . . Mathematics and mathematical science . . . *represents* the life-world, *dresses it up* as "objectively actual and true" nature. It is through the garb of ideas that we take for *true being* what is actually a *method*. (50–51)

Postmodernism's attempt to reintroduce meaning, purpose, value, and understanding explores the "why?" and understands the answer comes from us and our own way of seeing-as. By seeing dynamic holism, the unfolding of life, and the interconnectedness of all, we can't help but to feel awe and inspiration in New Science inquiry. The modern existential angst and the accompanying feelings of smallness and insignificance are dissolved as we appreciate the infinite complexity and relationships that are the dance of life.

When I first started studying the New Sciences over ten years ago and trying to apply New Science techniques to education, I became frustrated with the analytic tools of New Science that seemed just as reductionistic and arbitrary as applying measures like IQ scores to explore constructs like intelligence. I didn't know how to respond, ten years ago, when I was challenged with the admonishment "Chaos theory is useful to education only as a metaphor." After years of exploring the ideas of New Science and reading the research utilizing the techniques of New Science, I have come to realize that, perhaps, the metaphoric qualities of New Science are precisely the beginning of the power of New Science to help us see-as, to offer a change of aspect, and to give us new language to describe relationships and structures. The techniques of New Science must never be confused with the meaning and purpose of New Science as an attempt to explore our ideas about relationship, meaning, and systems, however, or the postmodern qualities are lost. We can't ignore any one of these three aspects of a postmodern logic without reverting back to a logic of domination and confusing New Science with its tools and methods.

The conversations in this book are explorations in New Science as a useful way of understanding educational contexts and cultures. The dynamics of a curriculum as the dance of meaning that precisely is the context of schooling will be explored from a variety of New Science perspectives. A form of Vico's poetic logic, New Science is a way of understanding our natural world not through analysis only but also through interpretation of our own imagery, stories, myths, and metaphors. Rather than emphasizing quantitative measure, poetic logic as postmodern logics of relationship, meaning, and systems encourages relational, social, and human approaches to meaning and culture.

Overview of the Book

I have to smile at the thought of offering an "overview" in light of the previous conversations of this introductory chapter. Serious challenges to modernist assumptions of privileged vantage points, no overview, no encompassing perspective is possible. The intent in this "overview" is to provide the initial "seed" or value of the recursive process that is the unfolding of the book itself. The book is presented as iterative patterns of ongoing conversation. The first iteration explores the historical streams of method (Doll) and logic (St. Julien). The poetic engages in conversation with the poietic (Trueit).

The second iteration explores the New Sciences of chaos and complexity. Within curriculum (Davis and Smitherman), historically (Stanley), and conversationally (Kahn), chaos and complexity have changed the conversational and cultural landscapes, offering more than new metaphors by challenging traditional ways of interacting with and seeing our world and ourselves.

The third iteration continues the conversation as complex dynamics are considered within the social realm. "Chiasmic" relations (Shotter) and critical paradoxes (Roy) address communications as social dynamics. In classrooms, these meaning-systems are played out in the language-games of and dynamics within traditional discourse domains (Reeder). Social systems theory (Rasmussen) offers a perspective on meaning systems as complex conversation, the complexity of which constructivist learning theorists have neglected.

The fourth iteration embraces both the poetic and the poietic, as aesthetics (Wang) and culture (Jewett) emerge from a recursive epistemology (Reynolds). Metaphors of chaos mathematics, fractaled geometries, and dynamical systems are the patterns that connect within this section, creating a resonance, a recursion, a self-similarity across the other conversations in the book.

To embrace the conversational focus, the editors have engaged the separate writings by embedding our own comments and insights within the text. Not intended as "editorializing," we hope to invite the reader into a similar conversation with the text. Chaos, complexity, curriculum, and culture are intertwined through these unfolding and recursing conversations.

Notes

1. Vico wrote an early version of *New Science* around 1710. His 1708–1709 previous work, *On the Study Methods of Our Time,* criticized Bacon and Descartes for their emphasis on reason. He developed these ideas further in his later book *New Science.* He revised *New Science* at least three times. The last revision occurred in 1744, the year he died. This version is the one used in most translations.
2. References to Vico's *New Science* (*NS*) are to the paragraph number (not the page).

References

Belenky, Mary F., Blythe M. Clinchy, Nancy R. Goldberger, and Jill M. Tarule. (1986). *Women's ways of knowing: The development of self, voice, and mind.* New York: Basic.

Bertalanffy, Ludwig. (1968). *General systems theory: Foundations, development, applications.* New York: Braziller.

———. (1975). The history and development of general systems theory. In *Perspectives on general systems theory: Scientific-philosophical studies,* (pp. 149–69). E. Taschdjian (Ed.), (Posthumous compilation of essays by L. Bertalanffy), New York: Braziller.

Bohm, David. (1980). *Wholeness and the implicate order.* New York: Routledge.

Burke, Tom. (1994). *Dewey's new logic: A reply to Russell.* Chicago: University of Chicago Press.

Capra, Fritjof. (1996). *The web of life: A new scientific understanding of living systems.* New York: Anchor Doubleday.

Colilli, Paul. (1997). *The idea of the living spirit: Poetic logic as a contemporary theory.* Buffalo, NY: University of Toronto Press.

Fleener, M. Jayne. (2002). *Curriculum dynamics: Recreating heart.* New York: Lang.

Gardner, Sabastian. (1999). *Kant and the "Critique of Pure Reason."* New York: Routledge.

Genova, Judith. (1995). *Wittgenstein: A way of seeing.* New York: Routledge.

Gleick, James. (1987). *Chaos: Making a new science.* New York: Penguin.

Griffin, Susan. (1980). *Woman and nature: The roaring inside her.* New York: Harper Colophon.

Husserl, Edmund. (1997). *The crisis of European sciences and transcendental phenomenology.* D. Carr (Trans.), W. Biemel (Ed.). Evanston, IL: Northwestern University Press. (Original publication in German, 1954; English, 1970).

Kline, Morris. (1982). *Mathematics: The loss of certainty.* New York: Oxford University Press.

Loder, James E., and W. Jim Neidhardt. (1992). *The knight's move: The relational logic of the spirit in theology and science.* Colorado Springs: Helmers and Howard.

Merchant, Carolyn. (1980). *The death of nature: Women, ecology and the scientific revolution.* San Francisco: Harper Collins.

Rorty, Richard. (1980). *Philosophy and the mirror of nature.* Princeton, NJ: Princeton University Press.

Osberg, Deborah and Gert Biesta. (2003). Complexity, representation and the epistemology of schooling. Paper presented by Deborah Osberg to the First Conference on Complexity Science and Educational Research, University of Alberta, October 16–18, 2003. (http://www.complexityandeducation.ca/pub03proceedings.htm)

Schwandt, Thomas A. (2001). *Dictionary of qualitative inquiry.* Thousand Oaks, CA: Sage Publications.

Vico, Giambattista. (1999). *New science: Principles of the new science concerning the common nature of nations*, 3rd edition. D. Marsh (Trans.). New York: Penguin Books. (Original publication, 1744).

Waldrop, Mitchell M. (1993). *Complexity: The emerging science at the edge of order and chaos.* New York: Simon and Schuster.

Warren, Karen J. (1996). The power and promise of ecological feminism. In *Ecological Feminist Philosophies*, (pp. 19–41). K. J. Warren (Ed.). Bloomington: Indiana University Press.

Whitehead, Alfred North. (1978). *Process and reality: An essay in cosmology.* New York: Free Press. (Original publication, 1929).

Wittgenstein, Ludwig. (1953). *Philosophical investigations.* G. E. M. Anscombe (Trans.). New York: MacMillan.

———. (1980). *Culture and value.* P. Winch (Trans.). Oxford: Blackwell.

First
Iteration

Historical Streams

The Culture of Method

Introduction and Educational History

As any professional educator knows, the practice and concept of educational methods is vitally important to the preparation (really schooling) of teachers-to-be. Of the usual professional triumvirate of courses taken by these teachers-in-training—foundations, methods, student teaching—methods are undoubtedly the most important and most criticized set. Educational methods are vilified as examples of what is wrong with teacher preparation, and yet administrators, educational reformers, and politicians emphasize more and more that teachers' success or failure depends upon the methods of instruction they use. The simplistic assumption operating here is that if teachers follow "correct" methods, all students will perform at levels above average. A well-defined method leads directly to good learning. The nineteenth century aphorism, "L'arn him good," may be more apt than we have realized.

Virtually no educational reformer today believes, as did Alfred North Whitehead, that the low level of student performance is due not to poor methods of teaching but to "good" ones (in Price, 1954, 63).[1] Just what are educational methods? Where did they come from? What assumptions underlie them, that Whitehead—an Anglo-American educator, mathematician, philosopher—would issue such a statement?

In this chapter, I wish to look at the history of method—its cultural embodiment—especially educational methods. I will begin with Peter Ramus (1515–1572)—Pierre de la Ramée, or Petrus Ramus (as he liked to be called), a Rector of the Collège de Presles, as well as Regius (King's) Professor, practicing at the l'Université de Paris. Ramus, of course, did not invent method; its history in Western thought goes back to the Latin *methodus,* itself a form of the Greek *meta* (pursuit, quest, follow) plus *odos* (way). In the melange of sixteenth and seventeenth century intellectual thought (high Renaissance, burgeoning scientific), a milieu of alchemists, charlatans, literati, mathematicians, pedagogues, philosophers, poets, rhetoricians, scientists, and theologians all caught in the swirl of Method, Ramus stands out regarding the art of teaching. Ramus set education on a particular path, one which leads, I believe, from his dawning Protestant frame of reference to our current concept of curriculum (Hamilton, 1990, 2003; Doll, 2002; Triche and McKnight, 2004) and the manner in which we, today, organize and instruct in those curriculum courses we call "methods." This path, or course (the original meaning of the word curriculum)[2] has been anything but linear. Our current concept of teaching, the methods it employs, and the organization of these into a set curriculum is by no means a direct descendant of Peter Ramus' ideas on method and curriculum organization, but there is a strong "family resemblance" between the two (to use Ludwig Wittgenstein's fortuitous phrase). As Walter Ong (1983/1958), the noted Jesuit scholar and Ramus historian, has pointed out (Ch. XIII), over the centuries Ramism became diffused throughout many countries, amalgamated with various other instructional procedures, and enfolded into and mixed up with scientific method and a strong enthusiasm about method in general.[3] After looking at Ramus and his influence on English and American Puritan thought, I wish to trace the influence of his curricular organization and teaching method through John Amos Comenius (1592–1670) and the German Didaktik tradition. Then I will look at a broader concept of method, particularly scientific method (which so captured John Dewey's imagination) in its various seventeenth century forms as expressed by Francis Bacon (1561–1626), Galileo Galilei (1564–1642), and René Descartes (1596–1650). Finally, I will look at what Jayne Fleener calls the current New Sciences and see if in this way of thinking there might be a frame for enlivening method, for infusing it with a new spirit, one quite different from the inert and barren one inherited from sixteenth and seventeenth century, "modernist" thinkers.[4]

Ramus: His Times, His Contributions, His Legacy

I believe it is important to realize, as a number of Renaissance scholars have noted (Randall, 1976/1940; Ong, 1983/1958; Gilbert, 1960) that the concept of scientific method, so important to us today and so much associated with the general notion of method—a procedure/process to be followed for acquiring (new) knowledge or developing (new) skills—was quite unheard of in Ramus' day.[5] J. R. Randall Jr. (1976), the medieval historian, notes that in Saint Thomas Aquinas' day (the 13th century), "genuine science . . . [was inspired not by the desire] to predict the future and control nature . . . [but rather by] seeking understanding [and] contemplation. Its goal was wisdom, a comprehension of the meaning and significance of things, above all of the chief end of man" (98). Quoting from the *Summa Contra Gentiles* (Book I, Ch. 37), Randall notes that Thomas continually uses the word "contemplation." After one particularly eloquent passage in St. Thomas, Randall (1976/1940) says:

> To be noted in this magnificent statement is that the aim is not the patient and never-ending search for truth, the careful investigation of nature that is the goal of modern science, but rather the contemplation of a truth static, fixed, complete, and perfect for all eternity The product, not the process, gives the joy. This notion, drawn like so many of Thomas' views and arguments from Aristotle, expresses the very inmost spirit of this medieval science. It explains why [medieval] method is dialectical rather than investigatory, drawing the consequences from truths already known rather than seeking new truths. It explains [medieval culture's] willingness to start from premises based on authority. "The philosopher"—Aristotle—found this truth; why question his achievement? It explains also the cardinal relation of faith to reason; the goal can be handed to men with the process. (95)

While today's science does not "contemplate a truth static, fixed, complete, and perfect for all eternity" (indeed just the opposite is true), it is interesting to note that educational methods, via its courses do not generally encourage "investigatory" procedures and, tacitly at least, assume that "the goal can be handed–on." In fact, I believe it fair to say that an underlying assumption of educational methods courses is that knowledge itself can be "handed–on." Students seem desirous of having such knowledge/methods handed to them and many a *methods* teacher is willing to comply. This sense of there being an accepted "it" to method is what so bothered Whitehead about "good" teaching.

Ramus (1515–1572) was born into the scholastic tradition—dialogical[6] not investigatory in its contemplation, first of the Christian Bible and then of Aristotle, who after the Bible was the source of all authority. In keeping with this scholastic tradition of method, medieval students were trained (for hours, days, weeks, years) in the art of dialectic/rhetoric: "arriving at a truth by *disclosing the contradictions in an opponent's argument* and overcoming them" (*American Heritage Dictionary*, 1969, 363; emphasis added).[7] This notion of "logic"—dialectic was logic in action—whereby truth came out of personal, oral, and often acrid disputations, had, naturally, strong tones of rhetoric in it. Logic and rhetoric, truth and persuasion, then, became inextricably entwined. Such conflation, later to bother both Bacon (1561–1626) and Descartes (1596–1650), was a feature of Ramus' wanting "to put the logical arts to use," to practical benefit (in Ong, 1983, 41, from Ramus' *Lectures on Dialectic*, Book IV). Of his studying for and practicing disputations, wherein persuasion not truth was the goal, Ramus has this to say:

> Never amidst the clamors of the college where I passed so many days, months, years did I ever hear a single word about the *applications of logic*. I had faith then (the scholar ought to have faith, according to Aristotle) that it was *not necessary*

to trouble myself about what logic is, and what its purpose is, but that it concerned itself solely with creating a motive for our clamors and our disputes. I therefore disputed and clamored with all my might. If I were defending in class a thesis according to the categories, I believed it my duty never to yield to my opponent, were he one hundred times right, but to seek some very subtle distinction in order to obscure the whole issue. On the other hand, were I disputant, all my care and efforts tended not to enlighten my opponent, but to beat him by some argument, good or bad: even so had I been taught and directed. The categories of Aristotle were like a ball that we give children to play with and that it was necessary to get back by our clamors when we had lost it. If, on the other hand, we should get it, we should not through any outcry allow it to be recovered. *I was then persuaded that all dialectic reduced itself to disputing* with loud and vigorous cries. (in Randall, 1976, 215–16; emphasis added).[8]

Ramus did indeed in his career, dispute with loud, vigorous cries. So loudly and so vigorously did he dispute, that for three years (1544–1547) he was forbidden to sell or reproduce his books, and was not "to teach publicly or write on philosophy without the permission of the king" (Ong, 1983, 24). The dispute Ramus had with his detractors was over Aristotle's *Organon* which Ramus asserted was not a "true" dialectic since Aristotle "did not start each book of the *Organon* with a definition," a universal proposition (24). Ramus' anti-Aristotelianism though—an attack in word only, since Ramus actually followed the Aristotle of his day in his own logic—was really an attack on the scholastic procedures of instruction utilized by virtually all university faculty in Paris (and elsewhere). Ramus was thus a reformer, albeit a conservative one, wishing to question and change the methods of instruction prevalent at the time. As a reformer, at both the university and college level, Ramus wished to bring order and serious dedication to the tasks of teaching and learning. Ong comments that the students of the time (teen-agers and younger) formed "a community which habitually lived in a state of unruliness which the modern imagination can hardly steel itself to reconstruct" (23). And indeed Ramus lost his head to students or ruffians who broke into his apartments at the Collège de Presles on August 26, 1572, and severing head from body threw both out the window. This St. Bartholomew's Day Massacre took the lives of many known or assumed Protestants.[9]

As a reformer, Ramus wished to, and indeed did, bring order and discipline to university and college life and study. He worked his college boys hard and was not above whipping them for laziness or incompetence. His pedagogical reform was to "textbookize" knowledge (if I may coin such an awkward word) by presenting any subject to be taught in the "reputedly scientific descent from 'general principles' to 'specials' by means of definition and bipartite division" (30). Such categorization and presentation of knowledge was Ramus' famous *method,* that which swept Protestant northern Europe and Puritan England and its American colonies in the seventeenth century.[10]

As Ong (1971) says, "His influence . . . in England and her American colonies, as elsewhere, was to be largely due to the textbooks with which he and his followers flooded the schools" (142).

Prior to Ramus' organization of knowledge for teaching and learning, one which Ong (1983) and others say was "superficially simple" (30), and intentionally so—since it was basically Latin grammar young boys ages 8 to 13 were learning—it was common for students either to memorize long lists of unconnected Latin phrases or to use Tarot card-like woodcuts (birds flying over sheaves of wheat in a field, etc.) with each figure representing an Aristotelian category. R. R. Bolgar, the medievalist, in his compendious *The Classical Heritage* (1954), says:

> [The schoolboys] made titanic efforts to remember the contents of the note-books they compiled. The Renaissance was the age of memorizing. Books were written outlining fantastic schemes. . . . Their ingenuity was misplaced; but their works survive to show the significance which was attached to the learning by heart of isolated facts—facts which could be arranged in lists. (274)[11]

Ramus' dichotomized patterning or charting, his "one and only way," the "one and only method" Aristotle teaches, "without interruption from universals to singulars" (in Ong, 1983, 251; in Triche and McKnight, 2004, 40) was a breath of fresh air into this nightmarish miasma. Instead of long lists of isolated facts, Ramus provided the student and the teacher with a branching chart of any subject (*ars*)[12] proceeding from the most general and universal to the particular and special.

Figure 1.1 A Ramist Map[13]

What this branching meant was that Ramus would dichotomize a subject, say mathematics into arithmetic and geometry, then branch arithmetic into numbers and fractions and branch geometry into plain and solid. This dichotomizing (ramifying)[14] would proceed until all knowledge in a subject was covered. Of this process Ramus himself says:

> Method is disposition by which . . . that enunciation is placed first which is first *in the absolute order* of knowledge, that next which is next, and so on: and thus there is an unbroken progression from universals to singulars. By this one and only way one proceeds. . . . This is the only method that Aristotle teaches. (in Ong, 249; from Ramus' 1569 edition of his *Dialectic;* emphasis added)

This simple method, just because of its simplicity, appealed to reformist educators, mostly Protestant and mostly Humanists, who wanted to provide young students with a shortcut way of learning the Latin they needed for university study and then for reading the Latin works with which the Renaissance university was filled. In developing a shortcut way to teach Latin grammar, again the prime prerequisite for all learning in the Renaissance, Ramus placed himself in the midst of a debate which had gone on for centuries, indeed for two millennia. Neal Gilbert, another Renaissance scholar, in his *The Renaissance Concept of Method* (1960), starts his book with Plato's *Phaedrus* (265D–277C) where Socrates "outlines what he would consider to be a true *art* or *techné* (*methodos*) of rhetoric, as opposed to the teaching of the Sophists or the superficial manuals of rhetoric" (3). Here Socrates argues that his method leads to wisdom, an understanding in depth, finding the *soul or spirit* of a subject; whereas the Sophists' method, "acquired by mere practice or routine" (4), never moves beyond looking at rhetoric superficially, as mere performance.

These superficial manuals with their emphasis on a routine of *efficiency* (Ong, 1983, 225) were subjects of heated debate for thousands of years. Galen, the physician (2nd century A.D.) says to Thessalus, one who advertised that he could teach the "art of healing" in a few months, that his was "the work of a tyrant, not a teacher" (in Gilbert, 19). Moving on to the Renaissance, Gilbert cites two contemporaries of Ramus who also advertised themselves as teaching in the spirit of efficiency. One, an Agostino Nifo (1473–1546), says that his method of interpreting Aristotle's *Topics* is "a shortcut that leads most quickly to the knowledge of anything"(59). Another, Girolamo Borro (1512–1592), says that his method is "the brief way under whose guidance we are led as quickly as possible to knowledge" (71). While there was good reason not to "grow old and grey in the study of logic," the equating of *meta+odos* (Greek) or *methodus* (Latin) with shortcutting did produce violent counteractions, all the way from Socrates to Galen, to many of the more traditional Humanists. One of these, a Mario

Nizzoli (1498–1566), banned the word *methodus* "as barbarous and not to be used in polite learned discussion" (64).

Why there was a history, two thousand years long—from Socrates to Ramus—of attaching method or *methodus*[15] to short-cutting, it is difficult to say. But it does mean that Ramus, "the greatest master of the short-cut the world has ever known" (in Ong, 1983, 3), was not alone in his emphasis on teaching efficiently. Such an emphasis, of course, appealed strongly to the newly rising, bourgeois groups of merchants, Protestant in orientation, who took to practicality, simplicity, and efficiency (Ong, 1971, Ch. 7). This was especially true of the Puritans who took to Ramism most enthusiastically. It provided for them a frame of both morality and simplicity—virtues they embraced. The Protestant and their Puritan brethren were not only practical people but moral ones as well. They took well to the Humanist reform movement, generally considered to have been given its frame by Desiderius Erasmus (1467–1536) who had the noble ideal that reading Latin authors (selected ones only) would produce men of virtue. Thus, young boys were to keep notebooks of phrases drawn from their readings, and the phrases, as Bolgar has pointed out, were then to be memorized, memorized, memorized.

As an alternative to the notebooks, Ramist charts—simple, clean, unembellished—appealed to the Puritans' desire for simple order, for "plain style."[16] This style accounted for much of Ramism's popularity in Colonial New England. Perry Miller, who encouraged Ong, while at Harvard, to study "the obscure figure, Peter Ramus," in doing research for his own book, *The New England Mind: The Seventeenth Century* (1954/1939), found "Ramism on every side" (in Ong, 1983, 4).[17] He also found, expressed in his *The New England Mind: From Colony to Province* (1953), that the New England Puritans tended to deify Ramus, whom Increase Mather called "that Great Scholar and Blessed Martyr" (117), and to whom "the Congregational theorist resorted, as with every vexing question." For the Congregationalist theorist

> found a satisfactory solution to any problem as soon as he could define the nature of a relationship; [and] once he could show that the terms were in disagreement (or agreement) with each other, he had demonstrated a law of God. . . . [For] once all forms of connection are specified and named and then ranged in schematic series, man has a logical transcript of the wisdom of God in so far as that is manifested in creation. (72)[18]

Such adulation, while it would have been most welcome to Ramus, was certainly not the reception he received among university scholars in Puritan England. There his work was looked upon as "juvenile," "fit only for youngsters in their early teens," and as Francis Bacon said, "already over within his day." Charles (or Charls) Butler, Oxford's most famous Ramist, was dismissed as only "an author of preparatory-school textbooks" (Ong, 1983, 299–303). Indeed, it is this legacy which Ramus has left us, the placing of knowledge for the purpose of teaching into simplistic, textbook form,[19] atomizing it into bits and pieces.[20] While our textbooks today and our educational methods courses where we learn how to teach, do not dichotomize the way Ramus did, they do, I hold, (1) accept the notion that knowledge can and should be atomized, structured simply for "ascertainable results"; (2) believe that a simple (and shallow) presentation is best; (3) prefer the dialectical over the investigatory; and (4) assume there is indeed "a best way": "the one and only way" that Ramus (and Aristotle) taught.[21]

It is easy to dismiss Ramus and his method, as does Bacon. To so do, however, is to miss the tremendous importance Ramus' method had on both the thought of his day and on subsequent centuries of teaching. John Schaeffer (1990) brings this point forward nicely in his book, *Sensus Communis,* on Giambattista Vico (1668–1744), a person I will draw on later, following Jayne Fleener. Here, Schaeffer talks of "the crisis of rhetoric" which Ramism brought to the Jesuit ideal of education, the *Ratio Studiorum,* in the 1660s almost a century after Ramus' death (31). Jesuit education, under this ideal, emphasized the performative aspects of rhetoric, which occurs when one is immersed in a situation "conversationally," when the debater or proponent is acting spontaneously and interactively with his opponent (see Trueit, this volume). Such an approach to rhetoric—improvisional declamations—"was useful for training the imagination in oral, especially extemporaneous performance" (34). Ramus played a major role in making this approach to rhetoric passé. His "one and only" method, a universal designed to fit all times and situations and subjects, rigidified rhetoric, gave it a set, formulaic form and a pre-set end goal. One now moved or manipulated a receiving audience toward a desired end. The personal humanness of Humanism was lost as "the discarnate mind *operating with fixed meanings* replaced the rhetorical imagination as the model of reason" (34; emphasis added). Such a model of "good" reasoning and "good" teaching, frightening to Whitehead, remains with us today. As I have said, while the lineage from Ramus to Tyler is not direct, the family resemblance is amazingly strong (Doll, 2002; Hamilton 2003; Triche and McKnight, 2004).[22]

Comenius and The Didactic Method

Another educational reformer who had a strong influence on our concept of method and who followed in the footsteps of Ramus was John Amos Comenius (Komensky, in Bohemian), born in 1592, twenty years after Petrus Ramus' unsightly death. Ong (1983) says that Comenius (1592–1670) "received his education and apparently much of the inspiration for his educational reform from his Ramist [and Protestant Reformation] teacher [Johann

Heinrich] Alsted" (298). Orphaned at an early age, Comenius went through what he called the "slaughter houses" of schooling where boys were routinely beaten,[23] where "a thousand and one rules" had to be learned by rote, where what learning did occur was made as complicated as possible—i.e., the seven genders of Latin: masculine, feminine, neuter, common of two, common of three, promiscuous, and doubtful (Keatinge, 2–3; 108–09). This sort of "education" Comenius described as "learning the unknown through the medium of the unknown" (110).

The education of the day was all rhetoric (declamation) since writing (prose especially) had not yet become a major factor in university life. Peter Sharratt (1976), describing Ramus' school, gives us an example of what school life was like:

> [T]he pupils were taught five hours in the morning and five in the afternoon, in each case made up of one hour's lecture on classical literature, two of 'ediscendi,' that is, studying or memorizing, and two more of debate and practice. (7)

This procedure went on for seven or eight years, until at the age of fifteen or sixteen, the student was himself able to teach or to go on to the doctoral study of law, medicine, or philosophy.

Comenius found this method of teaching lacked joy (the joy of Christian being). As an ordained Minister of the Moravian Brethren, he wanted to bring the joy of Christian piety to all. He felt that his own schooling, with its emphasis on physical beating and meaningless memorization, was dehumanizing and wasteful. So in the Ramist tradition of efficiency and in his own of Reformation, Christian piety, he wrote *The Great Didactic* (1638). On the frontispiece he states that this book is committed to helping youth "become learned in the Sciences, pure in Morals, trained to Piety," "Quickly, Pleasantly, & Thoroughly" (frontispiece to *The Great Didactic*). The notion of learning quickly was a hallmark of the times, to acquire the rudiments as quickly as possible and thus to be able to use one's knowledge. Here is seen the needs of a rising Protestant, capitalist class, learning not for its own sake but for practical and profitable activity. The notion of learning pleasantly was very much Comenius' own doctrine; certainly it was not Ramus'.

Comenius' sense of learning pleasantly was a Christian pleasantness, the happiness and joy one feels in committing oneself to a life of piety. As he says:

> Our schools, therefore, will then at length be Christian schools when they make us as like to Christ as is possible. (*The Great Didactic*, 226)

Comenius' *Didactic* was by no means the first didactic (plan for teaching) written. Nor is a didactic merely a "plan for teaching." Comenius searched mightily for the didactics of other Protestant educational reformers; Eilhard Lubin (1565–1621) and Wolfgang Ratke (1571–1635) were two upon whom he drew.[24] Comenius, however, was the one to set forth a Great Didactic, the didactic which would "teach everything to everyone" (*omnes omnia docere*) and with such certainty "that the result [useful learning] cannot fail to follow" (157).[25] The "teach to everyone" phrase is interesting here for, quite radical for the times, Comenius believed that education should begin on the "mother's knee"[26] and that young women as well as men should be "educated." On teaching young women, he says they should be educated to Christian piety but not to the point "*where curiosity shall be developed*" (220; emphasis added). He goes on to say:

> To sum up, they will learn to see, to praise, and to recognize God everywhere, and, in this way, to go through this life of care with enjoyment, and to look for the life to come with increased desire and hope. (221)

Just as Comenius believed that education for young women should be limited, so he felt for young men. The education both sexes were to receive was to be simple, with the complexities of the Bible saved for later years and with "the lascivious Latin authors" entirely removed. As he says:

> If we wish our schools to be truly Christian schools, the crowd of Pagan writers must be removed from them (383);
>
> [Writers like] Terence, Plautus, Catullus, Ovid . . . set before [our young children] jesting, feasting, drunkenness, amours, and deceits, from which Christians should avert their eyes and ears (394);
>
> Cicero, Virgil, Horace . . . are blind pagans, and turn the minds of their readers from the true God to other gods and goddesses. (395)

Finally Comenius concludes, "Christ loves those who believe easily," and so the idea of a simple, Christian piety became part of his (Protestant and Brethren) educational mission.

Comenius' didactic method was both simple and universal—one method for all. It was designed for the practical teacher, teaching boys and girls "of moderate intelligence" (Keatinge, 12–13). The method itself, one instructor, many learners—one instructor teaching hundreds of students at the same time from a properly authorized book, in a properly authorized manner, each student obviously on the same page at the same time—he calls not only doable but "essential," in order that no "miscommunication" takes place. Proctors, or mentors, or lower order teachers were to work in smaller groups helping the students acquire the proper knowledge properly. Comenius describes this system in the following way:

- A small number of masters would be able to teach a greater number of pupils than under the present system,
- These pupils would be more thoroughly taught,

- The process would be refined and pleasant,
- The system is equally efficacious with stupid and backward boys; and even masters who have no natural aptitude for teaching will be able to use it with advantage; since they will not have to select their own subject-matter and work out their own method, but will only have to take knowledge that has already been suitably arranged and for the teaching of which suitable appliances have been provided, and to *pour it into their pupils.* (*The Great Didactic*, 440; emphasis added)

To aid in this method which Comenius considered to be "universal, perfect, and natural," echoing Ramus' "one and only method," as well as a method of "ease, thoroughness, and rapidity," Comenius added proctors, mentors, division leaders from the students themselves. As he says, regarding the taking of dictation from the teacher:

> As soon as the leaders of divisions have secured attention, one scholar should be called upon to stand up and choose as his adversary any other scholar that he pleases. . . . At the end of each [copied] sentence the scholar stops, and his adversary has the opportunity of pointing out any mistake. (321–22)

Other class members may then point out mistakes in the sentence, followed by the teacher making the final points. In this way the teacher's words are recorded verbatim, "poured into the pupils." This method of teaching was what both the traditionalists and the humanists of the period would call "dialogical" not investigatory. In fact, the concept of investigation and its role in both pedagogy and intellectual thought was, historically, yet to come.

The Didaktik tradition, from Comenius to the present, has followed a circuitous path, has at times seemed a lost path, with many associated side trails and influences. Strong influences have come from philosophers such as Immanuel Kant (1724–1804) with his sense of moral duty and human progress; from G.W.F. Herbert (1776–1841) with his rigid formalism of preparation, presentation, association, generalization, and application (the "five windows" of the soul); and from Wilhelm Dilthey (1833–1911) with his sense of a softer, more humane "reform pedagogy," and emphasis on the phenomenological. Today, a certain renaissance seems to be occurring in Didaktik thought (see Gundem and Hopmann, 1998; Menck, 2000; Westbury, 2000; and Autio, 2002). Rudolph Kunzli, in Ian Westbury's *Teaching as a Reflective Practice: The German Didaktik Tradition* (2000) comments that today there is "no uniform conception of the object, method, and system of Didaktik within German educational research or teacher education, and indeed the word itself is used with a variety of meanings" (41). This is true, I believe, but the tradition does have a certain core, one which exemplifies its Protestant roots—that of relationship. Today that relationship is not the religious, Reformationist one of Comenius, but exists between and among content, learner, and agency (method).

In this relationship, agency (method) takes on a more interactive character than its Anglo-American curriculum counterpart. As Wolfgang Klafki (in Westbury, 2000) says, one of the great errors or "misconceptions," in teaching today is the belief that *"the search for method must be the final, albeit necessary, step* in good instructional preparation," the *"crowning element"* of instruction (143; emphasis added). Such a methodizing emphasis, historically rigid Klafki believes, overlooks the importance of both the learner (*currere* in curriculum theory, *bildung* in the Didaktik tradition) and the spirit of the content studied. This concept of content having its own "spirit" (my word, not Klafki's) is to me fecund and pregnant with developmental potential. Klafki talks of subject matter content having "an organic power," a certain vitality, "invisible but objective which needs to be mastered" (143) or "grasped" (153) before knowledge comes alive, becomes more than the collection of "dead, useless, lifeless" facts Whitehead so deplored. While Klafki's terminology of knowledge having an "organic power," "invisible but objective" which must be "mastered " is a bit strong for me, I do think there is a "spirit" to the subject matter we teach in methods courses and that finding and utilizing this spirit brings knowledge alive, liberating it from the banal. In any new renaissance or reformation of method, which I believe the authors in this book encourage us to envision, I would ask us to concentrate on finding the spirit of that which we teach.

Bildung—"character formation," "self-development," or "self-cultivation," all within a cultural frame (Westbury, 24 note, as well as all of his book's Part II)–runs throughout German (educational) thought and culture for much of the nineteenth and twentieth centuries. *Bildung,* if it does not arise from the thinking of Immanuel Kant, has at least a strong correspondence to his emphasis on the *practical,* the *pure,* and the *aesthetic.* As Klafki says, talking of classical theories of *Bildung:*

> There is general agreement that there are at least three main dimensions to this issue [that of *Bildung*]: a moral dimension [pure], a dimension of knowing or thinking [practical], and an aesthetic dimension. (96; addenda mine)

This notion of personal development within a culture, while appealing to an American pragmatist such as myself, does seem to emphasize an oddly strong sense of self, one that paradoxically entraps the individual within a universal (can one say national!) destiny.[27] To quote from one of many memorable phrases by Klafki in his article on classical *Bildung* and its relation to contemporary curriculum thought:

> Humankind must be understood as capable of free and reasonable self-determination; the realization of this possibility has been "assigned" as a destiny,

but in such a way that only each person, by himself or herself, is able, in the end, to secure this destiny; and finally that education is simultaneously the path and the expression of such a capacity of self-determination. (88)

Education designed to "secure such a destiny" appears *not to be* an education of choice, reciprocity, or freedom, especially the freedom to resist and reject. Without a strong notion of honoring "the other," and without the freedom to reject—even to reject that which one honors—morality for me hardly seems to be. So, fascinating as is the concept of *Bildung*, there appears a dark side to it, as Tero Autio (2002) has shown.

Before moving on to a broader concept of method, particularly scientific method with its emphasis on experimentation—absent in the Ramist and Didaktik traditions—I would like to make some general comments about these two traditions and their connection with what we call, in north America today, educational methods. While neither Ramism nor the Didaktik have direct connections with north American current teaching methods, Ramism's influence on colonial New England thought was great, as was the influence of German thought on both the American high school and university education a century later. Thus, I believe the cultural aspects of each have permeated our own curricular thinking in this and the last century. As we look at the textbook, factual approach to knowledge we offer in our methods courses, I believe it behooves us to recall both Ramus and Comenius and their desire to simplify. As we look at the notion of direct transmission, of a one best way, of all pupils learning in the same manner [time being the only variable here], I believe we need to consider how Ramus assumed that knowledge "logically" ordered was best learned that way, that "the one and only way Aristotle taught" was the only "natural" way, of how Comenius insisted that all pupils do the same activity in the same way to avoid "misconceptions," and that both Ramus and Comenius kept control very centralized. At a subtler level and indeed hidden too much today is a need for us to recognize that both Ramus and Comenius were humanists, much committed to a better and more humane world through education and the methods they proposed. They may have been simplistic in their consideration of these methods and what they could accomplish but the ideal is one worth bringing to fruition. The same might be said of the Didaktik tradition itself. While the framework in which I see character development placed bothers me,[28] I certainly applaud the notion of adding the aesthetic, the character-ful and spirit-ful to our present, too mechanistic concept of teaching.

Broader Concepts of Method

For having now my Method by the end,
Still as I pull'd, it came, and so I penned,
It down; until at least it came to be,

For length and breath the bigness which you see.
John Bunyan's "Apology" for *The Pilgrim's Progress*

But what, you ask, is this legitimate method?. . . . But do you suppose, when all the approaches and entrances to men's minds are beset and blocked by the most obscure idols . . . that any clean and polished surface remains in the mirror of the mind on which the genuine natural light of things can fall? A new method must be found. . . .
Francis Bacon, *Temporis partus masculus*

I have formed a Method, by whose assistance it appears to me I have the means of gradually increasing my knowledge and of little by little raising it to the highest possible points which the mediocrity of my talents and the brief duration of my life can permit me to reach.
René Descartes, *Discourse on the Method of Rightly
Conducting the Reason and Seeking for Truth in the Sciences*

[N]othing can escape our method . . . it spares the mind and the imagination; the latter, above all must be used sparingly.
Gottfried von Leibniz, *On the Method of Universality*

But science depends on demonstration, and the discovery of demonstrations *by a certain Method* is not known to everybody.
Gottfried von Leibniz, Preface to *The General Science*

The *true Method* taken in all of its scope is to my mind a thing hitherto quite unknown, and has not been practiced except in mathematics.
Gottfried von Leibniz, Preface to *The General Science*

As these quotations show, method, following the acrimonious debates over best method in the sixteenth century became a *modus operandi* for a much larger group of scholars–poets and philosophers as well as scientists and alchemists—in the seventeenth century. During this century, method moved from being a way (a shortcut way) for educators and teachers, theologians and humanists, to pass on their knowledge of the classical traditions to being a *new way of thinking*, embraced by virtually all intellectuals. Speaking of the Renaissance educators, Gilbert (1960) says: Method for them "did not even touch upon . . . gaining valid and useful knowledge," but concerned itself only with "transmitting an 'already established art.'" With the alchemists, philosophers, poets, and scientists of the seventeenth century this all changed. Method became, if not the experimentation of the nineteenth century, at least a precursor to it, a new way of thinking. As a movement, it swept across Western Europe and left its mark on subsequent centuries of all Western thinking. This movement not only distinguished Western thought from that of the rest of the world, it also separated Protestants from Catholics. Peter Dear in his *Discipline and Experience* (1995) comments, a lá Bolgar, that the Humanists (mostly Protestant) had in method "their own functional equivalent of the [Catholic] Holy Spirit" (121).[29] Method provided for the newly forming capitalist class, those (men) most attracted to Protestantism, a driving force, a sense of animation, akin to what spirit had done for Catholicism in previous centuries. While a Protestant/Method—Catholic/Spirit split is far too simple a dichotomy, there is a broad sense in which our American secular education system is method focused more than the American parochial system.[30] Further, the sense of method so prevalent in something like the Tyler rationale and all it has spawned has strong overtones of capitalist, commercial values in it (Triche, 2002; see also Pinar et al., 1995, especially remarks about the relation between Tyler's rationale and textbooks).

One branch of this new method, "scientific" or *methodus scientificus* "was only beginning to gain currency during the late Renaissance" (Gilbert, 222). With strong ties to the Aristotelian tradition of science as demonstrated knowledge, not as investigatory experimentation, this *methodus scientificus* was still a long way from our current concept of science as methodical "experimentation, measurement and verification,"[31] all done self-consciously (purposefully) and reflexively (looping back on itself). This "scientific" form of thinking S. J. Tambiah (1990) calls "Western civilization's . . . quintessential form of rationality,[32] "positivist" in outlook [33] (140). While such thinking was centuries in developing as a method (Dear, 1995, Ch. 1), it was beginning to develop in the works and writings of Francis Bacon (1561–1626), Galileo Galilei (1564–1642), and René Descartes (1596–1650).[34] These are but three from a host of thinkers who made the seventeenth century what Whitehead (1967/1925) called "The Century of Genius" (Chapter III). These three are often characterized as the inductionist (Bacon), the experimentalist/mathematician (Galileo), and the rationalist (Descartes). While such simplifications have some truth to them, they tend to mask the complexity which dominated this transitional age; and to obscure the pervasive influence Aristotle and medieval Christian thought continued to have on this dawning revolution. As Whitehead points out, induction—that mode of thinking attributed to Bacon and which indeed is the "quintessential form" of modern, scientific thinking—is itself based on a medieval, rationalist, and naive faith—i.e., that the universe is so universally and lawfully ordered that the particulars observed in one time-space can be extrapolated to other time-spaces. Without such a faith we have only isolated occurrences. In Whitehead's own words:

> Induction presupposes metaphysics. . . . It rests upon an antecedent rationalism.
> . . . The wider assumption of general laws holding for all cognisable occasions
> appears a very unsafe addendum to attach [to our limited knowledge of a partic
> ular occasion, no matter how carefully observed]. (44, addenda, paraphrase)

The important point here, educationally, is that our current belief in the rightness of simple, linear order and of a one best method, all enveloped in a mathematical frame did not originate with Frederick Taylor's industrial efficiency movement in the latter part of the nineteenth century,[35] but has roots that go back centuries to a medieval faith in the way God so ordered the world and universe. I will look at the concept of method in the writings of Bacon, Galileo, and Descartes, beginning with Galileo whom I believe we too often characterize as being a strong, if not the first, experimentalist.[36]

Galileo Galilei

That Galileo was obsessed with mathematics and its reality—its "real realness" to borrow a phrase from Whitehead—is quite indisputable. It is Galileo who gave us the famous statement:

> Philosophy is written in that great book which ever lies before our eyes—I mean the universe—but we cannot understand it if we do not first learn the language and grasp the symbols, in which it is written. This book is written in the mathematical language, and the symbols are triangles, circles, and other geometrical figures, without whose help it is impossible to comprehend a single word of it; without which one wanders in vain through a dark labyrinth. (in Burtt, 75)

And in his objection to Aristotelians:

> We do not learn to demonstrate [prove with certainty] from the manuals of logic, but from the books . . . which are the mathematical, not the logical. (in Burtt, 76)

That Galileo believed the universe to be ordered mathematically and simply—"nature . . . doth not that by many things, which may be done by few" (in Burtt, 75; from *Dialogue Concerning the Two Great Systems of the World*, 1661, 99)—is obvious, I believe. That he was an experimenter, in our sense of the word, is not only questionable, but also flies in the face of his faith in the mathematization of the universe. As E. A. Burtt (1955/1932) says about Galileo's view on experiments: "His confident belief in the mathematical structure of the world emancipated him from the necessity of close dependence on experiment" or on scholastic logic (76). In Galileo's own words:

> The knowledge of a single act acquired through the discovery of its causes prepares the mind to understand and ascertain other facts without the need of recourse to experiment. (in Burtt, 76)

Such a comment reinforces Whitehead's earlier comment that induction presupposes a rationalist metaphysics.

Peter Dear (1995) and others have pointed out that many of Galileo's experiments were not physical ones but "thought experiments"[37] (95) and much in the Aristotelian tradition.[38] Galileo did, though, make a major contribution through his "experiments": he combined mathematics with reason and so moved from the general notion of a ball rolling down a plane at an increasing speed, to a ball rolling down a plane at an increase of 32 feet per second per second, or of a cannon ball falling to the ground, not in straight line (as was believed) but in the form of a mathematical parabola. Galileo was certainly not the first to find a relationship between nature and numbers (or geometry),[39] but he is the first to mathematize nature, to assert that the reality of nature lay not in itself but in mathematics. This concept, that nature including all life, has a substratum of mathematical order to it remains with us to this day.[40] It lies at the heart of our concept of assessment, indeed of our concept of logic, as Jayne Fleener (this volume) points out.

Francis Bacon

A contemporary of Galileo's who, while liking detail and measurement, did not mathematize nature but dealt with it in and of its real physical self—and who believed he had a method for understanding "her" secrets—was, of course, Francis Bacon. Like Galileo and Descartes, Bacon was born when Humanism—with its admiration of a selected past and its belief that teaching was done by having pupils imitate selected orators and writers from that past—was losing its force and man's own power to reason was rising. This newfound power, well harnessed, Bacon believed could lead mankind to a New Atlantis, one wherein human misery was eliminated and Christlike charity reigned.[41]

A man of practical affairs, Bacon spent his life in service to his government, rising to the position of Lord Chancellor of England, thereby hoping to bring about his new Atlantis, not merely through his writings but also through practical actions. He believed a better life could be accomplished through a detailed understanding of Nature and an unlocking of "her" secrets. Scorning alchemy and magic, Bacon believed that "by expelling scholasticism and alchemy," one could replace these with "industrious observations, grounded conclusions, and profitable inventions" (in Farrington, 1964, 13). These words show Bacon to be a player in what has been called "the first industrial revolution" but he was also caught in the milieu of the times which honored the alchemy and magic it wished to supercede. Thus, as Farrington (1964) points out, a tone of the magico-alchemical pervades his writings (51). In the very first aphorism of the *Novum Organum*, Bacon talks of man being both the "servant and interpreter of nature," that he can do and understand "just so much," no more. Bacon's view of nature then is complex: he stands in awe of her and also believes (really hopes) that via "industrious observations, grounded conclusions, and profitable inventions," she can be subdued, controlled, bound and led to yield her secrets.[42]

Bacon is often considered to represent the practical aspect of human thought. A man of worldly affairs, Lord Chancellor of England,[43] he wished to deal with nature empirically, in itself, in its many real manifestations. He rejected Aristotelianism and Ramism, mostly because, in his view, these did not deal with nature itself. As he says:

> [W]e reject proof by syllogism, because it operates in confusion and lets nature slip out of our hands. . . . [T]here is a kind of underlying fraud here. (in Jardine and Silverthorne, 2000, 16).

And,

> The method of discovery and proof according to which the most general principles are first established, and then intermediate axioms are tried and proved by them, is the parent of error and the curse of all science. (*Novum Organum*, Book I, Aphorism 69)[44]

Further,

> The sciences we now have are no more than elegant arrangements of things previously discovered, not methods of discovery or pointers to new results. (I, 8)

As Dear points out, though, in his (1998) essay, "Method and the Study of Nature," for all his rejection of past scholastic practices, Bacon was most caught by that which he criticized. Bacon's method of "induction" was not experimental but Aristotelian, dealing with the relationship between axioms:

> Elicit axioms from sense and particulars, rising in a gradual and unbroken ascent to arrive at last at the most general axioms. This is the true way . . . (I, 19).

Timothy Reiss (1982) says there is here a sort of scholastic dialectic, a play between axioms and particulars—"the elaboration of 'axioms,' the 'descent to particulars,' and the return to the former" (203). Or, in Bacon's own words:

> [A]ll true and fruitful natural philosophy hath a double scale or ladder, ascendent and descendent, ascending from experiments to the invention of causes, and descending from causes to the invention of new experiments. (*AL*, II, VII.i)[45]

In these quotes, one sees that Bacon is still within an Aristotelian framework, that he is not a pure empiricist (as we would define such today), and that he wants that movement which goes from sense experiences/particulars to axioms/abstractions to be "gradual and unbroken." This sense of the gradual and unbroken, reminiscent of Ramus, prescient of Newton and Darwin (and tacitly underlying/supporting our current educational concept of method) is integral to the "new" method Bacon espouses. Still for all his tacit Aristotelianism and Ramism, Bacon's new way or order—he preferred not to use the term, *methodus*—did move European thought away from scholastic thinking and toward a more modernist, scientific one. In so doing, he left a legacy for educational methods.

Bacon believed that the methods of his day were clouded by the illusory radiance of four idols: the tribe, the cave, the marketplace, and the theatre. The tribe describes the idol wherein "human senses are the measure of (all) things"; the cave prevents individual men from seeing "the light of nature"; the marketplace is full of "words" which "confuse everything, and betray men into countless empty disputes and fictions"; while "in the theatre, philosophy stages productions of false and fictitious worlds" (*NO*, I, 39–44). The theme which runs through these four illusions is that while man has the ability, the power "which belongs to him by god's gift," to understand and control the natural world,[46] his own arrogance and culture prevent him from developing this power and from acquiring truth about the natural world.[47] Bacon's method for such development and understanding is to start, as Aristotle suggests, with that which is sensibly seen and hence obvious—that to which all rational and sightful *men* would agree. Second is to write down, to order in charts and tables, a form Ramus suggests, that closely observed. Such observation would be of both occurrences and non-occurrences. From this written procedure (*experentia literata*) one is able (or should be able) via reason to draw inferences, if, thirdly, one proceeds "without notions" (the illusory idols) and in "gradual steps." In Bacon's own words:

> There are, and can be, only two ways to investigate and discover truth. The one leaps from sense [sight] and particulars to the most general axioms . . . this is the current way. The other elicits axioms from sense and particulars, rising in a gradual and unbroken ascent to arrive at least at the most general axioms; this is the true way. (I, 19)

The concepts of (1) close, unfettered, unprejudiced observations, (2) the writing down of these observations and the procedures surrounding them for others to see, and (3) proceeding in analytical and gradual steps is, as we know, that which today we call the "scientific method." As already said, A.N. Whitehead (1967/1925) believed these scientific advances of the seventeenth century to be the "greatest intellectual success which mankind has achieved" (46). John Dewey, of course, was most enamoured of such a method, although he liked best the experimentalism that was to come centuries later. This process of observing well, writing down that seen and thought, and proceeding in gradual steps is practiced in virtually all our educational methods of instruction, especially those methods we associate with problem solving.

How new knowledge, that which Bacon wanted so desperately, is to proceed from this tightly controlled "racecourse" where "the finishing line" is "properly set and fixed" (I, 81) is not entirely clear.[48] The process seems constrained by itself. Surreptitiously, though, Bacon seems to have added insightful personal experience, into his concept of method. In discussing the fable of the huntress god Pan, Bacon says that in seeking truth about nature one needs to be like Pan, who drawing on "sagacious experience and the universal knowledge of nature, oftentimes, by a kind of chance, and while engaged . . . stumbles upon discoveries" (in Jardine, 1974, 144). Of this aspect of method, Lisa Jardine goes on to say that there seems to be "a 'sagacity,' a 'hunting by scent'" which is "a practical not a theoretical [or methodological] activity."[49] Such a *"pedagogy of practice,"* tacitly embedded in Bacon's method, has not been developed in the centuries following Bacon's vision of a Great Renewal but could possibly come from the twentieth century's new sciences and their "methods" that Jayne Fleener is asking us to look at.

René Descartes

The individual who, after Peter Ramus, represents (educational) method best, is René Descartes (1596–1650). Unlike Bacon who eschewed the word—too humanist for him—Descartes embraced method, as evidenced in the title of one of his major works, *Discourse on Method* (1950/1637).

Descartes is, as is well known, a towering figure in Western philosophical thought. In François Lyotard's phrase (1984), he is a developer of one of modernism's *grand écrits*—one which believes that God created our universe, along the lines of a machine,[50] and that we, through the power of our reason, can understand all there is to know about this universe and our place within it. This view is evident, I believe, in the following lines from his *Discourse*.

> [There are] certain laws which God has so established in nature . . . that after sufficient reflection we cannot doubt that they are exactly observed in all which exists or happens in the world. (1950, 27)[51]

To take on the challenge of analyzing Descartes' *grand écrit* would be beyond the scope of this paper. Instead I will focus on three issues I believe important for understanding the culture of method, particularly educational method. These are (1) certainty, (2) self, and (3) Descartes' method itself. I will start in reverse order. The full title of his discourse is *Discourse on the Method of Rightly Conducting One's Reason and Seeking Truth in the Sciences*. Descartes has four famous rules for directing one's reason in search for truth:

> *First Rule:* Accept only that which presents itself to the mind "so clearly and distinctly" that its truth is self-evident.

> *Second Rule:* Divide each difficulty "into as many parts as possible" for easier solution.

Third Rule: "Think in an orderly fashion," as did the geometers of old with their "long chains of reasoning," always proceeding by gradual degrees, from that which is "simplest and easiest to understand" to the more complex.

Fourth Rule: Review all the foregoing to be "certain that nothing is omitted." (1950, 12).

The connection I find between this methodization of reason and the Tyler rationale, I have already commented on elsewhere (Doll, 1993, 31 ff.). Both emphasize starting with the unquestioned (for Descartes, the "clear and distinct"; for Tyler, that approved or "authorized" by researchers and experts);[52] then move on, a lá Ramus, to a reductionist partitioning and linear organizing; and finish with a checking of the organizational frame to ensure that all has been properly done.[53] Efficiency and ease dominate all, a hallmark of the methodization movement.

The most important concept here, though, is that of certainty. His rational method is one Descartes believed would produce absolute certainty. He, in union with the English empiricists, has left us a legacy of certainty coming through "scientific rationality." For Descartes, of course, this rationality has its certainty tied in with the formalisms of mathematical thinking and faith in God's ultimate goodness. Today science and mathematics are both comfortable enough with themselves to live with and honor the spirits of probability and falsification (Popper, 1968), but in the sixteenth and seventeenth centuries when science and human reason were competing with Church authority and scholastic logic, "infallibility" was a necessity. As J. R. Randall Jr. (1976) says: "Certain knowledge was the paramount scientific problem of the sixteenth century" (219–20). Today, senses of the authoritative and infallible continue to linger on in the lay person's view of science and its methods. Often, too often I'd say, the phrase "Research tells us . . ." becomes definitive. The issue of multiple perspectives, so important to Gregory Bateson (*Mind and Nature,* 1988, Chs. 3 and 5) or the limitations of "one eyed reason,"[54] such a bother to Whitehead (1967/1925, Ch. IV)— who worried not only about the difficulties of "good" teaching but also of "logical" reasoning[55]—have yet to permeate the thinking of educational theorists. 'Tis time for a new view of both.

Descartes, like Bacon and so many others who went through scholastic training, found it wanting, both in practical applications to life and in opening up new realms of knowledge:

Nor have I ever observed that any previously unknown truth has been discovered by means of the disputations practised in the schools. (1950/1637, 12)

Whereas Bacon, though, found new hope in government and institutions ridding schools and society of the "idols" which hindered the true learning both believed could occur, Descartes turned inward, to self, to self-introspection. As he says:

> I gave up my studies entirely as soon as I reached the age when I was no longer under the control of my teachers; (6)

And, after travelling for a few years and observing life and others ways of being,

> I eventually reached the decision to study myself. (7)[56]

In this studying of himself, which lead to his famous *Cogito* ('tis I who think), Descartes showed a strong fascination with the individual and what the individual could accomplish by his own means.[57] As he says,

> There is less perfection in a work produced by several persons, than in one produced by a single hand. (7)

This emphasis on the individual has been a hallmark of modernist thought, separating subject from object, the person from nature (allowing the former to control the latter), and mind from body. Such separation comes out quite strongly in Descartes' "Sixth Meditation" (1951/1641) when he says, "I am only a thinking and not an extended (corporeal) being" (69). He continues; and since

> I have a distinct idea of the body in so far as it is only an extended being, which does not think, it is certain that this "I" (that is to say, my soul, by virtue of which I am what I am) is entirely (and truly) distinguished from my body and that it can (be or) exist without it. (71)

This view of Descartes' advocating our being pure cognition has certainly had a deleterious effect on our educational methods courses, their lack of attention to embodied knowing [58] and over attention to intellectual/willful knowing.

Tero Autio (2002), though, in his careful reading of Descartes, shows him putting forth a grand scheme, one wherein he wanted to blend the cognitive with the sensory in a manner which would control *The Passions of the Soul* (1985/1649) and develop a sense of human morality—all for the purpose of improving everyday life. Drawing on Stephen Toulmin's *Cosmopolis* (1990), which talks of the turbulent times in which Descartes lived—much of his life was framed by the Thirty Years War (1618–1648)—Autio says,

> The solipsistic interpretation of the self as a self-sufficient cognitive and *a priori* rational entity, *res cogitans*, strictly detached from its corporeal and social form, does not do full justice to Descartes' intentions. Rationality was not a ready–made property in an individual but a ("self-instructional") task in seeking balance in the interaction between the intellect and one's own bodily functions,

and between the intellect and the social and cognitive friction arising from the chaotic profusion of the volitional incentives in everyday life. (59)

While Autio makes a strong case for observing Descartes as a person, filled with existential doubts, hopes, fears, it has been more common to think of him as a stereotypical icon of Cartesianism. Michael Oakeshott (1967), preceding Autio, points out that while: "Descartes never became a Cartesian" (17), the concepts he brought to the fore were prominent during his lifetime. Descartes' dealing with certainty is one of these, straddling this line, being partly an expression of Descartes and partly of Cartesianism in its rationalism. Throughout his *Discourse* and *Meditations,* Descartes can be seen pandering after certainty but also desiring to honor his existential feelings. He wants desperately to move from doubt to certainty. As John Dewey points out in his *Quest for Certainty* (1960/1929), this historic quest has been a hallmark of Western thought since at least the time of Plato and it is to mathematical ideas that philosophers have turned to find certainty. Philosophers have believed that mathematical (often geometrical) ideas have a purity to them, since they are "unadulterated with material derived from experience." These ideas are "objects of the highest—that is, the most assured—knowledge" (140).

With Descartes, though, this quest seems to have taken a harder turn than with preceding thinkers. Ramus was indeed committed to Aristotle's "one and only way," and Comenius to a way of Christian piety, but only Descartes *reifies* his method into a procedure that produces not only "truth and right reason" but removes reason itself from this earth by making it part of God's domain. Here it resides, separate from the exigencies of human existence, but accessible to man through his rationality, reached via focused introspection and long chains of reasoning: "From the fact that God is not a deceiver, it necessarily follows that in this matter I am not deceived" (Sixth Meditation). This is the *"maximum maximorum"* move Serres satirizes.[59] In separating mind (where reason resides) from body, Descartes makes mind pure intellection, immaterial, unaffected by the extended world of body.

Mind and reason, then, become associated with a new (nonhuman) realm. Because of this association with God, Himself sheer perfection, Descartes' beginning assumptions, those "clear and distinct" ideas, lie beyond question. With the ends of human thought—knowledge, morals, values—allied with a fixed, static, certain "God,"[60] reason itself, its operations and methods, became mechanical, calculable, designed as Michael Oakeshott (1967) says, "of attaining given ends not themselves subject to the criticism of reason" (17, fn. 3). This sense of reason which is beyond the reasonableness of human doubt (Descartes' project) leads, paradoxically, to a limitation on knowledge—i.e., restricting it (a) to the formulaic, and (b) to that already known. Blaise Pascal (1623–1662), coiner of that fine *bon mot*—"the heart has its reason of which reason knows not"—realized that this quest for absolute certainty made knowledge only partial and took thinking out of the realm of the human. As Oakeshott says, Pascal knew

> the only knowledge that is certain is certain on account of its partiality; the paradox that probable knowledge has more of the whole truth than certain knowledge. (20)

The whole world of the probable, yet to come into existence—a world and logic both Pascal and C. S. Peirce explored so well—with its realization that all knowledge is forever incomplete, forever partial, forever open to further exploration, is by Descartes here closed.[61] In short, the world of rational certainty—a world our educational methods still inhabit, uncritiquing of its assumptions—is a limited, lifeless, spiritless world; and the God which created this world is "a medieval God" (Blumenberg, 1987, 314)—a *deus ex machina*—forever chained to the machine it created.

Giambattista Vico

Born (1668) a generation after Descartes death, Vico was, in the early part of his life, much taken with Cartesian rationalism and the certainty in thinking it produced. As he said (in *Universal Law*, 1721), recalling his earlier academic years (the decade 1699–1709), "All my life I had delighted in the use of reason more than in memory" [personal, felt experience] (in Bergin and Fisch, 1968, 37). In his later studies, Vico, drawn over time to the literature, fables, myths, and ancient histories of the Hebrews, Egyptians, Greeks, and Romans, came to realize that Descartes' *sum* (I am) was more a rational "mind" than a feeling, experiencing human, and that this mind/person, fully formed, fully rational was quite allied with a rational God. Both of these assumptions were an anathema to Vico: he felt the (hu)man was sensate, developed from wilder, more beastly forms and that all humanity was categorically separate from God.[62] In his *Scienza Nuova* (*New Science* [*NS*] 1984/1744),[63] Vico says, "Our treatment of it (humanity) must start from the time these creatures (the heroes and giants of which the myths of old tell us) began to think humanly." In the next paragraph he says: "But these first men, who later became the princes of the gentile nations, must have done their thinking under the strong impulsion of violent passions, as beasts do" (*NS*, 339, 340). In the beginning of Book II, he continues the same theme: "From these first men, stupid, insensate, and horrible beasts, all the philosophers and philogians[64] should have begun their investigations. . . ." (*NS*, 374).

What Vico is saying here is, first, that the rational man Descartes (and those before him) posits is really a development of humanity over long stretches of time—the ages of the gods, heroes, and giants, and finally the humans of which the ancient poets (such as Homer) speak. Second, Vico is asserting that rational man, categorically separate from and inferior to God (never knowing of His reason) developed as humanity developed, from the beasts of nature. Thus, for the mature Vico it is to history and myth, not to rational logic, that we should turn in trying to understand ourselves and our place in the cosmos. In this, Vico reaches across centuries to find common conversation with some contemporary (complexity) theorists. Further, Vico asserts that this rise from bestiality came from those few "among the Greeks (who have given us all we know of gentile antiquity)" who were "theological poets" (*NS,* 361). A few pages further in this chapter he says:

> Hence poetic wisdom, the first wisdom of the gentile world, must have begun with a metaphysics not rational and abstract like that of learned men now, but felt and imaged as that of these first men must have been, who, without power of ratiocination, were all robust sense and vigorous imagination. (*NS,* 374)[65]

In this statement lie not only patriarchal and racist sentiments, but a direct challenge to the rational thought which in one way or another influenced the scholastics, the humanists, the rationalists, the empiricists. Vico's *New Science* is truly a new science, one that honors the creative, the imaginative, the felt, the fearful.[66] Vico, in his way, has provided a new metaphysical base on which to build a concept of curriculum; a base which starts with sensate persons, not with rational minds.

Vico's *New Science* did not come easily. The version usually read (1744) is his third and came forth six months after his death in that year. Hayden White, in his Biographical Note to the International Symposium (commemorating the third century of Vico's birth) says that the 1730 and 1744 editions were so different from the first, 1725, edition "as to constitute a new creation" (1969, xxv). Bergin and Fisch, in their 1968 Introduction to Vico's *New Science* (3rd edition), comment that prior to the first edition there was "a quite different draft, since lost, which seems to have borne the title *New Science concerning the Principles of Humanity*"; and that the phrase "principles of humanity" appears in both the first and third editions, with Vico, in correspondence, referring to his book as a work "on the principles of humanity" (xxxviii). This bit of historical artifact is important because it is the concept of being human—more specifically the transformation of beasts of nature to men of nations—which makes the *New Science* new.

Breaking with those philosophers who preceded him—those who studied the logic of reason or the physics of nature, or the theology of God—Vico studied the origins of humanity. He looked at what he considered to be the history of humankind[67] and in so doing he elevated the concept of history itself (human experience) to the forefront. As Isiah Berlin (1969) says, upon reading Vico's *New Science,* one sees that he "had not enough talent for his genius. Too many ideas are struggling for simultaneous expression." Yet for all this toil and turmoil, Vico "uncovered a sense of knowing which is basic. . . ." This knowing is personal, experiential, historical; it is not a form of "knowing that," nor of "knowing how." "It is not analyzable except in terms of itself." It is neither inductive nor deductive. It "is the sort of knowing which participants in an activity [the experiencers] claim to possess as against mere observers. . . ." (373–76). For Vico, presaging Dewey's notion of the experiencer participating in a social situation, this knowing is first and foremost "poetic." Discovering this "Principle," says Vico, was the "master key" of his new science.[68] He goes on to say that

> The (poetic) characters of which we speak were certain imaginative genera (images for the most part of animate substances, of gods or heroes, formed by their imagination) . . . [and that these] allegories are found to contain meanings not analogical but univocal, not philosophical but *historical*, of the peoples of Greece of those times. (*NS, 34;* emphasis added)

The importance of this statement to Vico is brought forth in a quotation Donald Philip Verene (1993) posits, assessing Vico's thought:

> If only Italy had listened to Giambattista Vico, and if, as at the time of the Renaissance, it had served as a guide to Europe, would not our intellectual destiny have been different? Our eighteenth-century ancestors *would not have believed that all that was clear was true;* but on the contrary that "clarity is the vice of human reason rather than its virtue," because a clear idea is a finished idea. They would not have believed that reason was our first faculty, but on the contrary that imagination was. (3; emphasis added)[69]

Of all Vico contributed to Western thought (see also Fleener, Trueit, this volume) that which he offered most to educational thought was this concept of the role and power of imagination. An imagination born not of rational reason but of experiential doing. The sense of "being," which emerges here, arises from passionate involvement, not from dispassionate observation. This involvement is "poetic," in the sense that poets are doers, creators: "The very persons who by imaging did the creating," were called "poets," which is Greek for "creators" (*NS,* 374). In this act of creation, there is a certain primitive robustness and vigor, indeed a vitality that has a wildness, even barbarity about it. Ultimately this primitiveness needs to be tamed, controlled but never to the extent that the passion of the primitive is lost: " *Men at first feel* without perceiving, *then they perceive* with a troubled and agitated spirit, *finally they reflect* with a clear mind" (*NS,* 218; emphasis added).[70] This sense of knowing, indeed of being, is both dynamic and developmental; it presages Dewey's "plunging into experience," thus transforming experience into *an experience,* of Whitehead's feeling a situation, acquiring a "prehension," of Piaget's constructive process of re-equilibration, and is reminiscent of the struggle Plato describes as one tries to climb out of the darkness of the Cave into the light of Understanding. In Vico's view, this struggle is never ending, never "finished," it always recourses to retain its dynamic vitality, its power of primitive passion, and hence the cycle from primitive passion to rational reason must recourse back to primitive passion but at a higher, more conscious and complex level. (Vico, presaging Kant, was a true believer in the long-term progress of society.)

This dynamic and developmental view of knowing, really of understanding and being—indeed of educating—is, in its never endedness, never finishedness, a real alternative to Ramus' chart of all knowledge, to Descartes' method for discovering (God's) truth, and to Tyler's criteria for a good curriculum. This view of knowing, of realizing, leads to a different sense of curriculum, one which is not "methodized" but is transformative (Doll, 1993) or dynamic (Fleener, 2002). In this curriculum, which dances, knowing transforms itself, takes knowledge as knowledge beyond itself into that fascinating, aesthetic and spiritful,

> imaginative realm, born of the echo of God's laughter where no one owns the truth and everyone has the right to be understood. (Milan Kundera, in Richard Rorty, 1989, frontispiece)

Summary

In this section I have tried to show that *method*, a procedure so important to current curricular and instructional thought and practice, has a foundation of support well anchored in many centuries of Western educational and intellectual thought. Historically method has combined the simple with the certain, producing a crass simplicity and superficial certainty. All this was seen over and approved by a mechanical God. In the latter Renaissance ages, method became a movement, permeating virtually all intellectual thinking, and in the sixteenth and seventeenth centuries laid down a legacy—that of "the wild arrogance of reason"[71]—which remains with us today. In today's post-modern world, I suggest we need a new sense of method, one more lively, creative, imaginative, chaotic, and complex than that given to us by modernism. Vico, himself "an ancient not a modern," saw, centuries ago, the need to move beyond the rigidity of modernism's *scientific* rationality so as to include the power of the historically *storied* and the generative creativity of the *spiritful* and *spiritual*. In the last section, I would like to integrate these three S's to combine the strength of the Scientific with the power of the Storied and the vitality of the Spiritful and Spiritual to bring forth a new sense of method—one which helps develop the creativity, imagination, and intuition present in human experience and which honors these qualities as they appear in cosmic creativity.

Toward a New "Method"

> In order to learn you must desire to learn, and in so desiring not be satisfied
> with what you already incline to think.
>
> C. S. Peirce, "Lectures of 1898"

> The idea that . . . we can substitute "method" for deliberation . . . is just wishful
> thinking.
>
> Richard Rorty, *Consequences of Pragmatism*

In some ways it is not really a method I am going to talk about in this final section. Method, as has been shown in this paper, carries with it a sense of that which is formal, rigid, universal—a path or way for all to follow, the "one and only way." What I am going to talk about in this section, a new, livelier, spirit-filled method, is more like a habit—personal, private, varied according to circumstances and above all reflected upon. There is a similarity here between curriculum and currere—that which is laid out publicly and that felt, experienced personally.[72] Gerald Holton in his fine book on scientists and their methods (1973)—a forerunner to I. Bernard Cohen's rather monumental later work (1985), both a treasure trove of stories about scientists, really physicists—comments that

> Scientists themselves, by and large, have traditionally helped to derogate or avoid
> discussions of the personal context of discovery in favor of the context of justifi-
> cation. (17).

Holton goes on to label the science of justification (where one "drycleans" thought of all "personal elements") as S_2 and the "personal struggle" the scientist goes through in arriving at the point where s/he can present justification as S_1 (19–20). It is the S_1, the personal struggle, "the arena of one's own imaginative processes" I wish to focus on in this section. I believe spirit lies in personal struggle (Serres, 1997, 70–72), with all its complexities and chaotic happenings (irrationalities); and that in bringing forth this struggle and reflecting on it, a new, more humane, method can be found. This method used for curriculum design and instructional delivery has the potential, I maintain, for bringing professional education courses alive and of imbuing them with a spirit that is deep, rich, lovely and intellectually captivating. (Doll, 2004). This method is, of course, much allied with the pragmatist ones of Charles Peirce, William James, and John Dewey.

It is quite a leap to jump from eighteenth century Naples with Vico to late nineteenth and early twentieth century Boston with the pragmatists. But this is exactly what Max Fisch—a Vichean and Peircean scholar—does in his "Vico and Pragmatism" (1969) written for the three–hundredth anniversary commemorative of Vico's 1668 birth. The point of contact Fisch makes between Vico and Peirce (1839–1914) is the rejection, indeed disgust, each has with Cartesian rationalism. Fisch's point, though, is not merely that two philosophers, centuries apart, reject a third philosopher's way of thinking, but rather that in their rejection of the rigid formalism of Cartesian thought, each provides a similar life-breathing alternative. And for purposes of this paper, the rejection is not merely of a person and a time-centered historical movement, but of an educational paradigm that has dominated curriculum formation and delivery for the past three to four centuries.

Commenting on Cartesian logic and its embeddedness as a "standard" in university logic textbooks from the mid-1660s on, Peirce (in 1903) says: "*This approach* to logic standardized into textbook form *is a shameful exhibit* of what two and a half centuries of man's greatest achievements could consider as a good account of how to think" (in Fisch, 1969, 405; from Peirce 5.84; emphasis added).[73] Nothing much has really changed in the hundred years since Peirce made this comment; textbooks still present knowledge in a formalized, "dry-cleaned," manner, devoid of the personal struggles, doubts, intuitive leaps, guesses that brought knowledge to this S_2, refined and justified form. Unfortunately the "scientific methods" movement which educationists and social scientists in general abstracted from pragmatism's experimental and inquiry approach also drew out the very life spirit of this movement. The recent "Standards" movement in curriculum thought has done little to move us beyond the "shameful exhibit" Peirce saw, or the "deadness" of methods Whitehead saw (on "Standards" see Pinar, 2004, especially Ch. 9).

To understand the import of Peirce's remark and its relation to the alternative both he and Vico proposed, it is necessary to go back to Aristotle and his distinction (in the *Organon*) between *demonstrative* and *dialectical* reasoning. The former (demonstrative reasoning) is certain since it starts with "first truths known by intuition" and proceeds carefully step-by-step to "conclusions necessarily true" (Fisch, 1969, 402). This method was not only that of Aristotle but also that of Ramus and Descartes, and it has family resemblances with Holton's S_2 (formal presentation) and the scientific method used in both social science and educational circles. Aristotle's other form of reasoning (dialectical) deals with the probable, not the certain. It is "problem-centered and social" (402); experiential, practical knowledge crafted over time via a community of inquirers (neophytes and experts) in the field. In this method, really a practice and habit of inquiry, resides personalness (Holton's S_1), practice (pragmatism's active doing), probability (the contextualization of all knowledge and uncertainty of all knowing), and play (chaos and complexity's stretching of boundaries). Before going on to describe a "pedagogy of practice" which I hope amalgamates the foregoing, I'd like to make some comments on John Dewey's notions of both scientific method and process of inquiry.

Dewey's devotion to science, at times excessive,[74] is well known. He is considered, in educational circles at least, the father of the scientific method and rightly so, for a reading of his corpus reveals an early and long bias toward science.[75] In social science terms this method is generally considered as (1) collecting data, (2) forming hypotheses, (3) working out a methodology, (4) testing the hypothesis via experiment, (5) assessing the validity of the hypothesis. This method, often rigid in its application, certainly regarding its presentation to teachers (in terms of experimental design) not only has strong Ramist qualities to it but is also an aberration of what scientists do and a distortion of Dewey's "Five Phases, or Aspects, of Reflective Thought" (1933, 106–18).[76]

Paul Feyerabend, in his *Against Method* (1988), makes a number of points regarding scientists' ways of working (the S_1's of Holton). He states (1) that the conception of *a method* scientists would follow in "facing concrete research problem" is "much too crude" to be useful; (2) that scientists use and need "non-scientific" procedures—hunches, guesses, intuitions—as well as more formal ones; (3) that method actually constrains creativity and scientific progress (1–15). Hence, the only "method" which is really useful, and indeed which is used, is that of an "anything goes" approach. Such a "method" is, of course, more an attitude or habit of operation than a procedure to be followed.

Dewey, presaging Feyerabend, following Peirce, wants to develop a habit of mind in his "phases of reflective thought." About a *general method dulling* and restricting such thought Dewey (1966/1916) says:

> Nothing has brought pedagogic theory into greater disrepute than the belief that it is identified with handing out to teachers recipes and models to be followed in teaching. (170)

And three pages later he says:

> Imposing an alleged uniform general method upon everybody breeds mediocrity in all but the very exceptional. And measuring originality by deviation from the mass breeds eccentricity in them. (173)

While Dewey is against method as a recipe or rule to be universally followed, he is not against method itself. In fact, the quotes just given are part of his Chapter Thirteen, "The Nature of Method." Here he distinguishes general method, which he abhors—as dulling and restricting—from an individual's personal "way of attack upon a problem":

> The specific elements of an individual's method or way of attack upon a problem are found ultimately in his native tendencies and his acquired habits and interests. (173)

And,

Method . . . is the effective direction of subject matter to desired results. (165)

To understand Dewey's meaning in these two quotes—"problem," "habits," subject matter," "direction," "results" as well as his emphasis in his "Five Aspects of Reflective Thought," it is necessary, I believe, to go back to Charles Peirce's definition of pragmatism and forward to Dewey's expression of inquiry in his *Logic: A Theory of Inquiry* (1938). In the early 1870s, Peirce (1998/1913) and other "men of science" formed a group—called, "half-ironically, half-defiantly," the Metaphysical Club[77]—to study questions of logic and inquiry from a view that rejected both a metaphysical approach and a solipsistic, subjective one (399). In (probably) 1872, Peirce delivered a "little paper" (since lost) to this group wherein he brought forth his thoughts on these issues, particularly regarding Alexander Bain's (1818–1903) concept that belief was "that upon which a man is prepared to act." Thus was born pragmatism, the concept that the value of an idea lies in the consequences resulting from a person's acting on the idea.[78] This notion of acting, doing comes forth strongly in Peirce's 1905 statement that "the rational purport of a word or other expression, lies exclusively in its conceivable bearing upon the conduct of life . . . *there is nothing more to it*" (332; emphasis in original). In the ensuing years between Peirce's first putting forth the word in the 1870s and 1905 when he chose *pragmaticism,* a word "ugly enough to be safe from kidnappers" (395), much discussion ensued. But,

> all pragmatists of whatsoever stripe will cordially assent to the statement the meaning of hard words and abstract concepts . . . [lies, not in Aristotle or Ramus' first principles, nor in Descartes' personal intuitions][79] but in that experimental method by which all the successful sciences (in which number nobody in his senses would include metaphysics) have reached the degree of certainty that are severally proper to them today—this experimental method being itself nothing but a particular application of an older logical rule, 'By their fruits ye shall know them.' (400–01)

In this discussion of a method—again for Peirce such is really a habit of action, one which can and should be changed as ongoing evolutionary situations warrant—three characteristics stand-out: actions/doings, consequences, purposes. This might be expressed by saying that pragmatism honors not first principles, nor accepted authority, nor personal intuitions, nor. . . . but honors only the process whereby concepts (and precise language for Peirce) are developed by experimentation; truth (or validity or usefulness) being determined by the consequences of public acts resulting from intentional doings.

Dewey's particular take on pragmatism—more humanistic than either Peirce's logical validity approach or James' metaphysical, personal approach—is contained in his "Five Aspects of Reflective Thought"—again foundational for a pragmatic approach to education. He brings forth these aspects in his *How We Think* (1933). In the seventh chapter, "Analysis of Reflective Thought," Dewey states that all reflective thinking begins with some problem (to be solved), or some perturbation (to spur inquiry). Between the "perplexed, troubled, or confused *situation* at the beginning and a cleared-up, unified, resolved *situation* at the close" there lie "five phases of reflective thought":

1. A *suggestive phase* where the mind leaps forward, too quickly, to a possible solution;
2. An *intellectualization phase* where the *difficulty felt* is turned into a *problem to be solved;*
3. A *hypothesis forming phase* to act as a guide for close observation and data gathering;
4. A *reasoning phase (often mathematical)* where the mind logically examines, thinks;
5. A *testing by overt action* phase where corroboration, verification, failure occur. (106–18)

The ordering of these stages is "not fixed," far from it—all intermix continually—and the advantage of such a procedure, this "habit of reflective activity," is that "the person who really thinks learns as much from his failures as from his successes."

A number of issues stand out here. One is Dewey's commitment to problem framing; turning a felt discomfort or bother into a stated problem—here I would be happier had Dewey moved more toward inquiry and exploration, the "investigative" and creative, as I believe Whitehead did (Doll, 2004). Another is the commitment to action within a particular situation. Dewey's sense of theory is practically oriented; it is a *praxis* (Doll, 1993). A third issue is Dewey's recognition that such a method, born of situation, investigating situation, goes beyond such to become a habit of operation that frees one from the confines of dogma or past authority or personal prejudice. It is most unfortunate that this way of thinking, indeed of being, that Dewey thought would be so freeing to humankind has been rigidified by the schools into a set method—the very procedure Dewey wished to avoid. Virtually no one in the social sciences, including education, would envision the "scientific method," as freeing. Justifying yes, freeing no. Rather it, and its sister, "methods of instruction," are enslaving. Creativity does not live at this address.

Dewey, drawing heavily on Peirce, opens his *Logic: The Theory of Inquiry* (1938) with the observation that logic has traditionally been associated with "the relations of propositions to one another, such as affirmation-negation, inclusion-exclusion, particular-general, etc. (1). These propositions have historically been born *a priori* of ultimate first principles (those Ramus believed should guide curriculum design and implementation) or of personal, intuitive insights (those Descartes relied on). In this frame *reason* emerges "as the power which intuitively apprehends" first principles, or carefully guides (step-by-step) self-evident intuitions to conclusive certainties (10). Dewey, again following Peirce and his distrust of metaphysics, sees this framework (questionable at best) as no longer relevant. Once we adopt the pragmatic view that ideas are to be evaluated in terms of their consequences and we can test those consequences for their usefulness, the external and dominating standards/categories of logic no longer apply. As Dewey says: "postulating a faculty that had the power of direct apprehension of 'truths' that were axiomatic" becomes unnecessary. Instead, via the scientific method—observation, hypothesis formation, testing—much allied with reflective practice, we can devise a "self-corrective process of inquiry" in which logical standards and forms will emerge and "to which further inquiry shall submit" (5).

This continually, ongoing, recursive, opening/closing process whereby forms and standards *emerge* is much akin to the field of emergence so prominent in complexity theory today. This sense of an emergent "method," itself a "criticism of methods previously tried" and without "an external standard,"[80] begins in personal perturbation, in a *feeling* of discomfort. It is situation bound and ends up in personal belief or tentative knowledge which, when shared with others, becomes more refined and transformed into a cultural community's accepted beliefs, knowledges, practices. Dewey calls this process "warranted assertibility" (6–7), indicating both the process of warranting the belief, knowledge or practice has undergone and the tentativeness of the conclusion drawn. Done over time, this process becomes less a procedure to follow and more an internal habit—of doing, of being, of forming a personal "existential matrix." This matrix has both biological (Ch. II) and cultural (Ch. III) roots. Biologically, life is not only active, it is interactive, always dealing with the environment of which it is part, and forming "a delicate and complex system," which maintains a sense of stability over time as the living organism interacts with other parts of this delicate and complex system (26). Such a framing is quite consistent with the dynamic equilibria frame posited by both process philosophers and complexity theorists.[81]

Interaction with and within the environment is not merely physical; it is cultural as well. Bringing forth ideas into the light of cultural criticism and development is a key part of the scientific method, harkening all the way back to Francis Bacon.[82] Public discourse and verification is key if a personal idea, belief, knowledge is to have any value in a community arena. Education then needs to be democratic, as Dewey pointed out in his educational *magnum opus, Democracy and Education* (1966/1916). Each reinforces the other; each transforms the other. Classroom methods courses then should be interactive and communal, subject to ongoing questioning and verification, not didactic and formulaic. Alternatives here are not deviations but opportunities, just as "mistakes" may hide truths not seen.

In considering logic as a matrix of inquiry, with forms and standards emerging rather than being externally imposed, Dewey is very much developing an epistemology based on practice not on verification. In this, he is akin to Gerald Holton's S_1 and to Gregory Bateson's and A. N. Whithead's process epistemology—that of a dynamic system (Fleener, 2002). While Dewey is not usually thought of as a "systems" theorist, his use of matrix is indeed that of a systems thinker and when he makes comments such as "meaning is developed in relation to other meanings," or a proposition "has meaning as a member of a system not in isolation," or "as soon as a meaning is treated *as* a meaning, it becomes a member of a system of meanings" (301), he is indeed dealing with systems. In Dewey's sense of system two foci stand out: habit and situation.

In natural environmental interactions, an organism seeks a pattern for both its understanding and control within a situation. The back-and-forth of the organism-environment interactions is diffuse enough that habitual response "does not become completely rigid . . . but retains a certain amount of flexible capacity to undergo further modification as the organism meets new environing conditions" (32). In fact, only in "school and factory 'work' . . . are habits limited . . . to rather artificial conditions." Neither of these places is designed to foster creativity; both are too rigid, too mechanical.

Situation for Dewey is "not a single object or event or set of objects and events" (66); rather, it is "a contextual whole" wherein special objects (problems, issues) stand out for attention and investigation (67). Any situation, with all its contextual intertwinings, needs to be felt before the problem to be solved (or issue to be explored) is brought forth. Dewey's "method" (scientific and pragmatic) is neither rigid nor expedient. When done naturally, it is "the effective direction of subject matter to desired results"[83] and comes from an individual's "native tendencies" refined through "acquired [reflective] habits and interests." The development of these native tendencies, indeed their transformation into mature, reflective skills, is the whole purpose of education for Dewey (1933):

> The real problem of intellectual education is the *transformation* of more or less casual curiosity and sporadic suggestion into attitudes [habits] of alert, cautious, and thorough inquiry. (84)

A Pedagogy of Practice

> The Greek schools of philosophy . . . have not handed down any teaching on method in their dialectics because children learned more than enough method through practice. . . . The ancients believed that the ordering of studies should be left to prudence which is not governed by any art. . . . Only artisans instruct

that you do this first, that next, and then the other things in order: this method does not mold a man of practical wisdom, but some type of craftsman. (Vico, 1988, 98)[84]

A person of practical wisdom is more than a mechanic, fixing that which is, but is a creator, imaginative of insight. Helping such a person emerge and develop requires a certain pedagogy, not the pedagogy of mimesis (copying) but the "pedagogy of practice" wherein the practice is not mere repetition but the practice of doing, reflecting, visioning, doing yet again with a "difference." Such a pedagogy is one of transformation, of transforming an individual's nascent, natural instincts, interests, powers, abilities into mature, reflective, successful, and productive ones. A curriculum organized around such practice—itself honoring the play of performance and the performance of play—is dynamic, not stagnant. Like a play, the performance has structure but also flexibility as the performer (the "*currerer*" running the curriculum course) interacts with the audience and the other actors (the environment). The play (or curriculum) becomes transformed as it is produced by the players acting and interacting. In this sort of performative process, a semi-stable, semi-permeable structure and fluid habits continually and dynamically interact that new knowledge and new forms keep emerging. One might well call this not only a transformative curriculum but also an emergent one.

The concept of curriculum, given us by Peter Ramus and dominating our thinking (through Ralph Tyler) until William Pinar (1975, 1976, 1995, 2004) launched his reconceptualization movement, is a curriculum not only stable but simple (textbookish I call it), and assumes the learner to take in the qualities of the curriculum set forth. A dynamic, emergent curriculum, transformative in its processes, sees both the learner and the curriculum (child and curriculum, in Dewey's phrasing) having their own voice. The point-counterpoint of this duet/dialogue, with practice and over time, produces transformative results. Whereas Ramus' curriculum begins with first principles, a reconceptualized curriculum has no pre-set beginning,[85] the beginning is in the existential moment and as the experience, with communal help, plunges into a situation, a matrix of connections (rich, recursive, relational, and rigorous) emerge. In this way, child and curriculum, learner and teacher, self and text, person and culture dance together to form a complex pattern—ever changing, ever stable, ever alive.

Notes

1. The actual quotation is "I have a horror of creative intelligence congealing into too-good teaching—static ideas: [i.e., that] '*This* is the correct thing to know' . . ." (In Price, 63).
2. Curriculum originally meant a (circular) racetrack for running, I assume one like that at the Circus Maximus. John Calvin in the mid–1500s appropriated the word

for his notion of a course of life (*curriculum vitae*). See Doll, 2002, 28–32 and the *Oxford English Dictionary* (2ⁿᵈ edition, 1989). For an extended study of the word and concept of curriculum in the sixteenth and seventeenth centuries, see Triche and McKnight, 2004.

3. As I have said elsewhere: "No one word captures the tenor of the sixteenth and seventeenth centuries better than method. Method was the hallmark of the new Copernican science; it formed the heart of Descartes' treatise, 'On the Method of Rightly Conducting One's Reason and Seeking Truth in the Sciences,' and represented the vehicle by which a rising merchant and Protestant class could assert itself" (Doll, 2002, 30). Grafton and Jardine (1986) make this point strongly when they say:

> The individualism, verging on hero-worship [of the great teachers], of early humanism gave way in the early sixteenth century to an ideology of routine, order, and above all, "method" (123).

4. In the Introduction to *A Post-Modern Perspective on Curriculum* (1993), I explain the difference I see between modernist and postmodernist ways of thinking. Basically I see modernist thinking, that which originated out of both the Scientific Revolution of the seventeenth century and Enlightenment thought of the eighteenth, as focusing on closure and certainty—François Lyotard's *grand écrits*–while post-modern thinking focuses on openness and the possibility of achieving that which is not yet.

   Zygmunt Bauman in the Introduction to his *Postmodern Ethics* (1993) says that the modernist mind-set rallied around the twin banners of "universality and foundation" (8), and that now we realize such banners will not provide a standard for an ethics nor, I would say, for an epistemology or a pedagogy. "They have run their course" (10).

5. Method in Greek is a composite of two words: *meta* for pursuit, quest, follow and *odos* for way. The Greek and/or Latin notion of "following a way" (really imitating an authority; on this point, see Trueit, this volume) is quite different from our current sense of orderly arrangement. As the *Oxford English Dictionary* (2ⁿᵈ edition, 1989, Vol. IX, 690) says: "The sense of systematic arrangement [we use today for method] is foreign to Greek: it was developed through the special application of Latin method [methodus] by some logicians in the 16ᵗʰ century." Ramus was one of those logicians.

6. Aristotle in his discussions of logic (*Organon*) makes a distinction between dialectical logic (that dealing with probable truth) and "scientific" logic (that which could be demonstrated with certainty). For Aristotle making the probable certain meant a close and rigorous analysis of the probable and its alternatives. For the Renaissance humanists, with their strong interest in literature and existing in an essentially oral milieu, dialectic became the persuasive or rhetorical art of discoursing well. As Ramus was fond of saying, "*Dialectica est ars bene disserendi*" (Ong, 1983, 329, f. 18; Jardine, 1974, 41, f. 1). Thus, the reformist humanists moved rhetoric from its medieval position as ancillary to dialectic—being only the choice of phrasing and delivery in a thoughtful, well-reasoned (and hence correct) declamation—to the dominant position in the trivium as "the art of arts." Persuasion thus came to dominate truth, as rhetoric came to dominate logic.

7. I have used the *American Heritage Dictionary*'s (1969, s. v. *dialectic*) definition here as I think it expresses best the point I wish to make about logic and argumentative disputation fitting together. The OED (2ⁿᵈ edition, 1989), though, does make

the same point, albeit less strenuously. Under its first definition for dialectic it says "pertaining to the nature of logical disputation: argumentative, logical" (Vol. 4, 600). The OED etymological dictionary talks of "the investigation of truth by . . . argumentation or disputation," and then gives a history of this concept from Zeno through the Middle Ages.

The conflation of dialectic into rhetoric, the movement from truth to persuasion—one of the features of Ramus' humanism—is handled well by David Hamilton in his 2003 essay. In the trivium (taken from Boethius, who derived it from Aristotle), Grammar dealt with words, Dialectic (or Logic) with propositions and their logical sequence, Rhetoric with the organization of words and phrases for the purpose of persuasion (9). Ramus, following the lead of Agricola (1444–1485)—again "following" Aristotle, as always—focused more on how to arouse the emotion of an audience than with the details of logical sequence and validity. Thus, for Ramus, Dialectic or Logic became subservient to Rhetoric and moved away from scholastic disputation based on finding (*inventio*) and judging (*judicium*) to persuasion. In short, Ramus' method moved from *logical* validity to *psychological* persuasion. On this point, see also Ong, 1983, 100.

8. As stated in a previous endnote (#6), the disputation and argumentation of dialectic was originally meant as a way of arriving at truth. As the centuries progressed it became more and more a set of rhetorical skills and tricks, designed to have an individual win or beat his opponent, not to seek truth even if the opponent was "one hundred times right."

9. The fight between the scholastics (essentially Catholic theologians, interested in preserving the traditions of Aristotle and Aquinas) and the humanists (essentially Protestant reformers with a strong interest in the newly found humanistic [and pagan] literature of the ancient Greek and early Roman poets) was, as the beheading of Ramus shows, intense. The scholastics called the humanists such derogatory names as "poets," "Greeklings," and "Lutherans"; not to mention such unsavory names as "cranes, asses, beasts, blockheads and Antichrists." Not to be outdone in name calling, the humanists called the scholastics "beasts not human beings" . . . "rather like pigs or sows delighting in their own filth and treading on the pearls of others." Erika Rummel (1992) details all this colorfilled history in her article, "*Et cum theologo bella poeta gerit:* The Conflict between Humanists and Scholastics Revisted."

10. Ong (1983) points out that the "Methodists," adherents to the religion Methodism, founded by John Wesley, were also followers of Ramist logic and that Wesley was himself "the author of a logic textbook vaguely reminiscent of Ramism" (304). See also, Walter Ong (1953), "Peter Ramus and the Naming of Methodism," *Journal of the History of Ideas,* 14: 235–48.

   For a history of the sweep of Ramus methods in northern Europe and Colonial America, including an in-depth analysis of Ramus' universal method, see Triche and McKnight, 2004, *passim.*

11. It is these isolated facts, ones without context or relationship, which Whitehead called "scraps of information," "dead," "barren," "lifeless," "useless." See Doll, 2003; Whitehead, 1967, Chs. 1 and 3.

12. It is interesting to note that a subject was then looked upon in terms of the art of teaching it, not in terms of its content. Ramus' method was a teaching method. Hamilton, and Triche and McKnight make this point strongly in their works.

Ong, in his *Rhetoric, Romance, and Technology* (1971, 162–89), argues that a direct connection can be made between Ramus' branching, dichotomizing, atomizing of knowledge and current day computers with their information processing methods. See also, J. Campbell, *The Improbable Machine* (1989), which describes the evolution of machine logic from Ramus to Newell and Simon.

13. The Ramist map is reprinted with permission of the Special Collections, Glascow Unviersity Library, Glasgow, Scotland. It is copied from Peter Ramus' *Professio Regia* (Basile, 1576, folio 3 verso).

   The map—serving also as a table of contents—shows "the [seven] arts included in this volume" and provides a visual representation of the philosophy of Peter Ramus, "completely expanded," of which curriculum is a part. A teaching device, this map puts forth the discipline (of philosophy) "expressed in a Ciceronian manner, and, with examples from Cicero, rightly indicates a pure and genuine method provided to youth [and teachers] to exhort all toward a love of the liberal arts."

14. It is interesting to note that Peter Ramus' name and the word "ramify" come from the same Latin *ràmus,* meaning branching. The OED (1989) states that "ramification" is a sixteenth century French word (Vol. 9, 156).

15. Traditionally, in the sixteenth and seventeenth centuries method was taught as the last (fourth) part of a logic text. It was broken into *ordo* (the overall ordering of subject matter) and method (methodus) wherein "the more unknown and obscure parts of a discipline are explicated and demonstrated." Scholastic argumentation was most arcane and traditional scholastics relished the intricacies of the argument. To short cut this process was heresy. See Peter Dear (1998, 148).

16. Ramus' own style was anything but plain and simple. Ong (1983) says these "were tremendous rhetorical performances . . . attended by huge crowds . . . where even the groundlings or 'yellow beaks,' as the newcomers to the university were called, would have their souls torn out of them. . . . [His] remarks were salted with constant denunciation of the authors his fellow professors were teaching and peppered everywhere with 'Holy Jupiter!' and 'Good god!' and [he] roared all this out with the most spectacular declamation and gesture." Ong (1983) then goes on to say [medieval] "logic had never been like this" (33–34).

17. Samuel Eliot Morison, on whom both Miller and Ong draw, in doing his own research for Harvard's Tercentennary (1936), found such Ramist titles among the early Harvard theses as: "Rhetoric is the Garden of the Affections," "Dialectic is the Sun of the Microcosm, the Arguments are the Radii of Logic," and "Method is the Parent of Intelligence, the Mistress of Memory" (in Ong, 1983, 4). Triche and McKnight (2004) drawing on both Morison's works (1935, 1936) and on internet sites about Puritanism, provide storied examples of how useful New England Puritans found Ramus' method of "logical" analysis in their own declarations of teaching and learning.

18. Miller (1954) points out that the Puritan "simplisté view" of life "rested upon a deep-lying conviction that the universe conformed to a definite, ascertainable truth, and that human existence was to be had only upon the terms imposed by this truth" (5).

19. As an aside, it is interesting to note that Jacques Barzun in his Introduction to the 50th edition of Randall's *The Making of the Modern Mind* (1976) says that as an undergraduate forced to read this "textbook" he was "skeptical of surveys and summaries and pages marred by boldface headings at irritatingly short intervals," but found that this was a textbook "out of the common" (viii). Indeed he found

Randall's "textbook" equal in scope and depth to only two other "textbooks" he would recommend: Aristotle's *Ethics* and William James' *Principles of Psychology.*

Like myself, Hamilton (2003) talks extensively of Ramus' "textbookizing" (my word, not his) of knowledge, and presents the advantages and limitations of such an approach. This paper is devoted to finding an alternative to "textbookizing" knowledge, to letting knowledge flow forth in all its messy fecundity.

20. Peter Sharratt in his "Peter Ramus and the Reform of the University" (1976) states that one of Ramus' reforms of method was to ensure "that each art, each subject of the curriculum have a clearly defined scope, absolutely distinct from that of any other. Yet the method for explaining each art would be identical," thus ensuring that while the method would be the same in each science, each science would be separate from the other (7 and 14).

    Here is Ramus' sense of the universal. His method starts with universal propositions (those recognized by all as natural and valid) and is applied, universally, to all *ars* (subjects).

21. Regarding the "textbookizing" of knowledge, A. N. Whitehead has this to say: "In the schools of antiquity philosophers aspired to impart wisdom, in modern colleges our humbler aim is to teach subjects . . . to text-book knowledge of subjects . . . [and this] marks an educational failure" (1967, 29).

22. Hamilton in his 2003 paper, makes this point quite strongly when he says that Ramus transformed the trivium of scholasticism's *ars* (grammar, logic, rhetoric) "into [a set of] instructional methods . . . [which have] *served as paradigms in the subsequent history of modern schooling."* (Abstract; emphasis added)

23. Menck, in his *Looking into Classrooms* (2000) has a number of schooling woodcuts from medieval times. In one (44, figure 4.1) there is a picture of a schoolmaster, reed in hand, quizzing young boys on their Latin translations. The master obviously knows the translation by heart. On the left side of the picture, another master is beating the naked backside of one student while another holds him down. A coiled rope for more serious beatings lies in the corner.

24. It is interesting to note that in doing his didactic, Comenius searched for others' "method." Keatinge (1896) points out that he particularly sought out Ratke who did all he could to keep his "method," "a true method he was reported to have discovered," secret: "Ratke made as great a mystery of his method as was possible" (11). In reading these lines, I cannot help but think of the alchemists and their sense of secrecy.

25. Keatinge (1896) translates the Latin here as "the whole art of teaching all things to all men" (157). Considering, though, Comenius' interest in having girls as well as boys educated (*Didactic,* Ch. IX), it seems more accurate to use a generic translation.

26. For Comenius, the *Didactic* was more than just a series of lesson-books, although it was that. It was, as with the German concept of *Bildung,* to influence a person's whole character and was to start "at the mother's knee," and in the *Informatory of the Mother School,* a pamphlet written prior to the *Great Didactic,* Comenius lays down principles for the child's upbringing right from birth. Some of the chapters have titles such as "The greatest care should be taken of children," "God's most precious gift;" "Why God sends so many children into the world," "How their safety and health can be attained," "How they can be imbued with piety" (Keatinge, 15).

27. *Bildung* (formation) has roots deep within German culture. Hans-Georg Gadamer (1993/1960) talks of *Bildung* as the formative (historical) process of an individual "getting beyond his naturalness"; following G.W.F. Hegel, he asserts that *Bildung* is the finding of "universal viewpoints from which one can grasp the thing, 'the objective thing in its freedom,' without selfish interest" (14).

    Michael Wimmer (2001), with a Derridean slant, sees *Bildung* not so much in terms of finding a position as having one emerge, as "self-transformation without origin" (158). *Bildung*, thus, cannot be given, nor intentionally developed—hence unlike Gadamer is not to be allied with education, which has intentional purpose associated with it—rather *Bildung* is somehow experientially "bound up with the event of the experience of the other" (162). Such an experiencing—alienating and self-sustaining, transforming in a recursive manner—does have a transcendent value to it for both Gadamer and Wimmer. Both see *Bildung*, as do virtually all German dictionaries, "as intimately involved with the doctrine of man as "imago dei," as the image of God, and, in Vichean style, carrying man's "obligation to transform himself in the image of God" (160–61).

28. Rudoplh Künzli, the Swiss Didaktiker, in his article on "German Didaktik," (Westbury, 2000), says that in a forming of the individual through active participation in the cultural assets (of a society) . . . The initial task of the Didaktiker is *not* to ask how a student learns or how a pupil can be led toward a body of knowledge . . . Instead the initial task of the Didaktiker is *to seek the character-forming significance of the knowledge and skills that a culture has at disposal.* (46; emphasis in original)

    Künzli then goes on to say, in a footnote, that in "the classical expression of Didaktik . . . the unconditional validity of the material and its presentation by the *catechist* guaranteeing *orthodoxy* are central" (49; emphasis added).

29. The Dear (1995) quote runs: "Protestants would not accept the authenticity of Catholic tradition. Catholics held their tradition to be justified by the continual, behind-the-scenes guidance of the Holy Spirit. Just so, humanistically informed philosophers had their own functional equivalent of the Holy Spirit. It was something of consuming interest by the end of the sixteenth century: *Method*" (121; emphasis added).

30. While the Catholic parochial system relies heavily on memorization and its own sense of method, drawn from the *Ratio Studiorum* of the sixteenth century, Catholic education also has within its history of rhetoric a good deal of the oral and spirit-ful, even of the poetic. This sense of spirit has played a large role in the history of Catholic thought. See, for examples the works of Thomas Berry (1988a; 1988b, 1996). Especially noteworthy are his remarks on John Dewey's years in China (n.d.). Berry also spent time in China, recalled from there at the time of the Cultural Revolution.

31. Though I believe it is quite possible to see both the cybernetics movement (Hayles, 1999) and the Tyler rationale (Tyler, 1950) emanating from this general frame of experimentation, measurement, and verification, I believe it is also possible to see that the concept of experimentation—that which so attracted Dewey to the scientific method—is most prominent in cybernetics and most missing in the rationale. Education has borrowed only part of the scientific method, that of measurement and verification; the goals have come not from experimentation but from personal, metaphysical beliefs—a point Herbert Kliebard (1995) makes about Tyler's goals.

32. Jerome Bruner (1986) calls this form of thinking (the logico-scientific) "paradigmatic," (13) as it is the dominant mode of Western rationality. Alfred North

Whitehead (1967) calls this form of thinking the "greatest intellectual success which mankind has achieved" (46).

33. This positivist outlook, so influential in Anglo-American thought during the first and middle part of the twentieth century, was strongly influenced by the logical positivism movement of the Vienna Circle in the 1920s and 1930s. This group of practicing scientists and logicians, taking a misreading of Ludwig Wittgenstein's *Tractatus Logico-Philosophicus* (1919) as their Bible, were committed to the notion that the clarity of the scientific method could be applied to all philosophical propositions and that the real was what was scientifically verifiable—"to squeeze all apparently meaningful propositions into this verificationist straightjacket" (Edmonds and Eidinow, 157). Virtually dominant in English and American university circles during the early and middle parts of the last century, the movement died suddenly in Vienna in the mid–1930s. This death was due partly to the murder of its founder, Moritz Schlick, partly to Hitler's takeover of Austria and persecution of the Jews (the *Anschluss*), and partly to its own lack of validity. As A. J. Ayer, one of the Circle's non-Jewish members, later said: "Well I suppose that the most important of the defects was *that nearly all of it was false*" (157; emphasis added). The movement's origins were founded on nineteenth century physicist Ernst Mach's doctrine of "the economy of thought." Mach "became convinced that the ideals of simplicity in explanation had been of the greatest importance to Copernicus, Galileo, and Newton" (Mandlebaum, 306). For more on this movement see, in addition to Edmonds and Eidinow's (2002) *Wittgenstein's Poker*, and Mandlebaum's (1977) *History, Man, and Reason*, Janik and Toulmin's (1973) *Wittgenstein's Vienna*.

34. While Galileo and Descartes were both deeply Catholic, an important number of their writings were published by Protestant printers (in Leyden) who were "beyond the reach of the Roman Inquisition" (S. Drake, *Galileo Galilei: Two New Sciences*, 1974, xi).

35. For the history of this movement see Robert Kanigel, *The One Best System: Frederick Winslow Taylor and the Enigma of Efficiency* (1997), and for its effect on education, David Tyack, *The One Best System* (1974).

36. Much of this might come from the charming (maybe apocryphal story) of Galileo wanting the Bishops to look through his handmade telescope to observe the moons of Jupiter revolving but the Bishops refusing on the basis they had read Aristotle well on the issue of movement in the heavens. A clash of two paradigms here. For more on this clash see Maurice Finocchiaro (1989).

One of the interesting aspects to me of Galileo's "instrumentality" is that his telescope—not the first done in the medieval ages but by far the best—allowed him to see spots on the sun, the moons revolving around Jupiter, and crags on the moon; the hold of Aristotelian symmetry was so great, however, that the notion of these "irregularities" being *the very nature of Nature* did not occur until the twentieth century.

37. The belief that Galileo was a physical experimentalist, not a theoretical one, has been so pervasive that for centuries the story existed that Galileo actually carried two balls up the hundreds of steps of the tower of Pisa, one ball weighing one pound, the other weighing one-hundred pounds. Galileo, though, was not a husky man.

38. Peter Dear (1995) points out that Alexander Koyré (1978/1939) was one of the first to question "Galileo as a great experimentalist" (124) and preferred to think of Galileo as "a metaphysician" in the Aristotelian sense more than as an experimentalist in our current sense. Dear then goes on to state: While nowadays "there is

general agreement that Galileo did indeed develop his ideas on fall in concert with physical apparatus" . . . he "undoubtedly included a considerable number of thought experiments in his work"; and that "recent research has shown that Galileo aimed at developing scientific knowledge . . . according to the Aristotelian (or Archimedian) deductive formal structure" (124–26).

The important point for this essay is that experimentation—the self-conscious trying out of alternatives—so important to science today, actually came late to the "scientific revolution." Indeed as I have already quoted A.N. Whitehead (1967) as saying, the scientific revolution and its methods were based on a "naïve faith" (16), a "simple faith" (51). I believe this simple and naïve faith has remained with our educational view of scientific method, so that of the triumvirate processes of experimentation, measurement, and verification, only the last two have been prominent in educational methods.

39. Margaret Wertheim's *Pythagoras' Trousers* (1995) is worth reading on this point.

40. An interesting, albeit to me ultimately unsatisfying, book on this issue is Lakoff and Núnez's *Where Mathematics Comes From* (2000). The part of interest is the power they assign to humans to "metaphorize"—the foundation for all abstract thought, as they see it. The unsatisfying part is the sort of tacit reductionist tone I find in their writing.

41. Benjamin Farrington (1964), drawing on others, comments that in his time Bacon was a man "whose main passion in life was the good of mankind and the relief of the misery which belongs to his present state" (16). He goes on, that Bacon's having this vision, this passion, was overlooked in subsequent centuries, when he (Bacon) "was reduced in the nineteenth century to a debatable figure in the history of inductive logic" (17). Such seems to be our perennial tendency as revisionist historians to "read the past in terms of the present."

42. It has been pointed out by some current feminists (Carolyn Merchant, 1995) that Bacon often speaks disparagingly of nature (and hence of women). Merchant points out phrases such as "binding nature into service," making her man's "slave," and taking her "by the forelock" (81–82). These phrases do indeed exist in Bacon but so do one's (in the *New Organon*) where he talks of "man as Nature's agent" (Aphorism 1), of "being obedient to Nature" (Aphorism 3), and of "The subtlety of Nature far surpassing the subtlety of sense and intellect" (Aphorism 10). Bacon's many metaphors are always colorful, and his thoughts about Nature are partly masculine/industrial, partly feminine/alchemical.

43. For an account of Bacon's complex life see L. Jardine and A. Stewart (1998), *Hostage to Fortune: The Troubled Life of Francis Bacon*. London: Gollancz. Towards the end of his life, Bacon was convicted of abusing his power and ended his days in disgrace. Yet, as Jardine and Silverthorne, 2000, xxv, point out, some compared him to Moses. And, as his friend George Herbert said of him, "The alone only priest of nature and men's souls" (quoted in Farrington, 1964, 54).

44. It is interesting to read this quotation about the movement from general principles to the specific being "the parent of errors" and "curse of all science" alongside Ralph Tyler's four steps to organizing a good curriculum.

From now on I will cite, where I can, the *Novum Organum* aphorisms as the work, the book, the aphorism. So this quotation, in this form would be *NO,* I, 69.

The *Novum Organum* (1620) (after Aristotle's *Organum* or Instrument for Rational Thinking) is "the second part of the six-part programme of scientific inquiry assembled under the title *The Great Instauration,* or 'Great Renewal" of learning" (Jardine and Silverthorne, 2000, xiii). This project came at a time when practical experimentation in England—Gilbert, Harvey, Boyle, Hooke—was beginning to achieve prominence. Such experimentation was, though, as I've already said, more tied to medieval Aristotelianism than to our current practice of designing experiments "to test the truth or falsity of a scientific theory" (Jardine, 1974, 137).

45. *AL* refers to Bacon's *New Atlantis* (1605). The II refers to the second book, the VII to the section and the i to the paragraph.

46. These phrases, taken from the *Novum Organum*, (Aphorism 79), show an aspect of Bacon often missed: his Christian (*Genesis* oriented) belief that God had given man the gift of reason that man might dominate all for the benefit of all. This view comes forth strongly in Arthur Lovejoy's *The Great Chain of Being* (1965) and is well expressed in antiquity by Ovid's lovely phrase,

A holier creature than these and of loftier mind, capable of domination over the rest was still to seek. Then man was born. (*Metamorphoses*, I, 75–78)

For Bacon, a member of the English reformers who took to the Bible strongly, man had a duty to honor the honor God gave him. In Farrington's (1964) words:

For Bacon the new vision was shaped in a pronouncedly biblical mould . . . Man was not a child of nature but a superior creature . . . [S]ince God had made nature, the study of it was a religious duty, an act of worship, to be approached with humility and awe. There were virtually only two commandments—to worship God and love your neighbor. To love your neighbor meant actively doing him good. Science which was in one aspect, the worship of God, was also, by the application of knowledge to the relief of man's distress, the means of realizing the love of one's neighbor. (28)

The dictum, "knowledge is power," rightly attributed to Bacon, takes on a multihued emphasis when seen in the context of his vision. Power for Bacon is not mere personal aggrandizement; nor is the masculine control of feminine nature mere sexism: although both power and control do play a role in Bacon's patriarchal/Christian view.

47. Bacon, like Giambattista Vico who followed him, railed strongly against all past philosophical, scholastic, humanist learning. He is at times violent and abusive in his polemic against the "great" minds of Western thought—arrogant in their conceit and "idle chatter" which ignores the miserable plight of humankind. A reference to Aristotle suffices to show this tone of contempt:

Come, then, let Aristotle be summoned to the bar, that worst of sophists, stupefied by his own unprofitable subtlety, the cheap dupe of words. Just when the human mind, borne thither by some favouring gale, had found rest in a little truth, this man presumed to cast the closest fetters on our understandings. He composed an art of manual of madness and made us slaves of words. Nay, ore, it was in his bosom that were bred and nurtured those crafty triflers, who turned themselves away from the perambulation of our globe and from the light of nature and . . . spun out for us the countless quibbles of the Schools. But he, their dictator, is more to blame than they. He still moved in the daylight of honest research when he fetched up his darksome idols from some subterranean cave, and over such observation of particulars as had been made spun as it were spiders' webs which he would have us accept as causal bonds, thought they have no strength nor worth. (*The Masculine Birth of Time*, Chapter Two; in Farrington, 1964, 63).

48. Charles S. Peirce, in one of his last essays, the unpublished "An Essay Toward Improving Our Reasoning in Security and in Uberty" (1998/1913), has a long footnote (464) at the beginning of the essay, challenging Bacon's pessimism that nature is beyond human understanding. There he says of Bacon's (empirical) method, that which is to raise mankind above its inherent limitations (a point akin to so many writing in the methodist vein), that it is "somewhat like a method of bookkeeping," a point which, I believe, will resonate with many of today's scientific researchers. In contrast to Bacon, Peirce goes on to praise Galileo and those who labored so hard (if sometimes misguidedly) to understand Nature and the causes which produce *her* stunning effects. For Peirce, of course, the misguidedness was in working under the mantle of certainty rather than under the cloak of probability.

49. Michael Oakeshott, in his essay "Rationalism in Politics" (1947), talks of "two sorts of knowledge": technical knowledge which is rule governed and easily transmitted, and practical knowledge which resides in the act of doing. Practical knowledge "exists only in use," in practice, in doing. In this story of Pan, Bacon seems to be talking of that which Oakeshott (drawing on Wittgenstein) calls "practical." The irony is that the "scientific method" used in education is almost exclusively technical. The received history of this method seems to have missed the sagacious insight of Bacon—the father of the scientific method.

50. Gerald Holton, in his *Thematic Origins of Scientific Thought* (1973), comments that "on February 10, 1605—a date that might be taken to be historic for physics—[Johannes Kepler] revealed for the first time his devotion to the image of the universe as a physical machine in which universal terrestrial force laws would hold for the operation of the whole cosmos" (12). This mechanistic and anthropocentric view, as we know, held sway well into the twentieth century and the appearance of the quanta. The educational analogies of this view still dominate as is shown by such concepts as a universal IQ and such phrases as "time on task," or "gearing up," or in the simple, linear, direct cause-effect relationship we tacitly assume in our methods of instruction

51. It is ironic that Descartes came upon his "Method for Rightly Conducting Reason . . ." while in a trance-like state, alone in a "stove-heated room," as he served mercenary duty for the Duke of Bavaria in Germany, November, 10, 1619 (Doll, 1993, 30).

52. In both cases there is the notion of a hidden subjectivity. Kliebard (1995) says, referring only to the rationale, but with a comment I believe fits both Tyler's rationale and Descartes' method for right reason, Tyler's use of philosophical and psychological "screens" merely "passes the decisions on to a higher authority," (86): an authority which masks the ultimate arbitrariness and subjectivity of the choices made. In addition to Kliebard see Triche (2002), Ch. 1, and Autio (2002), Ch. V.

53. It is interesting to note in neither the rationale nor the method for right reason that the validity of the original assumptions is not checked. Tyler's phrase of checking to see "whether these purposes are *attained*" (emphasis mine), is most telling. Descartes' phrase is "that nothing is omitted"—in the long chains of reasoning. Questioning basic assumptions was not part of the methodization movement—a point brought home quite strongly by both C. S. Peirce (1992/1898) and by Kurt

Gödel (1963). Such questioning is still not a part of our teacher preparation "methods" courses (Doll, 1993, Ch. 2).

54. Whitehead points out that the overexuberance Western thought has placed in scientific rationality is really a carry over from the theological faith man developed in the middle ages. So the "narrow and efficient scheme of scientific rationality" which has dominated Western thought for the past four centuries is really "the product of a mentality" which found itself "extremely congenial" with medieval theology (1967/1925, 75). In this sense, our methods of teaching are still strongly tied to medieval scholasticism (see also, Trueit, this volume).

55. Whitehead's (1967/1925) statement about logical reason always needing to "transcend itself," (201) lest it become mired in dogma and methodization is most appropriate here.

56. There is, of course, in this idea of studying himself a certain degree of arrogance, but throughout his *Discourse,* Descartes talks of his intellectual powers as being only ordinary powers—of his and of all men's "simple and natural reasonings" (1950, 8). In this, Descartes, like Bacon, believes God has given all men the ability to reason well. This natural reasoning, though, needs direction, guidance, systematization—hence a method. While his method is purely personal, he does believe others may use it effectively. I believe carryovers from this sentiment of all having an innate ability to learn and judge well occurs in the U.S. government's *No Child Left Behind Act* (2001). Through God's act of creation, all humans can learn, 'tis only the right method that is needed for success. Method here, like reasoning, is simple, obfuscated only by the sophisms of the learned. God is thus, not only good; he is in a real sense simple. Along with worrying about good teaching and good thinking (logic), Whitehead also worried about a good God and a simple theology.

57. Michel Serres (1983), in a delightful bit of intellectual play, shows that rather than working alone, Descartes always had assistance in the games of life and logic, Descartes always had God himself as an aide. In the game of life, Serres says, this is indeed a "*maximum maximorum*" move and hence "error has been checkmated." (27).

58. The issue of "embodied knowing"—the bringing together of body and mind—is handled well by Francisco Varela, Evan Thompson, and Eleanor Rosch (1993), by Katherine Hayles (1999), and educationally by Brent Davis, Dennis Sumara, and Rebecca Luce-Kapler (2000).

59. See footnote 56.

60. As Alexandre Koyré (1967) notes, "Descartes' God is perhaps not the Christian God, but a philosophical one"—perfect logic and reason (122).

61. John Deely in a fascinating book—*New Beginnings: Early Modern Philosophy and Postmodern Thought,* 1994—proposes that Descartes' "new method"—"reliable rules," "easily applied," which if "followed" consistently would always produce certain truth (53)—was really a misguided detour in the history of western philosophical thought. Deely argues that in the later Latin period of the fourteenth and fifteenth centuries there was (in the Iberian peninsula with its Catholic spirit) an interest and development of "social, political and religious questions" (41) with particular emphasis on *being* (presaging Heidegger) and semiotics (presaging Peirce). In the popular adoption of Descartes' thinking, some of the key issues for the current post-modern turn, with its emphasis on the full spectrum of human experience (rational and irrational), were lost to Western philosophy for centuries.

62. In Section I of Book II, "Poetic Wisdom" (*NS,* 376), Vico says,

[T]he first men of the gentile nations, children of nascent mankind, created things according to their own ideas. But this creation was infinitely different from that of God. For God, in his purest intelligence, knows things, and by knowing them, creates them; but they, in their robust ignorance, did it by virtue of a wholly corporeal imagination.

63. References to Vico's *New Science of Giambattista Vico,* are hereafter noted as (*NS*) with the appropriate, numbered paragraph (rather than page numbers) which should correspond with other versions of the text; for example, see f.n. 63 below.

64. On searching for the origins of social institutions and humanity, which Vico links, he pays much attention to language. Language was what held a society together. As Vico says: "the first gentile people . . . were poets" (*NS,* 34), and "all the arts of the necessary, the useful, the convenient, and even in large part those of human pleasure were invented in the poetic centuries before the philosophers came" (*NS,* 217).

65. In reading Thomas Cahill's *Sailing the Wine Dark Sea* (2003), one can appreciate Vico, with his sympathetic honoring of the poetry and deeds of the ancient Gods and Heroes (especially as described by Homer), being disgusted by that which was to follow in the human age. Cahill brings forth the noble power of Homer's poetry and lets the beauty of Sappho's poetry sparkle in the brilliant light that bathed pre-Platonic Greece. He also let us see, indeed feel, how in the centuries following Homer and Sappho, both poetry and deeds descended to the vulgar and crass. There was nothing noble or beautiful about the "age of orgies" (my phrase, Cahill's description) that occurred in either ancient Greece or later in ancient Rome; but in both societies the ages of Gods and Heroes had a nobleness as well as primitive vitality to them. Creative but constrained force resided in both. This notion of force being both creative and constrained appears strongly in chaos and complexity theories.

66. The first men/creatures, "robust in imagination" but lacking in ratiocination were fearful of nature's mysteries and powers. From their imagination came myths and stories of appeasement and from these came reflective thought.

67. Vico saw this history as being recursive ("recourso" in Italian). R. G. Collingwood (1993) in his comments on Vico lays out this story quite nicely. Vico believed all gentile humanity began with the Gods and their fabled battles, pure strength. From this emerges the age of heroes (such as Ulysses) and its sense of imagination, cunning and "brilliant originality" which in turn leads to humans and their philosophical thought. This stage, however, always dries up, due to its lack of primitive force—this "thought exhausts its creative power and only constructs meaningless networks of artificial and pedantic distinctions"—and so humanity declines "into a new barbarism." This "cyclical movement is not a mere rotation of history through a cycle of fixed phases; it is not a circle but a spiral . . . thus the Christian barbarism of the Middle Ages is differentiated from the pagan barbarism of the Homeric age by everything that makes it distinctively an expression of the Christian mind" (67–68).

As an aside here, this cycle brings to mind Michel Serres' marvelous play on Roman history in his *Rome: The Book of Foundations* (1991); while the notion of "meaningless networks" and "pedantic distinctions" brings to mind A.N. Whitehead's "dead," "inert," "lifeless" ideas with which this chapter began, as well as scholasticism's convoluted logic.

68. Joseph Levine (1991) in his excellent article "Giambattista Vico and the Quarrel between the Ancients and Moderns," gives an overview of this "discovery," with an emphasis on the literary scholarship controversies surrounding early eighteenth century arts and letters, as well as an emphasis on Vico's own reading of (and being influenced by) Tacitus' "portrait of the barbarous early Germans" (67). The key here is to realize, as Levine says, that "it was not simply that the first men were primitive barbarians [a fascination all Europe had with the western "savages"] but that these (barbarians) were 'poets,' and of their kind supremely good" (68).

69. The statement is actually by Paul Hazard, a Vichian scholar, and appears in Verene's Introduction to Vico's *On Humanistic Education,* a collection of the first six commencement orations (1699–1707) Vico gave to the university community, as Professor of Rhetoric at the University of Naples—a position he held until his death in 1744. These orations form the basis of the thought Vico developed over his lifetime and eventually brought forth in his last and most mature version (1744) of *Nuova Scienza.*

70. This developmental sequence of feeling, perceiving, reflecting in Vico presages the American pragmatists developmental views. Peirce, Dewey, Whitehead all have complementary views of (cognitive) development. The relation between Vico and the American pragmatists is brought out nicely by Max Fisch—a Vichian as well as Peircian scholar—in his essay (1969) "Vico and Pragmatism," while Peirce's sense of creative development, foundational to pragmatist thinking, is well explicated in Douglas Anderson's (1987) *Creativity and the Philosophy of C .S. Peirce.* In the latter, Anderson makes a nice connection between the Dewey of *Art as Experience* and Peirce's notion of creative experience and Hartshorne's Whiteheadian cosmology. In the former, Fisch, quoting Peirce says, "Thus, the very origin of the conception of reality shows that this conception essentially involves the notion of a *community*" (417), a community wherein there is a play and interplay of feelings, perceptions, ideas.

71. This apt phrase is from Hans-Georg Gadamer, and is included in Cheng Zhongying's essay, "A Century Meeting: An Interview with Gadamer," in his *Ontological Hermeneutics,* Vol. 2. (2002). I am indebted to my friend Professor Zhang Hua of East China Normal University for providing me with the quotation and citation.

72. The concept of *currere*—the infinitive, verb, active form of curriculum—was brought forth to the curriculum studies world by William Pinar in his *Curriculum Theorizing* (1975), and by himself and Madeline Grumet in their (too much neglected) *Toward a Poor Curriculum* (1976). As a verb, active, *currere* focuses not on the structure of the course to be run, the curriculum, but on the experience of the individual running the course. In Grumet's own words: "*Currere* . . . seeks to know the experience of the running of one particular runner, on one particular track, on one particular day, in one particular wind" (1976, 36). For a fuller description of *currere* and its historical (mostly phenomenological) origins, especially its sense of "the immediacy and intensity of encounter," see Pinar et al., 1995, 414 and passim.

73. References to Peirce's own writings refer to the volume and paragraph of Peirce's writings in the *Collected Papers of Charles Sanders Peirce* (8 volumes, 1931–1958).

74. Richard Rorty (1999) makes the observation that the difference between pragmatism and neo-pragmatism, of which he is a leading exponent, focuses on pragmatism's fascination with science contrasting with neo-pragmatism's emphasis on the linguistic. He comments: after Quine, Feyerband, Kuhn it is "difficult to recon-

struct the foundationalist assumptions . . . required to take the notion of 'method' seriously" (34). He goes on "there is nothing like Descartes' [and I'd say Ramus'] 'natural order of reasons' to be followed . . . no activity called 'knowing' which has a nature to be discovered, and at which natural scientists [and their methods] are particularly skilled." For an elaboration of Rorty's view of the linguistic, see his *The Linguistic Turn* (1967).

75. A fine example of this bias is shown in Dewey's effusive support for the work of Frederick Matthias Alexander, founder of the Alexander mind-body technique. Trained in theatre, Alexander, in the late 19th century, found himself at times without voice. Doctors and coaches helped not. "F. M." (as he liked to be called) then undertook to study his face and mouth by enunciating before three mirrors. Here he discovered that in enunciation he had a tendency to "pull his head backwards and downwards" (Maisel, 1986, xiii). In correcting this bad habit, Alexander came to realize he needed not just a bodily change but a whole new kinesthetic awareness—a feeling of mind-body integration. It was this intellectual/sensory awareness—to be aware of one's unrecognized habitual physical acts—which constituted the heart of his technique.

John Dewey was most taken with this holistic integration of mind-body and for the last thirty-five years of his life followed the technique. He also wrote the introduction (and edited) one of Alexander's books, *Constructive Conscious Control of the Individual* (1923), and carefully read the manuscript for a second book, *The Use of the Self* (1932). Dewey was only one of a host of Alexander's admirers; George Bernard Shaw and Aldous Huxley also spoke eloquently on his behalf. Randolph Bourne, though, was just as forceful in his criticism of Alexander. Leonard Woolf, husband of Virginia, called him "a man who really has the gold brick" (Maisel, ix). In a time when conmen preyed on a gullible public, hucksters sold snake oil, séances were held for communication with those on "the other side of life," Dewey was bound to find it refreshing to find someone so committed to a *scientific* approach. (Whether Alexander was a scientific conman is an open question.)

In his 1923 Introduction, Dewey praises Alexander effusively and continuously for approaching his subject scientifically. What Dewey seems to mean by this is that Alexander has integrated doing-observing-reflecting in one continual, recursive pattern, always re-doing, re-observing, re-reflecting. In Dewey's own words,

> In some plans there has been a direct appeal to "consciousness" (which merely registers bad conditions); in some, this consciousness has been neglected entirely and dependence placed instead upon bodily exercises, rectifications of posture, etc. But Mr. Alexander has found a method for detecting precisely the correlations between these two members, physical-mental, of the same whole, and for creating a new sensory consciousness of new attitudes and habits. It is a discovery which *makes whole all scientific discoveries,* and renders them available, not for our undoing, but for human use in promoting our constructive growth and happiness. (1923, xxxi–xxxii; emphasis added.)

76. Prodded by writings and reports from the American Academy for Science and the National Research Council, and drawing heavily on the writings of both John Dewey and Joseph Schwab, a number of current science–methods textbooks have adopted an "inquiry" approach, distinguishing inquiry from method and focusing

on the ongoingness and tentativeness of inquiry and appreciating the personal "felt-ness" or "sensateness" inquiry needs.

Many of these texts appreciate the difficulty present in framing inquiry—its elusiveness and undefinability. A difficulty arises when these texts attempt such framing, resulting in a linear and too set set of procedures. For one example of such texts see Etheredge and Rudinsky (2003).

77. Louis Menand (2002) has written an engaging account of the Metaphysical Club (1872–1874) with a concentration on the lives of Holmes, James, Peirce, and Dewey (a nonmember but strongly influenced by the thinking of those in the club).

78. Pragmatism, a word adopted by Peirce as a practical way to make our ideas clear, comes from the Greek for "deed or act" ["behavior" says Fisch, 1969, 418]. Peirce, always careful (as a cartographer) of what he said and did and broadly knowledgeable, hence aware of the German use of the word in philosophy and history to convey "the evolution of causes and effects" (*OED Online*), chose not to use the German form *pragmatisch* nor the English *practicism* or *practicalism*. His choice of pragmatism (later pragmaticism) was because he wanted to bring in "some definite human purpose," realizing that the clear conception of "a word or other expression, lies exclusively in its conceivable bearing upon the conduct of life" (1998, 332–33). *There is,* he goes on to say, *"absolutely nothing more to it."*

In an earlier essay, "On Phenomenology" (1903), he states that while he finds it hard to state "the true definition of Pragmatism," he does believe that "it is a sort of instinctive attraction for living facts" (158).

79. Peirce, following Vico, in his "How to Make Our Ideas Clear" (1998/1878) points out that Descartes, in his desire to understand "clearly," never seemed to comprehend the "distinction between an idea seeming clear and really being so" (287). In this seminal article, Peirce goes on to argue for the scientific method, with its emphasis on practical verification, being the only way to make ideas clear. Thus, by neither personal intuition nor by rule-guided method, do we understand. For pragmatists understanding comes through communal action, through ideas being tested publicly in terms of results—or fruits.

Dewey (1998/1923) reflecting on Peirce's pragmatism comments that "a large part of our epistemological difficulties arise from an attempt to define 'real' as something given prior to reflective inquiry. . . ." (308). One could easily substitute the word "education" for epistemology and "knowledge" for real and have a truth that is with us today.

80. The notion of an external standard and the difficulties this has caused in western thought is taken up by Morris Berman in his *Wandering God* (2000), while the concept of order emerging from below, without standards, is handled in complexity theory by a number of authors, including Steven Johnson (*Emergence*, 2001).

81. I see the process "philosophers," Piaget (1971, with Garcia 1991) and Whitehead (1967/1925, 1978/1929) as precursors to the (now classical) complexity theorists, Bak (1999), Kauffman (1993, 1995, 2000), Marturana and Varela (1980, 1987), and Prigogine (1997, with Stengers 1984). For emergence theorists see Stanley (this volume).

82. As pointed out in footnote 47, Charles Peirce, in his essay "On Improving Our Reasoning," (1998/1913), aligns Francis Bacon's "method" of science with "bookkeeping" (464), not in itself likely to produce much insight into nature's secrets nor a method for improving our reasoning. For Peirce, such improvement comes from our close attentiveness in a situation (Wittgenstein's "seeing") and then reflecting

on that seen in the situation (Dewey's reflective development of experience). Although a solitary thinker, Peirce appreciated the role communal discourse plays in this developmental process (Trueit, this volume).

83. The phrase "desired results," while very much Dewey with his interest in practical problem solving, is unfortunate from a complexity point of view which wishes to see results emerging from interactions. This, too, is Dewey and it is this notion of emergence (and transformation) which makes him appealing to complexity theorists.

84. The practice referred to here is the practice of geometry. The Greeks believed firmly that in studying this discipline one acquired the art of thinking logically; one did not need to study method *per se*, for it was imbedded in the discipline.

85. To consider curriculum in terms of having a set (or pre-set) beginning is to consider curriculum in its noun form, as a collection and sequence of categories. In a *currere* frame, the notion of curriculum having such an external beginning, one outside a personal, existential moment, is nonsense. The beginning, as Dewey said so many times (especially in *The Child and the Curriculum*, 1990/1902), must begin with the individual and his/her personal experiences. The art of teaching is the process of helping the student develop and mature those experiences; to aid the student in appreciating and critiquing the (tentative) setness of knowledge if one were to put knowledge into a curriculum form.

References

Anderson, D. (1987). *Creativity and the philosophy of C. S. Peirce*. Dordrecht, The Netherlands: Martinus Nijhoff Publishers.

American Heritage Dictionary. (1969). W. Morris (Ed.). New York: American Heritage Publishing.

Autio, T. (2002). *Teaching under siege*. Tampere, Finland: Tampere University Press.

Bacon, F. (2001). *The advancement of learning*. New York: Modern Library. (Original publication, 1605).

———. (1985). *The new Atlantis*. Forward by Manly P. Hall. Los Angeles: Philosophical Research Society (Original publication, 1627).

———. (2000). *The new organon*. L. Jardine and X Silverthorne (Trans.). Cambridge: Cambridge University Press. (Original publication, 1620).

Bak, P. (1999). *How nature works*. New York: Copernicus.

Barzun, J. (1976). Introduction. In *The making of the modern mind* (50th anniversary ed.), J. H. Randall Jr. New York: Columbia University Press.

Bateson, G. (1988). *Mind and nature: A necessary unity*. New York: Bantam (Original publication, 1979).

Bauman, Z. (1992). *Intimations of postmodernity*. New York: Routledge.

———. (1993). *Postmodern ethics*. Oxford: Blackwell.

———. (1995). *Modernity and ambivalence*. Oxford: Polity.

Berry, T. (1988a). *The dream of the earth*. San Francisco: Sierra Club.

———. (1988b). *Creative energy*. San Francisco: Sierra Club.

———. (1996). Christianity and Ecology. *Private paper*.

———. (n.d.). Dewey's Influence in China. *Private paper*.

Bergin T. and M. Fisch (Trans. and Eds.) (1968). *The new science of Giambattista Vico*. 3rd. ed. Ithaca: Cornell University Press. (Original publication, 1744).

Berlin, Isaiah. (1969). Vico's concept of knowledge. In *Giambattista Vico: An international symposium.* (pp. 371–77). G. Tagliacozzo and H. V. White (Eds.). Baltimore: Johns Hopkins University Press.

Berman, M. (2000). *Wandering god.* Albany: State University of New York Press.

Blumenberg, H. (1987). *The genesis of the Copernican world.* R. Wallace (Trans.) Cambridge, MA: MIT Press.

Bolgar, R. R. (1954). Th*e classical heritage.* Cambridge, MA: Cambridge University Press.

Bruner, J. (1986). *Actual minds, possible worlds.* Cambridge, MA: Harvard University Press.

Bunyan, P. (1926). Apology. In *The Pilgrim's progress.* (pp. 3–10). London: Oxford Unversity Press. (Original publication, 1678–1690).

Burtt, E. A. (1955). *The metaphysical foundations of modern science.* Garden City, NY: Doubleday Anchor Books. (Original publication, 1932).

Cahill, T. (2003). *Sailing the wine dark sea: Why the Greeks matter.* New York: Doubleday.

Campbell, J. (1989). *The improbable machine.* New York: Simon and Schuster.

Collingwood, R. G. (1993). *The idea of history,* 2nd. ed. J. van der Dussen (Ed.). Oxford: Clarendon Press. (Original publication, 1946).

Comenius, J. A. (1896). *The great didactic.* W. W. Keatinge (Trans.). London: Adam and Charles Black. (Original Czech publication, 1638; Latin publication 1642).

Davis, B., D. Sumara, and R. Luce-Kapler. (2000). *Engaging minds.* Mahwah, NJ: Erlbaum.

Dear, P. (1995). *Discipline and experience.* Chicago: University of Chicago Press.

———. (1998). Method and the study of nature. In *The Cambridge History of Seventeenth-Century Philosophy,* Vol 1, (pp. 147–77). D. Garber and M. Ayers (Eds.). Cambridge: Cambridge University Press.

Deely, J. (1994). *New beginnings: Early modern philosophy and postmodern thought.* Toronto: University of Toronto Press.

Descartes, R. (1950). *Discourse on method.* L. Lafleur (Trans.). New York: Liberal Arts Press. (Original publication, 1637).

———. (1951). *Meditations.* L. Lafleur (Trans.). New York: Liberal Arts Press. (Original publication, 1641).

———. (1985). *The passions of the soul.* S. Voss (Trans.). Indianapolis: Hackett. (Original publication, 1649).

Dewey, J. (1923). Introduction. In *Conscious control of the individual,* F. Matthias Alexander. New York: Dutton.

———. (1933). *How we think: A restatement of the relation of reflective thinking to the educative process.* Boston: Heath.

———. (1938). *Logic: The theory of inquiry.* New York: Holt, Rhinehart and Winston.

———. (1960). *The quest for certainty.* New York: Capricorn Books. (Original publication, 1929).

———. (1966). *Democracy and education.* New York: Free Press. (Original publication, 1916).

———. (1990). *The child and the curriculum.* Chicago: University of Chicago Press. (Original publication, 1902).

———. (1998). The pragmatism of Peirce. In *Chance, love, and logic: Philosophical essays,* (pp. 301–08). M. Cohen (Ed.). Lincoln, NE: University of Nebraska. (Original publication, 1923).

Doll, W. (1993). *A post-modern perspective on curriculum.* New York: Teachers College Press.

———. (2002). Ghosts and the curriculum. In *Curriculum visions*, W. Doll and N. Gough (Eds.). New York: Lang.

———. (2004). Keeping knowledge alive. (Unpublished paper).

Doll, W. and N. Gough. (2002). *Curriculum visions.* New York: Lang.

Drake, S. (1974). *Galileo Galilei: Two new sciences.* Madison: University of Wisconsin Press.

Edmonds, D. and J. Eidinow. (2002). *Wittgenstein's poker.* New York: HarperCollins.

Ethredge, S. and A. Rudinsky. (2003). *Introducing students to scientific inquiry.* Boston: Allyn and Bacon.

Farrington, B. (1964). *The philosophy of Francis Bacon.* Liverpool: Liverpool University Press.

Feyerabend, P. (1988). *Against method.* London: Verso.

Finocchiaro, M. (1989). *The Galileo affair: A documentary history.* M. Finocchiaro (Trans. and Ed.). Berkeley: University of California.

Fisch, M. (1968). Introduction. In *The new science of Giambattista Vico.* 3rd. ed. T. Bergin and M. Fisch (Trans. and Eds.). Ithaca: Cornell University Press. (Original publication, 1744).

———. (1969). Vico and Pragmatism. In *Giambattista Vico: An international symposium*, G. Tagliacozzo and H. White (Eds.). Baltimore: Johns Hopkins Press.

Fleener, M. J. (2002). *Curriculum dynamics.* New York: Lang.

Gadamer, H-G. (1993). *Truth and Method.* J. Weinsheimer and D. Marshall (Trans.). New York: Continuum.

Galileo, G. (1939). *Dialogues and mathematical demonstrations concerning the two new sciences.* Henry Crew and Alfonso de Salvio (Trans.). Introduction by Antonio Favio. Evanston, IL: Northwestern University Press. (Original publication, 1914).

———. (1953). *Dialogue concerning the two great systems of the world, in the Salusbury translation*, rev. ed. Introduction by Giorgio de Santillana. Chicago: University of Chicago Press. (Original publication, 1661).

———. (1997). *Galileo on the world systems.* M. Finocchiaro (Trans.). Berkeley: University of California.

Gilbert, N. (1960). *The Renaissance concept of method.* New York: Columbia University Press.

Gödel, K. (1963). *On formally undecidable propositions of Principia mathematica and related systems.* B. Meltzer (Trans.), R. B. Braithwaite (Ed.). New York: Basic. (Original publication, 1931).

Grafton, A., and L. Jardine. (1986). *From humanism to the humanities: Education and the liberal arts in fifteenth and sixteenth century Europe.* London: Duckworth.

Gundem, B. (1992). Notes on the development of Nordic didactics. *Journal of Curriculum Studies, 24:* 61–70.

Gundem, B., and S. Hopmann. (1998). *Didaktik and/or curriculum: An international dialogue.* New York: Lang.

Hamilton, D. (1990). *Curriculum history.* Geelong, Victoria: Deakin University Press.

———. (1992). Comenius and the new world order. *Comenius, 46:* 157–71.

———. (2003). Instruction in the making: Peter Ramus and the beginnings of modern schooling. American Educational Research Association conference, Chicago, 2003, paper presentation.

Hayles, K. (1999). *How we became posthuman.* Chicago: University of Chicago Press.

Heims, S. (1991). *The cybernetics group.* Cambridge, MA; MIT Press.

Holton, G. (1973). *Thematic origins of scientific thought.* Cambridge, MA: Harvard University Press.

Janik, A., and S. Toulmin. (1973). *Wittgenstein's Vienna.* New York: Simon and Schuster.

Jardine, L. (1974). *Francis Bacon: Discovery and the art of discourse.* Cambridge: Cambridge University Press.

Jardine, L., and X. Silverthorne. (2000). *Francis Bacon: The new Organon.* Cambridge: Cambridge University Press.

Jardine, L., and A. Stewart. (1998). *Hostage to fortune: The troubled life of Francis Bacon.* London: Gollancz.

Johnson, S. (2001). *Emergence.* New York: Scribner.

Kanigel, R. (1997). *The one best way: Frederick Winslow Taylor and the enigma of efficiency.* New York: Viking

Kauffman, S. (1993). *The origin of order.* New York: Oxford University Press.

———. (1995). *At home in the universe.* New York: Oxford University Press.

———. (2000). *Investigations.* New York: Oxford University Press.

Keatinge, M. W. (1896). Introduction. In *The great didactic of John Amos Comenius.* London: Adam and Charles Black.

Kliebard, H. (1995). The Tyler Rationale Revisited. *Journal of curriculum studies.* (*27*)1: 81–88.

Koyré, A. (1967). *From the closed world to infinite universe.* Baltimore: Johns Hopkins University Press.

Künzli, R. (2000). German didaktik. In *Teaching as a reflective practice,* (pp. 41–55) I. Westbury (Ed.) Mahwah, NJ: Erlbaum.

Lakoff, G., and R. Núñez. (2000). *Where mathematics comes from.* New York: Basic.

Leibniz, G. W. (1951). Preface to the general science (1677). In *Leibniz Selections* (pp. 12–17). Philip P. Wiener (Ed.). New York: Scribner.

Leibniz, G. W. (1951). On the method of universality (1674). In *Leibniz Selections* (pp. 3–4). Philip P. Wiener (Ed.). New York: Scribner.

Levine, J. (1991). Giambattista Vico and the quarrel between the ancients and the moderns. In *Journal of the history of ideas,* (*51*)1: 55–79.

Lovejoy, A. (1965). *The great chain of being.* New York: Harper. (Original publication, 1936).

Lyotard, J-F. (1984). *The postmodern condition.* G. Bennington and B. Massumi (Trans.) Minneapolis: University of Minnesota Press.

Maisel, Edward. (1986). Introduction. *The resurrection of the body: The essential writings of F. Matthias Alexander.* Boston: Shambala.

Mandlebaum, M. (1977). *History, man, and reason.* Baltimore: Johns Hopkins University Press.

Maturana, H., and F. Varela. (1980). *Autopoiesis and cognition.* Boston: Reidel.

———. (1987). *The tree of knowledge.* Boston: Shambhala.

McKnight, D. (2003). *Schooling, the Puritan imperative, and the molding of an American national identity: education's "errand into the wilderness."* Mahweh, NJ: Erlbaum.

Menand, L. (2002). *The metaphysical club.* New York: Farrar, Straus, and Giroux.

Menck, P. (2000). *Looking into classrooms: Papers on didactics.* Stamford, CT: Ablex.

Merchant, C. (1995). *Earthcare: Women and the environment.* London: Routledge.

Miller, P. (1953). *The New England mind: From colony to province.* Cambridge, MA: Harvard University Press.

Miller, P. (1954). *The New England mind: The seventeenth century.* Cambridge, MA: Harvard University Press. (Original publication, 1939).

Miner, R. C. (2002). *Vico: Genealogist of modernity.* Notre Dame, IN: University of Notre Dame Press.

Misawa, T. (1909). *Modern educators and their ideals.* New York: Appleton.

Oakeshott, M. (1967). Rationalism in politics. In *Rationalism in politics,* (pp. 1–36). London: Methuen.

Ong, W. (1983). *Ramus, method, and the decay of dialogue.* Cambridge, MA: Harvard University Press. (Original publication, 1958).

Ong, W. (1971). *Rhetoric, romance, and technology.* Ithaca: Cornell University Press.

Ovid. (1976). *Metamorphoses.* Sir S. Garth (Ed.), John Dryden (Trans.). New York: Garland Publishing. (Original, first century B.C.).

Oxford English Dictionary. (2nd ed., 1989). J. A. Simpson and E. S. C. Weiner (Eds.). Oxford: Clarendon Press.

Peirce, C. S. (1931–1958). *The collected papers of Charles Sanders Peirce,* 8 volumes, M. Fisch (Ed.) Cambridge, MA: Harvard University Press.

———. (1988). On Phenomenology, in *The essential Peirce,* Vol. 2, (pp. 145–60). Peirce Edition Project, (Ed.). Bloomington: Indiana University Press. (Original publication, 1903).

———. (1992). *Reasoning and the logic of things. The Cambridge Conferences Lectures of 1898.* K. Ketner (Ed.). Cambridge, MA: Harvard University Press.

———. (1998). An essay toward reasoning in security and uberty. In *The essential Peirce,* Vol 2, (pp. 463–74). Peirce Edition Project, (Ed.). Bloomington: Indiana University Press. (Original publication, 1913).

Perez-Ramos, A. (1988). *Francis Bacon's idea of science.* Oxford: Clarendon Press.

Piaget, J. (1971). *Genetic epistemology.* E. Duckworth (Trans.). New York: Norton.

Piaget, J. and R. Garcia. (1991). *Toward a logic of meaning.* Mahwah, NJ: Erlbaum.

Pinar. W. F. (Ed.). (1975). *Curriculum Theorizing.* Berkeley: McCutchan.

———. (2004) *What is curriculum theory?* Mahwah, NJ: Erlbaum.

Pinar, W. F., and M. Grumet. (1976). *Toward a poor curriculum.* Dubuque, IL: Kendall/ Hunt.

Pinar, W. F., W. Reynolds, P. Slattery, and P. Taubman. (1995). *Understanding curriculum.* New York: Lang.

Pompa, L. (1982). *Vico: Selected writings.* Cambridge, MA: Cambridge University Press.

Popper, K. (1968). *The logic of scientific discovery.* London: Hutchinson.

Price, L. (1954). *Dialogues of Alfred North Whitehead.* Boston: Little, Brown.

Prigogine, I. (1997). *The end of certainty.* New York: Free Press.

Prigogine, I., and I. Stengers. (1984). *Order out of chaos.* New York: Bantam.

Randall, J. H. Jr. (1976). *The making of the modern mind* (50th anniversary ed.). New York: Columbia University Press.

Reiss, T. (1982). *The discourse of modernism.* Ithaca, NY: Cornell University Press.

Rorty, R. (1967). *The linguistic turn.* Chicago: University of Chicago Press.

———. (1982). *Consequences of pragmatism.* Chicago: University of Chicago Press.

———. (1989). *Contingency, irony, and solidarity.* Cambridge, MA: Cambridge University Press.

———. (1999). *Philosophy and social hope.* London: Penguin Books.

Rossi, P. (1968). *Francis Bacon.* S. Rabinovitch (Trans.). London: Routledge and Kegan Paul. (Original publication, 1947).

Rummel, E. (1992). Et cum theologo bellapoeta gerit: The conflict between humanists and scholastics revisited. *Sixteenth century journal,* (23)4: 713–26.

Schaeffer, J. D. (1990). *Sensus communis: Vico, rhetoric, and the limits of relativism.* Durham, NC: Duke University Press.

Scheurich, J. J. (1997). *Research method in the postmodern.* London: Falmer.

Serres, M. (1983). *Hermes: Literature, science, philosophy.* J. Harari and D. Bell (Eds.). Baltimore: Johns Hopkins University Press. (Original French essays published 1960s–70s).

———. (1991). *Rome: The book of foundations.* Stanford: Stanford University Press. (Original French publication, 1983).

———. (1997). *The troubadour of knowledge.* S. Glaser (Trans.). Ann Arbor: University of Michigan Press. (Original French publication, 1991).

Sharratt, P. (1976). Peter Ramus and the reform of the university. In *French renaissance studies: 1540–1570,* (pp. 4–21). Edinburgh: Edinburgh University Press.

Smith, N. K. (1952). *New studies in the philosophy of Descartes.* London: Macmillan.

Tambiah, S. J. (1990). *Magic, science, religion, and the scope of rationality.* Cambridge: Cambridge University Press.

Toulmin, S. (1990). *Cosmopolis: The hidden agency of modernity.* New York: Free Press.

Triche, S. (2002). Reconceiving curriculum: An historical approach. Unpublished Louisiana State University doctoral dissertation.

Triche, S., and D. McKnight. (2004). The quest for method: The legacy of Peter Ramus. *History of education,* (*33*)1: 39–55.

Tyack, D. (1974). *The one best system.* Cambridge, MA: Harvard University Press.

Tyler, R. (1950). *Basic principles of curriculum.* Chicago: University of Chicago Press.

Varela, F., E. Thompson, and E. Rosch. (1993). *The embodied mind.* Cambridge, MA: MIT Press.

Verene, D. P. (1993). Introduction. In *On humanistic education: Six inaugural orations, 1699–1707.* G. Pinton and A. Shippee (Trans.). Ithaca, NY: Cornell University Press.

Vico, G. (1969). *Giambattista Vico: An international symposium.* G. Tagliacozzo and H. White (Eds.). Baltimore: Johns Hopkins University Press.

———. (1984). The *new science of Giambattista Vico,* 3rd ed. T. Bergin and M. Fisch (Trans. and Eds.). Ithaca, NY: Cornell University Press. (Original publication, 1744).

———. (1988). *On the most ancient wisdom of the Italians.* L. Palmer (Trans.). Ithaca, NY: Cornell University Press. (Original publication, 1710).

———. (1990). *On the study methods of our time.* E. Gianturco (Trans.). Ithaca, NY: Cornell University Press. (Original publication, 1709).

———. (1993). *On humanistic education: Six inaugural orations, 1699–1707.* G. Pinton and A. Shippee (Trans.). Ithaca, NY: Cornell University Press.

———. (1994). *The autobiography of Giambattista Vico.* M. Fisch and T. Bergin (Trans.). Ithaca, NY: Cornell University Press. (Original publication, 1725–1731).

Wertheim, M. (1995). *Pythagoras' trousers.* New York: Random House.

Westbury, I. (2000). *Teaching as a reflective practice: The German Didaktik tradition.* Mahwah, NJ: Erlbaum.

Whitehead, A. N. (1967). *The aims of education.* New York: Free Press. (Original publication, 1929).

———. (1967). *Science and the modern world.* New York: Free Press. (Original publication, 1925).

———. (1978). *Process and reality.* New York: Free Press. (Original publication, 1929.)

Wimmer, M. (2001). The gift of *Bildung.* In *Derrida and education* (pp. 150–75). G. Biesta and D. Egéa-Kuehne (Eds.). London: Routledge.

Zhongying, C. (2002). A century meeting: An interview with Gadamer. In *Ontological hermeneutics,* Vol 2 (pp. 1–14). Beijing: Beijing University Press.

2

Watercourses

From Poetic to *Poietic*

Only in the stream of thought and life do words have meaning.

Wittgenstein, *Zettel*

In the Beginning . . .

I first read this Ludwig Wittgenstein statement several years ago in an essay by John Shotter, whose book, *The Cultural Politics of Everyday Life* (1993), inspired the course of my inquiry into "conversation." I think of conversation as the *stream of thought and life*, a flow of words and meanings, a stream of consciousness—a "jumble of thoughts and sensory impressions," the "flow and mixture of all past and present experience in the mind."[1] The turbulent flow of water, like wind flow, is chaotic, which is to say that it has not yet an identified, predictable pattern and yet it flows, as do life and thought and words. The metaphor of the river, the stream, the water, is not coincidental to the issue that John Shotter and I explore, but central to it: the fluidity and flux of life, meaning, and relations—"the fact that we do not understand life and the livingness of things at all" (Shotter, this volume).

According to Judith Genova (1995), when Wittgenstein refers to Heraclitus' phrase (that one cannot step into the same stream twice), he is commenting on the temporality of certainty and "established disciplinary forms of life" (Shotter, 1997, 45). Like Wittgenstein and Shotter, I regard schooling as such a disciplinary form of life, one that dams the livingness of life and creative spirit, leaving stagnant pools that soon dry up. I believe that in schools we are disciplined to speak and think in a rational and logical manner, to represent this as knowledge, and to reproduce these habits of thought. This form of representation, unlike the livingness of conversations, assumes a set, certain order.

By contrast, when I think of conversation, it is not as a disciplinary form, but quite the opposite; conversation runs and spills, in the present recalling the past and, simultaneously, anticipating the future. The action of conversation is that it plays with meaning and relations, transgresses, narrates and questions, and in so doing begins to recognize and then challenge the bounds of certainty. The disorderly current that pulls me alongside John Shotter, as I focus on interactions as a nexus of circumstances and events necessary for creativity, recognizes *conversation* as necessary for creative thinking. I find it significant that where education excels in producing orderly and systematic approaches to curriculum, it also limits the type of interactions and activities that lead to such creativity as often happens in conversation.

In her introductory essay, Jayne Fleener is inspired by Giambatistta Vico's (1744) idea of a new science to reawaken a poetic spirit that might infuse scholars, to temper their rational mathematization of nature. Fleener's reference to Vico provides a starting point for a historicization of the *poetic* and *logic*, to view modern rationality as an "established disciplinary form of life," a learned way of thinking. With Fleener I see principles of chaos and complexity theory providing the basis of a new logic, one that liberates modern Western cultures from the grip of certainty that logic has provided for centuries. Like Fleener—and Richard Rorty (1999), on whom she draws in calling for a poetic imagining for a better future (this volume)—I wish to move beyond a modern vocabulary. Inspired as well, by that sentiment, I wonder what is poetic imagining? Where does *the new* come from? My focusing on Vico in this chapter is not to challenge the call for the poetic—far from it—but rather to use this exploration of the word, "poetic" and its relationship to representation, to look at the interplay of language and thought, to understand the influences that give meaning to, and shape, discourses, and to question the taken-for-granted-ness of seemingly benign words that give voice to our thoughts. Vico's story is a focal point that allows me to move beyond a "naturalized present," that provides "temporal distance and perspective" (Robert Hattam, 2003, 137), to be able to bring forward questions about the relationship of representation to thought and to education.

My stream of thought and thinking flows from Giambattista Vico and his *poetic logic* to C. S. Peirce, whose pragmatism makes thinking *poietically*, creatively logical. There is a fine distinction between the words "poetic" and "*poietic*"; they have the same etymological root. Over time however, the "poetic" developed quite a different relationship to "representation." In this chapter, which has three main sections, I explore two different ways of thinking about that relationship. First, I situate Vico in the context of his time, explore his sense of "poetic" (*artful creation*), and the theoretical concepts underlying *representation* (*mimesis*) of the poetic. Remembering that all academic studies were conducted in Latin, passed down by scholastics from the neoclassical period, one understands that Vico was working from Latin translations many times removed from ancient Greek texts. The Greek word *mimesis*, "representation" in English, was interpreted, poorly, but in ways that suited the theological interests of scholastic teachers. Two influences underlie the metaphysical and theological interpretation of *mimesis* that are significant in Western rational thought. The first is based on a metaphysical separation of the natural and the supernatural. This separation, brought forth strongly in Vico's day (ironically, by Vico himself), was itself "un-natural." As G. E. R. Lloyd (1999, 33–58), tracing the history of scientific, rational thought in early Greece, explains, to understand "the concept of nature involves a corresponding development . . . [of] the notion of marvels or miracles: the category of the 'supernatural' develops . . . with that of the 'natural'" (50–51). The supernatural was excluded from logical rational thought—and its representation—to increase the likelihood of predictability and certainty.

A second influence on the interpretation of the word *mimesis* (representation) is Platonism,[2] which supports the moral and spiritual teachings of the church. Platonist ideas reinforced the separation of the naturalness of nature and the super-naturalness of ideal forms (ironically, that of which we could be certain, the *real*). Plato put forward that what is real in this world is *imitative* of ideal forms (the supernatural). For Plato, poetry is representation of *ideal forms*; for scholastics, representation is *imitative*. What is represented is a *re-presentation* (mimetic copying) of ideal forms; the works of the ancients were considered to be ideal.

Next, I present a contrasting form of "representation," also an interpretation of *mimesis*, but the premodern (re)presentation of "*poiesis*" (to create). The most obvious difference here is the difference between "imitation" and "creating." Both words, "poetic" and "*poietic*," are related historically to *mimesis* (representation), but each word deals with representation or (re)presentation in different ways. (Re)presentation—actually, *reenactment*—takes us back to the orality of ancient Greece and the participatory *creating*, not transmission, of knowledge. This distinction serves to show how modernist thinking moved away from complex appreciations of cosmological processes to simplistic, representational ones. Interpretations of the word *mimesis* (representation) after Plato and Aristotle, paradoxically, made the *poetic* less valuable as a source of "knowledge," but ideal as an approach to teaching.

Finally, I draw on the later philosophical writings of Charles Sanders Peirce, founder of American pragmatist thought, to suggest that *poietic* logic (not poetic) leads to the creating of new ideas. In Peirce's formulation of reason as a process of thought, I find strong implications for a revision of approaches to teaching and curriculum.

Giambatistta Vico: The Rhetoric of Poetic Logic

Vico was born (1668) in the year Isaac Newton constructed the reflecting telescope and Antony van Leeuwenhoek described accurately red corpuscles. In the same era, though in other parts of the world, Baruch Spinoza was writing philosophy (*Ethics*, 1675); Gottfried Wilhelm von Liebniz was writing mathematical logic and philosophy; medical, botanical and chemical scientists were identifying, quantifying and categorizing; astronomers such as Edmund Halley were mapping the heavens, and Olaus Romer was calculating the speed of light (1675). Scholars all around Vico were creating mathematically logical explanations of the miracles of nature—the heavens, the seas, the earth. For Vico, this trend to rational/scientific (and, indeed, abstract) knowledge, strongly influenced by René Descartes and European thinkers outside Italy, was a threat to the existing, ancient Roman culture—one with a rich history of oration in the style of the famous Roman, Cicero.

As Doll (this volume) explains, the mathematical/rational methods of Descartes and the mathematical/observational ones of Francis Bacon and Galileo Galilei swept all Europe during this century—north and south. Vico grew to maturity in this time of tumultuous transition between tradition and innovation, rhetoric and rationality, philosophy and literature, ancients and moderns.

There were two major quarrels between *ancients* and *moderns*; the first was "metaphysics" (which included theology) versus the new philosophies. The *new* philosophies were natural philosophy (which became the natural sciences—the "mathematization" of nature) and mechanical philosophy (which is otherwise known as Cartesian rationality). The second quarrel (*querelle*, in French), coming slightly later historically than the first, concerned the battle of the classics versus the vernacular (Levine, 1991). In literature, the moderns accused the ancients of imposing the "tyranny of the classics";[3] in philosophy the ancients found the moderns immoral and atheistic. In the literary dispute, Vico sided with the ancients, and in the philosophical dispute he sided with the ancients on the issue of morality. As Chair of Rhetoric at the University of Naples, Vico attended to these issues as they affected curriculum; as a rhetorician, he recognized that the classical education he so loved was at question. Vico's reaction was to resist the rising tide of the Protestant Reformation, with its humanism, and the mechanical philosophy and rational logic of Descartes. The culmination of that resistance was *The New Science of Giambattista Vico* (*NS*) (1744).

Vico's Rhetoric

As I read Vico, the *NS* is a rhetorical attempt to reestablish the ancient, not to explore the new. He perceived his culture, much as Plato may have perceived his culture, to be chaotic. Both men were aiming to bring order to their worlds; for Vico, order would be achieved with an instauration of theological metaphysics—the foundation of rhetoric (G. E. R. Lloyd, 1999).

Vico uses *new science* in his title to appeal to the moderns, to pull support for an ancient morality. As Robert Miner (2003) points out, when Vico writes of the "age of men,"[4] he considers it to be the age in which he lives, as an *ancient* among *moderns*. Miner describes Vico as the "physician" to a modern culture that he (Vico) indicates is in its "declinist" period ("the age of man"), suffering from the "'extreme ill' of utter individualism" which results in "hedonism" and "shameless dissolution" (Vico, quoted by Miner, 127).

Vico blames mechanical philosophers for the decline of morals, because the process of rational thinking—its humanism—distances man from God. For Vico, the rationalists are just plain wrong from that point forward. As Miner (2003) points out, Vico's *scienza nuova* contains "subversive historicizations of rationalistic and anti-theological metaphysics" (132). Miner notes:

> It is evident that the author of the *Scienza nuova* [NS] is something more than a descriptive historian who only wants to narrate the "facts," while remaining studiously neutral about their ethical implications. Vico makes no pretense to 'value-free' objectivity . . . (126)

Vico's purpose is to demonstrate scientifically the theological origins of man[5] (Fisch, 1969; Levine, 1991; Miner, 2003). For Vico, "the function of the true eloquence [rhetoric] . . . is to embody the *true* philosophy, to use it to prompt virtuous action, which . . . religious sentiment by itself cannot do in the [declinist] age of men" (Miner, 130, emphasis added). The *true* philosophy is *metaphysics*, which is "*without* power of rationcination" but rather "all robust sense and vigorous imagination" (*NS*, 375; emphasis added). "True philosophy" is a metaphysics that fits within a theological frame, as it had for centuries. Vico's metaphysics begins with the assumption of a direct relationship between God and man. Vico wants to reinforce God's supreme authority among the contentious discussion about "what knowledge is of most worth"; he wants to affirm a *natural* order that begins with God, secondarily situating man as authority in the civil world; and finally, validating *ancient wisdom* (which is the origin of rhetoric), as right reason. In so doing, he restores a rightful place for rhetoric and attends to the need to shore up flagging morality in the wake of the humanist, rationalist tide.

Vico's New Science

In the late 1600s, science was not yet a discipline, but the word *science* was used. Science, from the Latin word *to know*, was historically associated with the "seven liberal sciences" synonymous with seven liberal arts comprised by the *trivium* (grammar, logic, rhetoric) and the *quadrivium* (arithmetic, music, geometry, astronomy). Vico knew "science" from this longstanding tradition. For his *new science*, however, he draws upon the emerging Enlightenment "science," defined by its method, in the 1700s as:

> a connected body of demonstrated truths, or with observed facts systemically classified and more or less colligated by being brought under general laws, and which includes trustworthy methods for the discovery of new truth with its own domain. (http://www.oed.com; s.v. *science*)

Vico uses the terminology and language of Enlightenment science, "principles," "axioms," etc., which gives his new science the appearance of meeting certain criteria—criteria *for* certainty. Vico's intent is to provide a *scientific* genealogy that traces and proves, the divine origins of men and their institutions, the "rational civil theology of divine providence" (*NS*, 342, 385), (by which Vico intends to "heal" the sick, *new philosophies*, to put them on the right track). Because Vico admires the science of Francis Bacon, he wants his *new* science to demonstrate, to prove, to have evidence; however, logically, he cannot demonstrate the existence of God, because that requires one to create Him. Therefore Vico demonstrates the *historical origins* of man via his language (culture). Vico combines *science*—"trustworthy methods for the discovery of new truth"—with history, defined at that time as:[6]

> a continuous methodical record, in order of time, of important events; a chain of events dealt with as a whole and pursued to its natural termination; the study of the formation of growth of communities and nations. (http://www.oed.com; s.v. *history*)

History had regained value as a study by 1651, when Thomas Hobbes is quoted as saying, "the Register of Knowledge of Fact is called History" (http://www.oed.com; s.f. *history*, quotations). The history Vico provides draws on ancient written texts (Homeric epic poems), the Bible and other sacred manuscripts to demonstrate the poetic, sacred, origins of man—at the same time, in good rhetorical fashion, discrediting humanists and rationalists for their separatist views. For example, when Vico writes of the Epicureans (Locke, Hobbes, and Gassendi) and the Stoics (Descartes and Spinoza), he is providing for the reader the pagan roots of such modernists.

Given the definitions above, and that Vico is entrenched in the tradition of rhetorical, which traces its roots to the earliest metaphysics, it is reasonable that Vico would merge *history* and ancient *science* to explore his question concerning the nature of man. "Nature" was *the* hot topic of Vico's day. The way Vico pursues the question is not surprising, since (traditional) rhetoric concerns itself with the civil order of man, his institutions and government. In demonstrating a "civil theology of divine providence" (*NS*, 342, 385)

Vico creates his *Scienza Nuova* to appeal to the modern movement by providing a *scientific* genealogy that traces and "proves," *logically*, the divine origins of men and their institutions (344).

Vico's Poetic Logic

The easy part of outlining Vico's poetic logic, is to focus on *logos*, translated appropriately as *word, opinion, argument*, interpreted by Vico, in the sense of *rhetorical* argument. The Latin word *poiema*, referring to artistic *creation*, was the word Vico chose to describe his logic because in his research Homer's epic *poems* were the earliest known literary works of man. The poems are man's creations. Vico understands the *poetic* in the Aristotelian sense of art (including poetry) as a "re-presentation" (*mimesis*), an *imitation* of a universalized natural or historical event (Hardison, 1968: 291). For Vico, man's beginnings are God's creation—and he sets out to prove it. Therefore, most simply, when Vico uses the term *poetic logic*, he is talking about the logic of *poiema* (creation). There is more to his logic, however, and the *poetic* aspect is the direct connection between God and man, via *divine providence*, reconceived by Vico, as a Muse (the inspiration of poetry), also referred to as *imaginative genera*.

Vico determines that he can demonstrate, etymologically, the spiritual origins of man, and thus, the inseparability of man from God (thereby also undermining Cartesian rationality). The key to man's nature, that is, the relationship between God, nature, and humans, lies in the *sense* earliest man (in his "poetic wisdom," being closest to God's making) makes of *divine providence*, man's experience of natural phenomena. Man created his language through his senses, infused with the holy spirit which is *divine providence*; the etymological roots of language are proof, logically, of man's earliest beginnings.

Restated, this seems to be the path of Vico's poetic logic:

- God commands man through *natural* "signs" (*divine providence*);
- man makes sense of God's signs *metaphorically*, i.e., man sees that God commands by signs, therefore man learns to make signs. God's sign is thunder, man's response is to huddle in caves; man imitates God's signs, using them as a model;
- divine providence, God's "agent," *as nature*, was wild, brutish, and cruel—and so was early man;
- beastly man sought shelter from *nature* in caves, and the first institution evolved through his coupling with woman, creating family, a model for the institutions that would allow him to become fully human;

- man, learning to understand his own institutions (studying history, culture), since they mirror God's creation, will, through refinement, eventually come to understand God better—and this is the knowledge of greatest worth.

Within Vico's frame (and using his terminology), monstrous early man, deficient in reasoning powers, *made sense* physically, through his body, of the signs of nature—which were from God. In his fear, he learned the power and authority of God, to recognize the signs from God as commands. Through metaphors (a poetic device) he learned to make gestures, then symbols, letters, and words. Man makes imitations of God's creations, whose work is sublime and can never be known in its entirety. The logic Vico devises reflects man *imitating* God's plan in the creation of religious, civil, and governmental institutions. Vico's poetic logic is a logic of dual creation: man can really know only what *he* creates which validates cultural knowledge (*sensis communis*); only God can know His creations (nature, the cosmos). This logic reinforces the ultimate authority of God, and man in his image. It is a logic of domination, and of subjugation to authority—man to God, woman to man.

A Bridge: From Poetic to Poiesis

Revived in the neoclassical era by medieval scholastics, the Platonist version of *mimesis* (representation) unfortunately interpreted as "imitation, copy," informed and ordered the medieval curriculum. This appears to be the beginning of a *mimetic curriculum* (Trueit, 2002), that persists to this day, corresponding to Deborah Osberg's (2003) "representational epistemology" where "knowledge" stands for, or represents, a world that is separate, represented as "reality." The scholastic curriculum and even Vico's curriculum, involved many laborious hours each day, of students *copying* facts into their commonplace books, memorizing, Latin, arithmetic, and geometrical theorems, making sure that everyone was literally on the same page at the same time. Learning was associated with having the student reproduce, in exactly the same way, same order, that which comes before, never questioning, and always silent.[7] Students were disciplined (via drills and exercises) in a military manner, disciplined physically with beatings, strappings, for not conforming, as well as disciplined psychologically to normativity. Scholastics (clerics) adapted Plato's writings for their own purposes, i.e., to bring Christian morality to education, to associate education with progressive improvement of character through education, to bring forward a dialectical form of reasoning, in the Platonic/Socratic manner.

This imitative sense of the poetic exists today in education. As William Doll (1993, 2003, this volume), David Hamilton (2001), and Steve Triche (1999, 2004) have variously pointed out, many teaching methods and curricula in education today are based on this deadeningly dull, mimetic approach to curriculum. In addition, students are positioned in relation to authorities, their teachers, the texts, God or philosophers—to learn, by memorizing the word of others. This teaching-learning situation is one that defines schooling and is related to an assumed, but erroneous, direct relationship between the determined curriculum as input and test scores as outcome. A mimetic curriculum encourages rote learning of units of material, from discretely categorized disciplines, learning a logic of domination, learning to live with the paradox of a humanism that is dehumanizing.

Vico's poetic logic was not taken seriously in his time, but I have focused on Vico's "new science" and "poetic logic," as a way of calling attention to logical forms of representation that continue to shape our thinking, habits of thought that have become "natural," but have not always been so. For Vico, poetic logic would lead us to *true* knowledge as an imitation (*mimesis*) of God's creation (*poiema*). This logic inscribes a particular ordering of society, hierarchical society supported by a logic of domination (Fleener, introduction, this volume). As David Hamilton (2001) points out, drawing on Walter Ong, "'logic' became the subject a teacher taught to other coming teachers in order to teach them how to teach, in their turn, still other apprentice teachers, and so on *ad infinitum*" (9). The (re)production of an ordered, rational world is accomplished in part because we represent it in a particularly ordered and rational way. Order is a system of relationships of our devising. Logical representation is a disciplined habit of thought, reinforced, for example, in the "if-then," and "therefore" cause-and-effect grammatical structuring of our language.

Modernist forms of representation make it logical to speak and think about a "self," characterized by interiority (ego), individuality, autonomy (will)—separate from others, from nature, from God (spirituality)—the disembodied intellect, much criticized in poststructural and feminist theory. The "self's" of modernism evolved from an atomistic, reductive approach of scientistic thinking (Doll, 1993) which isolates the material from the spiritual; man from nature, mind from body. In the following section, a different organization thought is revealed, one that Vico might have discovered had he translated the word *poetic* from the (earlier) Greek (instead of believing that Roman Latin was the ultimate source of all knowledge). He might have understood *poetic* in the Homeric sense of *poiesis*, and invented, perhaps, a different logic.

Poiesis: Paideia of the Homeric Greeks

Exploring the concept of *poiesis* (to create, to make, to do) and its companion *mimesis* (translated from Homeric Greek as "reenactment") is to suggest that in the stream of thought and life, there is something prior to certainty, its representation as knowledge and its presentation as fact. *Poiesis* (*to create, to make, to do*), a word associated with a *process* that leads to a creation, perhaps a *poem*, but perhaps a tool or a song. Something that is poetic is a creation. When Vico says, "we can understand only by great toil the poetic nature," he refers to the creative nature of early man. Vico infers that these early beings, through innate *wisdom* (coming from God), are able to make gestures, sounds, words. From his perspective, that wisdom must have been inspired by God; it was the spirit of God infused into man. From Vico's perspective there must be a connection to bridge the separation between internal mental *representations* and real, external objects and events—man split from nature. Therefore, when Vico researched to the earliest known works, the Homeric *poems*, which he translated from the Latin *poiema* (creation), he knew that poems, as *creations*, were man's imitation of God's creation, because God inspired them. Vico "reads" the past from a literate and *representationist* perspective. His "poetic" lacks the spirit of the *poietic*; it is logically separate from that spirit because for Vico, man does not have the creative power of God.

An alternative form of thought brought to speech is "conversation," an archaic life-form of being in communion with, in-spirit-with. Being in-spirit-with brings one to experience language differently, not as a medium of transmission, but as a life-form of its own—a life-form alive and spirited. The poiesis of conversation is, I think, related to its most obvious characteristic—orality—and the accompanying archaic world-view that orients thought. Stanley Tambiah (1990) describes mythic and primarily oral societies, a view of the world prior to literacy, prior to a representationist world-view. Tambiah characterizes mythic societies by relations of complementarity, permeability, and continuity between natural, human and spiritual existences. Gods and humans have both weaknesses and the capacity for heroism. A mythic society, such as in the time of Homer, is characterized by contiguity, relations of existential immediacy, contact and shared affinities (105–10). In this mythic world, *poiesis* exists prior to language, in what Robert Bringhurst (2003) calls the music of the world: "a music we learn to see, to feel, to hear, to smell, and then to think, and then to answer" (163). A mythic world is (re)presented as "things divine *and* human" (Greenburg, 1961, 269; emphasis added).

To understand the ancient Greek (pre-Socratic) *poiesis* as "to create" in a mythic, oral society, says Gregory Nagy (1996), one must understand it as performance; to understand the value and purpose of performance, one must understand *mimesis* as reenactment; and embedded in this understanding of *mimesis* is the concept of *paideia*. The *paideia* (education, particularly, cultural education) of the community—its values, beliefs and attitudes—was influenced by the community's *participation* in the performance. Nagy explains that a "definite goal," a *telos*, is a part of *mimetic* (reenacted) performance. Nested in the semantics of the word *mimesis* is *deuk-/duk,* the Greek root word for education (*educere* in Latin), which means *draw continuously forward*—not pulling or pushing—*toward a definite goal,* in a future direction, toward maturity or, perhaps, to a stage of initiation, which marks achievement.

The interconnectedess of these words and concepts—*poiesis, paideia, mimesis*—is not surprising: in early Greek language and in oral cultures, meaning is highly contextual. Owing to the nature of orality, there is always a surplus of meaning (Ong, 1982) requiring interpretation. The major difficulty now, for us, is trying to represent *poiesis.* Brent Davis (2004) points out that "explanation" is a word that derives from Euclidian geometry, that it flattens out—planes—the object that is symbolically logical. How does one "logically" represent, or explain, dynamical processes? Modern Western forms of textual representation are inadequate for the task of explaining dynamic processes. An impression of poiesis, not isolated from this entanglement, but as a part of it, may be gathered then, from the following descriptions.

The composing of a poem, although formulaic in many ways, was also improvisational in its *reenactment,* in accordance with the dramatized myths and the memory of the community. The poet's ability to "read" and respond to his audience was crucial. From the audience's point of view, the poet's words, deeds, and portrayal of characters needed to ring true; he needed to meet their expectations—and he had to provide entertainment, therefore some element of novelty was needed in the telling (singing). The poet's livelihood depended on his ability to meet the demands of the audience, who were active, not passive, in their viewing of the performance.

Each *poietic* reenactment involves pulling the past into the present, *recollection,* and re-presenting *with variation,* since each performance was intended to improve upon the past, to have a sense of novelty. James Olney (1988), drawing on hermeneuticist Paul Ricouer, provides another perspective on *recollection* and *poiesis*:

> Memory creates the significance of events in discovering the pattern into which those events fall. And such a pattern . . . will be a teleological one bringing us, in and through narration, and by an inevitable process, to the end of all past moments which is the present. (47)

Poiesis, in the recollection, plays with time in that it "characterizes the story as made out of events"; and it "construes significant wholes out of scattered events" (Ricouer, in Olney, 47). The story pulls the past into the present, and in *poiesis,* the variation stands in relation to the future, for the future will draw on this variation.

Nagy (1996) explains *variation* as the "same thing but . . . a new instance of the same old thing" (52); seeing in different ways, as in seeing a sunset, different each evening. *Poiesis* entails a fundamental instability as regards form, but continuities evolve from "patterns of many kinds" (51–54), rhythms, rhyme-schemes, and patterns of events. Nagy's description of a "fundamental instability" might be likened to the "fluidity" of orally patterned thought developed by Walter Ong (1982). Ong discusses *continuity with change* in oral cultures as a "continuing present" (49). Since history is only as long as memory, the distant past must slip away, to be re-created in the present.

Further, there are these contributions to an understanding of the dynamics of *poiesis*:

- the Homeric "atmosphere" described by Paulo Vivante (1983): "everything is at once persuasive and mysterious, natural and marvelous, human and divine" (32);
- *poiesis* involves a plexus of actions and interactions: of the players, the poet, the chorus, *and* the audience; time: the mythic past, the present, and the future; the senses: speaking, hearing and seeing; intersubjectivities: gods, heroes, and mortals;
- *poiesis* has a "double nature": the first example is that the audience is moved between enchantment (captivated, under a spell) and "synthesizing" meaning, two different "states of mind" (George Walshe, 1984). The second example concerns the staging of the epic performance, highlighting the contrast between near and far, foregrounding and backgrounding characters against a sociohistorical context (Richard Martin, 1989); simultaneously, the chorus and audience, the "present" respondents/interlocuters, interact with the mythic past;
- meaning is not fixed as such, but is always in play.

The performance of Homeric epics, which served as a *paideia* (form of education) for several centuries, led to the development of a highly skilled, creative culture. In this mythically (dis)ordered society, the "knowing" of participation involves:

- *sociocentrism*, a person with(in) the world, a product of the world;
- continuity in space and time, through the process of recollection, variation and looking to the future;
- intersubjective understanding, pattern recognition and the totalization of phenomena, encompassing cosmic oneness;
- languages with a surplus of meanings, requiring interpretation and negotiation, necessitating contiguity of relations and the "*logic of interaction.*" (Tambiah, 1990, 109)[8]

Poiesis, from the audience's perspective is related to making sense *between* one's experience and the cosmos as it is presented/performed, connecting with one's history, culture and community. One is drawn out of oneself in enchantment with heroes, gods and goddesses, and alternately plunged into wrenching tragedy as one feels their pain as one's own. From the performer's perspective *poiesis* involves spontaneous interplay within the formulaic structure of the poem, between himself, the audience, the chorus and the muse.

The movement and fluidity of this form of life, this interpretive, responsive/adaptive *dance,* is the creativity that occurs in-between. In this sense, not unlike Hans-Georg Gadamer's (1998/1960) eloquent description (*Truth and Method*) of play related to the performance of *being* in just such terms: "Play does not have its being in the player's consciousness or attitude, but on the contrary play draws him into its dominion and fills him with its spirit" (109). Performing the task *presents* it. "First and foremost play is self-presentation. . . . All presentation is potentially a representation for someone" (108). Play before an audience becomes "*the* play" and "openness toward the spectator is part of the closedness of the play. The audience only completes what the play as such is" (109). He continues,

> The player experiences the game as a reality that surpasses him . . . all the more the case where the game is itself "intended" as such a reality—for instance, the play which appears as presentation for an audience. (109)

For Gadamer, the "in between" *is* play and the play involves a *self* in process of becoming. Likewise, in oral poetic performances, I suggest, the *play* is the action of poiesis (*creating*) involved in *doing* and *becoming.*[9] The difference in the process of "cognition" related to poiesis leads me to consider Tambiah's notion of *permeability* in regard to the concept of an autonomous self that has dominated Western philosophy. Permeable membranes allow the passage of molecules from rich concentrations on one side, to the area of lesser concentrations on the other side of the membrane to near equalization. Permeability denies a contained and boundaried Western self. It is a concept that fits with the idea from dynamic systems theory of a system being structurally closed but functionally open—a concept developed by Gregory Bateson (1979), also in relation to *play,* and in relation to his unique conception of "self."[10] Having permeability, the "self," is enriched or depleted by difference in the environment, always affected, continuously seeing things differently. As in the performance of epic poems, seeing involves elements of foregrounding and backgrounding (Martin, 1989); termed by Roger Ames and David Hall (2001) as "focusing the familiar":

> The language of focus and field expresses a world always in a state of flux, a world in which items cannot be fixed as finally *this* or *that,* but must be seen as always transitory states passing into other correlative states. (11)

What seems familiar, seen against a changing background, seen by one who is also in flux, is seen differently. As John Dewey (1958/1926) phrases it, in *Experience and Nature*: "The visible is set in the invisible; and in the end the unseen decides what happens in the seen; the tangible rests precariously upon the untouched and ungrasped" (43–44).

One might wonder at this point, what relationship there can be between the paideia of *poiesis* in mythic societies and contemporary (North American) cultures of education. The contrast between the *poietic* and the poetic are fundamental to representation—what can (and cannot) be said, thought, brought to discourse and to the classroom. Contemporary ways of speaking and thinking have separate realms for the spiritual, the illogical, and the extraordinary that sit outside of accepted representation (of logical forms) in modern academic and educational worlds. Western education, despite political, environmental, economic, and spiritual crises worldwide, insists on discourses which define and isolate rather than seek relationships, patterns, and connections. In contrast to the hierarchical ordering of Vico's world, where either God or logical method (Doll, this volume) authorizes, the *poietic* suggests a logic of interpretation which emerges from the interaction of doing and *becoming*.

When Fleener (this volume) refers to the "language of science [that] divorces us from the poetic logic of inspiration" she identifies what Plato called the "ancient argument," a dichotomy that he (Plato) instituted by separating and valuing differently, science and poetry. Working within modernist forms of logic and representation, however, it seems impossible to invent new ways, new understandings, and new interactions . . . "that celebrate and explore the interplay among matter and spirit, knowing and meaning, imagination and reality" (Fleener, this volume). It seems most likely that Fleener is suggesting, not that we even bridge the dichotomy, but that we learn to *play* with the constraints they place upon both thought and its representation, to move beyond the representational epistemology of a mimetic curriculum, and in new directions—post-epistemologically (see Fleener, this volume, and 2002).

Charles Sanders Peirce: Logic and Conversation

It may seem preposterous to think of flowing from *poiesis* to Charles Peirce, especially when the connection I make is related to Peirce's "logic." The point I wish to bring forward, however, is that Peirce makes it *logical* to think *creatively*, developing a logic of semeiosis that finds meaning infinitely interpretive, a concept of "mind" that, like the Homeric Greeks, is a "product" of interactions with/in the world, and a reasonable way to consider chance as the precondition for the emergence of the *new*.

Peirce, like Vico, is a cusp figure, but positioned at the other end of modernity, one of its first and finest critics. Peirce's pragmaticism leads to a reconception of the basic vocabulary and premises of education common in Vico's day. How? By insisting on inquiry to truth. His pragmaticist approach, focusing on the participatory process of acquiring knowledge, challenges the assumptions of mimetic schooling.[11]

My admiration for Peirce lies in his attempt to make obvious the flaws of logic in modern rationality.[12] As one of the preeminent logicians of his day, logic and the history of science were his realms; in addition, however, Peirce's "special business" (his phrase) was to bring mathematical *exactitude* to philosophical issues, which led to his interest in the intersections between language and mathematics and eventual development of a logic of semeiosis. In light of my previous criticism of modern rationality, it may seem surprising that Peirce's reasoning would appeal to one advocating consideration of *poiesis* and *poietic* thought; but I don't find it a contradiction. In favor of this pragmaticist brand of "right reason"—not rationality—I put forward these four points that distinguish Peirce, perhaps, as the first postmodernist. For Peirce:

- knowledge is fallible, contingent and never final—no determinism, no certainty;
- representation is never the "real," but an abstraction;
- there are differences—and possibilities—between the specific ("one") and the general (representation of the "many"): "it is the reality of some possibilities that pragmatism is most prepared to insist upon" (1998, xxviii); and,
- periods of time, change of perspective, and the play of thoughts ("Musement") leads to an appreciation of both difference and homogeneity: "that every small part of space . . . is bounded by just such neighboring parts as every other, without single exception throughout immensity." (1998, 438)

Peirce's lifework was to develop "scientific" methods of thought, consistent, well reasoned, and sure. Peirce's conception of pragmaticism is relevant to education, especially curriculum, since in his words, education is "an instinctive attraction for living facts" (1998, 158). The inference is that humans *make* sense; Peirce, as a pragmatist, wanted to capitalize on this instinct and advance the results of the process, the idea of starting where you are and working toward improvement. In the remainder of this paper I point to the *poietic* elements I see in Peirce's conception of scientific thought, and make connections to concepts from complexity theory that I think help to explain creativity and the need for conversation.

Science, says Peirce, "seeks to discover whatever there may be that is true" (1998, 86), a definition that corresponds with earlier uses of the word *science*, meaning "the state or fact of knowing; *knowledge* as opposed to belief or opinion" (http://www.oed.com, s.v. *science*). Peirce's body of writing is scientific in two senses: (1) influenced by his being a scientist, doing practical science; and (2) in his pursuit of advancing knowledge. His studies are an example of the *scientific* method he advocates, based upon painstaking historical background, careful, precise, and well-documented observations, and thorough reflection on findings. *Science* for Peirce is a deliberate inquiry, a way of getting at *truths*; scientific *method* is developed to provide consistency, but perhaps more importantly, as a way to ensure the quality (mathematical exactitude) of the process and to be as inclusive as one can be in consideration of the factors involved. Peirce explains a pragmaticist stance on *truth* in relation to states of belief or doubt; particularly, truth begins with a state of belief, not doubt (1998, 336).

Peirce's scientific inquiry has a *"common sensism"* to it, beginning with sensation, "percepts," awareness, noticing, leading to observation. About these first stages he says:

> To begin with, when a boy or girl first begins to criticize his inferences[13] . . . he finds that he has already strong prejudices in favor of certain ways of arguing. Those prejudices, whether they be inherited or acquired, were first informed under the influence of the environing world, so that it is not surprising that they are largely right or nearly right. He thus has a basis to go upon. But if he has the habit of calling himself to account for his reasonings, as all of us do more or less, he will gradually come to reason much better; and this comes about through his criticism in the light of experience, of all the factors that have entered into reasonings that were performed shortly before the criticism. (1998, 534, fn. 6)

As the scenario outlines, awareness grows, one begins to observe, to question, to reflect, and to consider in light of experience. For Peirce, we can move beyond this instinctive, commonsense approach, by training ourselves to observe as carefully as a scientist. Observation is key to thought, and all inquiry begins with an element of doubt—not Cartesian doubt—but a doubt that arises from external origins, a surprise, a sense of difference.

The inquiry of the pragmatist concerns the meaning of words and concepts, not just the received understanding, but how the idea, represented by the word, relates to or is connected with the inquirer, the environing world, the universes, passing from the specific to the general. *Knowledge*, he says, is "a plastic, applicable stuff," that advances as,

> the study passes from being a study of a single thing to being the study of a set of things; especially of a family of things. But a collection of existent individuals is itself an existent individual; so that the nature of the science is not radically altered until it becomes a study not of existent collections but of classes of *possibilities*. . . . The future is the practical part of life. Applicable knowledge, the

only knowledge deserving the name, is the anticipation of future percepts. (Peirce, in Eisele, 1985; emphasis added)

Lest the idea of "method" seem too rigid, structured, and confining— wait! The observations include the *relations between parts of systems, forms and ideas*. Peirce recommends that: "The highest kind of observation is the observation of systems, forms, and ideas" (1992, 187).

Peirce develops a logic of relations that acknowledges the role of "randomness"; later he develops the phrase "fortuitous distribution" to recognize "chance." Peirce was intrigued with both evolution and probability, both of which influenced his thinking. Randomness and chance are here suggestive of stochastic process, which sets the stage for emergence. About this he says: "I believe [science's] positively wrong conclusions are of small moment compared with its neglect systematically to consider *possibilities* among which there are likely to be keys to undiscovered treasures of truth" (1998, 466). Here is an indication of the difference between Peirce and methodologists prior to him. He provides a *logical* space for that which *might come forth*—in the future! Peirce's logic opens up the concept of probability to the consideration of what *may* exist. Probabilities are calculated on the number of actual occurrences; possibilities are defined in relation to "actualities." Between the sample (the specific) and the population (the general) is also *randomness* and *chance*, potentially even a miniscule difference that over time makes a difference.[14] There are always, in the present, the eventual effects of the past and potential for the future. For neo-pragmatist Richard Rorty (1999), this is the *hope* of the future.

Peirce is adamant that scientific thinking must not depend on a process that ends with the deductive conclusion as an endpoint. This is neither a linear nor deterministic process, but rather looks to future *percepts*. Ultimately, the deductive conclusion depends upon how that decision *rests*, how it sits with us, personally, and we are therefore recursively in the realm of qualities, senses, intuitions, memories, and the subconscious—the sum total of past experience which leads to abduction (which he also calls, in this recursion, "retroduction"). The process is not only recursive, beginning and ending with abduction, with the conclusion being evaluated, critically considered, now, in light of the inferences one started with—but presumably changed (in the habit of thought) because of the process. In this recursion, Peirce (presaging, John Dewey) reestablishes the connection between the sensate, experiencing knower and knowledge.

For Peirce, learning has to do with understanding relationships between the specific and the general, finding the probabilities and possibilities in between. He says, self is *inferred*; "self" is a general concept word, not a specific object. One knows "self" through experiences and through thought; all experiences, those that surprise us, draw us out of ourselves, allow us to create knowledge of our "self" and in this way—as with Bateson—we are self-creating. It is not the same as *autopoiesis*, but it is a way of reconceiving and rescuing the modern concept of self from the trap of *an embodied mind* (Varela, Thompson, and Rosch, 1993).

Finally, let the stream flow as words in a conversation, for it is "in the stream of thought and life" that words do have meaning: for Peirce, the connection between speaking and thought is "as intimate as that between body and mind" (1998, 474). Thought is nothing until it is brought to action, to a change of belief (habit of thought), into words. In speaking our truths, bringing them into "the public" (says Peirce), thought contributes to the growth of knowledge, as science depends upon a community of scholars. In this way, we develop social networks. As others hear, and we hear others, the possibilities for further creativity increase. An idea becomes part of a set, then a family, etc. As others make observations—absolutely critical for Peirce—we see differently, imaging, visualizing, with a new *perspective*, an activity Peirce calls Musement, governed only by the "law of liberty," making connections, free association, looking for differences and "homogeneities of connectedness . . . that every small part of space, however remote, is bounded by just such neighboring parts as every other, without a single exception throughout immensity" (1998, 438)—patterns of self-similarity which he says abound in all immensity—pointing to the interconnectedness of all living things.

In that moment, where Vico is poetic, Peirce is *poietic*. It is, as I said before, a fine distinction between words, but the distinction marks the way we are inscribed by culture and signifies that culture is not fixed and unchanging. These words reflect two different appreciations of worldly experience. For Peirce the interconnectedness and life in all of nature "proves" his connection to God, and in this view, he finds it "natural" that each inquiring person is *creating* meaning, recollecting the past, into the present with a focus on the future, as one converses with others, welcoming the surprise, the doubt, that will lead to further inquiry. If "only in the stream of thought and life do words have meaning" (Wittgenstein, 1981: no. 173), it is time, in this post-epistemological age, for education to change the way it conceives curriculum.

Delta: A *Poietic* Curriculum

I have explained how I see modern curriculum to be mimetic, based on a historicist account of ideas about *representation*. A mimetic curriculum produces and reproduces a particular cultural order, replicating simple forms of thought. Educational systems seem dedicated to normed, ordered thinking, which in turn, develops citizens that see a simple order—seldom choosing to see, but perhaps, incapable of seeing otherwise. Vico's story is a reminder of the inevitability of being a product of one's culture which functions to reproduce itself.

Within this system, doomed to repeat itself endlessly, there is no creativity—no newness—nor can there be in functionally closed systems (of thought). Nor can effective change proceed. I suggest that to move beyond this cycling system, which will eventually lead this system to implode, that we rethink "thought" in terms of *the poietic*, using a form of reason that makes it logical to think creatively.

I have hopes that chaos and complexity theories are tools to help us to think about and to deal with, change—not by rearranging what is present, but by looking for what was not there before, assuming the cosmos we live in, and its integral parts, to be creative. Can we begin to move beyond the liberal, humanist conception of an individualistic self—the "I am"—to envision complex cosmological systems of self-organizing actualization—the "becoming" of creatively functioning dynamical systems?

What might the implications be to consider poiesis and a *poietic* logic of interpretation for curriculum and for teaching? It is almost too ideal to bring forward, but I suggest that:

- the orientation and purpose of education changes from replication toward the recognition of thought as ongoingly interpretive and creative;
- approaches to teaching, to study, and to curriculum become fluid, active, even improvisational, as modernist structures and forms become permeable to allow a flow from disciplinary subjects and discipline specific content.
- *teaching* be reconceived to include establishing Peirce's *habits of thought*, a methodological approach to "study" that encourages both rigor and creativity in inquiry;
- *conversation* will be seen—and valued—as the play of thought, that leads to, and is necessary for, the genesis of ideas.

Notes

1. *Bedford Glossary of Critical and Literary Terms* (1997, 378. s.f. *stream of consciousness*).
2. "Platonism" in the sense in which I use the term does not denote the (very complex, shifting, dubiously consistent) thoughts of the genius who wrote the *Dialogues*. Instead, it refers to a set of philosophical distinctions (appearance—reality, matter—mind, made—found, sensible—intellectual, etc.): what Dewey called "a brood and nest of dualisms." These dualisms dominate the history of Western philosophy, and can be traced back to one or another of Plato's writings (Richard Rorty, 1999: xii).

3. The tyranny of the classics meant that students were required to read and write Latin; their texts were Latin classics. It also meant that the "vernacular"—the language spoken in their "ordinary" life—was not read in school.

4. Vico, in his *NS*, suggests that there are three "ages of man" (as Fleener outlines in her introductory essay): the age of gods, the age of heroes, and the age of man. Vico would idealize himself to be of the age of heroes.

5. The frequent and conscious use of "man," "men," in this essay calls attention to the use Vico makes of the word, and intends to criticize Vico's—and others—male (patriarchal) rationality that has contributed to a "logic of domination" (see Fleener's introductory essay) and to suggest forms of thought that will bring a change to such gendered language.

6. History was little valued after Plato, considered only *narrative* fiction; the origins of history were suspect because history was thought to be inspired by *Muses* (Clio), therefore mythic.

7. Stephen Halliwell suggests that Plato was probably responsible for "silent reading"; so strong was his prejudice against the sophists and the performances that they gave, that his students were required to read to themselves, silently.

8. The selections in this list are excerpted from a chart comparing concepts and characteristics associated with Tambiah's two orderings of reality, causality and participation. Tambiah places these "orderings" on a theoretical continuum.

9. Interesting that a "play," in current usage, is most often a scripted performance and a passive audience, much like lessons in school; or, the play of a rigidly structured game, often professional. Play is under-appreciated as an activity of thought, exceptions being Bateson, Gadamer, Peirce, Heidegger, and others who critique modern rationality.

10. For Bateson, it is a mistake to try to understand any biological phenomenon as an object: the *self*—really, there is no such "object"—cannot be isolated from a historical/cultural environment. Rather, one must view the organism as part of a functioning system. His chapter called Multiple Versions of Relationship (*Mind and Nature*, 140–55), depicts a "characterological self," developed as an accumulation of ideas about one's character, validated in interaction and relationship, between organism and environment. In that chapter he is interested in the delineation of the *self*. Where does *self* begin and end? *Self* is a collection of impressions gathered, in part, through play, exploration or other such contexts for *double description*.

11. It is interesting to note that Peirce was a pariah in the prevailing high-minded, Puritan culture of academia; he was even considered a bit odd within his own social circle. In later years he existed on the fringes, due in part to his irascible behavior. His papers, a prolific collection of writings at the time of his death, were placed in keeping at the Harvard library, much of it under limited access (on this point, and for a more complete understanding of C. S. Peirce, read his biography by Joseph Brent, or "autobiography" by Kenneth Ketner). From his marginalized and solitary position he produced some if his finest theoretical and philosophical work.

12. Peirce uses the word "ratiocination" (among others) to refer to his third stage of reasoning, deduction, which "traces out the ideal consequences of hypotheses." I suggest the purpose of doing so is that in this stage one is dealing with the ratio of one:many as, for example, one generalizes (statistically) from sample to population, or from a thing, to a set of things, to a family of things (see next page). For Peirce, deduction is a mathematical process involving iterations. The first two stages are abduction and induction. Abduction is the hypothesis forming stage; induction is

inference drawn "from experiments testing predictions based on a hypothesis" (1998, 97).

13. Inference(s) in this sense, is "the drawing of a conclusion from known or assumed facts" (OED online, s.v. *inference*).

14. C. S. Peirce precedes Alfred Korzybski and Gregory Bateson in recognizing a "map/territory" distinction; logically, it is the difference between conceptualization (abstraction) and a lived experience. Peirce and Bateson see this "between" as a space of possibility, an opportunity for growth of awareness, or reorganization (my term); Bateson frames this in terms of "levels" of learning, or context. Peirce's symbolic logic and philosophical speculation on this point is discussed in *Reasoning and the Logic of Things*, 60–61, and chapter 5.

References

Ames, Roger T., and David Hall. (2001). *Focusing the familiar. A translation and philosophical interpretation of the Zhongyong*. Honolulu: University of Hawaii Press.

Bateson, Gregory. (1979). *Mind and nature: A sacred unity*. New York: Bantam.

Bedford Glossary of Critical and Literary Terms. (1997). Ross Murfin and Supryia M. Ray. Boston: Bedford.

Berlin, Isaiah. (1969). Vico's concept of knowledge. In *Giambattista Vico: An international symposium*. (pp. 371–77). G. Tagliacozzo and H. V. White (Eds.). Baltimore: Johns Hopkins University Press.

Bringhurst, Robert. (2002). Poetry and thinking. In *Thinking and singing: poetry and the practice of philosophy*. Tim Lilburn (Ed.). Toronto: Cormorant Books.

Davis, Brent. (2004). *Inventions of teaching: A genealogy*. Mahwah, NJ: Erlbaum.

Dewey, John. (1958). *Experience and nature*. New York: Dover. (Original publication, 1926).

Doll, William E. Jr., and Noel Gough, (Eds.). (2002). *Curriculum Visions*. New York: Lang.

Doll, William E. Jr. (1993). *A post-modern perspective on curriculum*. New York: Teachers College Press.

Eisele, Carolyn. (Ed.). (1985). *Historical perspectives on Peirce's logic of science. A history of science*, 2 Vol. Berlin: Mouton.

Fleener, M. Jayne. (2002). *Curriculum dynamics: Recreating heart*. New York: Lang.

Fisch, Max. (1984). Introduction. In *The new science of Giambattitsta Vico*. T. G. Bergin and M. H. Fisch (Trans.). Ithaca, NY: Cornell University Press.

———. (1969). Vico and pragmatism. In *Giambattista Vico: An international symposium*, (pp. 401–24). G. Tagliacozzo and H. V. White (Eds.). Baltimore: Johns Hopkins University Press.

———. (1953). The academy of the investigators. In *Science, medicine, and history: Essays on the evolution of scientific thought and medical practice written in honor of Charles Singer* (pp. 521–63), London: Oxford University Press.

Gadamer, Hans-Georg. (1998). *Truth and method*. J. Weinsheimer and D. G. Marshall (Trans.). New York: Continuum.

Genova, Judith. (1995). *Wittgenstein: A way of seeing*. New York: Routledge.

Greenburg, Nathan. (1961). The use of poiema and poiesis. *Harvard Classical Philology*, 65; 263–89.

Hamilton, David. (2002). From dialectic to didactic. In *Paradigm 2002*, 2(5): 15–24.

Hardison, O. B. (1968). *Aristotle's poetics: A translation and commentary for students of literature.* L. Golden (Trans.). Englewood Cliffs, NJ: Prentice Hall.

Hattam, Robert. (2003). Review of *Curriculum Visions,* by Wm. E. Doll and Noel Gough (Eds.). *The Australian Educational Researcher, 30*(3): 135–38.

Levine, Joseph M. (1991). Giambattista Vico and the quarrel between the ancients and the moderns. *Journal of the history of ideas. 51*(1): 55–79.

Lloyd, G. E. R. (1999). *Magic, science, reason: Studies in the origins and development of Greek science.* Indianapolis: Hackett.

Martin, Richard P. (1989). *The language of heroes: Speech and performance in the Iliad.* Ithaca, NY: Cornell University Press.

Miner, R. C. (2002). *Vico: genealogist of modernity.* Notre Dame, IN: University of Notre Dame Press.

Nagy, Gregory. (1996). *Poetry as performance: Homer and beyond.* Cambridge: Cambridge University Press.

Olney, James. (Ed.). (1988). *Studies in autobiography.* New York: Oxford University Press.

Ong, Walter. (1982). *Orality and literacy: The technologizing of the word.* New York: Methuen.

Osberg, Deborah and Gert Biesta. (2003). Complexity, representation and the epistemology of schooling. Paper presented by Deborah Osberg to the First Conference on Complexity Science and Educational Research, University of Alberta, October 16–18, 2003. (http://www.complexityandeducation.ca/pub03proceedings.htm)

Peirce, Charles S. (1985). Reason's conscience: A practical treatise on the theory of discovery, wherein logic is conceived as semeiotic. In *Historical perspectives on Peirce's logic of science. A history of science,* (pp. 801–51). Carolyn Eisele (Ed.). Berlin: Mouton.

———. (1992). *Reasoning and the logic of things. The Cambridge Conferences Lectures of 1898.* K. Ketner (Ed.). Cambridge, MA: Harvard University Press.

———. (1998). *The essential Peirce. Selected philosophical writings,* Vol. 2 (1893–1913). The Peirce Edition Project (Ed.). Bloomington: Indiana University Press.

Rorty, Richard. (1999). *Philosophy and social hope.* New York: Penguin.

Shotter, J. (1993). *Cultural politics of everyday life.* Taranto: University of Toronto Press.

———. (1997). *Social construction as social poetics.* In *Reconstructng the psychological subject: Bodies, practices, and technologies.* Betty Beyer & John Shotter (Eds.). London: Sage.

Tambiah, Stanley. (1990). *Magic, science, religion, and the scope of rationality.* New York: Cambridge University Press.

Triche, Steve. (1999). *Reconceiving curriculum: An historical approach.* Unpublished Louisiana State University doctoral dissertation.

———. (2004). On two historical sources for a theory of curriculum: Gabriel Harvey's *Rhetor* (1574/1576) and William Ames's *Technometry* (1629). Paper presentation, American Association for the Advancement of Curriculum Studies conference, San Diego, 2004.

Trueit, Donna. (2002). *What is poiesis?* Unpublished paper. Louisiana State University.

Varela, F., E. Thompson, and E. Rosch. (1993). *The embodied mind.* Cambridge, MA: MIT Press.

Vico, Giambattista. (1984). *The new science of Giambattista Vico,* 3rd. ed. T. Bergin and M. Fisch (Trans. and Ed.). Ithaca, NY: Cornell University Press. (Original publication, 1744.)

Vivante, Paolo. (1983). *The Homeric imagination: A study of Homer's Poetic perception of reality.* New York: Irvington.

Walshe, George. (1984). *The varieties of enchantment: Early Greek views of the nature and function of poetry.* Chapel Hill, NC: University of North Carolina Press.

White, Hayden V. (1969). Biographical note. In *Giambattista Vico: An international symposium*, (pp. xxv–xxvi). G. Tagliacozzo and H. White (Eds.). Balitmore: Johns Hopkins University Press.

Wittgenstein, Ludwig. (1981). *Zettel*, 2nd. ed. G. E. M. Anscombe and G. Von Wright (Eds.). Oxford: Blackwell.

3

Complexity

Developing a More Useful Analytic for Education

> The best theory so far is that which transcends the limitations of the previous best theory by providing the best explanation of that previous theory's failures and incoherencies (as judged by the standards of that previous theory) and shows how to escape them.
>
> Alisdair MacIntyre, *Whose Justice? Which Rationality?*

Complexity. Do we really need to drag complexity into it? Do we need to talk about complex methods and analysis? Isn't education complex enough as it is? Isn't that the problem?

Yes, that is the problem. *Complexity* has emerged as the central problem of educational practice and educational theory. And we need to think about complexity because we haven't been making as much progress in either practice or theory as we would like. We are not able to accomplish the things with students that we dream of and we have not been able to fully understand why.

Education *is* complicated, everyone agrees. More precisely it is complex, complex in the still emerging sense that is central to this book—it is a recursive, open system characterized by emerging entities, the evolution of new capacities, and by developmental growth. Most importantly, complex systems are systems for which history matters. Something that was done yesterday, in yesterday's circumstances, with yesterday's students, does not have the same effect when repeated today. The situation is not stable. The seasoned teacher knows how to shift methods, content, and even the lesson's very purpose with the time of day, or the day of the week, or the mood of the students. The teacher recognizes the relevant pattern, makes sense of the poetics of the classroom. Such things are so commonplace as to "go without saying" among educators.

But these sorts of problems and the nature of the solutions teachers find are scarcely visible to researchers steeped in a traditional analytic. They are not seen and studied because the traditional mode of solving problems, focused on finding universal and certain solutions, has committed to a logic that depends upon a reductive, atemporal, and static—that is, simple—understanding of the problems themselves. This model does not yield helpful educational answers because the material world of education is not, in fact, simple. The elements of educational problems cannot be reduced to easily separable simples while change over time is at the heart of development and learning. Attempts to freeze the situation for the purposes of a reductive analysis necessarily obscure the dynamic relationships that are at the heart of learning. As a result, the bulk of educational problems—problems for which there may be good if not completely universal and certain solutions—are perceived as insoluble. And indeed, given the perspective and tools of the traditional reductive analytic, they are. But perhaps that need no longer be. This short chapter puts forward a simple thesis: that a new analytic, a different way of habitually addressing problems, is emerging and offers a much more useful context for analyzing educational problems.

The Educational Faces of Complexity

Across disciplines, the slippery systems that characterize complexity have proven resistant to traditional analysis. But the emergence of the "new sciences" (see Fleener, this volume) which take such uncertain systems as their subject encourage educators to recognize that new analytical tools are becoming available for their own slippery, less-than-certain, but nevertheless patterned systems.

We now have whole fields that are almost entirely "new" in the sense that their development has depended upon the use of new analytical tools and methodologies (see Doll, this volume). The oldest of these "new" modes of analysis is, perhaps not surprisingly, Charles Darwin's evolutionary theory. In Darwin's radical scheme, analysis focuses on small, random changes that compound over time to produce new types which survive—or do not—as they fit with a world dynamically changing around them. This contrasts dramatically with the preordained, static hierarchy of Linnaeus and with Newton's clockwork universe and inspires a model of habitual analysis in the biological sciences that is echoed throughout the new sciences (Mayr, 1988) As John Dewey noted, Darwin's integration of history into science changed scientific inquiry in fundamental ways (Dewey, 1929). Each of the traditional disciplines seems to be sprouting a fresh green branch that is involved with reasoning about its area in the new way.

Educators who are inspired by the new sciences approach them in a number of ways. There are those among us that are concerned with the nature of (for example, Fleener), or that we be prepared to teach the subject matter of, what has come to be called the new sciences of complexity and are working on how to best accomplish this (Jacobson, 2000). Closely allied, some want to make sure that our students can reason with the tools and techniques that these new disciplines offer (Resnick, 1994). Some educators want to understand the dynamic social systems of the classroom or the school with an eye toward developing stronger institutions of learning (for example, Rasmussen, Reeder, and Shotter). Others are most interested in the implications for how we conceive of curriculum and educational methods (for example, Davis, Doll, Trueit, Wang). Yet others, and I count myself among them, are most interested in understanding learning itself. We have scarcely begun to understand how and what our students learn and that is the first step toward reasoning about instruction within the constraints set by the materiality of human embodiment. But in this chapter I am going to ask the reader to step back from the fascinating particulars and consider the implications of the larger pattern that is emerging; to consider the possibility that the new sciences, the new media, and new intellectual tides in the humanities constitute something more than the standard fitful progress of human endeavor, something other than the advance of normal science (Kuhn, 1957). We will consider whether, when taken together, they represent the emergence of a different, broader, set of habits that come into play when we deal with difficulties. And we will examine whether they might prove more useful to the theory and practice of education than the earlier, reductive, habits of analysis. I will label the habituated complex of habits that people semiautomatically employ "an analytic" and regard the abstract description of that habitual activity as "a logic."

What Is an Analytic? What Is Logic?

Questioning the naturalness of the present usage of the terms "analytic" and "logic" by suggesting that they might be reconceived evokes the shades of more familiar concepts that posit a deep change of mind and/or society: examples include the German concepts of Zeitgeist and Weltanschauung; Reiss's discursive regimes (1982); MacIntyre's traditions (1988); Kuhn's paradigm change (1957); Toulmin's distinction between reason and ration (1990); Levi-Strauss' concrete/mythical reasoning (1966); Gadamer's historical consciousness (1976); Kant's Copernican revolution (1998); and Dewey's Copernican reversal (1929). Much of history and anthropology has also been devoted to disabusing ourselves of the idea that people differ only in minor ways. What unifies these disparate ideas is that they all point to the difficult idea that people might be stranger than we can easily understand in other times and places. These strains of thought are based on the assumption that profound differences in our modes of understanding are possible—and that the particular way the world is understood is profoundly important in the way people live their lives.

The differences between ways of understanding can be very hard to explore and express because we lose a secure place from which to reason. The tools that we use to make sense lose their natural and obvious qualities. As Ludwig Wittgenstein (1968) once remarked, "If a lion could talk, we could not understand him" (37). If, as I wish to suggest, we are at a point where new modes of analysis are emerging and coalescing then it is particularly *teachers* who will have the practical task of bridging this difficult gap. The purpose of teaching itself will require that those schooled and habituated in one mode of reasoning be taught another useful way of dealing with problems. A time-honored way of bridging such differences is to pull back to find a distance from which to develop a common framework within which the differences can be discussed. From a distance we can view all analysis as action— action that we trust will produce an answer that can be used to guide us as we pursue our goals. In the conception put forward here, "an analytic" refers to our habits of inquiry,[1] to the actual activity that we habitually engage in when we attempt to understand. "A logic" is the reified, normative abstraction of the activities in which we habitually engage. Both our current "reductive" analytic and the emerging "complex" analytic can be examined in this way. This activity-focused vision owes much to Dewey's foundational refusal of the traditional split between action and cognition (1929) and to his heirs in Thomas Kuhn and Stephen Toulmin. It is influenced, as well, by current work in the field of situated cognition (e.g., Clark, 1997; Wertsch, 1998) and interpretations of dynamic developmental patterns (e.g., Thelen and Smith, 1994) and neurologically constrained models of cognition (e.g., Rumelhart and Smolensky, 1986) that emphasize the interpenetration of development, cognition, and action in the world.

This is an unfamiliar way of thinking about analytics and logics; a short example may serve to make these concepts more concrete.

An Example: Recognition Research Within a Reductive Analytic

Consider the example of trying to understand something so basic as recognition. Let us suppose that we want to understand how facial recognition normally takes place because we hope to help youngsters make distinctions more fluidly. What habits of analysis would come into play? I believe the following story will sound familiar:

Brief consideration by the researcher leads to the conclusion that the youngster's difficulty probably arises as a result of the complexity and subtlety of the problem. The first order of business is to simplify the problem so as to isolate the basic factors. The researcher deems it obviously useful to look at a single instance of the problem and to examine it in a controlled environment. The topic chosen is the male-female distinction. He (let us presume this gender) locates a set of images chosen for how obviously they are found to be either male or female. From a large set of images the researcher selects those that are most clearly male or female, discarding all ambiguous cases. He may choose these himself, defer to the judgment of a panel of experts, or focus on those that are most quickly recognized as gendered by a sample of his population. The researcher must early settle on the level of certainty desired; in this case he decides that there must be only one chance in one hundred that his outcome could be achieved by chance. To make sure that the explanation is universal he takes great care to strip away any local variables and to eliminate the possibility that the history of the subjects or the history of their interaction during the procedures affects the measured outcome. Removing these effects statistically and increasing the certainty, in the guise of confidence levels, necessitates a large group of homogenous subjects.

Having set up these constraining conditions in order to enhance the universality and certainty of the eventual findings, the researcher is then free to reduce the problem to its constituent parts. The face is obviously composed of features (eye, ear, nose, and forehead, for instance) and careful attention must be paid to making sure that these are completely separated and involve no overlap. (How to separate the forehead from the eyebrows and the hairline might be an important issue.) The research is designed to determine if there is a single element, "a silver bullet," such as a feminine nose, that reliably explains recognition. Failing that, the key is sought in a single pattern of relationship between the constituent elements.[2]

The habits embodied in this condensed recounting are the "analytic"— the habitual habits of inquiry—that have become characteristic of Western and especially academic culture.

The Logic of Reduction

The associated "logic" is both derived from and normatively shapes this habitual analytic. The logic serves also to validate claims made by researchers—something is understood to be true, reliable, or certain based on arguments referring to the logic. The logic associated with the reductive story recounted above might be recounted in the following way: The most valuable knowledge is universal and certain. It is discovered—the truth preexists our experience and the particular context in which it is expressed can be expected to obscure the underlying rules. While other sorts of understanding might exist this discovered, certain knowledge is to be preferred in any realm. The world to be known consists of small, atomistic parts or features that in their combination comprise objects that we may know and invariant rules that relate them. Gaining knowledge depends upon a rigorous process of eliminating all features that are not universal and controlling for error and chance with the purpose of finding the feature or features that determine the object in question. Knowledge is embodied in theories and better, more

mature theories grow progressively simpler. This perspective has been discussed in the literature as the Newtonian or clockwork view (Doll, 1989). It
first established itself as an explicit basis for understanding in the realm of
physics and spread from that center.

Alternatives to Reduction: A Complex Logic

While a reductive logic has long had many detractors in other realms
(Blake, 1980), it is only relatively recently that its privileged position has
come under question from within the community of scientific inquiry. This
challenge is subtle and does not usually come in the form of an opposition to
the stated logic of justification but instead appears as a deviation from the
accepted habits of inquiry. People act differently while engaged in inquiry.
They pursue different aims using different tools. Their habits change. Their
analytic shifts. A change in their "logic," their way of justifying their activity,
may be—indeed likely will be—less noticeable. The older, prestigious logic is
used to justify new practices; the new logic emerges more slowly and only
where necessary to justify the pursuit of valuable understandings—or, and
this is crucial to the enterprise of the present book—when it is necessary to
induct new students into the community of inquiry.

This shift in habits constitutes an alternate way of practicing inquiry. If
we consider physics to be the center in which the Newtonian vision of scientific inquiry developed, then the alternative appears to be emerging in evolution and in the closely linked field of ecology. As this logic, in its turn, spreads
from its center in ecological analysis we may fairly label it a *complex logic*. In
a complex logic valuable knowledge is neither universal nor certain. Instead,
valuable knowledge grows out of the assumption that change and development are fundamental to life and that knowledge based on this world must
itself be changeable. What remains to make knowledge valuable is its usefulness—whether acting upon it helps us solve our problems. Valuable knowledge is pragmatic[3] knowledge. Knowledge is constructed and tentative; it is
not discovered but is a consequence of repeated testing cycles involving our
collective experience, action, and interpretation. Because there is no realm of
certain knowledge, developing methods of validating knowledge is not only
a serious endeavor but also an ongoing one. In this conception there is no
absolute chasm dividing truth and nontruth. The world is composed of relations, of patterns. The crucial questions revolve not around the reduction to
parts but around tracking the dynamically changing relationships that comprise the field of inquiry. Gaining knowledge depends upon a process of
developing models of these interactions and improving knowledge is a consequence of increasing to the number of factors that are taken into account in
order to better reflect the particular instances that are encountered by practitioners. Knowledge is embedded in these models and better, more mature

models are generally more complex, including larger numbers of relationships significant in increasingly rarer circumstances and hence are better able to reflect multiple, differing situations.

Comparing this "complex logic" to the "reductive logic" discussed above leads, one hopes, to instructive contrasts but falls short of presenting a picture of an alternate set of activities that comprise an habitual analytic of complexity. The earlier mentioned example of recognition can serve to fill that purpose.

An Example: Recognition Research Within a Complex Analytic

Brief consideration by the researcher leads to the conclusion that the youngster's difficulty probably arises as a result of insufficient or misleading experience. The first order of business is to examine the context and the individual's history to locate initial patterns of difference that will serve to guide further disciplined inquiry. The researcher deems it obviously useful to take as a beginning point an exploration of the range of field-based situations in which facial recognition appears as a problem for the caregivers who raise the question. The topic that arises out of this inquiry is rather broad: the child does not always appear to recognize the caregiver in new situations, leading to fear and confusion on the part of the young child. She (let us presume this gender) studies the situations in which this occurs most frequently looking for patterns that lead to nonrecognition and fear. From an already large set of circumstances the researcher expands her initial model of the field of inquiry to include situations that lead to recognition without fear in hopes of disambiguating broadly fearful circumstances and those that lead to nonrecognition. This fieldwork leads to new categories of possible explanations; for instance, the researcher begins to suspect that the more general issue is not recognition per se but the child's perception that this is "not the right person in the circumstance." She may choose to develop this "not-right" category (and others) herself, go to a group of reviewers to validate it, or return to her caregivers to confirm that this category makes sense in light of their experience. The researcher must early settle on the particular problem and circumstance to be considered; in this case she limits herself to understanding cases of not-right perception in young children.

Having set up these constraining conditions in order to enhance the value of the eventual findings, the researcher is then free to consider how the experiential basis of recognition affects the cases under consideration. The face is obviously recognized on the basis of the history of interaction between the child and caregivers in particular circumstances (at home, at daycare, and in the car for instance). The research is designed to find histories that lead to not-rightness in particular circumstances. The research is also designed to find as many different patterns that lead to these circumstances as is feasible and to integrate those patterns into the emerging model. The assumption is that there are likely multiple paths to similar ends. The researcher and caregivers group these paths based on which solution corrects the problem. A toddler might, for instance, not recognize a daycare worker and cry when being loaded into the car at daycare if the daycare worker does not usually perform the task. This is seen as a case of not-right perception if the mother taking over calms the child down. A different solution might be to vary the routine so that the daycare worker loading the child at daycare is an unremarkable part of the history of the child. It is then acceptable at daycare. (But it may still not be acceptable to be taken out at home by anyone but momma.)

Contrasting Styles Within a Broader Analytic

The most helpful way of regarding the two narratives I recount is to understand them as contrasting styles and not, in my judgment, as opposed narratives. If we believe, as I do, that shifting habits of inquiry are at the basis of our shifting analytic, then what I have discussed as the habits of a complex is a broader analytic in that it finds itself at home in a broader range situations. Viewed from within a broader complex analytic, the reductive habit set is useful and effective in limited but very real realms. There is no need to abandon it in those areas where its emphasis on certainty, simple cause, and quantifiable variables is valuable. Historically, the reductive perspective has been strongest in physics and mathematics, and it will surely remain important in engineering and any enterprises where focusing on certainty leads to greater safety. (The design and construction of bridges is one place where we might all hope for a dose of certainty.) The complex analytic, conceived of as broad set of habits, is more a predisposition to a set of habitual perceptions and actions than a set of rules that must be followed. As with other habits we might well expect that there will be many useful more or less local sets that prove valuable to differing communities of inquiry. Freed of a commitment to found truth, deductive certainty, and atomistically separate elements that operate in an "instantaneous," static setting, disciplined inquiry can become a much more comfortable part of disciplines ranging from biology to sociology to education.

While their opposition may not be the most productive way to think about the differing styles of reduction and complexity, there are certainly contrasts, contrasts whose significance lies in assessing the relative usefulness of these analytics in educational theory and practice. Education is an area in which the value of a reductive analytic is quite limited.

Reduction's fatal flaw for education's purposes is well worth noting: any recursive relationship between the elements that comprise the problem—and especially those changes that lead to changes in the patterns of relationships that comprise the situation studied—are ignored. This eliminates the core of educational problems of learning and development that are comprised of just such changes. This "overlooking" is not simply careless implementation–it lies at the heart of a reductive analytic that crucially depends upon formal logic (of the sort found in logic, geometry, or mathematics) to validate its truth claims with deductive certainty. In such systems the elements of analysis must be both separate and stable. Unless they can be distinguished from each other (separate) and unchanging (stable), no certain cause can be attributed to any element.[4] In many if not all natural systems and certainly in education, things do change over time; neither the relationships comprising the system nor the elements themselves are stable. We are not faced with the poor implementation of a good idea; we are faced with a habitual way of solving problems whose assumptions of separablity and stability are flawed at their root for any system whose most important problems concern development or learning.

Why? The Educational Value of Complexity

But even if the reductive analytic is inadequate, you may ask, why complexity? Why buy into analysis that implies that prediction is limited? Again, aren't things unpredictable enough in education? One reason is that complexity is an antidote to some of the specific problems with which the reductive analytic and its associated logic have left to education. All too often when a reductive analysis is applied to educational systems the result is either to so oversimplify the analysis of the system that the knowledge gained is obvious or to so simplify the experimental conditions under which the research is pursued as to lead to findings which, though stated confidently, do not actually usefully predict much in the messy world of practice. In the first instance we get research that proves that poor children lag behind in achievement or that boys do better than girls in algebra. These are true and even significant but do not tell teachers anything that was not obvious before the research was done. In the second case, that of simplified experimental conditions, the consequence is either that the "significant" finding is so small an effect size that the difference it would make is too small as to be impractical to even try and implement or—more commonly—the promised effect simply does not appear when teachers try to implement the findings "in the wild" of their classrooms. This latter consequence is a direct result of ignoring the way that recursion makes small differences important. This also helps explain why, in so many cases, a confident research finding vanishes when the test is rerun with even the smallest differences in conditions.

What is gained in moving to a complex analytic is a new and powerful way of understanding the patterns that appear in the world—and in ourselves. The same recursive processes that may lead to chaos provide the seed for emergence and a resulting self-organization. Emergent characteristics of complex systems are characteristics of the system that can be explained only on the basis of the interaction of the parts and which cannot be extrapolated from an analysis of the parts in isolation from each other. A familiar example is carrying capacity in ecosystems. The number of rabbits that a particular ecosystem can support is generally a pretty stable figure—but not one that can be inferred from the characteristics of rabbits (or of foxes). It is an emergent feature of the system.

Emergent features and recursion form the basis for self-organization in complex systems. One way of understanding emergent features is as a limit or boundary that is characteristic of a system. Such limits are very real; the system cannot assume all the states which would be possible if the parts were considered alone. There is no logical limit to the reproductive capacity of a pair of rabbits considered outside the context of a functioning ecosystem. Such limits and, of course, the material limits of the constituent elements themselves (rabbits cannot give birth to foxes) press systems toward stability.

Were it not for the effects of recursion, systems would tend toward either stasis or disorganization. But physical systems (as opposed to imaginary ones) are recursive. They are not isolated from their own ongoing processes as the reductive, linear analytic implicitly assumes. Recursion, as noted, can generate large changes from small differences causing the chaotic effects found in complex systems. In interesting cases this effect offsets the tendency toward stasis but does not drive the system to disorganization. Such systems are said to be balanced on the changing boundary between chaos and stasis. To stay at that edge, to persist as organized entities, such systems must link their internal structure to their environment in such a way that changes in the environment leads to structural changes that maintain the entity over time. These systems self-organize. They are characteristic of life, the weather, autocatalytic systems, and human thought. They are also characteristic, I contend, of the learner, the learner's development, and the classroom.

The benefits for education are not simply that a complex analytic helps clear away assumptions that are mistaken and habits that are misleading in educational contexts. A complex analytic also brings positive benefits in that it directs our attention to new phenomena and different aspects of familiar problems. A complex analytic suggests new tools—for example, a more central role for modeling—and directs our attention to those aspects of emerging disciplines—for instance, connectionist theories of learning—that seem best suited to informing educational purposes.

A complex analytic gives us new tools through which to view education, a way of viewing education that is as appropriate to our field as ecology was to biology.

Studies using a complex analytic allow us to evade the mind-body problem in learning and to refuse René Descartes' dualism when discussing mind.[5]

In development it becomes possible to both reject teleology and to gain the ability to assert that a child's developmental path is both broadly predictable and specifically unknowable. And it becomes much easier to analyze the classroom as a congeries of shifting entities. It is possible to envision educational tools that can track the shifting units of analysis that constitute the lived experience of teaching. It is possible to envision an analytic that can sharpen the intuition of teachers rather than deny it.

One example of a complex educational tool that would facilitate educational inquiry is the model. Explicit modeling of complex situations is widely used in the new science (e.g., ecology) and often substitutes for the axiom and rules form that theories take in more reductive and traditional analytics.

Modeling: One Example of a Complex Tool

Models are usually opposed to the more familiar laws of science. But in truth formal definitions of the two clearly overlap. Models and laws both function to guide inquiry and to embody in a usable form the valuable results of inquiry. They differ most markedly in *style*; they are regarded by their developers and used by the larger community in very different ways.

Their creators see laws as the found or distilled truths of an overly messy world. Users apply laws as, well, laws. They are understood to be basic truths and in any situation where they do not apply neatly and cleanly it is the situation that needs to be rectified and the confounding factors removed. Friction confounds the first law of motion. In an ideal world it is to be removed or at least minimized. Poverty correlates with reading difficulty. In an ideal world poverty is to be removed or at least minimized.

The makers of models and the users of models see and use their models very differently from the way that laws are seen and used. Their constructors view models as built things, as reflections of the world they represent. They are as complex as they need to be to model the development and change of those aspects that the community understands to be problems. As more situations are brought to the attention of the developers models typically become more complex. Users understand the models similarly—they are valuable only to the degree that they highlight local conditions and lead to effective action. There is little sense that a model should dictate the "purification" of a situation to which it purports to apply. It is much more likely to be assumed that the model needs modification to fit the local context. A drought changes the succession pattern in a recovering woodland forest. The solution is to change the model, not eliminate the drought. Poverty correlates with reading difficulty. The solution suggested by the tool of modeling is to further develop the model in search of finding a complex of factors that will enhance poor children's reading, especially along dimensions in which the poor differ from the wealthy.

These differences between the effects of centering on laws or models are not, of course, absolute differences. But they are differences in what differing habits of inquiry make sensible and natural solutions to issues that arise in practice.

Modeling allows for the sort of "soft prediction" that accommodates a teacher's intuition that a particular boy in her first grade class will have trouble with reading without demanding that she or he come up with the sort of simple, usually singular, causation that applies in all cases to all children that traditional researchers see as valid, universal knowledge. Instead modeling puts forward a complex web of causation that is, most often, made more complex and more subtle as additional factors are found to be important. Models can be and habitually are tweaked to accommodate local conditions—one locale might have a large number of native French speakers, for example. The "hard prediction" of laws predisposes us to policy that is simple—and simple policy is too often direct, brutal, and less than subtle. French can simply be forbidden.[6] A model, on the other hand, would tend to accept French speakers as part of the mix to be modeled and look for ways to turn that quality to the advantage of all.

Models develop the habit in their users and developers of seeking patterns of correlation and locating systemic constraints that over time that lead to more desirable results. It encourages policy makers to explore multiple paths and to look for points where a small difference may over time lead to disproportionably large changes. Good models are potentially powerfully *democratic* tools putting expertise at the service of people with less knowledge; they externalize "privately" held knowledge, making the assumptions and selective construction of the "real" visible and its implications readily available for selective manipulation by the user with little further intervention by the expert.

Having glimpsed the outlines of a complex analytic and how a tool associated with it may prove useful, one might find it helpful to examine one concrete case of a discipline that uses its tools to develop a framework of potential interest for education. The emerging branch of cognitive science alternately known as connectionist, neural nets, or developmental dynamics holds great promise for education and may be helpful in envisioning the influence of a complex analytic on the pursuit of educational goals

Connectionism, Re-cognition, and a Theory of Learning

Connectionism as an example of complexity has the virtue of being widely considered, especially by those who wish to model complex realms, to be one of the most complete extant examples of a complex discipline (Cilliers, 1998; Farmer, 1991). Because it is centrally concerned with explaining learning its centrality for education reconceived within a complex analysis is readily apparent.

Teachers know that knowledge is context-laden, slippery and changeable but that the current analytic has insisted that good knowledge is solid, unchanging, and context-free. How can a complex analytic explain the phenomena of learning in a way that not only confirms teachers' intuitions but also sharpens them?

Connectionism emerges from the interdisciplinary field of cognitive science through a profound disagreement with classical theories of mind. Connectionist theoreticians reject the current logical image of mind, with its computer metaphor, in favor of a metaphor of the brain. They postulate just the sort of networked architecture, recursive relations, and emergent features described above.

They find that logical strings are very hard to manipulate on models of this type but that perception and pattern completion are easy and blindingly fast. This certainly corresponds to the hard-won understandings of teachers—and their pupils. The long, linear logical strings of algebraic reasoning are notoriously difficult. The high school algebra graduation requirement is the most dreaded Carnegie unit[7] in American schools.

But connectionist learning theory can go beyond merely confirming the intuitions of teachers and giving them a language with which to communicate about these issues, as valuable as that would be. Connectionist models can also sharpen that intuition by directing attention to particular features of the learning experience. For instance, contrary to the counsel of traditional, reductionist theories of knowledge acquisition, connectionist models indicate that category formation is easiest when multiple members are presented to the learner that are weighted toward *noncentral* members of the category. The order of presentation also matters; a network can be led to over- or undergeneralize by a poorly chosen learning sequence. Further, as with pupils, it is much harder to unlearn an incorrect categorization than to learn it correctly in the first place. This all sounds more or less sensible, I suspect, but bear in mind that each of these results contradicts the implications of a traditional theory of knowledge acquisition. Teachers have, by brute encounter with students, developed intuitions that are more or less accurate. But these intuitions are at war with the culturally sedimented basis for current understandings of memory and the transfer model of teaching.

In addition, a new and more useful technical vocabulary may well emerge from connectionist models. For example, hysterisis is a term used to describe a state in which a less than optimal answer is found during thought but there is not sufficient difference in the learning set to disturb the previously learned relations. The learner is stuck. The term hysterisis encapsulates, in a way that "stuck" does not, that the current answer is good but not good enough, that it is in the student's learning history that the root of the problem is to be found, and that it is likely to take extraordinary new experiences to overcome the overlearned response.

Connectionist learning theories extend a teacher's intuition by providing principles such as the use of noncentral members in learning situations and a way to look at the effects of over- and undergeneralization and to develop new and useful ways of seeing and talking about learning.

Conclusion

The task of this short paper is to suggest that a new analytic is becoming available to education which is more suited to education's conditions and goals than the previous reductive analytic has been. This paper has laid out some suggestive characteristics of a complex analytic in terms of new organizational patterns which the perspective enables us to see. The value of the modeling as a tool in a complex context has been explored. Finally I have very briefly delved into one area, learning theory, where the current framework is woefully inadequate and have suggested that a particular complex analysis, connectionism, should be useful.

As Alisdair MacIntyre suggests in the statement that heads this piece, we judge a competing framework by how well it solves its progenitors' problems. By these standards, I believe, a complex analytic is to be preferred. It makes tractable problems that the previous perspective attacked but could not succeed in solving.

Complexity offers us a lens through which to productively re-view the complexity of our work and the work of other educators without succumbing to either mystification or reduction.

Notes

1. The phrase "habits of inquiry" is intended to reference John Dewey's formulation, particularly as he describes it in *Logic, the Theory of Inquiry* (1938) and particularly pages 103–19 of chapter six, "The Pattern of Inquiry." In his conception "habits" refers to all our habits of inquiry: habits of perception, habits of cognition, and habits of action.
2. Lest the reader suspect that this is an unlikely subject of inquiry or that the pattern of inquiry outlined is a bit too pat, he or she is referred to the very active facial recognition research—an area that includes a line of research often entitled "feature" or "parameter" based facial recognition.
3. I use pragmatic here in the philosophical sense; that the value, the meaning, the truth of a statement is to be found in the consequences of acting upon it—not in the security of its antecedent reference.
4. This formal insistence on separate and unchanging elements of analysis is, of course, often evaded or ignored. But the errors of the analytic doggedly follow us in practice. A painful example is the way that statistics are used in education (and the

human sciences more generally). In very few if any actual cases can factor independence or stability be realistically assumed in education—and yet we do not hesitate to rely on measures of significance that depend upon this assumption.

5. For a fuller treatment see Rumelhart and Smolensky's (1986) treatment in the "bible" of connectionism: "Schemata and Sequential Thought Processes in PDP Models."

6. Those familiar with the Louisiana context know that this was, prior to the last two generations, the policy of both public and catholic schools.

7. For those, perhaps thankfully, outside a US context, Carnegie units refer to a widely taught set of subject courses that in the aggregate are used to qualify students as high school graduates prepared to advance to university work. Algebra is among the subjects required.

References

Blake, W. (1980). *Songs of innocence and of experience*. Franklin Center, PA: Franklin Library. (Original publication, 1794.)

Cilliers, P. (1998). *Complexity and postmodernism: Understanding complex systems*. New York: Routledge.

Clark, A. (1997). *Being there: Putting brain, body, and world together again*. Cambridge, MA: MIT Press.

Dewey, J. (1929). The Copernican Revolution. In *The quest for certainty: A study of the relation of knowledge and action* (pp. 287–313). New York: Minton Balch.

Dewey, J. (1938). *Logic: The theory of inquiry*. New York: Holt.

Doll, W. E. (1989). Foundations for a post-modern curriculum. *Journal of Curriculum Studies, 21*(3): 243–53.

Farmer, J. D. (1991). A Rosetta Stone for Connectionism. In *Emergent computation: Self-organizing, collective, and cooperative phenomena in natural and artificial computing networks* (pp. 135–187). S. Forrest and Center for Nonlinear Studies (Los Alamos National Laboratory) (Eds.), Cambridge, MA: MIT Press.

Gadamer, H. G. (1976). *Philosophical hermeneutics*. Berkeley: University of California Press.

Jacobson, M. J. (2000). Problem solving about complex systems: Differences between experts and novices. In *Proceedings of ICLS 2000* (pp. xii, 388). B. J. Fishman and S. F. O'Connor-Divelbiss (Eds.). Mahwah, NJ: Erlbaum.

Kant, I. (1998). *Critique of pure reason*. P. Guyer and A. W. Wood (Trans.). Cambridge: Cambridge University Press. (Original publication, 1791.)

Kuhn, T. S. (1957). *The Copernican revolution: Planetary astronomy in the development of Western thought*. Cambridge, MA: Harvard University Press.

Levi-Strauss, C. (1966). *The savage mind*. Chicago: University of Chicago Press.

MacIntyre, A. C. (1988). *Whose justice? Which rationality?* Notre Dame, IN: University of Notre Dame Press.

Mayr, E. (1988). *Toward a new philosophy of biology: observations of an evolutionist*. Cambridge, MA: Belknap Press of Harvard University Press.

Reiss, T. J. (1982). *The Discourse of Modernism*. Ithaca, NY: Cornell University Press.

Resnick, M. (1994). *Turtles, termites, and traffic jams: explorations in massively parallel microworlds*. Cambridge, MA: MIT Press.

Rumelhart, D. E. and J. L. Smolensky. (1986). Schemata and sequential thought processes in PDP Models. In *Parallel Distributed Processing. Psychological and Biological Models.* Vol. 2. (pp. 7–57). D. E. Rumelhart, J. L. McClelland, and P. R. Group (Eds.). Cambridge, MA: MIT Press.

Thelen, E. and L. B. Smith. (1994). *A dynamic systems approach to the development of cognition and action.* Cambridge, MA: MIT Press.

Toulmin, S. E. (1990). *Cosmopolis: The hidden agenda of modernity.* New York: Free Press.

Wertsch, J. V. (1998). *Mind as action.* New York: Oxford University Press.

Wittgenstein, L. (1968). *Philosophical investigations.* (3rd ed.). New York: Macmillan. (Original publication, 1953).

Second Iteration

Chaos and Complexity

 # Interrupting Frameworks

Interpreting Geometries of Epistemology and Curriculum

In this chapter, I undertake a preliminary exploration of the possibilities for a new class of mathematical forms—namely, images drawn from fractal geometry—to serve as useful visual metaphors for pulling together and otherwise noting some of the common ground of various perspectives represented in current curriculum theorizing.

Before proceeding, I would like to make it clear that the suggestion that curriculum theorists might embrace a particular branch of mathematics should not be interpreted as an attempt to reassert the priority of the discipline in a time that we have become justly suspicious of the pervasiveness of mathematized sensibilities. I'm up to something quite different here. As will be developed, fractal geometry itself works to trouble the priority given to mathematics in academia. Powerfully demonstrating that, like all other realms of inquiry, mathematics is evolving and contingent, fractal geometry describes itself as one of many possible *models* of observed phenomena—as opposed to a singular definitive account (cf. Stewart, 1998). In the process, this geometry helps to highlight the pervasiveness of images that are drawn from classical geometries—visual metaphors that are evident in such commonsensical notions as "basics," "foundations," "constructions," "frameworks," "right," and "true."

Defining Geometries

Conventionally, the term "geometry" most often prompts thought toward the images and forms of Euclid's mathematics of the plane. For the ancient Greeks, however, *geometry* was actually more about a method of inquiry than a particular class of objects or system of assertions. The sign that hung above the door to Plato's academy, "Let no one who has not grasped the geometry enter here," for example, was not demanding a knowledge of established theorems, but an appreciation of a certain mode of thinking: the logical, deductive argument.

In fact, it was not until a century after Plato had erected his sign that Euclid developed his mathematics. Euclid's enduring contribution was a demonstration of how, using Plato's geometry, a range of already familiar forms and common assertions could be traced to a narrow set of definitions and assumptions. In the process, Euclid's geometry became a visual metaphor for the logical argument, offering a picture of how complicated truths could be built up from simpler, self-evident notions. In other words, it was through contributions such as Euclid's that Plato's geometry came to be regarded as not just a route to truth, but as exemplifying the structure of all knowledge.

While Plato's geometry languished between the time of Euclid and the dawning of the modern era, it was given a renewed impetus by Descartes and his contemporaries some centuries ago. Reassigning it the status ascribed it by the ancient Greeks, Descartes championed the logical argument. Through it, he made his major contribution to mathematical thought: analytic geometry. With the masterstroke of laying a grid onto the plane, Descartes demonstrated how the qualitative and the quantitative could be logically mapped onto one another. Shape could be translated into number, number into shape. This insight powerfully supported an emerging suspicion that all relationships could be understood in terms of linear equations—of direct causes, predictable outcomes, and prespecified paths.

Plato's direct, causal, logical geometry has since become a transparent backdrop too much of academic inquiry and to most of formal education. In the past few decades, however, considerable work has been done to render the privilege of this mode of argumentation more visible. Postmodern, poststructural, psychoanalytic, feminist, Marxist, deconstructionist, phenomenological, hermeneutic, ecological, and other perspectives have arisen, each of which offer their own particular critiques of the sensibilities implicit in the geometry announced by Plato, given form by Euclid, and championed by Descartes. While presenting compelling critiques of and alternatives to the linear, deductive argument, however, these discourses often invoke visual notions that rely on Euclidean and Cartesian geometries. References to circles, regions, domains, spirals, centers and margins, for example, are commonplace, and these bespeak a certain inability to escape our own situatedness. Even the increasingly frequent references to "nonlinearity" work only by calling forth what they aim to trouble. As limiting as logical rational thought might be, its associated images and forms are so woven through our language and our living spaces that it takes an effort even to notice them, let alone to invoke alternatives.

An illustration: the right angle.

Our modern uses of the word "right" derive from the ancient use of the right angle in measurement and construction. "Rightness" originally referred to the extent to which particular cuts or markings fitted to a preset standard of the perfect, ideal right angle. It's not difficult to imagine how such expressions as "That's not right!" might have drifted from their literal references in measurement to more figurative applications in matters of morality and ethics, especially given the attentions paid in ancient Greek and Roman cultures to ideals and absolutes. Notions of rightness, then, are Euclideanisms—metaphorical extensions of a particular geometric system and its underlying Platonic logic.

This point is not a small one, as the notion "right" is caught up in a complex web of associations in the English language. For example, it is closely related to words that derive from the Latin root, *rect* (which, depending on the dictionary you use, is translated either as 180°—straight—or 90°—right) that is tucked into such common terms as *correct, direction, rectify, erect,* and *rectitude.*

Paralleling these terms is a slightly more hidden (and perhaps more insidious) application of Euclidean rightness: notions that are clustered around the word "normal." *Norma,* its Latin root, originally referred to the carpenter's square, the instrument used to measure and create right angles for buildings and furniture. When incorporated into English, "normal" was used in very much the same sense as "right" was first used, to describe particular angles. "Not normal" and "almost normal" were references to the precision of cuts and constructions.

To make a long story short, the transformation in meaning of the word normal to its current, popular usages was prompted by a complex cascade of happenings, including a sudden need for standardized parts brought on by a rapid industrialization, the emergence of a new branch of mathematics (statistics) to deal with variations among such standardized parts and other measurable forms, and the application of the resultant statistical methods to less tangible phenomena such as intelligence and aptitude.

The manner of etymological play could be easily extended to other common terms and notions. The emergences of conventional meanings of "straight" and "true," for instance, have much in common with the roots of "right," "rect-," "regular," "rule," "line," "ortho-," "standard," and "normal." *Further,* so *far,* I have *strictly limited* myself in this *project* to words that are *explicitly aligned* with *prominent* Euclidean notions. I could easily *justify* an *extended list* that includes many, many other *ordinary* terms whose ancient roots and contemporary associations have to do with lines and linearities—including each of the words italicized in this paragraph. But the main point is that formal rational thought is structured into our language, at least in part, through the pervasiveness of Euclideanisms. And modern efforts to educate are entangled, entwined, implicated, and complicit in that web.

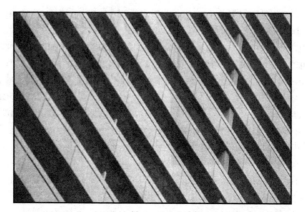

Figure 4.1 A Glimpse of Our Euclidean World

Of course, this phenomenon is not limited to the level of language. It is also built into our living spaces (see Figure 4.1)—as overwhelmingly embodied in both the physical and the conceptual organizations of the modern school. Buildings, classrooms, desks, texts, and the other objects used to organize learners' experiences are overwhelmingly *rect*angular. Similarly, the structures used for timetabling, for arranging curricula, for grading performances, and for marking progress are almost always based on rectangular grids.

The point here is not that the emergence of this particular web of association represents some sort of error or conspiracy. It is, rather, that these terms are pervasive. They are present in English-speakers' communications and infuse habits of interpretation—and, in the process, they do a particular sort of work in the projection and maintenance of a "normal" sense of how things are. Beneath the literal surface of these terms is a mesh of rightness and wrongness, of correctness and falsehood, of straightness and queerness. The priority of lines and linearities in the language is nested in the contested spaces of good and evil, truth and deception, morality and deviance.

The claim that lines and line-based interpretations are not neutral can be underscored through reference to any thesaurus. One such volume (Chapman, 1977) includes the following terms in its index, under "straight": accurate, candid, continuous, direct, heterosexual, honest, simple, thorough, trustworthy, undeviating, virtuous (1237). Anyone foolish enough to question the value or priority of such qualities would likely be seen as deliberately provocative and illogical. Associations have become pervasive and transparent. Their metaphoric worth and intent have been lost as they have become examples of what they describe: normal, standard, correct, orthodox. Analogical usage has decayed into illogical presupposition—a point that is cogently illustrated in the specific example of normal. Somehow a simple, plain tool used to make precise, square corners has evolved into a central idea in the analysis of social function, as framed by the normal curves as standard deviations that are deployed in quests for linear relations. (See Davis, Sumara, Luce-Kapler [2000] and Foucault [1990] for accounts of this twisted evolution.)

I could go on. Another obvious point of inquiry is *point* itself, a fundament of both Euclidean geometry and academic discourse. Other notions entangled in this web include *basic, fundamental,* and *structure.*

We humans are simply too given to the habit of making sense of things by associating new or poorly understood phenomena with the more familiar, comprehensible structures—a habit that, I believe, presents us with three modes of response: One is to do nothing—which can take such forms as a refusal to change, a clinging to some arbitrary set of basics or standards, or a going with the flow. Another response is deliberately reactionary: to set about to interrogate, to critique, to rebel against, and to otherwise dismantle the normative structures of language. The third way, I think, is to respond playfully: to delight in the irony of trying to do the *right* thing and to be *reasonable,* even while acknowledging the conceptual tyranny of such notions.

It's likely clear that it is my own conviction that the third choice is the most appropriate. I see it as a sort of mindful participation in the evolution of sensibilities. It is an acknowledgment of one's situatedness and one's complicity in the ways one is shaped and the ways one shapes.

Altering Geometries

It is thus that I argue that new visual forms are needed—ones that better embody emerging sensibilities and that, in the process, demonstrate the limitedness of popular visual interpretations. For me, fractal geometry seems to offer considerable potential in this project.

Over the last three or four decades, across most realms of formal inquiry, there have been decisive changes in perspective with the recognition that nature is relentlessly nonlinear (cf. Capra, 123). As with all large-scale shifts in thought, mathematics is on board with this transformation in sensibility—and, in fact, in some ways has led the way in the recognition that linear mathematics can describe only a special case of the world. Mathematics too has shifted from the quantitative to the qualitative in a recent subtle but pervasive move toward the geometric.

In particular, among many, many changes and emergences, the development of fractal geometry is an immensely significant event. Far closer than traditional geometries to the flexibility and rich texture of life (Stewart, 1998, 23), this elaboration of those previous geometries embodies the "new scientific" sensibility that the universe moves along according to a plurality of nested and overlapping rules, rather than a single universal system. These rules aren't pregiven, but emerge with complex forms and, in that emergence, create the constraints within which more complex forms and new categories of rules might arise. That is, rather than maintaining the frustrating quest for fundamental particles and basic principles, the new sensibility is to embrace the particularity and complexity of forms at whatever level of organism or organization one chooses to study—whether it be neuron, individual learner, classroom collective, social group, culture, species, or whatever.

To appreciate the potential of fractal geometry for interrupting and elaborating modern sensibilities and practices, it's important to understand a few key qualities—viz., recursivity, scale independence, and self-similarity.

Recursivity

To oversimplify, fractal images are produced by establishing a rule, applying that rule to generate a result, reapplying the rule to that initial result, and continuously reapplying the rule to results as they are determined in an unending, reiterative process. A visualized interpretation of recursivity is presented in the growth of the tree image (Figure 4.2). In each generation, the original "rule" (the grafting of four branches onto each limb) is applied to the product of the previous generation. In very short order, a very detailed—and surprisingly realistic—image arises.

Such recursive processes can give rise to tremendously complicated forms from very simple beginnings. Moreover, they seem to have a particular power to prompt attention toward and rethinkings of many natural processes. For example, since first playing with this category of recursive functions in the early 1980s, I have become increasingly unable to think of learning, growth, development, and other evolutionary processes in terms of progressions or accumulations—and I'm hardly alone in that regard. For many, these forms and events are more matters of a recursive, reiterative geometry.

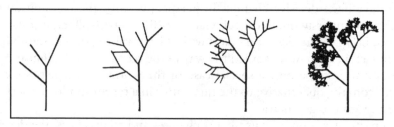

Figure 4.2 The First, Second, Third, and Sixth Iterations of a Simple Fractal Tree

Figure 4.3 An Illustration of Scale Independence (and Self-Similarity)

Scale Independence

In particular, and much in contrast to the figures and forms of more classical geometries, fractal images don't get simpler when you magnify them, nor more complicated when you pull back from them. Said differently, there is a *scale independence* to complex phenomena (Figure 4.3).

Since being proposed, the notion of scale independence has been applied to a wide range of phenomena—including notions that are generally thought to fall out of the purview of mathematics such as *time, memory,* and *life* itself. Following a suggestion by mathematician Rudy Rucker (1987), I've sketched out a fragment of my own life fractal (Figure 4.4), starting with what I'm holding at the moment of this writing.

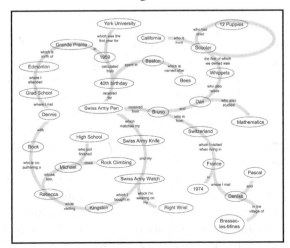

Figure 4.4 A Fragment of My Life Fractal. . . at the Moment

Figure 4.5 Bodies Enfolded in and Unfolding from Bodies

Closing in on any aspect of this web, or pulling back from the image, reveals another web that is similar in detail and form to this image (Figure 4.5). Each moment is a node, connecting and collecting a new weave of associations. There is no line joining birth to death. Rather, life is presented as a complex unfolding that is always renewed, always brimming with detail.

In various projects (e.g., Davis et al., 2000), I have worked with others to apply the notions of recursive embeddedness and scale independence to events of cognition. Whether examining, say, an individual body's learning of place value, or the emergence of a particular body of knowledge, the evolution of the body politic, or whatever body you find interesting, the bumpiness of detail remains constant.

Fractal images, which display the same level of detail whether one focuses on part or whole, are thus a cogent visual metaphor on at least one level. The relatively recent realization of the scale independence of human affairs is, I think, an important moment in our thinking about thinking. For instance, rather than allowing those dynamic phenomena that we call "thought" and "mind" to be lodged in individual bodies, we are enabled to realize the similar dynamics at play among cells and neurons, clusters of cells and neurons, bodily subsystems and systems, persons, social groupings, societies, and so on. Choosing any one as a focus immediately catches us up in every other level of phenomena. That means that we can think about *thinking* as the interactivity of neurons, or as a brain-based event, or as an individual's activity, or as a social event, or as a cultural linguistic event, or as a biological-evolutionary event, or (as I prefer) as all-of-the-above, all-at-once.

One of the upshots of the realization of scale independence is that it's vitally important for *all* of layers of organism and organization to be studied. However, rather than casting the resulting discourses of neurology, psychology, sociology, and cultural studies as, at worst, contradictory, or, at best, as simply complementary, the fractal imagery demands that they be seen as recursively embedded, caught up in and necessary to one another.

Self-Similarity

Said otherwise, as with many fractal images, there is a certain *self-similarity* to those events that have been identified as cognitive or as contributing to cognition. Self-similarity, the third quality of fractal images that I'd like to highlight, is connected to the notion of scale independence. In a nutshell, it refers to the way that particular parts of fractal images can closely resemble the original wholes. This quality is evident in the fractal tree (Figure 4.2), the fern leaf (Figure 4.3), and, in a less obvious way, in a "life fractal." It's also powerfully illustrated by a range of natural forms, four of which are pictured in Figure 4.6.

The discussion could go in any number of directions from here. Returning to my announced interests in matters of learning and curriculum, I've elected to focus on what this figurative device might have to offer current thinking around the "structures" of knowing and knowledge.

Figure 4.6 Some natural fractals: a River Valley (top left), a Tree (top right), a Brain Artery (bottom left), and Sludge (bottom right)

Knowing Structures

As a way into the topic of the structure of knowledge, let me go the route of a brief etymology of the word "structure."

Conventionally, the word structure tends to carry with it a sense of intentionality, deliberateness. Educators, for example, often aim to *structure* learning events, to *structure* arguments, to *structure* curricula, to in*struct*, to assist in the con*struct*ion of knowledge, and so on—following a sense of structure that draws from modern architecture. There is a sense of preplanning, deliberate implementation, step following, direct progress toward specific goals.

Biologists also use the word a good deal, but in a very different sense. When they talk about an organism's structure, it's in reference to the complex web of events that contribute to an entity's current form. Structure is both consequence and accident, inevitable and unrepeatable, familiar and unique, biological and experiential. Structures are matters of pattern and order, but not necessarily of deliberate invention. A tree, for example, is structured. One's sense of self is structured. Life is structured. But these are all complex matters, subject to the ever-renewing interplay of biology and circumstance.

The biologist's use of the term is more faithful to its origins. Sharing the same roots as "strew" and "construe," structure originally referred to the way things "fall" or "spread out" or "pile up" in ways that are not (and cannot be) predetermined, but that are not quite random either. When the notion of structure was first applied to buildings, it made perfect sense. Such forms, for the most part, weren't preplanned. Rather, they unfolded over years and uses as parts were added, destroyed, or otherwise altered. One built according to need, opportunity, and/or whimsy. The resulting edifices were thus not seen as permanent, but in flux, evolving—that is, they were structures in the biological sense of a form's immediate state of being.

For the most part, there is a very different attitude to architecture these days. Whereas the notion of "prespecified structure" would have been an oxymoron only a few centuries ago, today it makes perfect sense.

Unfortunately, that modern, deliberate sense has slipped into other uses of the term. The centuries-old notion of "structure of knowledge," for instance, today has a connotation of a carefully articulated order, rather than the perhaps-more-appropriate senses of unpredictable unfolding or complex emergence. This, unfortunately, is especially true in educational circles, particularly where mathematics and science are being discussed. Such bodies of knowledge are often treated as though they were pristinely structured in the modern architectural sense. Any close examination of the history of these bodies would suggest that a more biological interpretation is in order. That is, we're not fumbling along a more-or-less straight road toward a totalized and self-contained knowledge of the universe. Rather, we're all taking part in structuring knowledge—spreading out, piling up—and this requires a completely different image.

A similar, rigid notion of structure is often assumed in such phrases as "personal knowledge structure." One's sense tends to go toward modern buildings—and, once there, attracts such complementary notions as foundations, platforms, planks, scaffolds, building blocks, hierarchies, frameworks, and so on. Such habits of association, I believe, are the bane of constructivism, social constructivism, enactivism, and other discourses that use "structure" in the biological sense, but that tend to speak to audiences who work from more modern, technocratic understandings of the word.

There are, of course, alternative images available in the language—two prominent ones being the "tree of knowledge" and "bodies of knowledge." These are ancient notions—and, in terms of the biologist's and cognitive theorist's sense of structure, apt ones (Maturana & Varela, 1987). They suggest emergences that are unpredictable and uncontrollable, but, at the same time, ordered and familiar.

The problem is that this image is in competition with another more linear conception of the way complexity has emerged. Consider, for example, two conflicting images of the evolution of species. On the one hand, we have the familiar linear image, usually represented as some sort of steady progression toward optimality (and, most often, from scrambling simian toward a weapon-toting, Caucasian male). On the other hand, we have a more unruly, strewing tree-like fractal image. In one we have order, predictability, progress; in the other we have false starts, surprise turns, ever-mounting complexity.

That is, in one life is fitted into Euclid's geometry. In the other, life is poured into fractal geometry. In one there are implicit suggestions that endpoints are knowable and predetermined—and, hence, that totalized knowledge is attainable. One need only lay out the correct, logical sequence and then fill in the blanks. In the other, there is an immediate acknowledgment that knowledge is always partial—in both the sense of being fragmented and the sense of being biased.

Elaborating on this latter construal, one might think of the emergence of any complex form—whether a life or a mathematical understanding—as a structuring process that is similar to the generation of a fractal figure. One begins with some sort of seed: an experience, a premise, a rule, a simple image, and so on. From there, one structures—that is, one elaborates according to some particular constraints . . . and then elaborates those elaborations in an endless, recursive, ever-complexifying process like the ones that eventually give rise to the scale independence of fractal images.

What you end up with can't be predicted or controlled—but that doesn't mean it defies comprehension. It just means that the structure emerges or the path that unfolds has to be lived through for its endpoint to be realized.

What is suggested here, then, is a different image for characterizing the unfolding of any complex event—such as, for instance, a mathematics lesson or a research project. Rather than thinking in terms of a prespecified structure, one might think of a myriad of potentialities, one of which will be pulled into existence, but only by living through the event. I've found one image to be particularly useful in this regard: the flow of water down the fractal surface of a mountainside (Figure 4.7). The image generated by tracing out all the possible paths, often referred to as a "phase space," is itself fractal.

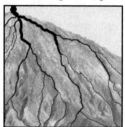

**Figure 4.7 A Phase Space Image for Characterizing
the Possible Unfolding of Events**

These sorts of images highlight the impossibility of predicting or controlling complex events. Even in this situation, which is vastly simpler than, say, a mathematics lesson, it's impossible to anticipate outcomes. We simply cannot expect to know in any definitive way where a particular droplet might go.

> If a system's potentialities are constrained, but not determined, by the system's qualities, really its antecedents, does this then lead us to a reconceptualizing of cause? If so, how would such be taught? For a social systems view of the relationship between a system's potentiality and its constraints, see Rasmussen (this volume).

Where it ends up depends on a host of uncontrollable events—including the influence exerted by the droplet on the surface that it passes over. Clearly, we can *prescribe* no outcomes in this situation. *However*, we needn't throw up our hands in despair. While the actual outcome is unpredictable, the range of possibilities is not. That is, the domain of potentialities is *proscribed* by the qualities of the system—the droplet must move downhill, it can't leap, and so on (Figure 4.8). This compromise of the unknowable and the knowable—which presents an important contrast to images of progress along lesson trajectories, through concept maps, along roads of life, or up evolutionary ladders—thus points to a different geometry of existence, a different shape to life.

The unpredictability, yet inevitable familiarity of a fractal landscape, for example, presents an interesting contrast to current metaphors of "obstacles" and "stumbling blocks" to understanding. Such images presume a knowable goal, and contingencies must thus be cast as impediments and resistances to be overcome in a grand competition. A geometry of surprise suggests that contingencies must be anticipated but, beyond a general expectation, cannot

**Figure 4.8 Euclidean Image for Progress versus Fractal Image
for Movement and Transformation**

be predicted in any dependable way. While metaphors of competition can be read into this image, one's movement might just as well be described in terms of mindful attendance to the texture of existence.

Unstructuring Curriculum

Having worked on these ideas for some years now, I always find it interesting to return to earlier writings—my own and, more importantly, some of the texts that most influenced my thinking in my early moments of graduate studies in education.

Inevitably, I get the feeling that someone else has already made all of these points, usually better than I have. In terms of the image of the waterfall that I used to end the previous section, for example, I must acknowledge Madeleine Grumet's (1988) influence in her description of curriculum as a "moving form." Drawing on Suzanne Langer's (1957) development of the waterfall as a dynamic form in motion, Grumet is clearly pointing to the many of the same sensibilities that I have attempted to highlight here. The same is true of William Doll Jr.'s (1988, 1993) discussions of the possibilities of chaos and complexity theories for interpreting matters of curriculum.

In an academic culture that continues to be preoccupied with the very Euclidean notion of territoriality, I am sometimes overwhelmed by the responsibility to cite and recite the work of others . . . and, of course, to demonstrate how my work is different. Inevitably, I end up feeling that I've failed in those regards.

In other moments, when I'm able to bring more fractal-ized sensibilities to bear on this worry, I realize that it can be more fruitful to think in terms of recursive elaboration than in terms of sitting atop a mound of past work. For some reason, I find the idea empowering—not in the least because it seems to recall the historical links of the notion of *empowerment* to acts of *improvisation* and goals of *improvement*. This realization does not free me from the responsibility to be attentive to who said what when—in fact, it seems to amplify the need to be familiar with what has come before—but it is liberating in that it highlights the importance of a repetition. Not a mindless mimicking, but a mindful reiteration.

I try to bring the same sensibilities to my thinking/doing/being around structuring curriculum. As I invite my own students into investigations of matters of learning or schooling or mathematics, it is always with desires to examine how we are implicated and complicit in their structures through something as simple and as invisible as our habits of association.

And, for some reason, regardless of the course or the specific topic, these investigations always come to involve a study of the geometries that we use and that we might use to structure our worlds.

References

Capra, F. (1996). *The web of life: A new scientific understanding of living systems.* New York: Doubleday.

Chapman, Robert L. (Ed). (1977). *Roget's international thesaurus*, 4th ed. Toronto: Fitzhenry and Whiteside.

Davis, B., D. Sumara, and R. Luce-Kapler. (2000). *Engaging minds: Learning and teaching in a complex world.* Mahwah, NJ: Erlbaum.

Doll, Jr., W. (1988). Curriculum beyond stability: Schön, Prigogine, Piaget. In *Contemporary curriculum discourses.* W.F. Pinar (Ed.). (pp. 39–47). Scottsdale, AZ: Gorsuch Scarisbrick.

———. (1993). *A post-modern perspective on curriculum.* New York: Teachers College Press.

Foucault, Michel. (1990). *The history of sexuality: An introduction.* New York: Vintage.

Grumet, M. (1988). *Bitter milk: Women and teaching.* Amherst, MA: University of Massachusetts Press.

Langer, S. (1957). *Problems of art.* New York: Scribner.

Maturana, H., and F. Varela. (1987). *The tree of knowledge: The biological roots of human understanding.* Boston: Shambhala.

Rucker, R. (1987). *Mind tools: The five levels of mathematical reality.* Boston: Houghton Mifflin.

Stewart, I. (1998). *Life's other secret: The new mathematics of the living world.* New York: Wiley.

DARREN STANLEY

Paradigmatic Compexity

Emerging Ideas and Historical Views of the Complexity Sciences

Complexity is the property of a real world system that is manifest in the inability of any one formalism being adequate to capture all its properties.

Donald Mikulecky, *Computers and Chemistry*

Opening Words

A growing number of scientists, scholars, and researchers from various disciplines and interdisciplinary domains have embraced a perspective on complexity that has extended and shifted their attentions toward envisioning certain questions and challenging problems differently. Currently, complexity is a notion invoked across a wide range of discourses, scholarly discussions and writings, and practical engagements with organizational or systemic structures: This can be seen in the proliferation of articles, essays, and books written on the subject that appear across most of the sciences, including biology, geology, ecology, physiology, the neurosciences, psychology, mathematics, computer science, and currently emerging technologies. These approaches also appear in the social sciences, education, urban studies, economics, organizational studies, politics, the military, and health care. This chapter is intended to illuminate some of the historical developments behind a collection of ideas, principles, and conceptualizations related to the complexity sciences, or in the language of mathematics, nonlinear dynamics.

A few key ideas lie at the heart of studies in the complexity sciences. Many writers, scholars and researchers will allude to notions like nonlinearity, chaos, complexity, self-organization, self-similarity, scale invariance, emergence, order and disorder, bifurcations, fractals, systems, parts and wholes, variability, and so on. These terms are frequently used to describe, interpret, and understand, and model particular phenomena that are commonly referred to as complex systems as opposed to other kind of phenomena variously described as simple and complicated or organized and disorganized. Before launching into a look at some of the more predominant ideas that can be found in contemporary framings of complex phenomena, a brief look at the kinds of structures and organizations described as complex and not-complex are in order. Thereafter, this chapter will continue with an exploration of some key ideas, principles, and conceptualizations that mark, both generally and specifically, complex phenomena.

Complex and Not-Complex

Reductionism has proven to be a very useful approach and means to understanding a wide range of phenomena. Reductionism (as when one views and interprets the world as comprised of parts) tends to frame the world as "out there," separate and separated from us through our bodies. However, besides the world, there is nothing else. There is only the world: Thus, there is no separation and the world is entirely connected. Ludwig Wittgenstein (1974) emphasizes this (grammatically with a comma for effect) in the first proposition of his *Tractatus Logico-Philosophicus*: The world is all that is the case, and all that happens to be the case.[1] This, though, runs counter to the almost "natural" assumption that many make about the world:

> It is a natural assumption about the world that it has its being "out there." That is to say, independent of experience, language, etc., the world is what it is ("the 'it' remains"). We may run into various difficulties understanding that world— under names such as illusion, hallucination, ambiguity, unclarity, equivocation, and the like. But these difficulties do not affect the fact that the world has its self-identical being out there, and such difficulties must be struck out of discourse if it is to be true to this being out there. Even in such striking out, the "it" remains, ever self-identical, ever calling for univocal discourse to give it a voice. (Jardine, 1998, 20)

It must be borne in mind that human beings are inseparable from the world. Our double-embodiment simultaneously separates us from the world and brings us into contact with the world (Varela, 1999). Our own collusion, then, brings us into a complex set of relationships—with our selves, in a self-reflexive manner, and the world. This is the *latus* in "relationship"—a reference to that which is at one's side. It is a kind of a direct connection with the world. It is, perhaps, in our minds that we become disconnected from the world through a particular conceptualization of that world. Thus, a different "mind-set" for drawing our attentions to the presence of various kinds of connections might give us cause to be suspicious of any kind of cutting up of the world that we might do.

One might argue that the world is already and always complex as would be suggested by various kinds of connections or relations that are present in the world. Moreover, our perceptions of the world are already complicitous in and creating a sense of complexity-at-work, as in the various and diverse perspectives and ideas that humans bring to one another in conversation, for example. It is, in fact, a conceptual sense of the world as a complex phenomenon or entity that is of importance in this paper. As the title suggests, it is the notion of complexity which will be explored here as a particular paradigmatic view—one that has not always been the case. Science and society at large are bearing witness to what would appear to be a new phenomenon, a particular intellectual orientation.

Still, there will be some who will say that not everything in the world is complex. The problem, becomes, then, how does one differentiate a complex phenomenon from one that is not? As suggested earlier, the domain of the complexity sciences is a relatively new, emergent field, and a transdisciplinary movement among researchers and scholars that originally came together around the realization that there are different kinds of dynamic phenomena which call for different interpretive and descriptive frames. Warren Weaver, an early cyberneticist and information theorist, was among one of the first prominent scientists to question and address, on a formal level, differences in the dynamics of different phenomena. In a seminal 1948 paper, Weaver outlined three different phenomena that are relevant to this paper and which have attracted the interest of many other scientists since.

Although no longer used, Weaver signaled an important early distinction among three kinds of different dynamical patterns that he termed "simple," "organized complexity," and "disorganized complexity." Framed in the language of systems, "simple systems" were thought of and discussed in terms of small numbers of independent parts or variables that determined the system. As such, the analytical tools available to enlightened thinkers like Newton and Galileo proved to be sufficient to understand and model such phenomena. Eventually, scientists and mathematicians encountered or created more complicated systems where the number of interacting parts or variables used to understand or model the system was increased slightly. Mathematician Henri Poincaré serves as an example of one individual who met up with the intractability of working with some apparently simple systems that fell outside the realm of computability, as when he considered the famous "three body problem."

In the nineteenth century, as individuals considered systems with increasingly larger numbers of interacting parts or variables, the need for special analytic tools became necessary. Thus, new analytic tools were introduced with statistical instruments along with the use of probabilities, just coming into prominence during this time. Weaver described these newer kinds of dynamical systems as "disorganized systems." As various systems became more complicated, individuals needed to rely more upon macro descriptions of these systems when the analysis of large numbers of agents in interaction proved computationally impracticable and sometimes impossible. This movement also coincided with the need for standardization of various industrialized processes and products. Moreover, these statistical tools subsequently were imported into domains like education, and remain quite familiar to individuals in the social sciences where such phenomena continue to be analyzed as disorganized complexity. The problem is that other kinds of phenomena that stretch across a wide range of organizational structure, including physiological systems, the human body, various social collectivities, and cultural and ecological phenomena, are not examples of disorganized complexity at all, but are what Weaver originally described as "organized complexity." Such "complex" systems involving, for instance, organizational coherence, the nervous system or traffic jams, do not easily surrender to those analytic tools that were originally designed to interpret chance events or statistical distributions of traits across populations or qualities of standards for large aggregates of machine parts.

Simply put, today the terms "simple" and "disorganized complexity" are not so prominent and have been reduced to the notion of "complicated" systems, and the term "organized complexity" has been reduced to "complexity." Thus, in today's contemporary terminology in the field of complexity science, systems are either complicated or complex. "Complicated" refers to events involving individual or collective independent actions, and this includes both simple and disorganized complex systems. "Complexity" generally corresponds to "organized complexity."

In the remaining sections of this chapter, a number of key ideas and principles pertinent to complex systems will be examined. Specifically, the notions of nonlinearity, emergence, and self-organization will be explored. As a way of framing the remaining sections, a collection of terms that generally fall under the umbrella term of "complexity" will be considered: not intending to be exhaustive, these include and are limited to chaos theory, catastrophe theory, and complex adaptive systems.

Under the Complexity Umbrella: Chaos

Human beings often tend to notice the accidental or even catastrophic more than the subtle changes that are constantly unfolding. Fitting for an introduction to chaos theory, one such "accident" is told about MIT meteorologist, Edward Lorenz who, in the late 1950s, discovered quite by accident a particular quality that is now referred to as "sensitivity to initial conditions." His "discovery," in the history of the complexity sciences, is often taken to be a critical marker and an often-told story in the evolution of chaos theory—actually, an old idea suddenly emergent in mathematics, physics, and information theory.

At the time of this story, Lorenz was using some sophisticated linear methods to model weather systems on his Royal-McBee LGP-30 computer

(Alligood, Sauer, and Yorke, 1997). The story of Lorenz's work is told in his own book, *The Essence of Chaos* (1995), as well as in James Gleick's well-known popular science book, *Chaos* (1988). More specifically, he writes about the experience that led to his discovery that the amplification of small differences in initial conditions could be the cause of chaotic behavior, a picture that suggests a lack of periodicity. After a cup of coffee and about an hour of printing from his dot-matrix printer, Lorenz returned to find that the numbers on his printout were nothing like his previous computational run. At that time in history, it was not unusual to think that a computer hardware glitch had happened, but Lorenz took a closer look at the numbers and realized that something else was happening. The problem proved to be the initial round-off errors that were amplified in the ongoing calculations of the program. "Chaos," thus, was born—but, not quite.

Although the allure of chaos would not take off until others took notice of Lorenz's work and the arrival of computers in the 1960s, the French mathematician Henri Poincaré (1854–1912) can certainly be counted upon as being one of the early pioneers who rebelled against the strong presence of Newtonian determinism in a nonlinear world at the end of the nineteenth century. In fact, Poincaré's 1879 doctoral dissertation paved the way for thinking about the formulation of (nonlinear) solutions to particular systems of differential equations (Eves, 1990, 571–72). Specifically, he noted that there could exist sequences of points through the intersections of trajectories with (what are now known as) Poincaré sections that are periodic in nature although those periods vary. Even more, he discovered that there could also exist simultaneously an infinite number of sequences that were not periodic. His methods proved to be useful in his solution to the problem of the stability of the solar system, but in particular, his insights opened the door to the study of "deterministic chaos."

A well-known and often discussed feature of chaotic structures, as previously mentioned, is their "sensitivity to initial conditions." His often quoted phrase, "*Prédiction devient impossible. . .*" Poincaré expressed in this way:

> If we knew exactly the laws of nature and the situation of the universe at the initial moment, we could predict exactly the situation of that same universe at a succeeding moment. But even if it were the case that the natural laws had no longer any secret for us, we could still only know the initial situation approximately. If that enabled us to predict the succeeding situation with the same approximation, that is all we require, and we should say that the phenomenon had been predicted, that it is governed by laws. But it is not always so; it may happen that small differences in the initial conditions produce very great ones in the final phenomena. A small error in the former will produce an enormous error in the latter. Prediction becomes impossible, and we have the fortuitous phenomenon. (Poincaré, 1905, 68)

This phenomenon, more recently, has been expressed metaphorically as a butterfly flapping its wings in some part of the world and affecting the weather conditions in another part of the world. The persistent use of this metaphor has created a certain amount of uncertainty about its origins. Nevertheless, Edward Lorenz's 1972 paper, "Predictability: Does the Flap of a Butterfly's Wings in Brazil Set Off a Tornado in Texas?" (mentioned in Lorenz, 1995) appears to mark the first appearance of this image. Hinging chaos to the condition of sensitivity to initial conditions still does not help much in determining whether or not a system is chaotic.

Mathematically speaking, a chaotic system must also be viewed from a macroscopic point of view. Chaotic systems exhibit particular qualities which can be described by features that are called attractor basins: These are forward-time limits sets of trajectories that attract a significant number of initial conditions (Alligood, Sauer, and Yorke, 1997, 240). Such attractors include structures known as "fixed-point limits," "periodic orbits," and "pathological monsters" known as "strange attractors" or "chaotic attractors." Thus, it is perhaps more important to attend not to individual points or localized trajectories, but regions of the chaotic system.

To be clear, small changes in the initial conditions are not enough to "define" a chaotic system. Not all systems are chaotic (hence deterministic, but unpredictable). Therefore, since not all systems are deterministic, small changes in the dynamics of the system change the system in very different ways. Changing the interactions of a complex system, for example, creates the possibility for new, novel patterns. For a chaotic system, though, in simply changing the initial conditions, the local trajectory in time may change; however, the overall, macro-description of the system does not change. That is, there can be no possibility for a pattern other than the one that is already enfolded into the system.

It is for this reason that chaos theory is not an entirely appropriate frame or collection of tools that can be applied to human systems or organizations of social interactions: They are not deterministic. Therefore, it is not so much that the mathematical tools are bad or outmoded. It is more in line with the idea that they are the right tools for another kind of problem. At

Chaotic systems are indeed determinist but due to the many and fluctuating factors involved in a system's development and its sensitivity to small perturbations, chaotic systems are inherently unpredictable. Traditional, Newtonian system models—those assuming predictability—are gross oversimplifications. In these models—deterministic and predictable—humanity's "free will" has been considered a special gift: a gift from outside the system by the system's designer. What happens to our traditional (albeit delusional) view of humanity in a chaotic/complex worldview? What does it mean to become post-human?

this point, however, chaotic phenomena, that is, phenomena with chaotic attractor sets, are important for particular qualities that do appear across a number of different organized structures. As such, it does make sense then to ask what chaos looks like.

Images of Chaos

In the age of the "new science," chaos and complexity have brought new perspectives to the way in which we frame, understand, and act within the world. This new perspective has extended beyond the technical achievements of science as well, moving into the realm of the arts, literary theory, philosophy, education, and politics with new voices emerging from within a "space" called "postmodernism." A whole new sense of ordering is emerging: It is not the older symmetrical, simple, and sequential ordering of a world, but rather something a bit more "fuzzy" (Doll, 1993, 3). Asymmetry, chaos, and "fractal" forms are the "new order" of the day.

While the "open vision" of postmodernism has, in some sense, come to include a slightly scientized view of itself, postmodern perspectives of the world and science in particular are somewhat shallow and suggest a mistaken or naïve view of science (Doll, 1993, 63). There is, nevertheless, a shared sensibility within and across the diverse postmodern mind-set that is reflected in a bifurcated fork of voices, ideas, and practices. This is not to suggest that the shared sensibility of chaos is the same across levels of discourse, let alone identical to the mathematical sense of chaos. It, most assuredly, is not. The colloquial notion of chaos is quite different from the technical, mathematical sense of chaos. This can be problematic as it can make for challenging conversations where the same words may be used but convey different senses or meanings. Still, it can be very difficult for some individuals to be open to other possibilities for understanding chaos. Put differently, natural scientists may be skeptical of certain uses of chaos theory, and find some nonscientific perspectives that invoke chaos theory to be questionable (Weingart and Maase, 1997, 465). At the same time, other "nonscientific" approaches, for example postmodernist approaches, challenge the privileged nature of science where it might be implied that certain meanings of "chaos" are better or more accurate.

The late twentieth century has seen some rather interesting and prominent shifts within the larger social collectivity. That is, after centuries of trying to straighten out the world, "new scientists" and "postmodernists" have moved toward trying to embrace the kinkiness of the world. There is, in fact, a certain natural, universal aesthetic preference for irregularity and roughness that human beings have: It is capturing the imaginations of scientists and artists (Spehar et al., 2003). The language and concepts attributed to the domain of complexity science, like "fractals" and "chaos," are popping up everywhere, from the interpretations of Jackson Pollock's abstract paintings involving paint drippings to computer graphics, music, and other wonderful strange attractions (Goldberg, 1999; Taylor, Micholich, and Jonas, 1999; Spehar et al., 2003).

The topic of "fractals" is a common one in complexity-related discussions and postmodern discourses. These patterns of chaos with common signatures like cracks and crevices, fractures and fragments, and wrinkles and warpings are a part of the "new aesthetic" for artists and scientists. There is a particular beauty about fractals and a certain perfection in their imperfections. The concept of a fractal has permeated into a larger collective understanding of the roughness and kinkiness of the world, its energy, and its capacity for transformation and dynamical change (Briggs, 1992, 23). That is, when one peers deeper into the structure or process of some phenomenon one might see continued levels of detail. Sometimes, we can even find a certain Byzantine architecture of similar structures with each level of magnification. Like a tree with its branches, smaller limbs and twigs, and the veins of its palmated leaves, we find scales of organized structures that bear a resemblance across all scales: the larger tree looks like a smaller limb with the smaller limbs and twigs on it. This pattern is called self-similarity or, more generally, scale invariance.

In a Euclidean world, one might experience a discontinuous jump of sorts from the single dimension of a straight line to the two dimensions of a plane figure to the three dimensions of a solid object, and so on. Fractals, on the other hand, are often described as "things" that lie in between these dimensions, and thus they are objects with fractional dimensions, depending on the nature of their crinkliness or crumbling nature. Nature, therefore, shows itself to us across many different scales where "evolutionary activity creates worlds within worlds, all moving, changing, feeding back into each other from small scale to larger scale, back to small scale" (Briggs, 1992, 23). Taken to either extreme—the very small and the very large, as well as everything in between—the whole and part play out in this image of scale-invariant detail, always a whole and a part in the wholeness of an all-at-once world.

Last, it would be good to pay attention to an important distinction between chaos and fractals. To be certain, they do share some common ideas and methodological approaches (Bassingthwaighte, Liebovitch, and West, 1994, 138). Deterministic chaotic equations can generate particular images in a mathematical object called a "phase space": when the image is said to be fractal, the corresponding time series is referred to as chaotic. But, as James Bassingthwaite and his colleagues remind us, "objects and processes studied by fractals and chaos are essentially different" (1994, 138).

As previously described, fractals have a particular quality called self-similarity whether these are objects or processes: analysis of possible fractal data is intended to determine whether or not this feature of self-similarity is present. Where this quality of self-similarity is present, appropriate fractal tools can then be used to characterize the dataset. In the case of chaos, however, one is concerned with knowing whether a given dataset is the result of a deterministic process that can then be analyzed for a closed mathematical form that takes the shape of a set of nonlinear deterministic equations. Where this is not the case, the time series dataset would suggest uncorrelated randomness.

The notion of "suddenness," however, is not captured in a chaos theoretic framework. In the history of the complexity sciences, other conceptual frames have been proposed that draw one's attention to the nature and notion of "change." Two conceptual notions in particular that address change explicitly are catastrophe theory and self-organized criticality.

Change and Opportunity: Crises, Catastrophes, and Criticality

How do people conceive and perceive of change? Is "change" dramatic? Slow to appear? All of a sudden? Progressive? It is, perhaps, both evolutionary and revolutionary in nature, and in nature both can be seen at work. Catastrophes and moments of crisis, in more usually-taken-for-granted ways, mark occasions for and of change: they are dramatic and all of a sudden, often "catching us off guard." But, of course, things like our bodies, the seasons, or the mountains change, too, but much more slowly and sometimes imperceptibly so. Still, what causes something to change?

Change would appear to be a process that unfolds across many different temporal scales.[2] A Chinese garden is a fitting example of a place where one might observe change across many such scales. Without much attention to the details of a Chinese garden, one might miss how the careful and deliberate framing of nature presents itself to us in the patterns of change: the turbulence of the waterfall; the blossoming of the Winter Jasmine flower; the stillness in the shadows of the trees caressing the white walls, moving gently across the open courtyard with the sun above; the rigid rocks with their life-like qualities that stare back in the shapes of oddly recognizable, familiar forms.

A Chinese garden might hardly come to mind as a place where catastrophes or crises might happen when viewed for its beauty and splendor. It bears a similar aesthetic quality to other fractal objects and processes. The world of ideas might unfold and appear in a similar way. That is, catastrophes and crises abound on many scales. But what gets noticed and how it is noticed is strongly shaped by our own perceptions. Those things that fall below our threshold of perception appear stable and unchanging: above such a threshold, a world of change appears.

A "catastrophe," as its etymology suggests, is a "turning" of some kind—like the "turning away" of a letter by the insertion of an apostrophe in a word; the turning over of a new leaf as when one changes one's behavior, throwing away an old one; or turning the corner to go in some new or different direction. A "turning point," therefore, appears that throws into question a certain prevailing view, and it can be a moment of crisis, or metaphorically, a crack in some foundation. A catastrophe, of course, need not imply throwing out one entire thing for another. In more postmodernist notions, a catastrophe may simply open up other possibilities for additional consideration.

Let us consider the work of mathematician Christopher Zeeman (1968, 1977). Questioning the notion that change happens gradually, Zeeman articulated his ideas in what he called "catastrophe theory" which examines the changes in the state-space of a system that describe sudden discontinuous changes. Certainly, the appearance of catastrophe theory in Zeeman's work didn't suddenly render null and void other theories and views of change. If anything, it opened up other ways of thinking about it. While the notion of a catastrophe in Zeeman's sense of the word is no longer prominent, it has been superseded by the notion of "criticality," as in Per Bak's "self-organized criticality" (Bak, 1999; Bak, Tang, and Wiesenfeld, 1987).

Whatever happened to Zeeman's work in terms of its influence on the scientific world's sense of change might be difficult to fully articulate; however, in evolutionary terms, one might say that it became extinct, although there are traces of its being in the ideas of other complexity-related concepts. Of the many terms that fall under the complexity umbrella, "self-organized criticality" is an exciting and relatively recent notion to appear. It seems to convey a sense of continuous change across many scales, and under the same underlying dynamics, it can bring forth big changes where the history of an entire system is affected. The canonical examples that are often raised in this context are sandpiles and earthquakes (Jensen, 1998, 2). From there, the idea spread to other phenomena like electrical breakdowns, magnetic flux, water droplets formations, and more recently to biological evolution. The basis for change in such phenomena is suggested by the idea of self-governance of the system itself and its own internal dynamics or self-organization.[3]

With the appearance of other new emerging ideas that are falling under the larger complexity frame, one might wonder if there is not some sort of crisis happening in the world of ideas. Indeed, on a much larger scale, we are seeing a broader shift in our collective worldviews. Some call this postmodernism: it is a thoroughly dynamic view of the world, and it is all-at-once seen as dangerous and destructive while opening up opportunity. It is, indeed, a crisis. In the Chinese sense of a crisis, *wei-ji,* in its iconographic composition, it is a combination of both "danger" and "opportunity"

(Capra, 1983, 26). As the eminent scientist and ecologist, Fritjof Capra suggests, society at large is finding itself in a crisis, at a turning point.

Since the appearance of chaos and catastrophe theories and self-organized criticality, a number of other ideas and concepts have come into play—complex adaptive systems, network theory, diffusion theory, artificial neural networks, complex responsive processes, systems thinking, and so on. The similarities and differences are much too vast for such a short exposition as this. Still, as Manuel De Landa would remind us, a sense of history infiltrated by physics would fare much better than a textual approach to the subject at hand (De Landa, 1997, 15). In fact, no textual approach could possibly "capture" the richness of the many complexity-related ideas that are discussed in the various literatures of today where it is being taken up in greater earnestness: in terms of a conceptual frame, a theory of complexity could never formally capture any "suitably complex" phenomena. Human beings are facing a time of immense opportunity for framing and enhancing a much richer view of the world than has been seen before.

One thing does appear to be invariant across various theoretical and conceptual frames of complex phenomena. That notion is "nonlinearity."

A Special Aspect of Complex Systems: Nonlinearity

The concept of linearity surfaces in a number of different guises and distinct contexts where meanings of the idea differ slightly although its overall abstraction is quite similar. Two properties, in particular, are frequently invoked: the *property of proportionality* and the *property of independence* (West, 1985, 5). Framed in the language of systems theory (as an example), a system or process is linear if the direct output of some operation is directly proportional to the input. More generally, if several factors are implicated in some system or process, then it is said to be linear if the end result is proportional to each factor. Mathematically speaking, it follows that each constant of proportionality is independent from one another.

Linearity is also often expressed in the form of a straight line on a Cartesian plane. In this manner, a particular phenomenon or event is often discussed as if it flowed or unfolded along a line. "Time" and "change," therefore, are conceived as "motion" along linear pathways. It is probably inevitable then that human beings would frame and understand events as linear happenings. As the proverb goes, "time and tide wait for no man"; however, no human being, to say nothing of tides, is that straight. That is, in a world of complex patterns, a capacity to adapt to a changing world requires a nonlinear being. Herein lies the importance of being nonlinear.

The idea of a straight line can be interpreted in a number of ways: algebraically, geometrically, or parametrically, for example. A straight line also constitutes a set of *ordered* points, an *arrangement* of points. With this notion of arranging and ordering points, as in a row, the idea of a sequence is not too far away. In more "postmodern" times, there is a sense that linearity is synonymous with order. Thus, there is this notion that events in the world can, should, or tend to unfold in a particular sequence. A nonlinear approach, therefore, is one that seemingly goes against a presumed, usually-taken-for-granted order. As has been observed on some occasions, the mere mixing up of things (as with a die to determine some order) should not be taken for being nonlinear. Random processes, however, are not nonlinear processes, as they tend to involve independent events. Here, some coherence is lost, and some misunderstanding is created with importing a mathematical idea into a different setting.

Complexity Concepts: Emergence and Self-Organization

Since the appearance of notions like chaos and fractals, other concepts have come into view, and the outlook has been of a largely scientific nature although elements of a philosophical and theological bent keep appearing as well. As an example, the concept of "emergence" is finding a new and exciting place in analytic thought, promising new ways in which to think about how novelty can happen in a very old universe. As Harold Morowitz (2002) suggests, emergence is the opposite of reduction: he continues:

> The latter [reductionism] arises from the whole to the parts. It has been enormously successful. The former [emergence] tries to generate the properties of the whole from an understanding of the parts. Both parts can be mutually self-consistent. (14)

The notion of "emergence" is a relatively new one in the modern-day writings of paradigmatic complexity. Donald Mikulecky (2001) suggests there are two kinds of emergence that one might distinguish which he describes as (1) the appearance of new things that arise through evolutionary processes and (2) the discovery of features in some phenomena that have always been there although they have been invisible in light of reductionist paradigms or simply more dominant formal frameworks for understanding a system (344). (This is not to say that there are *only* two types.) Also with the discovery of nonlinear dynamics, and specifically with the discovery of chaos, the concept of emergence and novelty began to appear although it was not the strongest form of emergence. Moreover, the association of emergence as a feature that should appear "at the edge of chaos" was quick to appear in biological and ecological terms—in co-evolutionary terms (Kauffman, 1995, 26–28). Computer simulations have also played a role in the claim for "emergent properties" owing to the lifelike qualities of genetic algorithms, cellular automata, neural networks, and other computational concepts and tools. Last, there are many natural phenomena that warrant the description of emergent phenomena. As Mikulecky (2001) writes: "Complexity is the property of a real world system that is manifest in the inability of any one formalism being adequate to capture all its properties" (344).

Like complexity science, emergence has no universally accepted definition. The notion of emergence remains hard to measure or explain since it lacks a certain concreteness that might be useful for recognizing it when one might see it (Corning, 2002, 22). Rather, as Jeffrey Goldstein (1999) suggests, "emergence functions not so much as an explanation but rather as a descriptive term pointing to the patterns, structures or properties that are exhibited on the macro-scale" (58). Emergence also appears, for example, in the writings of physicists to describe phenomena like convection patterns, organizational theorists to explain the formation of network patterns, economists to explain the behavior of the stock market, and philosophers to examine consciousness. The origins of the term, however, go back to pioneer psychologist G. H. Lewes (1874) and his work *Problems of Life and Mind*, although to be certain, the underlying idea was stated by Aristotle almost 2000 years ago in his *Metaphysics* (Corning, 2002, 18–19).

In addition to the notion of emergence, the term "self-organization" has also proven to be a frequently invoked term in the complexity-related literature. Self-organization describes how a system may bring itself into being on its own with a minimum of external direction or assistance. Kevin Kelly (1994) refers to this sort of process as "bootstrapping" (450). It is not a new concept: One can go back to what now are called the "Macy Conferences" to find scientific researchers like Gregory Bateson, Norbert Wiener, Margaret Mead, Warren McCulloch, and John von Neumann engaged in lively conversation and debate over the notion of "self-organizing systems." The 1959 conference is of particular note with its primary focus on self-organization (Kelly, 1994, 451).

Where self-organizing phenotypes are visible, the descriptions of the phenomenon cannot be deduced from the individual interacting parts of the systems to account for features that can only be observed at the level of the self-organized whole. In other words, the behavioral complexity of a self-organizing system depends on interactions, and not its individuals or parts (Solé and Goodwin, 2000, 176). In particular, the type and variety of interactions has a great deal to do with the behavior of the emergent system.

The individuals of a larger system have no idea how to build a collective organized structure. An ant, for instance, has no idea how the ant colony is taking shape. Moreover, depending on the environment, the same collection of interacting agents—ants, cars, people, for example—can create a variety of different emergent patterns. Nevertheless, the same agents in the system can and do interact with one another without some key organizing figure to bring forth, in a self-organizing manner, continuously generated novel forms. For this reason, we see a variety of widespread self-organized forms and universal patterns. No two trees, two flocks, two rivers, two cities, two brains are ever the same. Of course, many human-made organizations are created by design. For example, urban planners have tried to create neighborhoods and communities—sometimes from scratch; curriculum developers and health administrators attempt to define prescriptive educational outcomes and health care systems.

It would be a bold statement, indeed, to suggest that a social system—any system that operates far-from-equilibrium—could be constructed in some "appropriate" manner with the aim that it might "construct itself." Kauffman (1994, 86) argues that human beings organize systems for human purposes. Concerning the emergence of living systems, however, Kauffman adds:

> In the deepest sense, we seek universal principles governing the emergence of nonequilibrium, self-organizing, living, evolving systems on the earth and else-where in the Universe. It is life, after all, which has yielded our only natural examples of complex adaptive systems (CAS). (85)

Emergence, therefore, is driven by the self-organizing nature of a system far-from-equilibrium. It is in this manner that the notions of emergence and self-organization are linked. Thus, in the context of human beings, the self-organizing nature of local interactions gives rise to globally emergent, coher-ent patterns.

In the final section of this chapter, another approach will be presented that proposes a radically different view and approach to social interactions. It is, in some sense, rather new, although it is rooted in a number of ideas that come from Norbert Elias and George Herbert Mead. Complexity scholar and group psychotherapist Ralph Stacey (2003) offers a view of social interactions that *simultaneously* questions the usefulness of recent complexity science ideas and asks that we pay attention to human interactions the patterns that arise in the "living present." He calls this view "complex responsive processes" (Stacey, 2001, 4).

The Emergence of Meaning in Social Interaction

In his most recent book, *Complexity and Group Processes*, Stacey (2003) explores an alternative way to understand human interaction. In particular, as he writes, he is concerned with three questions:

- "Who am I and how have I come to be who I am?"
- "Who are we and how have we come to be who we are?"
- "How are we all changing, evolving and learning?" (43)

These questions are fundamental to understanding social relations. Stacey's notion of "complex responsive processes" offers a radically different way of thinking about how the identities of individuals and collectives emerge, how they are interrelated and how they change. Stacey's concerns arise from a need to explain what is going on when human beings are engaged in interactions. Whereas many other complexity frames offer prescriptive ways for directing or creating the conditions for certain possibilities, Stacey questions the possibility of doing such things.

Stacey's work, to begin, immediately raises some questions about a perennial worry concerning the import that a theory has for practice. This is an often discussed and debated topic where it is assumed that theory and practice are two different aspects—one involving thinking and the other action. The split, as with many other dichotomies, is often perceived as problematic. But theory and practice are inseparable. As one thinks differently, one acts differently and vice versa.

Human actions have no inside nor outside: there are no boundaries. And in this way, the human mind gives form to and is formed by social interactions. This may not seem particularly radical: some postmodernists frequently try to "push" the mind "out of the body." What is different about complex responsive processes is a need to posit a notion of wholeness, and hence parts. The inherent spatiality of other complexity-related theories is not present in Stacey's theory of social interactions. Thus, there is no system, no "internal world" (and by extension, nothing "outside"). His is a theory of temporal, dynamic processes involving gestures and responses. As such, human interactions create nothing above or below. A human interaction produces only "further interactions and is its own reflexive, self-referential cause" (2003, 5).

Stacey's work evolved from the idea that certain metaphors were becoming problematic for talking about social phenomena. Human beings participate with others in interaction, not as parts in a system outside their own interactions. This, of course, renders Stacey's approach incompatible with other complexity-related perspectives. But this is not to say that one should take Stacey's approach and combine it with another since combining inconsistent theories obliterates difference and eliminates paradoxes and ultimately the evolution of novel possibilities. Synthesizing two inconsistent views does not seem acceptable to him.

The complexity sciences, however, have a great deal of appeal, analogically speaking, for Stacey's process of relating. The problem, however, is not so much that human beings use analogies and metaphors to describe and explain various phenomena, but rather that we forget we are doing so in the first place. Emergence and interaction, for example, can be extended to Stacey's approach. As he suggests:

[A] key insight from the complexity sciences is that interaction between entities has the intrinsic capacity to produce emergent coherence in the absence of any blueprint or program. In other words, local interaction between entities can pattern itself into local and widespread coherence without any causal agency above or below it. (2003, 14)

Additionally, the notion of nonlinearity in interactions can also be brought into Stacey's approach to understanding human interactions. Novelty, therefore, emerges in the nonlinear interactions between diverse entities.

Certainly, the complexity sciences have called for a reevaluation of how we might understand and explain social interactions. We should not think, however, that this shift will improve our "social organizations"—Stacey would say there are no such things. It would suggest that we might be able to create the actual conditions for a particular outcome or arrangement. One might be suspicious if someone came along selling a method to create the right conditions for a particular outcome to appear. Should one be suspicious of curriculum designers and developers, for instance? What is important to remember about Stacey's work in this context is that it is not a prescription for action, but a means for thinking about human interactions and working with it rather than trying to change it.

Closing Words

Chaos. Complexity. And, to some extent, culture. But as the title of this collection of essays also points to "curriculum," attention to it might be appropriate here. Perhaps, taken as a whole, the various and varied written pieces in this collection of papers add up to include all four "c's"—"chaos," "complexity," "curriculum," and "culture." Read together, something more is bound to emerge from the reading of this work. But perhaps, in these closing words, a few thoughts on curriculum would be nice, in the very least, so as to touch upon all four "c's" in this piece.

In the field of curriculum theory—in the historical traces, anyway—it has been acknowledged on several occasions that it has experienced its own breakdown or crisis. We have heard that the field has been approaching death—a crisis of sorts, a point of bifurcation or symmetry-breaking, to use two complexity terms. Attributed to Joseph Schwab in 1970 and repeated by Dwayne Huebner a few years later, the sentiment was that the curriculum field was "near death," or in a "crisis"—in a word, according to Schwab, "moribund" (Doll, 1993, 161; Pinar, 1999, xxvi). How this crisis should be characterized has not been agreed upon. Recent offerings, however, have been made drawing upon complexity science notions as a possibility for framing the curriculum field in terms of its health—fitting since we are talking about its death (Stanley, 2003). But if curriculum is just about dead, if not actually dead, an appropriate burial should be in order. In the very least, one might take a pulse or place a stethoscope upon its chest and place a mirror to the mouth to check for any signs of shallow breathing before making such pronouncements of death and ordering coffins and such.

As this modest history lesson might point out, there is a little "chaos" and "complexity" in the midst of all of our lives that might help us to understand what is going on in some very different and useful ways. That is, theories and conceptualizations like chaos theory and catastrophe theory, complex adaptive systems, and complex responsive processes have opened a significantly different view of various diverse worldly phenomena. It should not be forgotten that these are "ideas"—a collection of mappings for an already and always changing world. There is an Irish saying that warns, "Always be suspicious at the corner." In this manner, we might be just a bit wary about the next complexity-inspired idea. In any event, one can almost count upon other new ideas coming into the mix at some point in time.

Notes

1. The exact quotation in German is: Die Welt ist alles, was der Fall ist (*The world is all, that is the case*). Quoted in Bearn, 1997, 47.
2. Readers are referred to Hongyu Wang's contribution to this volume on Chinese gardens for some further insights into the fractal aesthetic of Chinese philosophy and art forms like gardens.
3. Although external forces frequently contribute to the evolution of the system, such processes happen more slowly than the internal processes that tend to relax the system (Jensen, 1998, 3).

References

Alligood, Kathleen T., Tim Sauer, and James A. Yorke. (1997). Chaos: An introduction to dynamical systems. In *Textbooks in mathematical sciences*. T. F. Banchoff, K. Devlin, G. Gonnet, J. Marsden, and S. Wagon (Eds.). New York: Springer.

Bak, Per. (1999). *How nature works: The science of self-organized criticality*. New York: Copernicus.

Bak, Per, Chao Tang, and Kurt Wiesenfeld. (1987). Self-organized criticality. An explanation of $1/f$ noise. *Physical Review Letters* 59(4): 381–84.

Bassingthwaighte, James B., Larry S. Liebovitch, and Bruce J. West. (1994). *Fractal physiology*. New York: Oxford University Press.

Bearn, Gordon C. F. (1997). *Waking to wonder: Wittgenstein's existential investigations*. Albany: State University of New York Press.

Briggs, John. (1992). *Fractals: The patterns of chaos. A new aesthetic of art, science, and nature*. New York: Simon and Schuster.

Capra, Fritjof. (1983). *The turning point: Science, society, and the rising culture*. Toronto: Bantam Books.

Corning, Peter A. (2002). The re-emergence of "emergence": A venerable concept in search of a theory. *Complexity* 7(6):18–30.

De Landa, Manuel. (1997). *A thousand years of nonlinear history.* New York: Zone Books.

Doll, William E. (1993). *A post-modern perspective on curriculum.* New York: Teachers College Press.

Eves, Howard Whitley. (1990). *An introduction to the history of mathematics.* 6th ed. Fort Worth, TX: Saunders College Publishing.

Gleick, James. (1988). *Chaos: making a new science.* New York: Penguin Books.

Goldberg, Ary L. (1999). Chaos theory and creativity: The biological basis of innovation. *Journal of Innovative Management* 4(3): 17–25.

Goldstein, Jeffrey. (1999). Emergence as a construct: History and issues. *Emergence 1*(1): 49–72.

Jardine, David William. 1998. *To dwell with a boundless heart: Essays in curriculum theory, hermeneutics, and the ecological imagination.* New York: Lang.

Jensen, Henrik Jeldtoft. (1998). *Self-organized criticality: Emergent complex behavior in physical and biological systems,* Vol. 10, *Cambridge lecture notes in physics.* P. Goddard and J. Yeomans (Eds.). Cambridge: Cambridge University Press.

Kauffman, Stuart A. (1994). Whispers from Carnot: The origins of order and principles of adaptation in complex nonequilibrium systems. In *Complexity: Metaphors, models, and reality.* G. A. Cowan, D. Pines, and D. Meltzer (Eds.). Cambridge, MA: Perseus.

———. (1995). *At home in the universe: The search for laws of self-organization and complexity.* New York: Oxford University Press.

Kelly, Kevin. (1994). *Out of control: The rise of neo-biological civilization.* Reading, MA: Addison-Wesley.

Lewes, George Henry. (1874). *Problems of life and mind.* London: Trübner.

Lorenz, Edward N. (1995). *The essence of chaos.* Seattle: University of Washington Press.

Mikulecky, Donald C. (2001). The emergence of complexity: Science coming to age or science growing old? *Computers and Chemistry 25;* 341–48.

Morowitz, Harold J. (2002). *The emergence of everything: How the world became complex.* New York: Oxford University Press.

Pinar, William F. (1999). Notes on the relationship between a field and its journal. In *Contemporary curriculum discourses: Twenty years of JCT.* W. F. Pinar (Ed.). New York: Lang.

Poincaré, Henri. (1905). *Science and hypothesis.* London: Walter Scott Publishing.

Solé, Ricard V., and Brian C. Goodwin. (2000). *Signs of life: How complexity pervades biology.* New York: Basic.

Spehar, Branka, Colin W. G. Clifford, Ben R. Newell, and Richard P. Taylor. (2003). Universal aesthetic of fractals. *Computers and Graphics 27*(5): 813–20.

Stacey, Ralph D. (2003). *Complexity and group processes: a radically social understanding of individuals.* New York: Brunner-Routledge.

———. (2001). *Complex responsive processes in organizations: Learning and knowledge creation.* New York: Routledge.

Stanley, Darren. (2003). The body of education: What might a 'healthy' education system look like? First Complexity Science and Educational Research Conference, University of Alberta, paper presentation.

Taylor, Richard P., A. P. Micholich, and D. Jonas. (1999). Fractal analysis of Pollock's drip paintings. *Nature 399;* 422.

Varela, Francisco J. (1999). *Ethical know-how: Action, wisdom, and cognition, writing science.* Stanford, CA: Stanford University Press.

Weaver, Warren. (1948). Science and complexity. *American Scientist 36;* 53–76.

Weingart, Peter, and Sabine Maase. (1997). The order of meaning: The career of chaos as a metaphor. *Configurations* 5(3): 463–520.

West, Bruce J. (1985). *An essay on the importance of being nonlinear.* New York: Springer-Verlag.

Wittgenstein, Ludwig. (1974). *Tractatus logico-philosophicus.* D. F. Pears and B. F. McGuiness (Trans.). London: Routledge and Keegan Paul.

Zeeman, Eric-Christopher. (1977). *Catastrophe theory: selected papers, 1972–1977.* Reading, MA: Springer-Verlag.

———. (1968). Lecture notes on dynamical systems. Aarhus: Aarhus Universitet.

Chaos and Complexity Theories

Wholes and Holes in Curriculum

Everything we do is a structural dance in the choreography of coexistence.
Maturana and Varela, *The Tree of Knowledge*

In the mind's eye, a fractal is a way of seeing infinity.
Gleick, *Chaos: Making a New Science*

Current Western scientific and mathematical thought is predominantly associated with the work of Isaac Newton and René Descartes. Notions of linear, cause-effect correlations, and predictability of "natural" patterns are important aspects of the scholarly investigations performed by researchers. A different perspective, however, is emerging in science, mathematics, and other fields. This approach is based on nonlinear relations and transformations. Rather than following Descartes' notion of dichotomies of looking at either/or relations, nonlinear dynamics utilizes interrelations and connections. Rather than agreeing with Newton that time is irrelevant and that patterns can be followed both forward and backward, nonlinear dynamics maintains that patterns are developed through time and that time is irreversible (Prigogine and Stengers, 1984).

> The significance of change in ideas about time cannot be overemphasized. Modernist views of time as an external measure are challenged by chaos and complexity views that see time in relational and dynamic ways.

A significant contribution that sparked research in nonlinearity is the work of Henri Poincaré. At the turn of the twentieth century, the King of Sweden put forth a challenge: accurately predict the motions of three interacting bodies (e.g., the Sun, Earth, and Moon). This is known as the three-body problem. While many scholars labored to find a solution, relying on Newtonian modeling using calculus, Poincaré put forth a proof that, in fact, a three-body problem cannot be predicted or solved with accuracy. This proof rejects Newton's theory that all of nature can be determined linearly. At that time, however, few scholars recognized the "gravity" of this solution and Poincaré's work was not followed for more than fifty years.

I situate this story and these thoughts within a Western frame because Western thought has been greatly influenced by Descartes' "I think, therefore I am" separation of mind and body and by Newton's deterministic approach. These perspectives are pervasive in Western society, in literature, spirituality, philosophy, education, etc. The creation of the world, whether through evolution, Genesis, or other such ideologies, is framed within a cause-effect narrative. Nonlinear dynamics is a field of study that creates an opportunity for a paradigm shift in which interrelationships, connections, and blends of similarities and differences are primary areas of research. These notions are not based on dichotomies of difference; rather, a blend of similarities and differences work together to create and maintain living systems. Therefore, the following presentation of nonlinear dynamics is a tale of new concepts that are defined, developed, and transformed through a different approach but still within a Western frame. Nonlinear dynamical systems are perceived as an alternate method of research in science and mathematics that incorporates a perspective of connectivity, not dichotomy. Two main components of nonlinearity now under investigation are the notions of chaos theory in mathematics and complexity theory in science. These two areas of research are strategically separated so as to present a history of current conceptual underpinnings and applications, but the fields of chaos and complexity are interconnected and related in many ways.

Chaos Theory

In the *Oxford English Dictionary* (2002), the word "chaos" is defined as (1) "complete disorder and confusion," or (2) "the formless matter supposed to have existed before the creation of the universe" (236). Common thought in current Western society identifies the meaning of "chaos" with the first definition, associating it with pandemonium, mayhem, bedlam, and the like. In the field of mathematics, the word "chaos" has come to mean something different, more in line with the second definition. This idea originally emerged out of the work of Edward Lorenz (1963) but was not termed "chaos" until the publication of Tien-Yien Li and James Yorke's (1975) "Period Three Implies Chaos" paper.

Lorenz (1993) tells his story of how he came to recognize nonlinearity in his weather research, specifically the idea that a small change can make a big difference. He had written computer code to calculate and predict weather patterns based on data input of wind, barometric pressure, temperature, and other influences. He was working on a particular project and had printed out his results to study. He decided to rerun one part of his study, but when he entered the data he only submitted numbers significant to three decimal places, though the earlier analysis was significant to six. He went to get a cup of coffee while waiting for his computer to go through the program. When he returned, much to his surprise, the results were significantly different from his previous analysis. At this moment, Lorenz realized that he had discovered something important, that something as small as only three decimal places can result in amazingly different results. He presented his findings in 1963, recognizing a system's sensitive dependence to initial conditions (24). Most mathematicians and scholars did not recognize his perspective as contrary to their Newtonian, linear perspectives; however, a few did, and they began to research nonlinear behavioristic systems.

More than a decade later, Li and Yorke (1975) published a paper that demonstrates how deterministic equations could produce unpredictable values. They named this idea of unpredictability as "chaos," and that word has remained as the defining term ever since (though many mathematicians have tried to present new words and different names, but to no avail). Li and Yorke (1975) proved that if a function has a period of three, it will also have infinitely more periods. According to Robert Devaney (1992), Li and Yorke presented a special case of Sarkovskii's Theorem[1]—a theorem that was first proved in Russia in 1964 but was unknown in the West (134). Both theorems rely on systems of patterns generated by iterated functions. Simply stated, iterated functions involve the process of taking an output of a function and using that value as the next input. The set of values that result is then analyzed as a pattern of the function for the given initial input. Patterns may change as new initial values are selected.

While Li and Yorke (1975) were working primarily on algebraic patterns of functions, Benoit Mandelbrot was working with the Julia sets—a discovery of two French mathematicians, Gaston Julia and Pierre Fatou, in the 1920s—to generate geometric interpretations of patterns that result from iterated complex functions. (For a distinction between fractals and chaos, see Stanley, this volume.) Mandelbrot (1977) published his book, *The Fractal Geometry of Nature*, to display his geometric mapping of a more generalized version of the Julia sets. This map is known as the Mandelbrot set and is a primary focus of study for scholars in chaos theory. Each point of the Mandelbrot set represents the behavior of a Julia set. The Mandelbrot set is, therefore, a set of behaviors of sets. This complex set, itself, reveals many interesting dynamics. Figure 6.2 displays a more colorful version of Mandelbrot's original black and white graph.

The function $F(z) = z^2 + c$ (with z and c as complex numbers) is a generic equation used for all of the Julia sets.

The relationship and arrangement of Julia sets on the complex plane reveal the "bulbs" of the Mandelbrot as self-similar, emergent, and dynamic as borders are transversed.

Each Julia set uses one value for c, but Mandelbrot made his first contribution by varying both z and c. For example, Figure 6.1 shows one particular Julia set, called Douady's Rabbit, and is defined by the function $F(z) = z^2 + c$ where $c = -0.12 + 0.75i$ (NUI Maynooth, 2004). Figure 6.2 displays the Mandelbrot set, which includes Douady's Rabbit but also includes all other Julia sets. This set of sets is a display of dynamic interactions that occur in iterating functions.

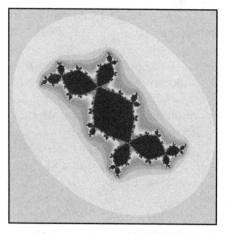

Figure 6.1 *Douady's Rabbit*
(NUI Maynooth, 2004)

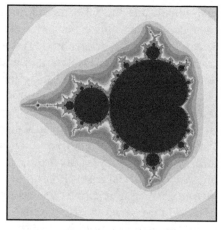

Figure 6.2 *The Mandelbrot Set*
(Azuma, 2000)

Figure 6.1 and Figure 6.2 are illustrated in color as a way to display various sets (called *orbits*) that occur when the function is iterated. These orbits display fixed, periodic, and chaotic behaviors. Fixed implies converging toward one value, while periodic means moving from one to another (the period value shows how many numbers the orbit moves between). Chaotic behaviors are values in which the output does not display any indication of an emerging pattern, for predicting what future iterated values will be is impossible. Another example of different types of orbits displayed within one graph can be shown in logistic functions.

Logistic functions are generally expressed as the function: $x_{k+1} = \lambda x_k(1-x_k)$ and are used to display patterns associated with population growth and decline, where the minimum value is zero and the maximum possible size is one (1). The

The logistic function, used as an alternative to exponential functions to simulate population growth, provides a more realistic pattern of behavior as feedback, through the recursive process, displays, for certain values, complex system behavior. See Kahn's interview with Lord May for more information about the logistic function and possible uses in the mathematics curriculum.

constant λ is used as a parameter to account for different species (see Devaney, 1992, 12). Values less than zero (0) and greater than 1, when iterated, are going to move toward (negative) infinity, thus the scale to display should focus mainly between $x = 0$ and 1. The line $y = x$ is used as a reference point for each iteration, since the resulting y becomes the new x.

The process of iteration displays a relationship between the initial seed and its ensuing values for the function (Figure 6.3). This function shows some points converging toward a value somewhere between 0.5 and one (1). A few points will move to zero (x = 0.5, 1), while any initial value less than 0 or greater than 1 moves to negative infinity. Noticing that a certain pattern occurs around a particular value of the function, the point at which the function and the line $y = x$ meets is called a critical value. [F(0.75) = 0.75.] More iterations of values between 0 and 1 exhibit a "dance" around 0.75. What results is a variety of orbits with some fixed points, some periodic points, and other iterations with no distinct pattern, thus displaying chaos. The patterns that emerge depend upon the initial seed selected.

Together, the works of Lorenz, Sarkovskii, Li, Yorke, and Mandelbrot—along with many others—provide us with a branch of mathematics that focuses on the patterns of iterated functions. Their ideas come together, encouraging mathematical investigations based on the idea of inputting various numbers, real and complex, into different equations. This branch of mathematics focuses on concepts such as initial conditions, sensitive dependence, small changes can make big differences, randomness generated by deterministic equations, iterations, bifurcations, attractors, and complex patterns.[2] Some applications that could be listed in conjunction with nonlinear dynamics and based on some of the conceptual underpinnings are located in other areas of study, such as science and social science. Weather systems and their unpredictability, geologic formations, chaotic patterns of Saturn's rings, populations of biological systems, and sociological patterns of behavior are a few examples. These applications draw on conceptual understandings of mathematics based on nonlinear patterns of research.

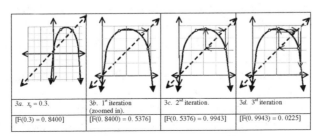

3a. $x_0 = 0.3$.	3b. 1st iteration (zoomed in).	3c. 2nd iteration.	3d. 3rd iteration
[F(0.3) = 0.8400]	[F(0.8400) = 0.5376]	[F(0.5376) = 0.9943]	[F(0.9943) = 0.0225]

Figure 6.3 Orbit Analysis for the Function $F(x_{k+1}) = 4x_k(1-x_k)$ with the Initial Seed, $x_0 = 0.5$

Three specific ideas that draw on conceptual understandings associated with nonlinear dynamics could relate to the classroom: fractal patterns, bounded infinity, and unpredictability. These ideas incorporate various perspectives of chaos theory that exhibit patterns of nonlinearity that relate as metaphors for patterns that emerge in classrooms. The idea of "chaos in the classroom" connotes a nonlinear, fractal-like pattern of relationships that does not focus on conformity or rigidity but on emergence, sensitive dependence, and recursion.

Three Aspects of Chaos

The study of nonlinear dynamical systems can lead to a metaphorical interpretation of patterns in the classroom. Rather than focusing on cause-effect relations and predictable models of behavior, a perspective stemming from chaos theory lends itself to analyzing relationships that are emergent and sensitive to the system of the classroom. Such relationships can relate to fractal patterns, bounded infinity, and unpredictability.

Fractal Patterns

Fractals are patterns of self-similarity that are generated using iterated functions. Mandelbrot coined the word fractal as a way to describe geometric patterns that do not become more simplified (reduced) as one zooms in or out. Brent Davis and Dennis Sumara (2000) define a pattern as self-similar "if, under magnification, a portion resembles the whole" (826). The Mandelbrot set, as shown above, is an example of a fractal. The complexity of the Julia sets within the Mandelbrot set exhibit patterns of complexity, no matter the magnification.

Similarly, patterns of behavior in a classroom can relate to these fractal patterns. Some patterns of behavior seem to be fixed, like asking kindergarten students if they want to play. Some are periodic, like students showing either a fascination or disgust for certain subjects. Still others are chaotic, like the behavior of students that are performed each day in the classroom. These fractal-like patterns display dynamic relations that occur within a classroom among teachers, students, subject material, and the classroom environment. By relating conversations in the classroom to fractal patterns, teachers can embrace a rich metaphor as a picture of what is occurring. The initial seed will have an impact on what conversation will ensue, the format of the discussion will affect the type of interaction, and the patterns of the resulting conversation may in fact display differing "orbits." Some conversations could be focused on one particular venue, others could move between different aspects of a topic, while still others might be hermeneutic moments in which no participant (including the teacher) knows where the conversation might lead. Kauffman (2004) explores a creative conversation, one that echoes the sentiments of Davis's (1996) hermeneutical listening and Pinar's (2004) complicated conversation. All three scholars encourage an incorporation of structure and flexibility, a conversation in which all participants listen and engage in the activity of reciprocal relations. The resulting dialogue becomes a beautifully constructed fractal pattern of interconnectivity.

Bounded Infinity

A second concept that can relate to the classroom is that an infinite set of numbers can occur within a fixed region. Imagine all the numbers that exist on a number line between the integers of zero and one. That is one example of a bounded set of an infinite amount of members. Another example is the fractal image of Koch's curve (Figure 6.4). Mandelbrot reconstituted our ideas about dimensionality by redefining dimension as a relationship between self-similarity over recursion and the number of pieces across scales of similarity. He developed a general formula to describe fractal dimension, defining dimension as the log of the number of pieces created (k) divided by the log of the magnification factor (M), written mathematically as d = (log k) / (log M). Look at the equilateral triangle inscribed in the circle below (Figure 6.5). For each side of the triangle, divide the side into three parts. Then insert a fourth part of equal length to create a new form. Each time this procedure occurs, the perimeter of the triangle increases. In the case of Koch's curve, the dimension would be d = (log 4) / (log 3) ≐ 1.262, which is larger than one but less than two—a fractional dimension. The area of the triangle remains within the boundary of the circle (the area of the circle remaining fixed), while the perimeter of the triangle increases to infinity. Therefore, bounded infinity is illustrated in this image.

Figure 6.4 *Koch's Curve (Spännare, 2003) Circumscribed*

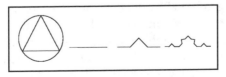

**Figure 6.5 *An Equilateral Triangle Inscribed in a Circle;*
*Iterations That Occur to Form Koch's Curve***

Teachers can connect to this notion of bounded infinity in their classrooms. A teacher may be restricted (bounded) by the national initiatives, state mandates, district criteria, school instructions, and curricular concerns, but within these boundaries are infinite possibilities. The potential relationships between teacher and students, among students, and how a teacher chooses to implement the subject material are boundless. This grants freedom to the teacher to not feel constricted by the limits that are imposed by outside sources but rather to be creative within them.

Unpredictability

Chaos theory incorporates the notion that sensitive dependence to initial conditions is an important component needed to generate chaotic behaviors. Small variations in conditions may lead to large differences in nonlinear dynamical systems (Gleick, 1987; Peterson, 1998). One well-known statement is presented by Lorenz (1993): "Does the flap of a butterfly's wings in Brazil set off a tornado in Texas?" (14). Nonlinear, open systems are divergent and generative, not closed and limited. An immediate consequence of sensitive dependence in any system is the impossibility of making perfect predictions, or even mediocre predictions sufficiently far into the future (10–12). Predicting becomes problematic beyond certain ranges of time. This leads to new perspectives of behaviors, for "what is important here," according to Doll (1993), "is that instead of looking at the relationship of parts or variables to each other, one sees the system related to itself over time" (92). The logistic function is one such example of sensitivity to initial conditions and changes that occur over time.

This leads to a continually posed question in education, one that is a subject of (sometimes hostile) debate. How can a teacher "guarantee" that learning is occurring in the classroom? (For a critique of this perspective, see Kahn, this volume.) This question assumes a linear, cause-effect relation between teacher and student. Fleener (2002) presents a different perspective, one that focuses the question on how a teacher might engage learning through interaction. She draws on the work of Mandelbrot to argue that "system dynamics can be captured through the geometry of recursive presentation. Rather than trying to eliminate the 'noise,' control the system, or predict system behavior, Mandelbrot developed a geometry to explore the patterns that emerged" (115). Mandelbrot connects the deterministic with the random so as to exhibit unpredictable yet beautiful patterns. Similarly, pedagogy can be seen as a combination of the deterministic and the random, the patterned and the emergent. In a classroom, a teacher may have established objectives and pedagogical goals, but in the act of instruction the teacher responds to the random interactions of the students. Davis (1996) qualifies unpredictability in curriculum as opportunities to plan but not predetermine (273). Linking pedagogical goals with the unpredictable behavior of students generates a curriculum that is emergent, generative, and open. Rather than averting the "noise," a teacher can imagine "chaos" as patterns that emerge as teachable moments, embracing the notion that not everything that occurs in the classroom can be predicted.

A Pedagogical Example

As a current instructor for elementary education majors, I implemented the constructs of fractal patterns, bounded infinity, and unpredictability in my own classroom. I began by placing the number "1/3" on the chalkboard. I asked the students to take one minute to write down whatever thoughts resulted from what I had written on the board. (I did not even say "one-third.") At the end of the minute, I asked students to share their thoughts. The class discussion ranged from the idea that 1/3 means one of three equal parts, to comparing 1/3 to 1/2, to converting fractions to decimals and percents. As students used terms such as numerator, least common denominator, and reciprocal, I wrote them on the board. After the class shared for about thirty minutes, I suggested that an assignment could emerge from the conversation that occurred, whether it would be to define all the terms on the board, or to provide a new question that related to what was discussed so as to begin the next lesson with what was concluded that day. (In chaotic terms, that question would be the next iteration for the new lesson, where 1/3 was the initial seed from the first day.) The conversation that ensued was not dictated by me, but as the instructor I did have a role. I had two specific objectives. One was that the conversation would cover several concepts associated with the National Council of Teachers of Mathemtics, or NCTM (2000) *Standards*—which they were—and the other was that students would become more comfortable in speaking in mathematical language—which they did. (In fact, one student shared that when 1/3 appeared on the board, she cringed. By the end of the thirty minutes, however, she felt more comfortable with fractions.)

This example displays how a classroom can be analyzed using the chaotic notions of fractal patterns, bounded infinity and unpredictability. The use of 1/3 was my choice as the initial seed. Other choices would have resulted in different patterns. And the conversation that did take place was not the same when performed across two different semesters. Though there are similarities, there are also rich distinctions among students and between classes. Also included were certain structures, such as writing in journals, writing on the board, taking turns talking, the mathematics involved, the contributions of the students, and the role of teacher as facilitator. However these structures played a part, there is still an infinite amount of potential that could occur. This leads to the unpredictability of what might occur. While some parameters could be envisioned (such as the fact that most other topics, e.g., whales, would likely not come up in the conversation), there is still an unimaginably rich opportunity for a different learning experience in which students become engaged in the actual discussion of mathematics, rather than the teacher acting as a translator.

My creation of a classroom format that opened up discussions about fractions generated different experiences for students. By creating dialogues about mathematics, I intended to allow for students' experiences to become part of the discourse. This type of discourse is different from most mathematics classrooms; something Fleener (2002) suggests should be changed:

> Mathematical discourse can be expanded to broaden our visions of relationship, combat notions of mechanistic determinism, reconnect us and our students with a mathematics of pattern and relationship, explore complex and dynamical systems, and embrace intuition and experience as meaningful in mathematical investigations and explorations. (116)

Granting and inviting student participation, a class that uses this open-ended format embraces student intuition and experiences. This setting allows for a less rigid but still rigorous method for instruction. Traditional mathematical classrooms entail presentations of predefined and predetermined mathematical concepts and strategies. In contrast, by allowing students to enter into a conversation about "1/3," their ideas are valued and inform the direction of the dialogue.

These metaphors and descriptions of chaotic patterns that can occur in a classroom are only a glimpse of some ideas that can be produced from a nonlinear perspective in the classroom. Following concepts of chaos theory, I now turn to present a brief history and explanation of current concepts and applications of complexity theory. Because the notions of nonlinearity incorporate both chaos theory in mathematics and complexity theory in science, an understanding of complexity theory might assist in the elucidation of chaotic concepts. The two areas are not mutually exclusive and should not be interpreted as such. Rather, taking chaos and complexity theories together, a more holistic approach to research in either designated area is enriched. Thus, I present some ideas of what is meant by complexity theory.

Complexity Theory

While chaos theory is located within mathematics, complexity theory situates itself in science. The term "complexity" is an umbrella term for much work that has been performed by scientists in numerous fields of research. This concept of complexity stems from an "attempt to understand nature," which Prigogine (1997) claims "remains one of the basic objectives of Western thought. It should not, however, be identified with the idea of control" (154). Recognition of emergent patterns and descriptions of interrelationships become the focus of this science. A new consortium that has emerged, the New England Complex Systems Institute (NECSI, 2000), frames complexity in the following way:

> Complex Systems is a new field of science studying how parts of a system give rise to the collective behaviors of the system, and how the system interacts with its environment. Social systems formed (in part) out of people, the brain formed out of neurons, molecules formed out of atoms, the weather formed out of air flows are all examples of complex systems. The field of complex systems cuts across all traditional disciplines of science, as well as engineering, management, and medicine. It focuses on certain questions about parts, wholes and relationships. These questions are relevant to all traditional fields.

NECSI gives a synopsis of the similarities found in complexity theory research. Research in complexity theory offers a "new kind of science" (Wolfram, 2002) that can generate a different way of perceiving patterns. Another troupe of complexity scientists can be found in New Mexico at the Santa Fe Institute, a consortium of scholars in diverse fields who in the 1980s collaborated to explain and expound on their works in seemingly disparate areas of research, such as physics, economics, and politics, as a way to "name" their approach to methodology. Waldrop (1992) gives a thorough, historical review of many of the scholars associated with the Santa Fe Institute in his book, *Complexity: The Emerging Science at the Edge of Order and Chaos*, highlighting some of the work generated as a result of their interactions. Significantly, the title "complexity theory" became the name for the work in systems theories that explores the concepts of feedback loops, interrelationships, dynamic systems, parts and wholes as interactively involved that cannot be separated, and structures as continually renegotiated.

Stuart Kauffman, a longtime participant at the Santa Fe Institute, calls for a constructive rather than a reductive science. Kauffman (2000) perceives complexity theory as a different perspective, a different methodology[3] for science:

> It is not always that everything is hidden and science must ferret out the mysteries by scouring for unknown facts, although often science proceeds in the manner of finding new facts. Rather it can be the case that the world is bluntly in front of us, but we lack the questions of the world that would allow us to see. (81)

Complexity theory is an emerging field in which scientists seek patterns and relationships within systems. Rather than looking to cause and effect relations, complexity theorists seek to explicate how systems function to rely upon feedback loops (reiteration, recursion, reciprocity) so as to (re)frame themselves and thus continue to develop, progress, and emerge. Humberto Maturana and Francisco Varela (1987), two Chilean biologists and complexity theorists, propose that life is a complex choreography. They focus on the notion of structures (see Davis, this volume) as fluid boundaries that continuously change as interactions occur. These interactions rely upon feedback. For example, the "nervous system's organization is a network of active components in which every change of relations of activity leads to further changes of relations of activity" (164). This describes the reliance of feedback in the process of (re)organization and relations. In addition, they propose that "everything we do is a structural dance in the choreography of coexistence" (248). This dance is one that is continuously negotiated through all components and aspects—a dance that moves, changes, and develops as each move, change, and transformation occurs.

Complexity scientists argue that the time of Newtonian physics, though once considered progressive, has passed (Prigogine and Stengers, 1984). Complexity does not mean the same as complicated. A complicated system can be broken into parts, like an airplane. In complex systems, there are no parts, only patterns that we recognize in that moment (Capra, 1996; Waldrop, 1992). The patterns mean something in relation to the entire whole, and the patterns inform what that whole might be.

Historically, systems thinking emerged in science in the 1930s. Scientists looked to relationships and properties of systems, recognizing that a systems approach becomes necessary. In the next decade a group of scholars from different fields interested in the "mind" entered into a series of conversations, now referred to as the Macy Conferences (1946–1953). At these conferences, researchers from the "hard" and "soft" sciences generated a systems approach to conceptualizing "mind." In addition, a new concept of cybernetics emerged out of these meetings as a new scientific process, eventually leading to artificial intelligence. Von Bertalanffy (1968) presents an example of the "hard" aspect of science in his book, *General System Theory*, in which he assumes the role of defining and framing system theory along with potential applications, not only in science but in education and social science as well. He believes systems thinking becomes necessary when trying to analyze concepts:

> A certain objective is given; to find ways and means for its realization requires the systems specialist (or team of specialists) to consider alternative solutions and to choose those promising optimization at maximum efficiency and minimal cost in a tremendously complex network of interactions. (4)

His work exhibits the incorporation of complex notions of systems, but still maintains a mechanistic purview. This mode of thinking is still continued today, for "objects themselves are networks of relationships, embedded in larger networks" (Capra, 1996, 37). One such scholar who applies a similar mechanistic perspective to complexity theory is Ilya Prigogine, recipient of the 1977 Nobel Prize in chemistry for his work on the thermodynamics of nonequilibrium systems.

Prigogine published various papers but eventually put his ideas into his book, *Order out of Chaos* (Prigogine and Stengers, 1984). Three important concepts in this book include the notions that time is irreversible; there is order among chaos; and, systems can be perceived as dissipative structures. Each concept is significant because each differs from contemporary scientific thought. First, the notion that time is irreversible implies that Newton's Method cannot be used to explain the past and predict the future in one demonstration. Instead of perceiving systems in linear causalities, Prigogine and Stengers (1984) explain that systems are constantly reinterpreting and relating to structures of patterns both within and outside of its constructs so as to select certain paths from a pool of potential results. Also, time is an important concept to consider because it keeps everything from happening at once. Chemical reactions occur as "time oriented" events; at each moment, the resulting chemical bond is different. Second, Prigogine puts forth the notion that within perceived chaos there are moments of order. (This is converse to chaos theory, which studies the randomness that emerges out of structured order. The two do not contradict each other; rather, they work together as a way to describe the interconnectivity of order and chaos.) Order, according to Prigogine and Stengers (1984), occurs when a structure undergoes an activity and reacts by producing a coordinated, stable result (131). Stability does not imply a static system; stability describes a moment of equilibrium in a dynamic system.

This leads to a third concept, the notion of dissipative structures. Dissipative structures are described as systems that may transform into new patterns when caught in far-from-equilibrium conditions (12). Prigogine reconceives concepts associated with the Second Law of Thermodynamics (hence, his subtitle of "Man's New Dialogue with Nature") through dissipative structures. Systems may be in conditions that are termed at-, near-, or far-from-equilibrium, and these states will exhibit diverse properties. Systems that are found to be in an at- or near-equilibrium state will maintain certain parameters and functions. However, if the system undergoes far-from-equilibrium conditions, the system may transform into a different arrangement that becomes the new at-equilibrium state. Dissipative structures are the new structures that arise out of interactions in a system that is experiencing a far-from-equilibrium situation.

Prigogine (1997) continues his argument for a new dialogue with nature in *The End of Certainty*, in which he focuses on the arrow of time as irreversible. While Einstein dismissed this notion as somehow irrelevant, Prigogine recognizes that "it is precisely through irreversible processes associated with the arrow of time that nature achieves its most delicate and complex structures" (26). Simultaneously, Prigogine (1997) commends Einstein and Descartes for their contributions to science as he also contextualizes their work within their historical situatedness. Prigogine (1997) claims that now science is looking to include instability, which changes the meaning of the laws of nature, "radically, for they now express possibilities or probabilities" (4). This call for a scientific frame that includes instability and probability as key components moves the dialogue toward understandings, not control. This frame also includes human experience and metaphysical ideas as intertwined within the conversation.

Ilya Prigogine passed away in May 2003, but he leaves a legacy of seeking innovation and creativity. His passion to convince others that "the future is no longer determined by the present" (Prigogine, 1997, 5–6) still lingers. In his latest book, *Is Future Given?*, Prigogine (2003) continues his argument. What started in 1984 for him, a quest to persuade the scientific community to consider that the irreversibility of time is significant, continued for the duration of his academic career. His vision for a new scientific perspective, one that intertwines historical conventions of science with emerging ideas, is best surmised in his conclusion from *The End of Certainty*:

> What is now emerging is an "intermediate" description that lies somewhere between the two alienating images of a deterministic world and an arbitrary world of pure chance. Physical laws lead to a new form intelligibility as expressed by irreducible probabilistic representations. When associated with instability, whether on the microscopic or macroscopic level, the new laws of nature deal with the possibility of events, but do not reduce these events to deductible, predictable consequences. (Prigogine, 1997, 189)

Scientific description that relies on probabilities and resists predictions is significant for complexity theorists. This new dialogue that Prigogine started in 1984 (or even before) continues on in the contributions of other scientists who are concerned with systems and complexity.

For example, scholars in the field of biology take notions of complexity as a way of seeing patterns in living systems. Prigogine's work with dissipative structures displays patterns of self-organization. In relating chemical and physical structures to geological patterns of fossils, Prigogine and Stengers (1984) recognize that the "early appearance of life is certainly an argument in favor of the idea that life is the result of spontaneous self-organization that occurs whenever conditions for it permit" (176). The notion of self-organization also is presented in the work of Maturana and Varela (1987), biologists who study living systems as autopoietic (self-making) structures. Their work presents a biological argument for how living systems interact, change, transform, and adapt: "Our proposition is that living beings are characterized in that, literally, they are continually self-producing. We indicate this process when we call the organization that defines them an *autopoietic organ-ization*" (43). Organization occurs at many levels, from cellular to biological structures (such as human beings) to social systems of cultures. Maturana and Varela (1987) move through these levels as they reconceptualize "structure" in biological terms, associating the idea with living systems that continually shift and change internally as they interact externally. This contrasts architectural notions of structure that presume a set, established, fixed boundary that will not shift or change, like a wall or a foundation. An example of a different perspective of structure is a beach. A beach is defined by the interactions between the sand and the water. This boundary is always in flux, for the waves and sand are in constant motion. The complex interactions of elements of a beach allow for a continual renegotiation of its dynamic structures.

Another biologist working with the notion of self-organization is Stuart Kauffman. In his book *The Origins of Order*, Kauffman (1992) conveys thirty years of ideas and thoughts in working through the impact of self-organization and the origin of life. He includes in his working thesis the evolutionary idea of natural selection as not the nemesis of self-organization but rather a force that interacts with self-organization (256) as a way to describe how ecosystems coevolve. A key component in his premise of living systems is the notion that living systems are very close to the "edge-of-chaos phase transition" (Waldrop, 1992, 303). He continues his working hypothesis in his *Investigations*, postulating that "communities of agents will co-evolve to an 'edge of chaos' between overrigid and overfluid behavior" (Kauffman, 2000, 22). Kauffman parallels Prigogine's (1996) assertion that the future is unpredictable. Kauffman (2000) suggests, as an alternative, to consider biospheres. But he does not pose this suggestion in what might be called a "traditional" scientific manner. Instead, Kauffman claims that we need stories.

> [I]f we cannot prestate configuration space, variables, laws, initial and boundary conditions of a biosphere, if we cannot foretell a biosphere, we can, nevertheless, tell the stories as it unfolds. Biospheres demand their Shakespeares as well as their Newtons. We will have to rethink what science is itself. (22)

By sharing stories of his conversations with others as well as his own personal musings about the origin and patterns of life, Kauffman communicates his notion of co-construction by example, as a way of demonstrating a coevolutionary approach to scientific research. His *Investigations* intertwine questions and answers as a way to "know and make our world together" (*xii*). Kauffman participates in what Prigogine hopes might be a new dialogue with nature.

Complexity theory is a field that tells stories as a way to reflect how these stories might (re)consider science. Open, living systems are nonlinear, generative, and coevolving. How we might construct our understandings of these systems depends upon our methodology. Three specific concepts within complexity theory, cellular automata, dissipative structures, and autopoietic systems, are explored below as examples of complex relations framed within complexity theory.

Three Aspects of Complexity

Overall, complexity theory offers a different kind of discourse, one of connectivity and potentiality. A nonlinear perspective embraces a way of knowing that is consistent with Maturana and Varela's (1987) purview that "knowing how we know does not consist of a linear explanation that begins with a solid starting point and develops to completion as everything becomes explained" (244). Learning occurs in nonlinear patterns, emergent, divergent, convergent. The three ideas of cellular automata, dissipative structures, and autopoiesis can be used to examine and relate a nonlinear perspective to a curriculum that functions as an open system.

Cellular Automata

Participants at the Macy Conferences generated specific models in their own research, but they did "agree in seeing randomness not simply as the lack of pattern but as the creative ground from which pattern can emerge" (Hayles, 1999, 286). Von Neumann created a simple machine that would display patterns of cellular automata that undergo specific properties as a way to show random patterns emerging out of simple rules. Each cellular automaton is an on/off switch that changes according to the conditions of its neighbors' states. The grid of cellular automata displays the states of each automaton as they are updated by the conditions of the neighboring cells. Though this sounds simplistic, what emerges are patterns of complex behavior that give the "uncanny impression of being alive" (240). The patterns are dynamic and continually changing as the automata reiterate and update their states. Stephen Wolfram devotes a full chapter to the work he generated with respect to cellular automata. Wolfram (2002) continues the work of those from the Macy Conferences with his recognition of "complex behavior from simple underlying rules" (862). He relates his work in computer-generated patterns of cellular automata to biological processes in living systems (something Kauffman and Varela previously stated—see Hayles, 1999). Cellular automata, according to Wolfram (2002), can be classified as one of four types. The first class is convergence to one fixed value; the second class displays a set of fixed values; the third class appears to have some structured patterns and some random as well; and the fourth class displays completely random patterns (231–49). These classes relate to the orbits of nonlinear iterated functions as presented in the section on fractal-like patterns. Amazingly, a grid of "on/off" switches can move through many displays of patterns that could result in spontaneous, emergent behaviors.

L. Charles Biehl (1998, 1999) elaborates on cellular automata in his two-part mathematics lesson on forest fires. He explains cellular automata in simple terms and applies its concepts specifically to the unpredictable patterns of forest fires. This lesson allows students to participate in activities that will produce many kinds of results, for probability is a component of how the results emerge. No two sets of answers should be alike. Taking this perspective more generally, components for what constitutes "curriculum" can be conceived in terms of cellular automata. From learning theories to pedagogical practices, new research to textbook information, teachers to students, state mandates to district goals, each such category of automata can interact to create patterns of various types. The beauty lies in the inability to predict the emerging behaviors. Curriculum is an open system that retains its vitality through its complex relations. The context and the processes involved are important to the system, but these relations are dynamic and continually changing as interactions continue.

Dissipative Structures

Systems will display certain classes of patterns, depending on the current conditions of the system's structure. Most often, class four patterns emerge "at the edge of chaos," when the system is at a state of far-from-equilibrium. This relates to dissipative structures, as developed by Prigogine, in which systems are analyzed with respect to equilibrium in three different states: at-equilibrium, near-equilibrium, or far-from-equilibrium. Sawada and Caley (1985) describe these three states as contextual. For equilibrium and near-equilibrium, systems appear stable. However, "when systems approach the far-from-equilibrium state (on the threshold of Becoming) they are subject to spontaneous, dramatic reorganizations of matter and energy" (14). In these moments of spontaneity, on the threshold of becoming, new interactions and relations emerge in this dance of coexistence. For example, the human body exhibits how organisms come to exist in equilibrium. I can go on many diets and exercise vigorously, but if I maintain my weight within certain parameters, that weight will eventually move back to where it is most stable. It might only be in drastic measures in which my body experiences far-from-equilibrium status that my shape and form might change. Then a new point of equilibrium would emerge, one which my body would seek to maintain. Populations of species also display different moments of being at-, near-, or far-from-equilibrium. Complexity theorists use mathematical models generated in chaos theory as ways of displaying patterns and changes in a population, illustrated with logistic functions.

As demonstrated in Figure 6.3 earlier, logistic functions illustrate changes in the values as interrelated, changes in the system across time. This change is not displayed linearly but rather "on top of" each other, occurring within certain boundaries. Depending on the values selected, some functions will converge to a particular value, others will oscillate between two values, and still other functions will display chaotic behavior. Another way of analyzing a logistic function is to use a table. Table 6.1 is a spreadsheet that displays some of the patterns that exist for $\lambda = 4$ when different seeds are selected. Notice the similarity between certain seeds, such as 0.2 and 0.8, 0.3 and 0.7.

In addition to using Microsoft Excel as a way to generate orbits computationally, there is a Java Applet online that generates the first 2000 iterates for any specified x and λ. One can go to the Internet URL: http://math.bu.edu/DYSYS/applets/Iteration.html, select the logistic function, specify x_0 and λ, and the display will show the numerical values and a linear graphical display of these values. The linear display exhibits patterns of behavior that differ for changing initial seeds. The initial seeds influence the stability of the population, and the graphs display how close or far from equilibrium the population might be.

Dissipative structures could be used as a tool of analysis for classroom conversations. Certain topics are discussed, considered, and debated, yet the conversation does not necessarily stay on one topic. For example, using the illustration of the class discussion of 1/3, the class started with the idea of fraction, what is a fraction, what are terms associated with it, what fractions symbolize. Then someone brought in the relationship between fractions and percents, and a new topic was discussed, around the connection between fractions, percents, and decimals. These different aspects were considerations, topics of focus for the students, around which the conversation revolved. After the conversation, the students were required to describe and analyze the lesson in a journal. The result was interesting, for different students focused on various aspects of the conversation. They were each transformed in their own ways of thinking of fractions and about teaching, recognizing that the conversation was open-ended, not fixed, and close.

$F(x) = 4x(1-x)$									
x_0	0.1	0.2	0.3	0.4	0.5	0.6	0.7	0.8	0.9
x_1	0.3600	0.6400	0.8400	0.9600	1.0000	0.9600	0.8400	0.6400	0.3600
x_2	0.9216	0.9216	0.5376	0.1536	0.0000	0.1536	0.5376	0.9216	0.9216
x_3	0.2890	0.2890	0.9943	0.5200	0.0000	0.5200	0.9943	0.2890	0.2890
x_4	0.8219	0.8219	0.0225	0.9984	0.0000	0.9984	0.0225	0.8219	0.8219
x_5	0.5854	0.5854	0.0879	0.0064	0.0000	0.0064	0.0879	0.5854	0.5854
x_6	0.9708	0.9708	0.3208	0.0255	0.0000	0.0255	0.3208	0.9708	0.9708
x_7	0.1133	0.1133	0.8716	0.0993	0.0000	0.0993	0.8716	0.1133	0.1133
x_8	0.4020	0.4020	0.4476	0.3577	0.0000	0.3577	0.4476	0.4020	0.4020
x_9	0.9616	0.9616	0.9890	0.9190	0.0000	0.9190	0.9890	0.9616	0.9616
x_{10}	0.1478	0.1478	0.0434	0.2979	0.0000	0.2979	0.0434	0.1478	0.1478

Table 6.1 *Example of Analysis Using an Excel Spreadsheet*

Autopoiesis/Open Systems

A conversation that is considered open and transformative relates to Maturana and Varela's (1980) notion of *autopoiesis*, a word used to describe what they believe is a key characteristic of a living network, defined as the ability of a system to continually produce itself. A literal translation of autopoiesis is "self-making" and is defined as "a network pattern in which the function of each component is to participate in the production or transformation of other components in the network" (Capra, 1996, 162). A dance is an example of a structural, self-making experience that is mutually negotiated between parts of the whole. The network of relations that occur within this dance functions in a feedback loop so as to continually move, change, and develop in relation to an even greater context (or whole).

As a way of exhibiting a curriculum that could be autopoietic, I draw on Doll's (1993) four R's, *richness, recursion, relations,* and *rigor,* which are offered as new criteria for curriculum. Each curricular concept is connected with the others, and together they form an alternative to the schismogenic path (Bateson, 2002/1979) that education is currently taking. Doll (1993) provides a new context for a richly related curriculum that rigorously challenges students as they recursively reflect on their connectedness and express their creativity.

First, richness "refers to a curriculum's depth, to its layers of meaning, to its multiple possibilities or interpretations" (Doll, 1993, 176). Curriculum strands, content standards, these all have richness within them. The method with which this richness is engaged is the difference that makes the difference (Bateson, 2002/1979, 27). Instead of focusing on how to impart factual knowledge transference, educators should employ hermeneutic methods. Doll (1993) suggests, "Another way to state this is to say that the *problematics, perturbations, possibilities* inherent in a curriculum are what give the curriculum . . . its richness" (176). Students can "play around" with ideas, concepts, and information, and interrogate underlying assumptions associated with knowledge. No matter the subject, "dialogue, interpretations, hypothesis generation and proving, and pattern playing" (177) can all be used as pedagogical practices that transcend simple transference of information and move toward a rich curriculum.

Second, recursion is a transformative process that relates to the mathematical operation of iteration. "In such iterations," claims Doll (1993), "there is both stability and change; the formula stays the same, the variables change (in an orderly but often nonpredictable manner)" (177). This notion of transformative looping is different from repetition. Repetition "is designed to improve set performance. Its frame is closed. Recursion aims at developing competence—the ability to organize, combine, inquire, and use something heuristically. Its frame is open" (178). Recursion is significant because it allows for continual reflection that stimulates and generates new information.

Doll (1993) relates this process to Dewey's secondary (reflective) experience, to Piaget's reflexive intelligence, and to Bruner's statement that it is necessary "to step back from one's doings, to 'distance oneself in some way' from one's own thoughts" (177). In the classroom, dialogue becomes an important tool for recursive experiences. Doll (1993) emphasizes this point: "Without reflection—engendered by dialogue—recursion becomes shallow not transformative; it is not reflective recursion, it is only repetition" (177). A transformative curriculum allows transcendence, creativity, and reflexivity to occur within recursive dialogues. These dialogues are simultaneously generating new experiences and knowledge on which participants can continue to reflect. This process is an open, unpredictable, generative method for learning.

The third "R" is relations, and the concept of relations directly connects with richness and recursion. Doll (1993) categorizes relations as pedagogical and cultural. Pedagogical relations are considered "conditions, situations, relations [that] are always changing; the present does not recreate the past (though it is certainly influenced by the past) nor does the present determine the future (though it is an influencer)" (179). Relations of a rich and recursive nature can be developed between different learners, between a learner and information, and within the learner herself. Cultural relations can occur within discourse, narration, and dialogue. These relations are important in the curriculum because *discourse* now becomes what Jim Cheney (1989) calls "contextualist" (123)—"bound always by the localness of ourselves, our histories, our language, our place, but also expanding into an ever-broadening global and ecological network" (Doll, 180). We are all contextually bound—not bound in the modernist restrictive sense, rather our situatedness that is ever-changing, ever-shifting, and dynamic. Thus, we must consider how "on the one hand, to honor the localness of our perceptions and, on the other hand, to realize that our local perspectives integrate into a larger cultural, ecological, cosmic matrix" (181). Allowing these considerations to affect how curriculum is shaped and developed creates moments for learning to become a rich and recursively related experience.

The fourth "R" that Doll (1993) presents is the notion of rigor. "Here rigor means purposely looking for different alternatives, relations, connections" (182), providing curricular opportunities for students to critically analyze concepts and deconstruct the assumptions and frames within which these concepts are defined. Functioning within this rigorous frame, allowing for a dialogue that is meaningful and transformative, and "combining the complexity of indeterminacy with the hermeneutics of interpretation[,] it seems necessary to establish a community, one critical yet supportive" (183). Postmodern ideals do not discount the importance of learning information; in addition to learning, critical thinking becomes an essential component. Deconstructing the underpinnings of knowledge and the assumptions that accompany information allows for interpretive frames to expose the limitations of such knowledge as well as to stimulate new perspectives and new approaches to learning. "Facts" no longer remain absolutes but are (re)considered in the context within which they were generated. This allows for a content-rich curriculum that considers the relationships of knowledge. Knowledge is not eliminated, and learning still occurs. However, students are able to recursively reflect on the connections with which this knowledge came to be determined, and put forth how these patterns could be (re)considered. (See also Davis's notion of unstructuring curriculum, this volume.)

One example of a rigorous curriculum is the subject English. Currently the national language for the United States is English. Grammar, mechanics, spelling, and the like are still important for students to learn in order to be literate in American society. In addition, though, students should analyze the history of how the United States came to determine English as the predominant language, recognize the limitations that accompany this, and consider how the rising population of Hispanic speakers in the United States could affect this in the future. By considering these issues, students can critically interpret how their current situatedness as learners in an English-speaking country affects them locally and globally. Their relationship to language and discourse becomes analytical and more open to diverse learning situations. This could be a different state of equilibrium for them as they experience a more transnational life than prior generations have known.

Wholes and Holes: The Cantor Set

Nonlinear dynamical systems are analyzed in chaos and complexity theories. Both theories involve connections of parts and wholes, relationships, interconnectedness, and patterns. A metaphor for the classroom and for curriculum that depicts concepts associated with both chaos and complexity is the Cantor set. The Cantor set is a fractal that can be constructed by shrinking a line segment by one-third.[4] As this function reiterates, what results is a series of smaller and smaller line segments, and increases in the number of gaps in between (Figure 6.6). Continuing to infinity, this set would seem to disappear; however, that is not the case. Devaney (1992) remarks that

> one of the remarkable features of the Cantor set [*K*] is the fact that there are many, many more points in *K*. In fact, *K* is an *uncountable set*. To explain this remark, we recall that a set is called *countable* if it can be put in one-to-one correspondence with the set of positive integers, that is, we can enumerate the points in the set. A set is *uncountable* if it is neither finite nor countable. (76)

With this uncountable set, its dimension can also be calculated using Mandelbrot's formula. The Cantor middle-thirds set is defined as creating two pieces ($k = 2$), and the magnification factor is three ($M = 3$), Thus, the

Figure 6.6 The Cantor Set

dimension of a line segment that undergoes the recursion in the Cantor set is $d = \log 2/\log 3 \approx 0.631$. Notice that this dimension is less than one but greater than zero. The line segment does not disappear, though there are uncountable many "holes" in it.

Using the Cantor set as a metaphor for curriculum, one can look at the movement from smaller to larger segments (creating wholes) or larger to smaller (creating holes). First, looking in the direction of creating wholes, education can be seen as an opportunity for students to make meaningful connections that have a magnification to a greater connection. In this way, knowledge acquisition becomes as Bateson (2002/1979) describes, "uniting with other similar systems to make still larger wholes" (136). This process moves from the smaller, more disconnected segments, toward a larger, more completed connection. Understanding and knowledge are re-created in these connections that link parts to a larger whole, and this continues on to larger wholes and more connections. Whitehead (1967/1929) theorizes that "fragmentary individual experiences are all that we know, and that all speculation must start from these *disjecta membra* as its sole datum" (163). Similarly, students begin their academic career with these fragments (prior knowledge and experiences) that are recorded as pieces. Through educational experiences, students connect information so as to synthesize their fragmentary pieces. An example is a child learning to read. A student will have exposure to letters and to words, then these words are read in a sentence. Their prior knowledge of verbal language connects to the sentences that are read, allowing comprehension to occur when students connect what they are reading with their own verbal language and life experiences. Reading becomes meaningful and patterns continue to connect.

Second, creating holes is a process that never ends. Though knowledge may be bounded at some level temporally, it is uncountable. A student proceeds through school and makes more connections, but within these connections are still uncountable gaps. Just as on a number line there are uncountably many numbers between 0.15 and 0.16, so the information that can lie within a connected pattern is uncountable. For example, a student learns multiplication facts. Then in algebra, multiplying variables is presented. Following, the student learns that there are imaginary numbers that have interesting properties when multiplied. In addition, the understanding of simple multiplication forms new meanings for the student. This process can

We tend, in teaching, to treat content as finished and complete packets of information to be "transferred" from "us" to "them," often directly or tacitly conveying this notion to our students. What we may be ignoring—or failing to recognize—in this simple transfer approach is the complex "poetry" of learning. Extending Smitherman's analogy about parts and wholes, what might be hinted at is that the rhythm, pattern, and rhyme, the way the hearer receives the pattern of presentation, against the backdrop of their own experiences, and uses the interplay to create meaning, *is* the prosody of learning.

continue. Within the understanding of multiplication, there is a depth to more concepts and information that will always arise, an uncountable amount of knowledge that can be acquired.

Education then becomes an experience that provides opportunities for connections but also reveals these holes that lie within. The student acts as an arranger who continually attempts to make connections but also is shown "those cracks in the smooth surface of our conceptual world that may suggest new interpretations of human experience" (Grumet, 1999, 29). These "cracks" generate quests for new knowledge, new understandings, and springboards into an open-ended curricular vision.

Springboards of Uncountable Possibilities

Valentine: "She did not have the maths, not remotely. She saw what things meant, way ahead, like seeing a picture."

Tom Stoppard, *Arcadia*

In Tom Stoppard's (1993) play, *Arcadia*, Valentine is a character in our current time period who studies chaos and complexity theories. What he has discovered is a journal of a young woman from England in 1809, and in this journal she theorizes about the effects of iterations in mathematical equations and how they change over time. What Valentine observes is her mathematical intuition and that she had diverged from what was considered "normal," accepted mathematical thought of her time period. He also mentions that she could not fill the pages of her journal with enough iterations to see the chaotic patterns, which can now be easily and quickly computed with computers. He later shows the graph of her equations on his laptop to a colleague and discusses how insightful she was, though in another part of the play her tutor cannot accept what she has proposed because he does not understand. This story demonstrates how inundated our culture has been with Newtonian concepts. The creativity utilized and unorthodox approaches undertaken could not be accepted because they were "outside" of the norm, the accepted way of doing mathematics. Similarly, mathematical research in general has affected our scientific methodology and, in turn, our societal and educational perspectives. Nonlinear dynamical systems provide a new springboard in which our purview can change.

Through metaphors associated with chaos and complexity theories, new visions for curriculum can emerge. Rather than viewing education in a sequential form in which the teacher is a dispenser of knowledge, one could envision theories and practices of education in nonlinear ways. Fractals create a beautiful and dynamic picture that continually transform. Constantly seeking new knowledge is what humans experience in daily life. So in schools, curriculum may be viewed as a blend of determinism and randomness, reciprocally related, and infinite within current boundaries. Knowledge is socially constructed, bound by time and current interpretations (Bateson, 2002/1979; Davis, 1996; Trinh, 1990; Weedon, 1998). As continual seekers of information, humans (re)form what knowledge is. A simplistic example is the change in how humans perceive the shape of the Earth. Before the fifteenth century, many assumed the Earth was flat. That changed into the assertion that the Earth is a sphere. Now scientists argue that the Earth is actually not a (perfect) sphere, that the shapes at the North and South Poles are more flat in form. Thus, what is perceived as accepted knowledge has shifted through many centuries.

Perspectives of curriculum that stem from nonlinear dynamics spark new notions of epistemology and pedagogy. Working with bounded infinity and reciprocity with respect to knowledge acquisition, a teacher can create a chaotic learning environment, where open and divergent ideas are generated. Coupling determined goals with random interactions forms a system in which all involved become influential participants in the transformation of understandings and information. Just as chaos theory stems in part from challenges toward Newton's assumptions, so should assumptions associated with educational theories and practices be challenged.

Chaos and complexity theories describe systems that are sensitively dependent to initial conditions and propose ways in which a system can relate to itself over time. Parameters are continuously negotiated, and predictability is limited. Conversations can be chaotic in behavior. The beginning words and final farewells could appear quite disjointed. Following the conversation as it transpires, however, shows the relationships and the interaction, and each transition into new topics relate (in some way, to the conversants, at least). In this same manner, phase space captures moments in a nonlinear dynamical system and relates the changes over time. The focus becomes the process as to how the system changes in stages, not the beginning and end. Importantly, no matter how small the time intervals, there will always be more moments between—uncountably more—that could be exhibited.

Metaphors of complexity in curriculum elucidate in interesting ways how the process of learning could be changed. The idea of self-organization, allowing students to reconceptualize knowledge, melds with what Whitehead (1967/1929) problematizes as a predicament—that we try "to fit the world to our perceptions, and not our perceptions to the world" (165). Negotiating knowledge and interacting as co-contributors to the conversation contribute to changing perceptions as well. What will be produced, opened up, generated, is unpredictable. How exciting!

Chaos and complexity theories easily lend metaphorical analogies for education. There are connections within each student, but these are difficult and sometimes virtually impossible to ascertain. Instead of isolating students into one specific situation, "what is important, epistemologically and pedagogically, is a comparison of the patterns an individual develops operating in a number of different situations—this is an ecological, holistic, systemic, interrelated view. Within this view, lie patterns otherwise unseen" (Doll, 1993, 92). These patterns allow students not to suspend part of who they are in order to participate but rather encourage the development of oneself, and thus produce even richer and more meaningful interactions.

Notes

1. Sarkovskii first ordered all of the natural numbers as the odds, then products of 2 times each odd, then 2 squared times each odd, continuing to 2 raised to the n power times each odd, then listed each power of 2 in descending exponential power from 2 raised to the n power down to 2 then 1 was reached (i.e., $3, 5, 7, 9, \ldots, 2 \cdot 3, 2 \cdot 5, 2 \cdot 7, \ldots, 2^2 \cdot 3, 2^2 \cdot 5, 2^2 \cdot 7, \ldots, 2^n \cdot 3, 2^n \cdot 5, 2^n \cdot 7, \ldots, 2^n, 2^2, 2^1, 2^0$). Using the natural numbers in this order, Sarkovskii then posed his theorem, that for a function F that maps the Reals onto the Reals ($F: \mathbf{R} \rightarrow \mathbf{R}$) is continuous, if F has a periodic point of period n and that n precedes k in the Sarkovskii ordering, then F also has a periodic point of prime period k (Devaney, 1992, 137). A periodic point means that the iterations will repeat a pattern of size n. The significance of this theorem lies in the fact that if a function has a period of size 3, then all other periods will be present, implying that there are an uncountable number of patterns, hence chaos.

2. Chaos theory has many components that are interconnected. As a way to create a possible frame in which categories can be constructed for developing different aspects of chaos theory, I present a list of such categories. This list is an amalgamation of my own creation, stemming primarily from two texts that present concepts of nonlinear dynamical systems and chaos theory (Alligood, Sauer, and Yorke, 1996; Devaney, 1992).

     A.   Orbit Analysis (orbits, critical points, periodic points, period doubling, strange attractors)
     B.   Initial Conditions and Sensitive Dependence
     C.   Recursion, Iteration, Feedback
     D.   Complex Numbers and Functions

    E. Logistic Equations
    F. Mandelbrot set and Julia sets
    G. Applications and Connections with Complexity Theory
        (cellular automata, Pascal's Triangle)

This list is only one perspective for qualifying components of chaos theory. Others have offered different ways of categorizing concepts in chaos theory as a way to organize curriculum (see Bedford, 1998; Devaney, 1992; Fowler, 1996; Frame, 1996; Peitgen and Richter, 1986).

3. In this context, I am drawing on Sandra Harding's (1987) definition of methodology, which she distinguishes from method and epistemology. Harding (1987) posits that "discussions of method (techniques for gathering evidence) and methodology (a theory and analysis of how research should proceed) have been intertwined with each other and with epistemological issues (issues about an adequate theory of knowledge or justificatory strategy)" (2). Kauffman (2000) presents his interpretation for what I perceive as a methodology, how research should proceed.

4. The actual mathematical formula that can be used to calculate the Cantor set is $F(k) = (1/3)k + (2/3)$.

References

Alligood, K., T. Sauer, and J. Yorke. (1996). *Chaos: an introduction to dynamical systems.* New York: Springer.

Azuma, D. (2000). Lesson 1: A Mandelbrot set viewer. *GLOW Tutorial.* Fremont, CA: SourceForge. Retrieved online on October 24, 2001, from http://glow.sourceforge.net/tutorial/lesson1/mandel_small.jpg.

Bateson, G. (2002). *Mind and nature: A necessary unity.* New York: Bantam. (Original publication, 1979).

Bedford, C. (1998). The case for chaos. *Mathematics Teacher, 91*(4): 276–81.

Bertalanffy, L. V. (1968). *General system theory.* New York: George Braziller.

Biehl, L. C. (1998). Forest fires, oil spills, and fractal geometry: An investigation in two parts. Part 1: Cellular automata and modeling natural phenomena. *Mathematics Teacher, 91*(8): 682–87.

———. (1999). Forest fires, oil spills, and fractal geometry: An investigation in two parts. Part 2: Using fractal complexity to analyze mathematical models. *Mathematics Teacher, 92*(2): 128–37.

Capra, F. (1996). *The web of life.* New York: Doubleday.

Cheney, J. (1989). Postmodern environmental ethics. Ethics as bioregional narrative. *Environmental Ethics,* 11 (summer), 117–134.

Davis, B. (1996). *Teaching mathematics: Towards a sound alternative.* New York: Garland.

Devaney, R. (1992). *A first course in chaotic dynamical systems: Theory and experiment.* Cambridge: Perseus.

Doll, W. (1993). *A post-modern perspective on curriculum.* New York: Teachers College.

Fleener, M. J. (2002). *Curriculum dynamics: Recreating heart.* New York: Lang.

Fowler, D. (1996). The fractal curriculum. In *Fractal horizons: The future use of fractals* (pp. 17–34). C. Pickover (Ed.). New York: St. Martin's Press.

Frame, M. (1996). Fractals and education: Helping liberal arts students to see science. In *Fractal horizons: The future use of fractals* (pp. 35–74). C. Pickover (Ed.). New York: St. Martin's Press.

Gleick, J. (1987). *Chaos: Making a new science*. New York: Viking Press.

Grumet, M. (1999). Autobiography and reconceptualization. In *Contemporary curriculum discourses: Twenty years of JCT* (pp. 24–30). W. F. Pinar (Ed.). New York: Peter Lang. (Original paper published in 1980).

Harding, S. (Ed.). (1987). *Feminism and methodology: Social science issues*. Bloomington: Indiana University Press.

Hayles, N. (1990). *Chaos bound*. Ithaca, NY: Cornell University Press.

———. (1999). *How we became posthuman: Virtual bodies in cybernetics, literature, and informatics*. Chicago: University of Chicago Press.

Kauffman, J. (2004). Education as creative conversation. *Education Week, 23* (28), 38.

Kauffman, S. (1992). *The origins of order*. New York: Oxford University Press.

———. (2000). *Investigations*. New York: Oxford University Press.

Li, T., and J. Yorke. (1975). Period three implies chaos. *American Mathematical Monthly, 82,* 985–92.

Lorenz, E. (1963). Deterministic nonperiodic flow. *Journal of Atmospheric Science, 20,* 130–41.

———. (1993). *The essence of chaos*. Seattle: University of Washington Press.

Mandelbrot, B. (1977). *The fractal geometry of nature*. New York: W. H. Freeman and Company.

Maturana, H., and F. Varela. (1980). *Autopoiesis and cognition*. Dordrecht, Holland: Reidel.

———. (1987). *The tree of knowledge: The biological roots of human understanding*. Boston: Shambhala.

National Council of Teachers of Mathematics (NCTM). (2000). *Principles and standards for school mathematics*. Reston, VA.

New England Complex Systems Institute (NECSI). (2000). *What is the study of complex systems?* Cambridge, MA: Retrieved online on September 3, 2002, from http://necsi.org/guide/whatis.html.

NUI Maynooth. (2004, March 10). *Douady's rabbit*. Department of Mathematics, NUI Maynooth. Kildare, Ireland. Retrieved online on March 26, 2004, from http://www.maths.may.ie/images/rabbit.html.

Oxford English Dictionary. (2002). *The concise Oxford English dictionary*, 10th ed., J. Pearsall (Ed.). New York: Oxford University Press.

Peitgen, H.-O., and P. Richter. (1986). *The beauty of fractals*. New York: Springer-Verlag.

Peterson, I. (1998). *The mathematical tourist*. New York: Barnes and Noble.

Pinar, W. F. (2004). *What is curriculum theory?* Mahwah, NJ: Erlbaum.

Prigogine, I. (2003). *Is future given?* River Edge, NJ: World Scientific.

Prigogine, I., and I. Stengers. (1984). *Order out of chaos: Man's new dialogue with nature*. New York: Bantam Books.

———. (1997). *The end of certainty: Time, chaos and the new laws of nature*. New York: Free Press.

Sawada, D., and M. Caley. (1985). Dissipative structures: New metaphors for becoming in education. *Educational Researcher, 14*(4): 13–29.

Stoppard, T. (1993). *Arcadia*. London: Faber.

Trinh, M. (1990). *Women, native, other*. Bloomington: Indiana University Press.

Waldrop, M. (1992). *Complexity: The emerging science at the edge of order and chaos*. New York: Simon and Schuster.

Weedon, C. (1998). *Feminism, theory and the politics of difference*. Malden, MA: Blackwell.

Whitehead, A. N. (1967). *The aims of education.* New York: Free Press. (Original publication, 1929).

Wolfram, S. (2002). *A new kind of science.* Champaign, IL: Wolfram Media, Inc.

Prospects for Nonlinear Education

Reflections from Lord (Robert) May

Robert May, now Lord May of Oxford, currently President of the Royal Society and former Chief Scientific Adviser to the UK government, has long believed that nonlinear systems should be taught earlier in both secondary and university courses in mathematics, biology, and theoretical physics. Furthermore, he has emphasized, "such nonlinear systems are surely the rule, not the exception, outside the physical sciences" (May, 1976, 467).

> When will a nonlinear *habit of analysis* become the rule in both the physical sciences and in curriculum design?

Of particular interest is May's (1987) assertion that the existence of chaotic systems "invalidate standard techniques for analyzing population data 'in situations where linearity' had been falsely assumed" (26). Imagine the impact on classroom teaching, tutoring, and educational research if it were to be recognized that linearity has often been falsely assumed in teaching and learning! The manner in which population biology and ecology have changed from linear to nonlinear disciplines is an interesting precursor of what might well happen in curriculum studies. Strikingly, that change was guided by theory, with field practice then implementing the change in theoretical perspective. (See Real and Levin, 1991; Cushing et al., 2003.)

This interview focuses on the educational implications of May's work. He has already provided two readily available reflections on his earlier work (May, 2001a, 2003). What is offered here supplements, rather than repeats, the earlier reflections.

We met in his office at the Zoology Department at Oxford University, where he spends each Friday and Monday, actively engaged in research and teaching, while continuing to work at the Royal Society in London from Tuesday to Thursday. The informal style of the interview has been retained.

The Unpredictability of Simple Things

Robert Kahn (RK): What would you want educators to know about your work and the potential applications to education?

Lord May (LM): I think the main implication for education is that most of the things that still today are done both in school and college, in secondary and tertiary education, are focused on linear systems. You can take linear systems apart; you can fit bits of them together. It's much simpler. There are a whole set of techniques that have been around for a long time; and it's only relatively recently that we have learned that there are some general underlying principles in nonlinear systems (cf. May, 1994).

One of the things that does emerge from the study of "chaos," which has a fairly precise meaning (unlike "complexity" which is often used in a vacuous way, meaning little more than that things are complicated) is that really simple, completely deterministic systems can behave in ways that look effectively random. I think that is an enormously important message to get across. Furthermore, it can be got across very simply. You can have a ten-year-old playing with a quadratic map. Just think of a number between naught and one, take it away from one, multiply it by one unvarying constant; and you can see what it does when the constant is chosen to be big enough. That can be done pretty easily, and what you get flies in the teeth of intuition. I think the implications of the quadratic map, and its best-known application as the ecologist's discrete logistic equation, are very important. (See May, 2003, 33fn. for a full description of the logistic map. To create a computer program that explores the logistic map, see G. Baker and J. Gollub, 1990, 168–70.)

I am drawing a distinction between the vague sense of "complexity" and that rather precise notion of what we mean by "chaos"—simple, purely deterministic low-dimensional systems, behaving in a way that not merely looks random in some parameter regime, but is so sensitive to initial conditions that long-term prediction (in technical jargon, prediction outside the Lyapunov horizon) is effectively impossible, even though you know all the rules. (For an explanation of the Lyapunov Exponent, see Peitgen, Jurgens and Saupe, 1992, 516f.)

I think that has very profound implications, not least philosophical implications, because most intuition and most of what people learn in secondary and tertiary education is that: "Yes, the world obeys rules. If the rules are really simple, as they are in some systems in physics, then you can make predictions. If the rules are extraordinarily complicated, as in much of biology, then it's very complicated, and it's harder to understand and make predictions."

Too often, for example as in *Jurassic Park,* where you get this idiot "chaoticist" person, chaos is presented in a vulgarised and completely misleading way. The so-called "chaotician" in *Jurassic Park* runs around spending most of the movie telling people that modern chaos theory says that the park is going to be unstable. What he's really doing is saying that the world is very complicated, which we always knew. You don't need chaos theory to tell you that the world is complicated. What chaos theory tells you is that sometimes really, really simple things—not like Jurassic Park—can be unpredictable. I couldn't wait until the dinosaurs ate him.

The End of the Newtonian Dream

RK: What are the "philosophical implications" that you are drawing here?

LM: The Newtonian dream is that the world is not at the whims of gods, ghosts, or goblins. The world is governed by underlying rules. When the rules are simple enough, you can understand what's happening in the system, and make clear predictions. Unpredictability arises when you have a large number of rules operating, as in the roll of the ball in a roulette wheel.

Chaos theory in some ways is saying, it's the end of the Newtonian dream. Things can be about as simple as you can imagine, albeit nonlinear, but otherwise as simple as you can imagine, like the quadratic map, and yet you may be effectively unable ever to make long-term predictions. For example, when I was young, one thought local prediction of the weather beyond twenty days or so was just a matter of increasing computational power and more weather stations and satellites. Now it seems very likely (although technically it's not a completely solved problem) that predicting local weather conditions beyond ten days or so will never be possible in general. I think that is quite a revolution in the way that we think about the world.

Exploring the Implications of the Quadratic Map

RK: One college teacher commented, "I see a lot of students who are studying biology and other sciences who have never heard of Lord May or use any chaotic techniques." The point she was making was that, "You can tell me all this academic stuff, that says how important chaos theory is, but, in practice, how are we actually going to reach these students?"

LM: The trouble with the quadratic map as a model for biological populations is that it has the rather irritating property that once "x" is bigger than one, it goes negative, but you can get round that by saying that if "x" ever gets bigger than one, the population is extinguished. Alternatively, you can just use a different mathematical function. Either way you then have something that is an obviously oversimplified metaphor for how populations of discrete nonoverlapping generations may behave.

Such models have been put in the literature as oversimplified metaphors for how salmon populations or various insect populations might behave. But if you do have a population like that, with a propensity to grow at low densities from generation to generation and to decrease at high densities, then if these nonlinear effects are not too severe it will settle to some steady value, as intuition suggests. What is more surprising is that such a population can have self-sustained oscillations if the nonlinearities are more severe, and what is most surprising is that it can do all these random-looking, "chaotic" things if the nonlinearities are even greater. I think that is very interesting and can be expounded just by using the quadratic map, as I have already explained. It is illustrated by the experiments on flour beetles (see Cushing et al., 2003), and it bears a more debatable relevance to certain phenomena seen in the real world like the erratic, "quasi-periodic" fluctuations in cases of measles in big cities before vaccination, or the oscillations in the populations of Canadian lynx and hare over the past 150 years.

Learning to Think in a Nonlinear Style

RK: Do you think you can learn to think in a nonlinear style, to look for nonlinear data?

LM: I don't see why not. In fact, it's the distinction between linear and non-linear phenomena that I think is itself an important one to learn. The whole notion that you can decompose a complicated musical note by Fourier Analysis into a weighted summation of pure notes is itself an interesting one, and arguably a not completely valid one. (For an explanation of Fourier Analysis, see Peitgen, Jurgens, and Saupe, 1992, 261–62.)

Thinking Outside the Box

RK: Many of the contributors to this book think that classroom teaching is still far too linear. It could be argued that the requirements for lesson plans and syllabi create a situation where it is very difficult to move beyond these preset teaching goals into adapting to the teaching moment as it arises in actual experience. What do you think?

LM: I think such predetermined goals are based on thinking very rigidly within a circumscribed box. If you were thinking of teaching significant mathematical concepts in secondary and primary schools at earlier ages than we usually do, consider the relative difficulty of introducing calculus and the relative difficulty of introducing discrete systems. Discrete systems are very simple, simpler than continuous ones. They do not involve notions of time intervals tending to zero, or Zeno's Paradox, and other such semi-philosophical ideas. They simply say: here's the number of animals in this generation, or at this time step. Here's the simple formula that takes us to the next time step. Look at what the equation does; at how the time series plays out. Then you can even begin to build up a graphical understanding of the quadratic map. That requires much less in mathematical sophistication than elementary calculus. I don't see that there's much in the way of an inherent block to such teaching and learning.

RK: So you think it is possible both to teach about nonlinearity and to teach in a nonlinear style at earlier ages than we usually do?

LM: I don't see why not, provided you use discrete systems rather than continuous ones. With discrete systems, where there is only one variable, you can see chaotic phenomena with the very simplest of nonlinear terms. By contrast, with continuous systems you need at least three dimensions—three variables—before chaotic dynamics can appear (in two dimensions, you cannot have orbits crossing, which in effect means chaotic behavior is not possible). If you think about dynamics and teaching simple systems, look at the harmonic oscillator. It's really com-

> It does seem useful to present the simplest forms of chaotic math first. Might the principle of simplifying the learning situation be misleading, however, for education more generally? We learn complicated nonmathematical topics quite easily. Consider the complexity of simple recognition. The youngest child quite easily learns to recognize its mother's face in differing conditions—a task which computer science has found forbiddingly complex. There is reason to believe that the habit of simplifying tasks for instructional purpose is generally a mistake and that it is more effective to make the learning context richer and more ambiguous. See St. Julien, this volume, for such interpretations.

plicated. You've got to know calculus; you've got to be able to integrate; you've got to be able to understand trigonometric functions. There's quite a lot there to be able to understand the simplest rules of dynamics.

It's an historical accident that so much of what is done in physics is continuous systems. A lot of what happens in the real world is actually discrete systems; and they can be much easier to handle. (Cf. Goldenfeld and Kadanoff, 1999; Sugihara and May, 1990.)

Integrating Basic and Applied Science

RK: Let's turn to what's happened in chaos theory, as you reviewed in the Princeton Landmarks in Biology edition of *Stability and Complexity in Model*

Ecosystems (May, 2001a). What I was struck by in your 1976 *Nature* article was how you were interested in the first-order difference equations in the context of the "delicate mathematical aspects of the fine structures of the trajectories" and yet at the same time you were interested in "the practical implications and applications" of the resulting mathematical insights. That's an unusual combination of basic and applied science. It requires rather different perspectives, doesn't it?

LM: It's also very revealing, as I found out when I wrote that independent review article for *Nature*, that at least five different people or research groups had already independently discovered these properties of quadratic maps (May, 2003). Each of those sets of people found it was a curious mathematical phenomenon, and that was it. They had not realized the wider implications.

Jim Yorke is fond of saying that we were not the first people to discover these properties of quadratic maps, but rather were the last (See May, 2002; Li and Yorke, 1975). We were the last in the sense that we came at it in a different way, not as a problem in mathematics but as a metaphor for real-world phenomena. Our mind-set was: what are the interesting practical messages to emerge from the properties of this caricature of a biological problem? With this mind-set—this focus on the larger world—then the wider practical implications are immediate. Whereas others saw only a mathematical phenomenon, we saw wider, immediate practical implications. I think it very much depends on your motives for working on a particular problem.

Incidentally, these discoveries had very little to do with the advent of computers. That came very quickly afterwards. But the stuff that Jim Yorke did, and George Oster and I did, was essentially completely analytical (see May, 2003). It's a question of context.

RK: I remember how in that 1976 *Nature* article you wrote of how nonlinear systems were clearly the rule and not the exception. Do you still think that's true after all your work in science policy?

LM: Science policy is something else entirely. Science policy is complex because it's complicated. When I was appointed Chief Scientific Advisor to the [UK] government, one of the tabloids said, "The new Chief Scientist is an expert on chaos. He is about to discover he has a lot to learn."

Some Applications of Chaos Theory

RK: What impact do you think your work has had on biology as a science?

LM: I do think the '76 review [in *Nature*] served a purpose in speeding up the recognition of certain phenomena. All sorts of people took off from that review—Pierre Collet (1980) in France, Mitch Feigenbaum (1983). It was useful to produce what was simultaneously a synoptic and certainly a deliberately evangelical review at that point.

This is something that could have happened years and years earlier. It's almost puzzling that it didn't. As long as you're working continuously in at least a three-dimensional system (because you can't in two dimensions have orbits cross) chaos can emerge; whereas in discrete time, you can have a one-dimensional system that is chaotic. And I think that observation was immensely helpful in demystifying what chaos is. It's something that is very accessible.

It is true I think that it was the conjunction of this work with the advent of fast computers, that made the understanding of various systems explode. People could now go back and do things in all sorts of systems in quite explicit contexts—chemistry, biochemistry, physiology, neuroscience, cardiology—some a bit flakier than others. You could combine a rough idea you had about an equation that operates in continuous time and more than three dimensions with computational power. Now with this underlying simplicity of understanding, you weren't puzzled by what was happening. And I think that's why things exploded over the subsequent ten years [from 1976].

Chaos Theory and Social Systems

RK: Do you have anything to add about social systems?

LM: My view basically is that physical science is relatively simple because at heart most systems in physical science are relatively low-dimensional deterministic systems. The life sciences are more complicated because there are very often very high-dimensional systems. Social science is the most difficult, because it's a high-dimensional system that acts on the operant observer in different ways from time to time; things really behave differently by virtue of the role of the observer (and, lest there be misunderstanding, this is not at all like the Heisenberg uncertainty principle). So I just think there are very few examples of low-dimensional systems in the social sciences.

Nonetheless, I still think even with that being said, it is useful to have the background recognition that even if there were some caricature of a social system that was purely deterministic and low dimensional, its behavior can nonetheless be extraordinarily complicated and effectively unpredictable. There are indeed examples in what is arguably the central problem of the social sciences, which is the question of how you evolve and maintain cooperative behavior in the face of the benefit that accrues to the cheats—the people who take the benefits without paying the cost.

I think some of these metaphors for the evolution of cooperative behavior (the so-called Prisoner's Dilemma) do demonstrate that you can get internally organized cooperative behavior, even though there is an advantage to cheats. The metaphor can become more robust when you add a spatial dimension to the Prisoner's Dilemma. This is a very simple deterministic metaphor, with very simple deterministic rules about the interaction of cells, and defined by extremely simple behavioral rules. But it generates amazingly complicated behavior, and that would be an example of a relevant metaphor in the social sciences, which involves spatial rather than temporal chaos. Earlier, you might have been able to see such phenomena in a computer simulation, but you wouldn't have been able to understand what was going on. Now you can understand it. More generally in the social sciences, however, things are just plain complicated.

Changes in Ecology

RK: Turning to ecology, what changes have occurred there?

LM: If you go back to the '70s that marked an interesting transitional stage in ecology, because it had been up to that point a largely descriptive subject. It's a relatively young subject. The British Ecological Society is the oldest ecology society and it's less than a century old. There were some mathematical things back in the '30s, but they were rather abstract and they were too metaphorical in a way.

If you looked in the early 70s there was just the beginning of a more theoretical physics style of approach. For example, what is the relation between the topological structure of a food web and the ability of species within it to withstand disturbance? Or, how similar can species be yet continue to coexist? There were theoretical things being done then, but there were many people who said, first of all, that you didn't even have a right to theorize unless you'd served a twenty-year apprenticeship slaving in the field. On the other hand, there was a degree of uncritical enthusiasm. There was quite a range of opinion.

If you pick up a basic general ecology text today, it will have a lot of mathematics, although not much of it will be related particularly to chaos and complexity. The current texts have the balance between theory and observation and experiment that is characteristic of more mature disciplines (see Galison, 1997). You need to seek out the underlying simplicities—that means defining them mathematically and then pursuing conclusions.

If you look at a subject that is highly descriptive, such as immunology, it's more like ecology was thirty years ago. People ask questions. The average immunologist works brilliantly at a molecular level, describing how individual viruses interact with individual immune system cells. On that basis we can successfully design drugs that suppress viral replication—the antiretroviral drugs used against HIV. You can do a great deal, but what you can't do—

what has not yet been done—is to understand why there is so long and variable an interval between being infected with HIV and coming down with AIDS. To understand this, I believe we will need to understand the dynamical interplay between entire populations of different kinds of HIV strains and entire populations of different kinds of immune system cells. Personally, I think it unlikely we will be able to have an AIDS vaccine until we understand the nonlinear dynamics of these population-level interactions (May, 2004).

RK: Why do you think that change has occurred in the consciousness of ecology?

LM: I don't know. There has been an observational ecology for about a century that posed relevant questions (cf. Zimmer, 1999). In contrast, the descriptive basis of immunology is really only about a couple of decades old. In another twenty or thirty years an immunology textbook will have a lot of mathematics in it.

Current Research Interests

RK: So what are your current research interests? Are they linked to chaos theory?

LM: Not very much. Some of my interests are in conservation biology. We're actually thinking about some of the problems associated with properly cataloguing the record of species that have been recorded, and speeding up the cataloguing of the untold number of species that haven't yet been identified. This involves, amongst other things, sorting out the problems of synonyms. It is very mathematical, but there are problems with estimating the rate at which synonyms arise and are uncovered—the same species discovered separately, placed in separate catalogues. There are interesting problems in the questions of what synonymy involves, and in the statistics of that awareness (see May, 2001b).

Other topics I am interested in have to do with currently fashionable things such as the structure of the World Wide Web and the Internet. The underlying questions are something like those about the structure of food webs: how does the structure of the information network relate to its ability to resist viruses? How do you design an immune system as a defense for a particular virus? How do you best protect information systems from targeted attack?

Conclusion

The breadth of May's interests in basic science, applied science, and science policy is exciting, as is his concluding suggestion that the development of ecology as a discipline is a model of what might well happen in immunology and the search for an AIDS vaccine (cf. May, 2004).

However, in one respect, May's successful search for appropriate models and laws in the context of population biology could be a somewhat misleading guide for curriculum theorists. As May himself has recognized, in educational matters, models can often be used to gain new insights into teaching and learning processes, but the creation of a theoretical model in a discipline does not necessarily lead to new "laws." Certainly, Lorenz's various models of the atmosphere demonstrated both the impossibility of long-term weather predictions as well as the importance of understanding the underlying patterns of order (Hunt, 1995; Lorrenz, 1993). It is these patterns of order, or "patterns of organization" that Evelyn Fox Keller (1985) points out are of interest, whether they are "spontaneous, self-generated, or externally imposed," rather than natural laws with their "coercive, hierarchical, and centralizing tendencies" (132).

The meaning of insight and understanding is the crux of the issue. As Stephen Kellert (1993) suggests:

> In the face of the nonreductionist, nondeductivist, diachronic methodology of chaos theory, it does violence to the actual practice of this science [of chaos theory] to force it into the mold of a law-seeking activity. Moreover, the conception of understanding as the discovery of laws has deep connections to the doctrine of determinism as total predictability. Far better to consider chaos theory as a search for *order*, a concept broader than law. (112; italics in original)

Chaos theory may well offer the metaphors and tools to reshape curriculum studies, but not necessarily to build the models in the manner of ecology (Kahn, 1998).

Many of the contributors to this book are indebted to Lord May for the immense contribution that he has made in many fields for more than forty years. His interdisciplinary perspective, his ability to "think outside the box," and his sheer good-natured willingness to teach, to share and to learn are an inspiration to many.

References

Baker, G. L., and J. P. Gollub. (1990). *Chaotic dynamics: An introduction*. Cambridge: Cambridge University Press.

Collet, P., J.-P. Eckmann, and H. Koch. (1980). Period doubling bifurcations for families of maps on R^n. *Journal of Statistical Physics, 25,* 1.

Cushing, J. M., R. F. Costantino, B. Dennis, R. A. Desharnais, and S. M. Henson. (2003). *Chaos in ecology: experimental nonlinear dynamics*. London: Academic.

Feigenbaum, M. J. (1983). Universal behavior in nonlinear systems. *Physica 7D*, 16–39 [Reprint in D. Campbell, D. and H. Rose, H. (Eds.). *Order in chaos*. (1983)]. Amsterdam: North-Holland.

Galison, P. (1997). *Image and logic: A material culture of microphysics.* Chicago: University of Chicago Press.

Goldenfeld, N., and L. P. Kadanoff. (1999). Simple lessons from complexity. *Science, 284;* 87–89.

Hall, N. (1994). *Exploring chaos: A guide to the new science of disorder.* New York: Norton. (Original publication, 1992, *The new scientist guide to chaos.* New York: Penguin.)

Hunt, J. C. R. (1995). Review of *The weather revolution: Innovations and imminent breakthroughs in accurate forecasting* by J. Fishman and R. Kallish. *Nature, 374:* 23.

Kahn, R. E. (1998). Exploring chaos: Can chaos theory inform the curriculum? Doctoral dissertation, University of Missouri-Kansas City, 1998. Abstract in *Dissertation Abstracts International. DA9900318.*

Keller, E. F. (1985). *Reflections on gender and science.* New Haven, CT: Yale University Press.

Kellert, S. H. (1993). *In the wake of chaos: Unpredictable order in dynamical systems.* Chicago: University of Chicago Press.

Li, T., and J. A. Yorke. (1975). Period three implies chaos. *The American Mathematical Monthly, 82:* 985–1022.

Lorenz, E. N. (1993). *The essence of chaos.* Seattle: University of Washington Press.

May, R. M. (1976). Simple mathematical models with very complicated dynamics. *Nature, 261:* 459–67.

———. (1987). Chaos and the dynamics of biological populations. *Proceedings of the Royal Society of London. A, 413:* 27–44.

———. (1994). The chaotic rhythms of life. In *Exploring chaos: A guide to the new science of disorder* (pp. 82–95). N. Hall (Ed.). New York: Norton. (Original publication, New York: Penguin, 1992, *The new scientist guide to chaos.*)

———. (2001a). *Stability and complexity in model ecosystems,* with a new introduction by the author. Princeton, NJ: Princeton University Press. (Original publication, 1973).

———. (2001b). Biological diversity: Causes, consequences and conservation. Asahi Glass Foundation 2001 Blue Planet Prize Presentation. Web site: www.af-info.or.jp/eng/honor/hot/enr-may.html.

———. (2003). The best possible time to be alive: The logistic map. In *It must be beautiful,* G. Farmelo (Ed.). New York: Granta Books.

———. (2004). Uses and abuses of mathematics in biology. *Science, 303;* 790–93.

Peitgen, H.-O., H. Jurgens, and D. Saupe. (1992). *Chaos and fractals: New frontiers of science.* New York: Springer-Verlag.

Real, L. A., and S. A. Levin. (1991). Theoretical advances: The role of theory in the rise of modern ecology. In *Foundations of ecology: Classic papers with commentaries* (pp. 177–91). L. A. Real and J. H. Brown (Eds.). Chicago: University of Chicago Press.

Sugihara, G., and R. M. May. (1990). Nonlinear forecasting as a way of distinguishing chaos from measurement error in time series. *Nature, 344,* 734–41.

Zimmer, C. (1999). News. Life after chaos. *Science, 284,* 83–86.

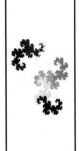

Third
Iteration

Systems and Communications

Bringing Corporeal Life Back In

Chiasmic Relations and Poetic Understandings

[B]ut they [the children of a nascent humankind], in their robust ignorance, did it by virtue of a wholly corporeal imagination.

Vico, *The New Science of Giambattista Vico* [1]

Our attitude to what is alive and to what is dead, is not the same. All our reactions are different.

Wittgenstein, *Philosophical Investigations*

The purely corporeal can be uncanny.

Wittgenstein, *Culture and Value*

I want to discuss the rethinking of teaching and learning in a new context, a new context that comes into view when we admit something which, it seems to me, we are not currently admitting to ourselves: the fact that we do not understand life and the livingness of things at all. We might feel that our ignorance here is no big deal. After all, we live in the midst of it, i.e., life, without too much trouble. And look at what we have achieved in biology, genetics, medicine, physiology, cell biology, and so on. Surely we must, to an extent, understand something of its nature. But, what if Giambattista Vico (1968) is right, and it is a "property of the human mind that whenever men can form no idea of distant and unknown things, they judge them by what is familiar and at hand" (*NS*, 122)? And what if, because of this, there are some phenomena crucial to our learning and understanding of ourselves and the world around us whose character we are totally failing to acknowledge for what they are. Indeed, to go further, what if it is precisely the amazing success of our current methods that is *standing in the way* of us recognizing that certain of the phenomena occurring around us—phenomena crucial to us understanding human communication, particularly in its instantiation in us teaching each other how to do things—are in fact truly mysterious, and not understood by us at all? Then, I suggest, our currently partial understandings can in fact radically mislead us into thinking that, with just a bit more and a bit more research along current lines, all that is still unknown to us will ultimately become clear. After all, understanding life is just a matter of finding the right combination of elements, isn't it?

> In education this often gets played out in much of the traditional scientific research arena—if only we could control the messy conditions of learning we cold better ensure student achievement. This is the hope of educational policy makers.

Well. Perhaps it isn't. Perhaps our dream that we can understand human phenomena—such as communication, teaching, development, and learning—by finding the right kind of elements and by placing them into the right kind of sequential pattern, into the right codes, principles, or laws, isn't too far away from the dreams of witches and magicians in the power of spells and word-magic. Why should a certain pattern of ink-marks on paper in themselves play such a crucial role in our lives? Aren't we forgetting something? As Ludwig Wittgenstein (1953) remarks: "Every sign *by itself* seems dead. *What* gives it life?—In use it is *alive*. Is life breathed into it there?—Or is the *use* its life?" (no. 432). Whatever answer we might give here, it is clear that, as Wittgenstein (1981) puts it elsewhere: "Only in the stream of life and thought do [our] words have meaning" (no. 173).

We seem to have forgotten both the ineradicable responsiveness of our bodies to events occurring around us, and to the fact that such events themselves only occur embedded within a continuously ongoing, immensely complex stream of spontaneously occurring, living activity within which we have our embodied, human, being at every moment in our lives. And it is only at certain crucial moments both within and in relation to this spontaneously occurring flow, that such ink marks can have their significance. What matters is how they are interwoven into it, not just spatially, but also temporally. Indeed, it is especially in the sequential or temporal unfolding of a person's living, responsive, bodily activity, that they seem to be able to influence the actions of the others around them in their meetings with them. For, in addressing their own responsive living movements toward others, they seem able to arouse within them anticipations and expectations of what might be coming next, hence, to *express* to them meanings in their actions.

It is this special kind of interweaving or intertwining of living activities occurring only in meetings between two or more living activities in which they influence each other's temporal flow by creating between them (and around themselves) a unified temporally unfolding flow of activity to which they can all be responsive in their own way. It is the organized dynamic complexity of this unfolding, emerging stream of life that I want to discuss. To characterize its unique chronotopic (time-space) nature, I shall say that it is a *chiasmatically* organized flow of living activity, where, in using the word *chiasm*, I am following Maurice Merleau-Ponty (1968) who in his posthumously published last book remarks at the beginning of Chapter 4, entitled "The Intertwining—The Chiasm":

> If it is true that as soon as philosophy declares itself to be reflection or coincidence it prejudges what it will find, then once again it must recommence everything, reject the instruments reflection and intuition had provided themselves, and install itself in a locus where they have not yet been distinguished, in experiences that have not yet been "worked over," that offer us all at once, pell-mell, both "subject" and "object," both existence and essence, and hence give philosophy resources to redefine them. (130)

In other words, what Merleau-Ponty is suggesting here is that I can learn about the world, others, and my own nature, only from within my own actual engagements with the others and othernesses around me. The only way I know of language is from within my actual use of it; and that it makes itself manifest to me in ways that continually reverse the relationship between subject and object, between speaking and listening, of signifying and the signified, and so on. "In my experience of others [more] than in my experience of speech or the perceived world," he notes, "I inevitably grasp my body as a *spontaneity which teaches me what I could not know in any other way except through it*" (1964, 93).

The most obvious example of what the chiasmic intertwining of two activities within our own bodies can teach us occurs, of course, in binocular vision. Both Merleau-Ponty (1962, 1968) and Gregory Bateson (1979) take binocular vision as paradigmatic of the special chiasmic nature of our living relations to our surroundings. To quote Bateson (1979):

> The binocular image, which appears to be undivided, is in fact a complex synthesis of information from the left front in the right brain and a corresponding synthesis of material from the right front in the left brain. . . . From this elaborate arrangement, two sorts of advantage accrue. The seer is able to improve resolution at edges and contrasts; and better able to read when the print is small or the illumination poor. More important, information about depth is created. . . . In principle, extra "depth" in some metaphoric sense is to be expected whenever the information for the two descriptions is differently collected or differently coded. (68–70)

In other words, in such chiasmically structured relations, much more is happening than the mere blending or interweaving of separate constituents which remain identifiably separate even when complexly interwoven. Something utterly new and novel is being created. As I move my eyes around to fixate first on the far corner of my room, and then on the keyboard in front of me, I gain a shaped and vectored sense of my surroundings in relation to my possible bodily actions within them—some of their aspects are *distant* from me, others are *near*. Our relations to our surroundings are not just simply relations of a causal kind, or of a systematic, logical, or rational kind

either, but are *living,* dynamic relations. My understandings do "not
arise from the 'I think' but from the
'I am able to,'" says Merleau-Ponty
(1964, 88).

> How might this shift, this under-
> standing, change our expectations
> for classroom curriculum? The "new
> analytic" or poetics of this ask us to
> explore precisely these kinds of in-
> between spaces.

Although we have separated
body and mind, subject and object,
passivity and activity in our philosophical reflections and debates, in our living
activities—and all but forgotten our bodies completely in the Cartesian
emphasis on just our mental abilities and capacities—there are no such sepa-
rations between activity and passivity, and so on. All such seemingly polarized
phases in reality simply flow into each other. I begin to feel the surface of the
skin on my passive left index finger with my active right one, but gradually I
begin to move my left finger more actively over my right and the surface of
its skin begins to become present to me. And such dynamic intertwinings or
chiasms as these are manifested in the relationship between my body, mind,
and world, between my past and present experiences and future anticipations,
between my incarnate self and the others and othernesses around me, and
between my language and all of these experiences. Our understandings, our
truths, our questions, are formed in the lived present where all these chiasms
take place. What is the nature of such chiasmic or chiasmatic relations? We
can only just begin that investigation here, but already, it seems, one thing is
clear: they can only occur within and between already living bodies.

Vico and the "Poetic Wisdom" Embodied in a "Sensus Communis"

I want to pursue the connections between the study of our bodily activities, and the recent focus on the study of chaos (disorder) and complexity in
dynamic, growing systems occasioned by current theoretical developments in
meteorology, biology, and physics further, by following up a connection that
Jayne Fleener brings forward in her introduction to this book. For there, she
sees "the promise of New Science [of chaos and complexity]" as being "in
reconnecting us with a geometry of relationship, a poetry of interconnectedness, and an emergence of meaning. Like Giambattista Vico's *New Science,*
written almost three hundred years ago, New Science is an approach to
meaning that goes beyond the myopic perspective of Modernism or the
techniques of modern science" (Fleener, this volume). Indeed, we shall find,
just as she suggests, that many of the themes Vico introduced in his *Scienza
Nuova,* are crucial themes too in the new sciences of complexity. Thus,
instead of directly turning toward developments in the new sciences of complexity, I want rather—now that the new sciences have made us familiar with
and more able mentally to cope with heterogeneity in dynamic systems,
diversity, otherness, unfinished-ongoing-unities, dynamic stabilities within a

flow, stable disorder, systems of similar differences, and many other seemingly oxymoronic concepts—to show how these notions have always been
"there," unheralded, in the background to all our intellectual inquiries. Thus,
I want to make the "uncanny" (Wittgenstein) nature of our spontaneous corporeal activities the central focus of my article because, to repeat, chiasmic
relations occur only within and between our living bodies, and as such, they
underwrite, so to speak, all the crucial distinctions and relations in terms of
which we conduct our more deliberately formulated intellectual inquiries as
self-conscious individuals in the world. It is this that Vico (1968) tries time
and again to make clear to us:

> It is true that men have themselves made this world of nations . . . but this world
> without doubt has issued from a mind often diverse, at times quite contrary, and
> always superior to the particular ends that men had proposed to themselves;
> which narrow ends, made means to serve wider ends, it has always employed to
> preserve the human race upon this earth. (*NS,* 1108)

And he continues at this point with a long list of human activities in
which people, in the attempt to pursue their own personal ends at the
expense of others, are still nonetheless forced to invent socially shared forms
of activity within which they, and those they mean to exploit, can mutually
influence each other's actions in an intelligible manner. In other words, what
is always already there, unobtrusively flowing away in the background to all
that we do, is what Vico (1968) calls our shared *sensus communis* (commonsense). Such a common sense is, he says, "judgement without reflection,
shared by an entire class, an entire people, an entire nation, or the entire
human race" (*NS,* 142)—and we continually display such a sensus communis
in the (philosophically unnoticed) characteristic ways in which we spontaneously respond to events occurring around us, not in terms of their objective actuality, but in terms of shared anticipations of possible next happening
events.

Indeed, in this connection, it is worth mentioning the distinction Vico
(1988) makes between what we take to be *certain* (certum) and what we take
to be *true* (verum): while the true is what is made (his *verum-factum* thesis),
the certain is always a part of the truth (his *certum est pars veri* thesis). In
other words, although nowhere does Vico make this radical distinction thoroughly clear (Berlin, 1976, 99), a crucial aspect of what is *certain* for us, is
the shared common sense basis of our social practices in terms of which we
"go on" in an anticipatory fashion with each other. But what Vico clearly
does point out, as mentioned above, is that this crucially shared background
to our lives is created between and around us whether we feel we are participating in it or not. Hence the difficulty we have in paying attention to it, and
hence the magnificence of Vico's achievement in bringing its existence into
light, for we have no sense of our own involvement in it—and it is precisely

this shared sense of what is fitting and what is not in what we say and do in our social lives together, that Wittgenstein (1953) is attempting to highlight in the *grammatical* remarks he makes in conducting his philosophical investigations.

It is true that philosophers in the past have been aware of this primordial life-world, but they have mostly taken it for granted, and (mostly) deemed it as unworthy of their serious and disciplined attention as part of a cooperative inquiry. Indeed, since the time of Plato, with only very few noteworthy exceptions, they have discounted it—not as a chaos embodying deep and complex forms of order—but as something utterly confused, unstable, subjective, and with no intelligible order to it at all, requiring replacement by more rational forms of life. Only Vico, as Jayne Fleener notes in her introduction, saw early on the importance of *poetic* events in creating the special kinds of relations between people productive, ultimately of a civil society and a human cultural history. But, as the early peoples were mute, what could possibly be the form of a mute poetry? As itself a poetic image here, we can, Vico suggests, imagine such early peoples as acting, say, toward thunder claps in the sky *as if* they are the voiced roars and bellows of a gigantic but invisible being somewhere above them. Whether as a matter of fact this was so, is beside the point. The point is that in doing so, they would exhibit "a wholly corporeal imagination" (*NS*, 376)—and it would be in the active bridging of the gap occurring between a circumstantial event and a living human body by a living, expressive reaction to it, that is the essence of a poetic relation. In the act, a chiasmic intertwining of the event and the bodily response to it occurs, such that an anticipation of possible future events is manifested in that response. Indeed, here too "inner" feeling and "outer" expression are chiasmically intertwined within an indivisible living unity, so that it makes no sense to ask whether all concerned *chose* to express their feelings of fear in the same way.

Hence Vico's (1968) claim that "the certain [the *certum*—our taken for granted, shared, *anticipatory sense* of things] began in mute times with the body" (*NS*, 1045). Thus we find, he said:

> [T]he principle of [the] origins both of languages and of letters lies in the fact that the early gentile people, by a demonstrated necessity of nature, were poets who spoke in poetic characters. This discovery, which is the master key of this Science, has cost us the persistent research of almost all our literary life, because with our civilized natures we moderns cannot at all imagine and can understand only by great toil the poetic nature of these first men. (*NS*, 34)

And he continues:

> In the night of thick darkness enveloping the earliest antiquity, so remote from ourselves, there shines the eternal and never failing light of a truth beyond all question; that the world of civil society has certainly been made by men and that

its principles are to be found within the modifications of our own human mind. Whoever reflects upon this cannot but marvel that the philosophers should have bent all their energies to the study of the world of nature, which, since God made it, He alone knows; and that they should have neglected the study of the world of nations, or civil world, which since men made it, men could come to know. (*NS*, 331)

In other words, although the world of everyday civil society is a vastly rich and massively complex and dynamically developing and changing world, nonetheless, Vico thinks that because we ourselves have made it, we ought to find it easier to understand than, say, the world of physics, which is not our own creation. For our civil society is concerned, not with a realm of abstractions, which may or may not be true according to evidence, but with the actual social reality in terms of which we live our lives. Its subject matter is thus more sensuous and concrete, less abstract and mental than that in the natural sciences. To that extent, however, to us moderns, situated in a scientific, geometrical universe, conducting our inquiries as disinterested, disembodied, external observers, they are in fact *less* rationally visible to us. We must begin to think of conducting our inquiries into its nature in quite a different way, in a manner that, for a start, begins to take into account "the human necessities or utilities of social life" (*NS*, 347). For the primordial world of our everyday, common sense activities is not accessible to the highly abstract and selective methods of the natural sciences; it is more intricately built than any of these sciences allow. But this does not mean that its peculiar structures are not open to other methods of inquiry and modes of understanding.

Everyday Life within a Chiasmically Structured Reality

We moderns have grown used to having a subjective mind inside our heads, and to being surrounded (we think) by a world of inert objects. In such a world, we take our language to be a kind of representational instrument of mind, working to give names to the objects around us. We have also grown used to thinking that the key to understanding ourselves and the world around us lies in our discovering principles, orders, repetitions, regularities, or rules—where it is the task of specially trained individuals, scientists or other experts, to do such discovering for us. In Vico these matters are all entirely reversed. Mind does not precede language but arises within it, and both in turn are the necessary outcomes of certain first-time, spontaneously occurring, bodily urgencies, the need to respond in some already humanly meaningful way to startling or striking experiences. At first like mere indicatory gestures or mimes, such expressive responses—in which the chiasmic intertwining of "inner feeling" and "outer expression" is already shared in common with the others around one—work as *socially constitutive* poetic images is beginning to give our lives together a socially shared order. And in time, from such spontaneously responsive beginnings, such orders can be developed from within by internal differentiation, into complexly articulated institutions. It is in this mute, corporeal poetry, in the chiasmic intertwinings that occur when two or more living activities meet, that all the possibilities lie for our developing new understandings of ourselves and our world lie. And what is special in Vico, as in all the other thinkers upon whom I now shall draw—Wittgenstein, Merleau-Ponty, Bakhtin, and Vygotsky—is that, instead of the refined theories of special intellectuals and academics, we must now turn to the messy concrete but immensely complex details of the everyday life-world that their predecessors have mostly spurned. A world in which its gods and heroes, its customs and laws, its words and its sciences all depend just as much on the common and collective sense of the people for the mean-ing that they have for each one of us, as on the refined notions of intellectu-als. And what is also common to them all, is that we can find, they suggest, a new starting point for our inquiries in our first-time bodily responsiveness to startling, surpris-ing, or striking events.

Indeed, just like Vico, so for Wittgenstein (1953), the meaning-fulness of our language does not initially depend on its systematicity, but on our spontaneous, living, bodily responsiveness to the others and othernesses around us. As he puts it: "The origin and primitive form of the language-game is a reaction; only from this can more complicated forms develop. Language—I want to say—is a refinement, 'in the beginning was the deed'" (1980a, 31). By the word *primitive* here, Wittgenstein (1981) means that " . . . this sort of behavior is *pre-linguistic*: that a language-game is based *on it*, that it is the prototype of a way of thinking and not the result of thought" (1981, no. 541). In saying this, again just like Vico, Wittgenstein (1969) remarks: "I want to regard man here as an animal. . . . As a creature in a primitive state. . . . Language did not emerge from some kind of ratiocination" (no. 475).

> Like Gleick's description of chaos, the interesting and startling lie not in the smooth and rounded, but in the bumpy and scabrous. This point comes forward in Rasmussen's con-clusion; the teacher provides a per-turbation that disrupts the student's cognitive system. C. S. Peirce makes the point that all inquiry proceeds from a "surprise," a disruption. The bumpy and scabrous is found in specifics—the complex details of life-seldom in universals.

In other words, rather than supposing that the source of our activities is hidden away inside us somewhere so that we can only approach it indirectly, in terms of hypotheses and theories, like Vico, Wittgenstein (1953) suggests that "nothing is concealed . . . nothing is hidden" (no. 435). Everything we need to understand a person's meaning is shown or displayed by them out in the world between us, in the unfolding course of our living involvement with them. Thus, we should begin our studies by attending to the special character of the interplay of spontaneously responsive bodily activity occurring between people, for it is only *from within* this interwoven involvement that the kind of understandings of importance to us will emerge. Elsewhere, I have discussed this kind of activity in terms of "joint action" (Shotter, 1980, 1984), and under the influence of Mikhail Bakhtin's (1986) work, I have also called it *dialogically structured* activity (Shotter, 1993a, 1993b), but now, as already mentioned, I want to go further, to emphasize first the special forward looking (anticipatory) nature of its temporal sequencing and, second, its intertwining with both other living activities and its surroundings, by pointing to its chiasmically structured character.

There is much, as I have already mentioned, that is special about this kind of activity. But a number of features deserve to be especially highlighted: To begin with, because we cannot not be responsive both to those around us [others] and to other aspects [othernesses] of our surroundings, in such a spontaneously responsive sphere of activity as this, instead of one person first acting individually and independently of an other, and then the second replying, by acting individually and independently of the first, we act jointly, as a *collective-we*, with all involved—as in dancing—in a common, unfolding, rhythmic movement. Thus we do this spontaneously and bodily, in a "living" way, without us having "to work out" when and how next to act if we are to coordinate our actions with an other's. As Bakhtin (1986) points out:

> All real and integral understanding [within our everyday talk] is actively responsive. . . . And the speaker himself is oriented precisely toward such an actively responsive understanding. He does not expect passive understanding that, so to speak, only duplicates his or her own idea in someone else's mind. Rather, the speaker talks with an expectation of a response, agreement, sympathy, objection, execution, and so forth (with various speech genres presupposing various integral orientations and speech plans on the part of speakers or writers). (69)

Thus, even during the voicing of their utterances, speakers look for nods of recognition, for the appropriate signs in the responses of those around them that they are "following" them. But this means that when someone acts, their activity cannot be accounted as wholly their own—for a person's acts are partly "shaped" by the acts of the others around them—and this is where all the strangeness of the dialogical begins. For, in the intricate "orchestration" of the chiasmic intertwining occurring between our own outgoing, responsive *expressions* toward those others (or othernesses) and their equally responsive incoming *expressions* toward us, both a special phenomenon and a special kind of understanding of it occurs.

The special phenomenon in question is the creation within the responsive interplay of all the events and activities at work in the situation at that moment, of distinctive, dynamic forms, dynamic forms in which all of those involved in them are participant parts. And in the special kind of understanding that becomes available to us, we understand these dynamic forms as, to use Steiner's (1989) term, "real presences."

In other words, we grasp these real presences, not as passive and neutral objects, as representations, but as real agencies that can enter into our activities both to structure and to guide them—as well as "its" in their own right with their own requirements, they also function as "the witness and the judge" (Bakhtin, 1986, 137), requiring us to take an "evaluative attitude" towards events in which we are involved.

I shall call this a *relationally responsive* understanding to contrast it with the *representational-referential* understanding more familiar to us in our traditional intellectual dealings. This does not occur in all our exchanges with each other, only in our truly reciprocally or mutually responsive ones. One thing that is special about such a form of understanding is that, although it relies on learning, once learned, it occurs immediately and unhesitatingly, without us having to pause to check among a number of possible interpretations as to what is occurring. As with learning our

> The distinction Shotter makes here is similar to Trueit's regarding representation having a double life, one being *poietic* (relationally responsive), the other mimetic (representational-referential).

mother tongue, this kind of learning is very basic, and is usually—given the Cartesian biases at work in our current modes of inquiry—mis-defined. I shall call it participative learning. One aspect of its non-Cartesian nature is well expressed by Mead (1934), when he notes that:

> The mechanism of meaning is . . . present in the social act before the emergence of consciousness or awareness of meaning occurs. The act or adjustive response of the second organism gives to the gesture of the first organism the meaning it has. (77–78)

In other words, long before anything occurs in our heads, in our conscious experience, we can find the *precursors* or *prototypes* for what later we shall talk of in mental or cognitive terms, in our responsive, bodily activities. We can, perhaps, begin to see why this is so, if we explore the general nature of dialogically-structured activity further. As space is very limited, this must be in the form of a list:

- Such activity constitutes a distinct, third realm of activity with its own characteristic properties.
- It is not simply *action* (for it is not done by individuals; and cannot be explained by giving people's *reasons*), nor is it simply *behavior* (to be explained as a regularity in terms of its causal principles).

- Indeed, as a distinct third sphere of activity, it involves a special kind of sensuous, nonrepresentational, or embodied form of understanding, which is prior to and determines all the other ways of knowing available to us.
- Activities in this sphere lack a finalized specificity; they are only partially determined.
- Indeed, many of the important "structures" in this sphere cannot properly be thought of as *things* at all: they must also be conceived of as *activities,* as regions of structurizing activity, within which not strictly localizable dynamic stabilities are continually reproduced by other activities . . . which depend in their turn, upon dynamic exchanges at lesser and greater levels (Prigogine, 1980).
- Thus what is produced in such dialogical exchanges is a very complex mixture of not wholly reconcilable influences.
- Activities in this sphere have neither a fully orderly nor a fully disorderly structure, neither a completely stable nor an easily changed organization, neither a fully subjective nor fully objective character.
- Indeed, it is precisely their lack of any predetermined order, and thus their openness to being specified or determined only *by those involved in them,* in practice—while usually remaining quite unaware of having done so—that is their central defining feature.

Many others have expressed similar ideas. Merleau-Ponty (1968) puts it thus: "In a sense, if we were to make completely explicit the architectonics of the human body, its ontological framework, and how it sees itself and hears itself, we would see that the structure of its mute world is such that all the possibilities of language are already given in it" (155). Lev Vygotsky (1986) also discusses the emergence of "higher" mental functions from our already existing "lower" ones, by us learning how to "orchestrate" them into a deliberately sequenced, complex ordering. In this way:

> Awareness and deliberate control appear only during a very advanced stage in the development of a mental function, after it has been used and practiced unconsciously and spontaneously. In order to subject a function to intellectual and volitional control, we must first possess it. (168)

As we have already noted above, Wittgenstein also suggested that the origins of our "language-games," and of our prototypes for new ways of thinking, could be found in our spontaneous bodily reactions.

This focus on our spontaneous, bodily responsiveness to events in our surroundings changes completely the way in which we make sense of many terms of importance to us in the conduct of our daily human affairs. In particular, such terms as learning, understanding, knowing, communicating, meaning, organizing, etc., will all have to be used in a wholly new way. They will all now have to be used in a *participative* manner, a manner which in the past was thought of as "primitive" by Levy-Bruhl (1926), and is now thought of as an aspect of our *primordial* being by Merleau-Ponty (1962) and is talked of as *primeval* by Wittgenstein (1980).

Conclusions: Rethinking Teaching and Learning

Central, then, to the rethinking of teaching and learning suggested by the remarks above are three major themes: One is that we should look first to the elicitation of new bodily responses from pupils, prior to any attempts to teach abstract forms or principles. The use of striking examples that, in providing poetic images, provide not only prototypes for new ways of thinking, but also in making a bodily difference to those they strike, they provide memorable moments in which it is possible to "re-feel," so to speak, the mattering differences they made in the lives of those experiencing them. Another is that such moments occur when two or more living activities meet up with each other, and in such moments another chiasmically structured activity occurs both between and around the other activities—an unmerged unity of still distinct processes, a "unity of heterogeneity" rather than a "unity of homogeneity" in Prigogine's (1980) terms. This is what it is for the relevant events to be events of a poetic kind: two familiar events in an unfamiliar juxtaposition occasion the chiasmic creation of a living relation between them—a new relational dimension that matters to us in our lives together. Finally, a third: To say that we are spontaneously responsive in our bodies to events in our surroundings is to say, as Garfinkel (1967) puts it, that we are continuously responsive in our daily discourses with each other to *seen but unnoticed* events, and it is due to these "seen but unnoticed features of common discourse [that events in our] actual utterances are recognized as events of common, reasonable, understandable, plain talk" (41). In other words, what we are learning when we learn our mother tongue is not a piece of knowledge or an item of information that one might later apply intellectually, but an immediate, unhesitating way of seeing and acting. One is learning how to be a proper participant in one's linguistic community—how, as Vygotsky (1978) puts it, "to grow into the intellectual life of those around [us]" (88). And this is done by those around us, who already know the kinds of connections we must learn to make, stopping us in our tracks, startling us with the need to make a creative connection between things still unconnected by us, and by aiding us further in articulating and chiasmically intertwining and interconnecting such events into the rest of our everyday lives together. Much of this, it seems to me, is summed up by Vygotsky (1986) in the following claim:

> What served as a postulate in the old psychology—the interconnectedness of mental functions—must become a problem in the new one. The changing inter-

functional relations must become a central issue in the study of consciousness. It is this new approach that must be used in tackling the lack of consciousness and deliberate control in school children. The general law of development says that awareness and deliberate control appear only during a very advanced stage in the development of a mental function, after it has been used and practiced unconsciously and spontaneously. In order to subject a function to intellectual and volitional control, we must first possess it. (168)

By "changing interfunctional relations," he means that, instead of allowing the relations between perception, attention, memory, thought, language, etc., to remain under the spontaneous control of circumstances, we can, by taking control of our own surrounding circumstances, take control of ourselves, by sequencing them into a structure of our own devising. Just as others can call us to "Stop," "Look," "Listen," "Notice connections not noticed before," "Respond to *them* as like *this*," and so on, so we can come to call out such responses in ourselves.

Taken together then, what all these comments on the rethinking of teaching and learning amount to is a need in the West to shift our current focus on learning as a result of explicit teaching on it as a matter of the one-way transmission of information by an expert toward another kind of learning altogether. For there is another, much more basic and important kind of learning that occurs without teachers, spontaneously within our everyday engaged involvements with the others around us. In current Western, Cartesian influenced notions of knowledge and learning, what is learned is thought of as a matter of gaining explicit knowledge, an epistemological matter. The kind of knowing of concern to Vico, Wittgenstein, and so on is to do with the kind of person one has learned to be, something ontological, a new way of being in the world.

Such new learning is achieved when, to repeat, abilities that are exercised spontaneously, as something that children already know how to do without knowing that they know, are first "called out" from them by the words of others, which later they learn to "call out" from themselves by their own words. In such circumstances as these, learning occurs as just one moment in an otherwise continuous, multiparty involvement, in which a shared field of creativity emerges in which all alike, often all unawares, are collaboratively engaged. To turn this around into a process more under our own control than it is at present, we all must become more sensitive in our dealings with each other to the new beginnings offered us by our bodies in their responses to the events occurring in our surroundings. To emphasize this, I will end with a remark of Merleau-Ponty's (1962) to this effect:

My body is not only an object amongst all other objects . . . but an object which is *sensitive* to all the rest, which reverberates to all sounds, vibrates to all colors, and provides words with their primordial significance through the way in which it receives them. . . . [The body] is that strange object which uses its own parts as a general system of symbols for the world, and through which we can consequently "be at home in" that world, "understand" it and find significance in it. (236–37)

Note

1. References to Vico's *New Science* (*NS*) are to the paragraph number.

References

Bakhtin, M. M. (1986). *Speech genres and other late essays.* Vern W. McGee (Trans.). Austin: University of Texas Press.

Bateson, G. (1979). *Mind in nature: A necessary unity.* London: Dutton.

Berlin, I. (1976). *Vico and Herder.* London: Hogarth.

Garfinkel, H. (1967) *Studies in ethnomethodology.* Englewood Cliffs, NJ: Prentice-Hall.

Levy-Bruhl, L. (1926). *How natives think* (*Les Fonctions Mentales dans les Sociétés Inférieurs*). L. A. Clare (Trans.). London: Allen and Unwin.

Mead, G. H. (1934). *Mind, self and society.* Chicago: University of Chicago Press.

Merleau-Ponty, M. (1962). *Phenomenology of perception.* C. Smith (Trans.). London: Routledge and Kegan Paul.

———. (1964). *Signs.* Richard M. McCleary (Trans.). Evanston, IL: Northwestern University Press.

———. (1968). *The visible and the invisible.* Evanston, IL: Northwestern University Press.

Prigogine, I. (1980). *From being to becoming: Time and complexity in the physical sciences.* San Fransisco: Freeman.

Shotter, J. (1980). Action, joint action, and intentionality. In *The structure of action* (pp. 28–65). M. Brenner (Ed.). Oxford: Blackwell.

———. (1984). *Social accountability and selfhood.* Oxford: Blackwell.

———. (1993a). *Cultural politics of everyday life: Social constructionism, rhetoric, and knowing of a third kind.* Milton Keynes: Open University Press.

———. (1993b). *Conversational realities: Constructing life through language.* London: Sage.

Steiner, G. (1989). *Real presences.* Chicago: University of Chicago Press.

Vico, G. (1968). *The new science of Giambattista Vico.* T. G. Bergin and M. H. Fisch (Trans. and Eds.). Ithaca, NY: Cornell University Press.

———. (1988). *On the most ancient wisdom of the Italians.* Lucina Palmer (Trans.). Ithaca, NY: Cornell University Press.

Vygotsky, L. S. (1986). *Thought and language.* Alex Kozulin (Trans.). Cambridge, MA: MIT Press.

Wittgenstein, L. (1953). *Philosophical investigations.* Oxford: Blackwell.

———. (1969). *On certainty.* Oxford: Blackwell.

———. (1980). *Culture and value,* P. Winch (Trans.). Introduction by G. Von Wright. Oxford: Blackwell.

———. (1981). *Zettel,* 2nd. ed. G.E.M. Anscombe and G. Von Wright (Eds.). Oxford: Blackwell.

 # Learning, Teaching, and Complexity

Within the last decades systems theory has proved to be a strong candidate when it comes to understanding and handling the kinds of problems within education that are characterized by complexity, chaos, unpredictability, unintended effects, individuality, pluralism, and reflexivity. In this chapter I will focus on the relationship between learning and teaching that is connected to the relation between learning as an individual phenomenon and teaching as a social phenomenon, that when brought together change each other mutually. The exploration of this issue will be based on the German sociologist Niklas Luhmann's (1927–1998) systems theory, and I will begin by presenting the background on which his theory has been developed.

Theoretical Background

Luhmann draws on various theoretical tools in the development of his theory. He has a firm grounding in sociology, which serves as his primary source of inspiration, but is equally influenced by systems theory, cybernetics, biology, and phenomenology. He was one of the earliest proponents of the concept of systems and is therefore often labeled a systems theorist, but this designation is all too narrow. His theory is rooted in his wide reading in a great number of disciplines and characterized by exceptional creativity in his application and synthesis of these.

The notion of self-reference occupies a central place in Luhmann's development of his theory of society early on. In the beginning of the 1980s, this notion was supplemented with the concept of autopoiesis, meaning self-production. The concept was introduced in the early 1970s by the Chilean biologist Humberto Maturana (1928–) based on his work on the organization of living systems and nervous systems. According to Maturana, a living system is autonomous by virtue of being self-producing or autopoietic, and he defines autopoietic systems—for instance, a nervous system—as systems that are organized as networks of processes that produce the elements making up the network. Through their interaction, these elements contribute to the realization of the network of processes that produced them as well as to the continuous generation and realization of the system as a concrete unit in physical space (Maturana, 1975, 317f). One conclusion Maturana drew from this was that autopoietic systems must be closed in relation to their environment. No information is transferred from the external environment to the nervous system, because that which is seen or sensed by the nervous system is determined by the nervous system itself. Thus the external environment merely functions as a disturbing factor for structural changes that are already determined by the structure of the system, and the nervous system itself determines what it considers a disturbance.

This line of reasoning serves as an inspiration for Luhmann and is incorporated into his theory through his stress on the concept of *self-reference* as a consequence of viewing systems as autopoietic: autopoietic systems are self-referential in their organization and self-referential systems operate autopoietically. One might say that Luhmann establishes self-reference as the central concept in his theory of autopoietic, closed systems by viewing it as almost synonymous with autopoiesis. But for Luhmann, the concept can be expanded to include other systems

> The word closure seems strange in a book devoted to openness and "open systems." Any open systems thought (an autopoietic one for Luhmann as well as for Maturana and Varela) is structured by the dynamic of the interactions occurring *within* the system. Hence closure here refers somewhat paradoxically to a system's internal interconnections and their dynamic organization. It is this internal, ever-shifting (dynamic) organization that gives a system its uniqueness.

than living systems, since a system can be termed autopoietic if it can be established that it operates in a specific manner that only applies to the system in question. Autopoiesis is not confined to living systems: psychic and social systems, too, are autopoietic. Psychic systems operate by means of cognitive activities such as thoughts, feelings, impressions, etc., while social systems operate by means of communication, and they reproduce themselves based on thoughts and communication. The fact that autopoietic systems are operationally closed means that all operations take place within the boundaries of the system: there can be no production of cells outside a living organism, no thought or feeling outside consciousness, and a social system is made up of communication. As a result, a social system is not made up of, for instance, human beings or psychic processes: these constitute the social system's (external) environment.

Luhmann was particularly inspired by Edmund Husserl (1859–1938), who is regarded as the founder of modern phenomenology. Luhmann's interest was initially sparked by Husserl's critique of science and of modernity as presented in the late work *Crisis of European Sciences and Transcendental Phenomenology* (1936) and further developed in *Experience and Judgement* (1954), which was published posthumously. But Luhmann also draws on the early Husserl's seminal work *Ideas Pertaining to a Pure Phenomenology and to a Phenomenological Philosophy* (1913), which marked a turning point in Husserl's phenomenology after *Logical Investigations* (1900–01), and on the fifth meditation in *Cartesian Meditations*, which was originally published in French following a series of lectures at the Sorbonne in 1929 (a German edition was published in 1950).

Luhmann builds on Husserl's reflections on knowledge as an intentional act whereby reality is invested with meaning and validity in the mind (Rasmussen, 1998). This line of thought paves the way for a constructivist reformulation of Husserl's basic ideas (Luhmann 1996, 39–40). Thus, in Luhmann's work, intentionality is transformed into the idea of marking a distinction. The glance that *observes* the world and the glance that observes its appearance, noesis and noema in Husserl, are designated other-reference (what) and self-reference (how). And the synthesis of individual *intentional* acts, which according to Husserl occur within a horizon of expanding possibilities, Husserl's conception of the world is reformulated by Luhmann as the concept of *world*, based on the distinction between system and external environment, as *reality*, based on the applied difference between object and cognition, and as *meaning*, based on the distinction between the actual and the possible.

This reinstatement shows the ways in which Luhmann veers from the path set by Husserl. Luhmann's reformulation stops precisely at Husserl's explanation of the crisis of European science. Husserl's thesis that science must never lose sight of the life-world lies at the heart of his critique. The life-world is conceived as the shared or common horizon that encompasses the meaning and validity of unanimous, that is, coherent experience, which is manifested in intersubjectivity through continuous adjustment(s). It is here that Luhmann diverges from Husserl, since Luhmann unequivocally rejects any concept of life-world as a satisfactory solution to the problem of a unified first and final resort. Luhmann not only rejects such a solution, he considers it to be theoretically weak to the extent that it can only be regarded as a manifestation of perplexity, "indeed, as an admission of defeat" (Luhmann, 1995a, p. xli). "'Intersubjectivity' is not a concept at all, but a formula of embarrassment, which indicates that one can no longer endure or determine the subject" (Luhmann, 1995b, p. 169).[1] The subject inevitably stands alone.

Husserl's difficulties in determining the social are due to the fact that his attempt at overcoming objectivism rests on an absolute foundation, a fundamental unity, namely the transcendental subject, which is given *a priori* and exists prior to experience; but according to Luhmann, there can be no inter-subjectivity based on the subject. If one applies the concept of life-world, it must be coupled with an awareness that every system has its own life-world, because the sphere of familiarity appears through observation. Thus one individual's life-world is not and cannot be shared by another, because collective familiarity is an impossibility. Truth and being are not guaranteed by several observers apparently observing the same thing, and the social cannot be explained by adding up transcendental subjects and designating the sum, or rather the plurality, a transcendental intersubject.

Luhmann replaces Husserl's inadequate notion that scientific results must never lose sight of the subject and the life-world, as that "lies beneath" (Luhmann, 1993)[2] objectivism, with the concept of observation as an operation that marks a distinction. A scientific result, for instance, is that which is being observed under the influence of an observation by an observer and that which lies beneath is that which cannot be observed in the observation, namely the other and the observation itself; thus one might say that Luhmann radicalizes the phenomenological project. Knowledge has no absolute foundation, but is based on the unity of the actual operation of observing and the recursive reference that facilitates its unity precisely here and now—that is to say, in the form of the above-mentioned paradox.

Luhmann's use of the British logician George Spencer-Brown (1923–) deserves a mention here. In a little book called *Laws of Form* (1969) Spencer-Brown proposed a calculus for the observation of the world; a formalism that aids the expression of Luhmann's ideas about difference and self-reference. Spencer-Brown showed that any observation of the world, that is to say, any construction, is based on distinction. Knowledge presupposes drawing a line in the sand, so to speak, marking a distinction dividing space into two sides, as in, for instance, the distinction between system and environment, and one of these sides can and must be indicated: system or environment. With the aid of Spencer-Brown's calculus of difference Luhmann can thus formulate the following formula: "When something is the case, something else lies beneath—that is to say the distinction between that which is not indicated when something is indicated" (Luhmann, 1993, 257),[3] which is the separation itself (the observer) and the unmarked state (cf. Baecker, 1999, 45). Form is a conceptual tool for drawing a boundary, but form does not equal either one of the two sides, nor does it equal the boundary. Form constitutes the two sides *and* the boundary. With this calculus it becomes obvious that the epistemological foundation of modern society can neither be found in ontological certainty nor in the certainty apparently afforded by intersubjectivity.

Learning and Teaching in the Knowledge Society

In the knowledge society or, as it is also called, the learning society, teaching is not a popular topic. In the learning society, it is not teaching but rather learning which is referred to, and learning is something that the individual does, on his or her own, or nearly on his or her own. In any case, there will no longer be teachers that organize teaching and who teach by conveying knowledge to students. The driving force behind the learning society is the learning students who take responsibility for teaching and their education themselves, who make the agenda and who build up their own competences (e.g., Ranson, 1994).

Throughout the 1990s, we have observed serious efforts to discredit the notion of teaching, especially on the part of advocates of the learning society and of those who are wholeheartedly optimistic about the possibilities for information technology (IT) in the educational system, but these efforts have also been encouraged in the field of international educational policy-making. Furthermore, the idea of the learning society appeals to progressive pedagogical notions about putting focus on the student and taking students' individual needs and interests as point of departure. Both IT-optimists and reform pedagogues can thus agree on the idea that IT makes it possible for the individual student to work with problems related to subject matter at his or her own pace and at a degree of difficulty appropriate to the student. In this way, it is claimed, teaching staff is free to give more effective assistance to those students who may need it. Teachers will to a greater degree be able to become consultants and advisors and support each individual student on his or her own terms. It is envisioned that teachers will be able to assume the roles of advisors, consultants, resource people, coaches, or facilitators for students' independent learning.

This approach is based on the distinction between learning and teaching: learning is compared with teaching and the part of learning is taken on the assumption that learning has a greater impact than teaching. My aim in writing this chapter is in part to point out that teaching, as the other side of the distinction between learning and teaching, is also significant. I also aim to show that teaching and learning are entwined, and that they do not have to be seen as part of a distinction in which each side mutually excludes the other. I will do this by first presenting a constructivist concept of learning that is equal to the problem of complexity in modern society and then defining teaching as a social process intended to stimulate learning.

Operative Constructivism

The leading question is how we set about handling complexity and the immediate response is by learning. Learning is in other words the handling of complexity. However, this answer needs a definition of the concept of learning that can do this. Such a definition is found in the theory of operative constructivism as developed by Luhmann.

Operative constructivism is thus named because knowledge is regarded as an operation: the operation of indicating a difference, namely the difference between what attention is directed at and everything else. When this first difference, the difference between the system and the external environment has been indicated, it is possible for the system to introduce the separated external environment into the system. This is what Luhmann, with reference to Spencer-Brown's Laws of Form, calls reentry. The system is not more important than the external environment; the system and the external environment are what they are by virtue of the existence of each other, but systems can operate and they do this by indicating differences.

According to Luhmann, systems are autopoietic, that is, closed and self-referential. Luhmann includes the concept of autopoieses, which means self-production, in his systems theory in the beginning of the 1980s as a description of the fact that knowledge cannot operate beyond its own boundaries.[4] Autopoiesis replaces Piaget's concept of equilibrium: systems do not strive for equilibrium; rather they strive for their own maintenance. With the concept of autopoietic systems, Luhmann achieves a clarification of the concept used up till now of self-reference: autopoietic systems are self-referentially organized and self-referential systems operate autopoietically. A closed system means that each unit used in the system is determined by the system itself. Systems can be irritated or disturbed by *their* external environments, but such interference is always a selective contribution of the system (Luhmann, 1995c, 17), which can start the operations of the system.

When a system establishes contact with *its* external environment, it cannot take place through a point to point harmonization between the system and the external environment, as this will, of course, neutralize the difference and lead to the system and the environment becoming identical. Furthermore, such an attempt will quickly encounter the barrier set by the capacity of the system. Therefore, systems must put themselves in contact with their external environments through some form of neutralizing of the difference of complexity, and they can do this by *selecting*. A selection is something made actual on the basis of what is possible for the system:

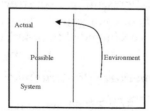

Figure 9.1 System Selection

Systems therefore use their own operations alone to connect themselves to their external environment: nothing moves from the outside into a system. A system constantly produces its own unit and thereby also its own boundaries through its own operations. This means that systems constantly self-reproduce increasingly greater parts of the external environment in themselves while performing operations, for which reason they also extend their boundaries accordingly. In this sense, knowledge can be defined as the increasing of the inner complexity a system gains through the operations it uses to reduce the complexity of the external environment. Knowledge can, in other words, be defined as the *activating of a difference.* (See Reynolds, this volume.)

What Spencer-Brown demonstrates is that underlying every observation of the world, that is, every construction, is a distinction. Knowledge presupposes that a line is drawn in the sand, so to speak; that a distinction that separates two sides is indicated and that one of these two sides at the same time must and can be indicated (Spencer-Brown, 1972, 1). In this sense, distinction and indication can be understood as the fundamental elements in observation and conceptualization. For this reason, "the laws of form" can be regarded as laws about the way the world can be described and thus for knowledge, which Luhmann formulates pointedly in this way: "By observation on the other hand, I mean the act of distinguishing for the creation of information" (Luhmann, 1990, 82). Systems learn by choosing between deviations from their own state, which, however, does not imply that systems follow a purposive course toward increasingly better knowledge.

An operation is a selection or an observation, since every observation is a selection through which something is distinguished from something else. An observation is an operation with two components that cannot be separated. First, there is the selection of side, and secondly, the boundary that separates what is selected from what is not selected. The first component is the selection of side: something is made present, while something else becomes absent, or as Luhmann puts it, something is made actual and something else remains possible. The other component is the selection of boundary: the "line" that separates what is selected from what is not selected. Learning consists therefore of being able to make a distinction through which it is possible to describe one thing and not another. Learning must be understood as a process by which the person, who is learning himself or herself actively, through operations, constructs his or her own knowledge. This was also the conclusion of constructivist theories like those of Piaget and von Glasersfeld, but they drew it on the basis of concepts of adaptation and equilibrium; concepts which are not found in operative constructivism.

The boundary which separates what is actual from what is possible is drawn by the cognitive system itself with reference to itself,[5] in that the unit of a difference (form) that is used for an observation, is, as mentioned, stipulated by the system that is observing. It can therefore be said that the indication of a difference never occurs arbitrarily, because the observer is always deeply rooted in his or her previous experiences, knowledge, interests, needs and values. In short, the line is drawn on the basis of the prerequisites of the system. In this way, the boundary can be understood as an expression of the complexity of the learning system, and all knowledge becomes unique for each individual system.

Teaching

What is teaching? Teaching is a social phenomenon. Teaching cannot be performed in solitude. Teaching is a reciprocal interplay or interaction between several people with the aim of making someone wise in the sense of being well informed, knowledgeable, or competent. Teaching is an intentional activity whose intention is to change people in such a way that they become more well informed, knowledgeable, or competent; in other words, learn.

Teaching as Communication

With the point of departure in communication's theoretical turn in sociology from action to communications (see Stichweh, 2000; Leydesdorff, 2002)—which Luhmannian systems theory emphasizes—the social element is understood as communication. On the basis of this understanding of the social element, I will not define teaching merely as an intentional activity, but as the special case of communication whose intention is to change participants in teaching (see Luhmann, 1995a, 463). I thus see teaching as a communicative phenomenon. Using the difference between teaching and learning as a basis, the same definition could also be expressed in this way: teaching is the specialized form of communication aimed at stimulating learning. Although it is the intention of teaching through deliberate disturbances to change the learner, this does not mean that this intention is always achieved. Whether or not it happens depends entirely on the learning person. Learning is the student's own output. It is erroneous, however, to conclude that just because it is not possible to "learn" someone something, one should not teach, and the teacher should avoid the prominent role of educator and instead assume the unobtrusive role of facilitator. In any case, such assertions are far too general to be able to capture the manifold forms of teaching. It may, of course, be an advantage for the teacher to assume unobtrusive roles as support, consultant, supervisor or resource, for the learning activity of the learning person in certain teaching situations, in certain parts of a teaching sequence and on certain occasions, but far from exclusively.

Teaching is generally seen as bringing about a connection between the student and the information, and the teacher is seen to be the one who establishes this connection. On the basis of this perception of communication, which is known from the traditional communications model (Shannon and Weaver, 1964), in which communication is regarded as a transmission of information from a source of information through a channel to a receiver, the connection between the student and the information that the teacher is expected to produce will often be seen as a process through which the teacher conveys information in the form of teaching content to the students. It is not this understanding of communication that makes the basis of the definition of teaching I use.

Luhmann introduces a concept of communication (Luhmann, 1995a, chapter 4) that consists of a synthesis of three selections: (1) information, (2) utterance and (3) understanding of the difference between information and utterance. One party in the communication must carry out the first two selections, while the second party must carry out the third selection. Communication occurs when I (ego) understand that another person (alter) has *uttered information*. It is the third selection of understanding that realizes the difference between information and communication. The addressee is part of the communication. It can therefore be said that understanding is the success criterion of communication and thereby also educational communication.

The clear differentiation in operative constructivism between psychic systems and social systems introduces an equally clear differentiation between learning and teaching, and on the basis of the fundamental difference in operative constructivism between system and external environment, it is made clear that psychic systems belong to the external environment of social systems and that social systems belong to the external environment of psychic systems. The communication of teaching is, in other words, the external environment of the conscious operations of students and teachers, and their conscious operations are the external environment for the communication of teaching.

Teaching, regarded as a social activity, does not comprise psychic systems. Teaching does not comprise students and teachers, who in their own processes make use of consciousness. Teaching exclusively comprises *communication*, for teaching as a social activity makes use in its processes solely of communication. The premises for the continuous processes in teaching must be established in teaching and this can only happen through communication, but what the teacher does in his or her teaching on the basis of his or her planning leads to reactions in the teaching, which cannot or can only with difficulty be planned because teaching as a social communicative system operates autopoietically. The only thing which is transparent and which the collective attention can concentrate on is the communication that at any time occurs between participants, in that communication is here understood as a selective organization that reaches out for something in the current horizon of reference that the communication itself has first constituted, and disregards something else.

Understanding is not something the teacher simply can introduce to the student in the social context of teaching. Each individual student's understanding of the information the teacher communicates (the student's perception of the teacher's selection of information and communication) is a product of the student's own selections, and thereby also a construction. Similarly, the teacher's understanding of what the student says (the teacher's perception of the student's selection of information and communication) is his or her selection of understanding and thereby also a construction. The teacher does not convey anything to the student, just as the student does not convey anything to the teacher; however, the communication of teaching as the external environment for the students' and teacher's consciousness triggers learning by irritating these people's conscious operations and both parties, or rather all three—the student, the teacher, and the social system of teaching—learn. This means that understanding, and therefore also misunderstanding, are inevitable aspects of communication.

Teaching as a self-referential communicative process is made possible by the continuous testing on the part of the parties involved in the communication of whether the previous communication has been understood. This occurs through the observation of the other party's way of joining the communication; in other words, through a form of evaluation of whether what one has said seems to have been understood by the other party, judged on the basis of what the other continues to say.[6] This test is also carried out as a selection, namely, as the observation of the way the person with whom one is communicating joins the communication.

This means that part of one's attention must always be spent on checking understanding, and if this turns out to be negative, it usually leads to a change in the nature of the communication to reflexive communication, that is, communication about communication. In reflexive communication, the course of the communication can be thematized by one party asking, for example, how something was meant, or through an attempt to communicate information in another way. The drawback of such reflexive communication may be that the teacher, when he gets the impression that he has not been understood, talks even more, repeating himself with other words or attempting to use examples and analogies. The idea behind this is, of course, to increase the redundancy in the communication and thereby increase the possibility of entering the conversation and of being understood, but the result can very well be that the continuation of the communication only gives rise to new understanding problems. It cannot be certain, for example, that the examples used are understood as examples of the theme that is being communicated; there is a risk that they will extricate themselves as independent stories and thereby lead to a shift in the theme of the communication.

Teaching in Schools

The operational, constructive concept of learning I advocate here does not support the claim that learning takes place only in special contexts. On the basis of this concept, learning is something that can take place at any time and at any place a system is aggravated by its external environment into making a differentiating operation, which leads to a change in its structure of expectation. This concept of learning thus cannot be used as an argument for asserting that organized teaching in schools is the only place where learning is possible. Learning can occur anywhere, although sometimes as socialization. However, teaching is the historically well-known form of a social arrangement and organization aimed at intensifying possibilities for learning and the results of learning. There are three special features of educational communication: first, it provides an organized and arranged communication system in which the roles of the student(s) and teacher(s) are complementary; second, communication in such a system can proceed with reference to previous themes, which makes it possible to build upon previous communication; third, it thereby becomes possible to reduce the arbitrariness and sporadic nature that characterizes the communication aimed at upbringing which is found in families or the unplanned, unsystematic, and ad hoc form of learning that takes place in everyday social contexts.

Teaching can thus be defined as being the special form of communication that is characterized by the fact that it is carried out with a special intention in mind, which is usually embedded in historical and societal ideals. Teaching usually takes place in an institutional, organizational setting that contributes to the conditioning or framing of the educational endeavors so that they are not just based on individual decisions that must repeatedly be debated. In addition, educational communication is usually also seen as planned communication in which special methods are applied which can help strengthen the connection between aim and result, that is, between teaching and learning. Framing of educational communication, insofar as it has developed from an historical point of view with the aim of relieving the pressure from educational communication, is the theme of the following section.

The Framework of Teaching

Symbolically Generalized Communication

As noted previously, everything that happens in teaching must be determined communicatively, and therefore the concept of communication is of crucial importance in dealing with the question of teaching. As indicated, according to Luhmann the concept of communication can be understood as a synthesis of three selections. However, as each of these selections alone is a contingent event, the synthesis of all three selections is highly improbable. Luhmann draws attention to the fact that there is a multitude of problems or obstacles which communication must overcome in order to become communication at all. He points in this regard to three *improbabilities*. The first improbability is connected to the problem of double contingency, in which two completely undecided communication participants face one another and it is "improbable that ego *understands* what alter means" (Luhmann, 1995a, 158). The second improbability relates to the question of making contact with the addressees of the communication, in that it is unlikely that communication will affect others than those who are present in the concrete communication situation. The third improbability concerns the question of *success*, which refers to the question of whether the addressee takes on "the content selected by the communication" (158) and makes it the object of further communication and communication linkage. Luhmann (1997) indicates, therefore, that historically, special communication media have developed, which contribute to render improbable communication probable:

> When we speak of media of communication, we are always referring to the operative application of the difference between mediating substance and form. Communication—and that is our answer to the problem of improbability—is only possible as the processing of this difference. (195)[7]

He distinguishes between the media of dissemination (*Verbreitungsmedien*) and the media of accomplishment (*Erfolgsmedien*). Media of dissemination, which shall not be dealt with in this connection, have the function of increasing the probability of communication which has been made improbable because of geographic distance, in that such media help determine and expand the sphere of receivers of any given communication. Dissemination of communication can occur orally in interactions between participants who are present to one another, it can occur in writing, which with the appearance of the printing industry expands the circle of receivers but at the same time also makes it impossible to know who has read what texts and whether they can remember the contents of them. Modern mass media, including electronic mass media, are significant media of dissemination today.

Media of accomplishment is used as an umbrella term for symbolically generalizing communication media whose function is to "produce a novel connection between conditioning and motivation" (203).[8] This happens by adjusting the communication to special conditions determined by the media, which increase the chance of acceptance. The symbolically generalized communication media help motivate potential communication participants to actually participate, by making it possible for them to orient themselves toward reliable assumptions: in the economic system toward money, in the political system toward power, in the scientific system toward truth and in the pedagogic system toward the child, or today, toward all stages of life. In addition, the symbolically generalized communication media are ensured through codification, that is, the fact that connected to each media is a binary schematic, which in relation to the media money is payment/nonpayment, in relation to politics is the possession of power/lack of power or government/opposition, in relation to science is true/false, and in relation to upbringing and education is better/worse. Finally, the symbolically generalized communication media are ensured through programming. Programming concerns the elucidation of the themes that the communication can be expected to follow in a given system, and it thus helps give the participants of communication the possibility of adjusting their potential contribution to the communication, in that contributions which suit the theme or which are perceived to be appropriate in relation to the theme have a greater chance of meeting acceptance. In the economic system, budgets and accounts have program status; in the political system, it is the governmental and party programs; in the scientific system, theories and methods fulfill this function; and in the pedagogic system, teaching plans and curricula are used for this purpose. The combination of symbolically generalized communication media, codes, and programs helps make probable the improbable communication in society's functional systems, in that they narrow the field of what can be expected.

Teaching takes place within the framework made by the symbolically generalized communication media *child* or in the modern world the *course of individual life*, with the ensuring of this by that inherent in the pedagogic system's code and program use. However, the symbolically generalized communications media of the pedagogic system do not have the same capacity as other systems' symbolically generalized communication media. This makes the pedagogic system dependent on other relief factors with regard to the ability to simplify the educational complexity and contingency that is a result of the communicative arrangement of three selections, which furthermore are placed in the social form of the double contingency. For this purpose, special system formations present themselves, namely interaction systems and organization systems, respectively. Interaction systems and organization systems represent two different ways of dealing with improbable communication and double contingency.

Interaction and Organization

Interaction systems and organizations are not formed outside of society, but they cannot be understood as a part of society (compare with the abandonment of the partial/complete understanding in Luhmann's theory). In other words, it cannot be said that society consists of or comprises organizations and interaction like a nest of Chinese boxes. Society, organizations, and interactions are unique types of systems, which are determined on the basis of their unique ways of dealing with the problem of double contingency.

Interaction systems are defined as the type of social systems in which participants in the communication are present and physically present to one another (Luhmann, 1995a; 1997). This means that a system may be called an interaction system when the communication sets limits between itself and the external environment that are determined by who is present in the communication and who is not, even though it is, of course, possible in an interaction system to communicate about someone who is absent.

Interaction systems are, in contrast to functional systems and organizations, to a greater degree limited by time. The communication in an interaction system can be interrupted and resumed at a later time, which gives interaction systems the advantage of being able to build on repeatability to the extent to which the participants in the communication are able to remember the theme and the contributions that have been communicated within its framework. Precisely through the setting of limits between present and absent participants, interaction systems form a system/external environment balance, within which they produce their own story, which helps determine what participants in the interaction system can regard as probable. Structures emerge in interaction systems, which are solely structures of the system in question, which mean that the patterns of expectation that develop are solely connected to the communication among the participants of communication who have been present to each other in the communication.

Educational communication takes place predominantly as interaction, which is a major reason for the possibility of teaching succeeding, but is also a source of overtaxing, in that everyone present has the possibility of contributing to the communication with their own individual contributions and thematizations and at any time they choose. This fact emphasizes the significance of structural linkage between conscious processes, which cannot be monitored, and education communication, which can only be monitored in an interaction system through communication between the participants who are present to one another. It becomes important that everyone hears what is actually said in order for the next speaker to refer to what has been said and, regardless of whether it has been understood in the same way by all participants in the communication; it becomes important that everyone joins in on the same theme of the communication; and it becomes important that the individual participant in the communication shows consideration for the others, so everyone does not talk at the same time.

In the interaction of the classroom, structural linkage can be extremely difficult if the theme of the communication is not clear. This can be the case, for example, if what was intended as an example is not understood as an example, but rather as a new independent theme which can be joined, or if the students—or the teacher, for that matter—let their thoughts and associations run wild, so that they are introduced without adjustment to the communication. If it were possible for every participant who is present in the communication to contribute with exactly what they happen to be thinking of at the moment, the educational interaction would break down.

An interaction system regulates itself through the adapting on the part of participants of their contributions to the theme of the communication and through the timing on the part of participants of their contributions, in such a way as to avoid overlapping each other. In an interaction system, such regulation can only take place communicatively, for example, by pointing out that a contribution does not fit the subject of the communication, or by requesting that someone waits until another participant has finished speaking. A considerable portion of educational communication is taken up by such regulations.

In schools, some of the pressure on educational communication can to a certain extent be relieved by the fact that it takes place in an organizational setting. This makes it possible for the participants in the communication to orient themselves, not just according to the difference between being present and being absent, but also according to the special differences that characterize organizations. These include in particular membership and non-membership as well as the difference between person and role. Furthermore, there are additional rules and regulations that can be included as part of the decisions made in the organization and not just between the participants in the communication who are present to each other. Teachers and students in the school can, by orienting themselves according to their special expectations of roles and according to the rules decided upon in the organization, reduce the scope of possibilities for what can be expected, because these factors help reduce complexity.

However, despite these pressure-reducing factors, educational communication is to a great extent reduced to orienting itself according to interaction, in that the organizational roles and decisions as well as the function and performance determined by the functional system must constantly be communicated in the interaction system *teaching* if it is to any degree to be observable and guiding for participants: roles must be confirmed through illustration, decisions must be re-updated for reasons of both remembering and understanding, and the idea behind the teaching must continuously be thematized for reasons of conditioning and motivation. Modern society's conditioning of teaching as interaction in the organization school in an educational system helps make the results of teaching efforts more predictable because the organizational conditioning regulates roles and expectations of roles through its creation of a framework and regularity by defining the group of people who enjoy membership in the organization. The organizational conditioning contributes to the self-simplification of teaching, in such a way that it can be liberated from a dependence on individual's personal values, opinions, and tastes. All of these characteristics of educational communication as interaction between participants that are present to one another form the framework for this type of communication. However, such framing of educational communication should not be perceived as a limitation, but rather as the form of limitation that simultaneously increases the possibilities for teaching to produce its anticipated output.

Teaching and Understanding

The criterion of success for communication when it is perceived as a synthesis of three selections is *understanding* and therefore also of educational communication. Discussion about teaching implies therefore a concurrent reflection on understanding. This criterion of success is in accordance with the fact that there has been general agreement since the first formulations of modern pedagogy in the mid-1700s that the foremost goal of teaching is understanding. Despite their differences in their perception of the role of pedagogy in modern society and of what methods are most appropriate for the achievement of understanding, the founders of modern pedagogic theory are concerned with the same problem: how can it be ensured that the student does not just acquire a knowledge of the subject matter being taught, but that he or she also understands it. In addition to the cognitive theoretical problem about how the world is constituted in knowledge, this ideal raises the pedagogic question of how the teacher can ensure that his or her efforts are understood, in other words, the question of the relationship between intention and effect in teaching.

Traditionally, understanding has been regarded as a relationship between the teacher or the content of the teaching and the student's brain. In this view, it becomes the teacher's task to make himself comprehensible, to ensure that he has been understood and finally to attempt to understand whether the students have understood the material that has been worked with in the teaching. This concept of understanding is strained by its basic subject philosophical view—the world versus people or, in this case, teacher/content versus student. In the conceptualization of teaching as a social and thereby communicative self-referential process presented here, it must constantly be tested in the communication whether the prior communication has been understood. The teacher must constantly orient himself toward the difference consisting in whether the communication has been understood or not understood. The process of understanding is required to be able to link back to whether the previous communication has been understood, but such a linkage presupposes that the teacher knows or is aware of why and to what purpose, in other words, on the basis of what differences, he communicates something as information. This is a condition for whether the teacher can ask himself whether the student has understood him as a system in their external environment.

It may be possible if the teacher-student ratio is one-to-one, but in modern schools, where it is more likely to be one to twenty or more, it becomes extremely difficult, if not impossible, for the teacher to test understanding. These conditions have led to the formulation of the thesis of *a deficit* of *understanding in teaching* (Schoor, 1986). Luhmann therefore attempts to re-form the problem of understanding on another level. Instead of perceiving understanding as a category which deals with the relation person-person or person-thing, he sees understanding as a general method of observation, control, and operation between self-referential systems: "Understanding is understanding of the handling of self-reference" (Luhmann, 1986, 72).[9] According to this definition of understanding it can be said that only self-referential systems can understand.

Self-referential systems are systems that can handle a difference between themselves and everything else (system/external environment difference) and which can deduce consequences of this for themselves; they are, in other words, systems of opinion. This means that understanding in teaching cannot be limited to social interaction or the ability of the teacher to empathize. Understanding also deals with the dimension of content and communication (information and communication): the teacher must understand whether he or she has been understood and the student must strive to understand. As noted, this is difficult and improbable in large groups of students. The production of understanding in schools today takes place, to a great extent, at random.

The old problem concerning the effect of teaching is thus thematized in a new way. The teacher teaches, but there is no guarantee that his efforts will lead to understanding on the part of the students. An attempt has been made through time to solve this problem by developing teaching methods that are more sensitive to students. According to Luhmann, however, this is unlikely to be of much help to teachers when what is essential is the establishment of a firm connection between the intention of the teaching and its result. At the same time, the problem is one-sidedly related only to the teacher's system reference, and therefore the question of understanding is raised for the teacher as a question of whether and how he can be understood and whether he has been understood or not. However, teaching is an element of a difference that arises on the basis of double contingency both in relation to the teacher's behavior and the student's behavior. This means that there is double contingency on both sides, and that each side must reflect this doubling in order to reflect himself or herself in the social communication of the teaching.

Deficiency of understanding in teaching is in reality an expression of a paradox: at the same time that teaching shows a lack of understanding, understanding is a prerequisite for the educational communication's operations. Such a paradox can nearly be understood as what Douglas Hofstadter calls *strange loops*. These loops are characterized by the fact that when one moves up (or down) in a hierarchical system, one unexpectedly finds oneself back where one started (Hofstadter, 1979, 10). Hofstadter exemplifies strange loops by Bach's fugues, in which we suddenly find ourselves back at the beginning, even though the tones have moved upwards; Escher's drawings of hands, that are drawing themselves; and Gödel's theory that it is impossible to make a theory of whole numbers that at one time is consistent and complete: all consistent axiomatic formulations of number systems contain judgments which cannot be settled. The paradox in Gödel's evidence lies not in the evidence itself but in the fact that as soon as one believes that one has established a system of thought that includes everything and is complete, one suddenly discovers that this system is an expression of one's description, rather than of what one was describing. The system refers back to itself; it is self-referential. When systems become so complex that their structure allows self-reference, paradoxes arise of the type in which the conditions for the possibilities presuppose their own results: understanding must be used to establish understanding. This paradox is usually handled through feedback processes between the student's learning and the educational communication in the sense that the communication adapts itself to the student's development in terms of understanding on the basis of the student's contribution to the communication. A connection is, so to speak, formed between two processes, namely, on the one hand, the process in which the educational communication attempts to create understanding and on the other hand, the process which runs as a feedback loop between teaching and learning.

> Hofstadter's "strange loops," the basis for his "tangled hierarchies," disrupt our usual sense of hierarchy in favor of a *vision of difference*, one which leads to emergence, adaptation, and sentience. This concept of difference is similar to Maturana and Varela's concept of operational closure and Prigogine's concept of dissipative structures. All these authors—Hofstadter, Maturana and Varela, and Prigogine—struggle with the problem of creating and maintaining difference in a world whose intricately interconnected systems threaten to overwhelm difference.

> One might go so far as to suggest, as does Roy, the value of "paradoxical inquiry."

Gödel's evidence does not provide a basis for correcting or repairing a system's limitations; however, one can learn from Gödel how to deal with the *expectations* that are placed on a system. All ideas about paradoxes being avoidable in a complex system must therefore be regarded as pre-Gödelian thinking. The question is not *whether* paradoxes can be avoided—in this particular case, whether the deficit of understanding can be avoided in teaching. The question is *how* one can deal with and work with this paradox.

When the teacher does not have the possibility of understanding whether he has been understood, the interaction in the school can intervene compensatorily. When the goal of teaching is to achieve understanding, there is no point focusing one-sidedly on the participants who are involved in the teaching. It is precisely their structurally built-in specific characters that produce the deficit of understanding. The participants can no longer understand each other because the teaching situation exceeds the individual's capacity for understanding.

According to Luhmann, this means that in order for a realistic pedagogy to become really modern, that is, in accordance with the conditions that prevail in a modern differentiated school, it must liberate itself from the old European notion of teaching as an interpersonal subject/subject relation. It is much more productive to regard the formation of system and structure in the educational communication as an emergent effect of the mutual communication instead. Precisely because of the deficit of understanding, a social system is developed as an autonomous communicative reality (Luhmann, 1986), which consists of that which occurs as communication and which with reference to itself reproduces communication.

This supraindividual system, which the participants in teaching create through their communication, can affect the participants and lead to effects, which cannot simply be explained by subjective intentions. Possibilities arise in the communication for additional joining, which is a reality that exists in and because of the educational communication. The teacher must regard the problem of understanding from the perspective that he is himself a part of the social system that he helps reproduce. In order to influence learning, both teacher and students must glide smoothly into the communicative flow of teaching. Any attempt at changing psychic systems, which is, of course, the purpose of the special communication of the teaching, must take as its point of departure whatever has happened in one way or another because of oneself.

Teaching and Complexity

To recapitulate, teaching is to be understood as the intended form of communication that is aimed at changing psychic systems. That which is intended is, in other words, the learning that the student has brought about himself or herself. This means that even though learning is performed by the student himself or herself, teaching can be adjusted in order to support the student's efforts at learning, which in the modern complex society chiefly means that the most crucial task of teaching becomes the support of the students' handling of complexity through communication.

On the basis of the concept in operative constructivism of operations of observation and on the basis of von Glasersfeld's interpretation of Piaget's concept of the learning scheme (Glasersfeld, 1995, chapter 3), it becomes possible to lay down certain principles for teaching that take the abilities and aptitudes of the students into account, and which give the teacher a systematicism, which can be used when planning or carrying out teaching. Operative constructivism follows Spencer-Brown's guidelines, or rather imperatives, for the handling of complexity, which in short are aimed at indicating a difference. Such an operation, indicating a difference, can be divided into two phases: first, the reduction of complexity through selection, and then the reduction of unavoidable concomitant contingency through reflection. Von Glasersfeld's concept of schema operates with three steps, which naturally are interwoven in the psychic system of the student, but which it can be useful to distinguish from one another in educational communication: Recognition in the current situation, production of a result through comparison with already established expectation structures, and finally checking of this result on the basis of the established understanding of learning. On the basis of this systematicism, the following separation into phases of educational communication can be put forward: first, a phase in which new material is introduced as a point of departure for the student's necessary reduction of complexity, then a phase for the student's selection of understanding, and finally, a phase for the student's reduction of contingency.

> Another interpretation, taking a completely different stance, is to embrace the complexity and use it to "complexify" learning. Indeed some argue that the complex context is crucial to the sorts of learning humans do best; see St. Julien (this volume) speaking about connectionism.

The introduction of new material is and will continue to be an important task of teaching. It is faced with the paradox that the prerequisite for learning is that the student already must know something, to which the new material can be connected, a fact that hearkens back to the systems theoretical rule that only complexity can reduce complexity (Luhmann, 1995a, 26). In this phase, educational communication may fittingly be able to introduce a complex field of study in a planned way in an appropriate order and by so doing, reduce the overwhelming nature of the material. This may, for example, be done by presenting new material in the form of an overview, which shows how the new subject area relates to other similar subjects, by pointing out differences and similarities in relation to these topics and by introducing basic theories and new concepts in the field of study. Such an overview of a new subject area should help increase the possibilities of the student being able to see the connections that are obvious to someone who already has an overview, and to open the student's eyes to familiar elements in the new subject area which he or she can latch onto and in this way increase the likelihood that the students can join the communication.

The phase that comprises the student's own selection of understanding is a phase in which the student must concentrate upon material, within the framework of the field of study that has been presented. This is chiefly an independent activity; however, it does presuppose that the student knows enough about the subject area to pose questions about it. The establishment of such basic knowledge is one of the major intentions of the presentation of the field of study.

The phase comprising the reduction of contingency concerns the question of the reduction of uncertainty the student may have in relation to his or her selected understanding. Teaching can disturb the consciousness of students and trigger new thoughts, ideas, or emotions; it can introduce new topics; it can present complex and confusing material in a planned way and in an appropriate order, which makes the material less overwhelming; and it is in the social communication of teaching that the students' understanding can be tested.

Above and beyond, and as a supplement to the factors that relieve pressure in the educational interaction discussed above, special forms of self-simplification that can support the reduction of complexity and contingency have developed. These forms likewise concern the question of expectations and especially the possibility for the narrowing of the scope of *what* can be communicated as well as *how* communication takes place *when*. What remains when this sphere of possibilities has been limited is what can be expected. In the dimension of facts, the *what* of teaching is determined through the choice and sequencing of themes and through the adaptation of contributions to the chosen theme. In the social dimension the scope of *how* things can be communicated in teaching through the choice of method and the determination of roles that follows this choice. In the time dimension, the *when* of teaching is decided through the organization of starting times and finishing times.

Themes and Contributions

Through the difference between themes and contributions, educational communication becomes a process. Contributions can be compared with themes, which are of a longer duration. Themes, which typically control communication processes, are characterized by having a factual content, which serves to coordinate contributions (the subject dimension); a time-related aspect, which makes it possible to return to earlier contributions or themes (the time dimension); and a social aspect, which more or less "binds" the participants, in that they make themselves known through their opinions, attitudes, and so on (the social dimension).

Themes help reduce the complexity of communication, in the same way as sequences help reduce the complexity of the contents of teaching. In the fact dimension, considerations on sequencing concern the curricular question about the content of what the teaching is to be about, whether the teaching should take point of departure in the concrete or the abstract, move from the simple to the complex, or the complex to the simple, or perhaps from simple complexity to compound complexity. In the time dimension, consideration is directed at when a given topic of teaching can be introduced and concerns therefore the question of progression. In the social dimension, consideration may by given to whether and how the teaching can take into account the readiness of the students and their needs and interests, and it is also in this dimension that understanding tests are established through students' discussion with each other, the correction of mistakes, exemplification, the putting forward of hypotheses, confirmations, or corrections. In such tests, one's own as well as others' understanding is observable.

Sequencing is thus an internal pedagogic matter, which concerns the problem about reduction of complexity. The purpose of the selection of sequences is to help coordinate the relationship between system and external environment. By reducing the complexity of the external environment through sequencing, it becomes possible to increase demands in the social system in the context of teaching and the psychic systems. The traditional curriculum question of to what extent teaching should take its point of departure in the general, that is, in material and curriculum of the knowledge dimension or in the specific, that is, in the student's need and interests, is in the theory of self-referential, autopoietic systems replaced by the view that the student's "acquisition" of the external environment is a process that presupposes both system and external environment, and the "acquisition" consists of the systems reconstructing the external environment in its own structure.

In research on the quality of teaching, one of several factors which is emphasized in repeated studies as being decisive for the quality of teaching is *clarity* (for an overview of research on this topic, see Einsiedler, 1997). The category *clarity* is usually used in relation to the communication of information in teaching. However, in this case, the definition of this category is made more specific and deals with a communicated *clarity* in choice of theme, including questions, references, and explanations, in that such a communicated clarity is a prerequisite, but not a guarantee, that as many students as possible are able to join the current communication. It is therefore not sufficient to have made a choice of theme once; even this choice of theme must constantly be thematized, reinterpreted, and renegotiated with the aim of reducing uncertainty about what the educational communication in reality is about.

Methodology

Constructivist theories of learning like radical constructivism (von Glasersfeld) and operative constructivism (Luhmann) make it impossible to indicate a specific, preferred method of teaching. The teacher must be capable of mastering a wide range of methods, which he can use according to where the individual students are in their learning process. This means that the teacher

> Doll (this volume) argues for a new sense of method, one which focuses less on clarity of communication and more on the habit/practice of shared inquiry. Such inquiry never ends, never resolves itself. Luhmann's perspective on communication provides the basis for an interesting problematic here.

must be able to switch between different degrees of control in teaching, from teacher-controlled class teaching through organization of teaching activities of a more independent nature to completely free forms of working.[10]

Moreover, the teacher must be aware of the value of the students' own initiatives in relation to the form and contents of teaching. Not all of the contents of the teaching need necessarily be initiated by the teacher. The theory of the acquisition by autopoietic systems of the external environment through communication gives no explicit instructions about how good teaching can be planned. However, it indicates that learning is activated through disturbances or irritations. Therefore, the possibility of teaching is to stimulate learning through intentional disturbances. The learners' self-referential processes are actualized because the learner distinguishes himself from other things; this distinction is used in the tapping of knowledge through the learner's constant use of inner unrest and vibrations to explore his or her external environment, or conversely, through the effect of planned educational communication on internally structured expectations.

On the one hand, when based on the difference between system and external environment, teaching constitutes a possible, but undefined stimulating disturbance from outside (from the side of the external environment), while on the other hand, it is the learner alone (from the side of the system) who, on the basis of the limitations that the situation and conditions set, decides whether or not the disturbance is observed. Learning and teaching take place as recursive processes in their respective system types, which means that the two sorts of systems take as their basis for their future operations previous operations, conscious operations, and communicative operations, respectively, which they can mutually observe and adapt themselves to. In this regard, psychic and social systems, consciousness and communication, are mutually dependent: they are interdependent. As Luhmann (1995a) describes:

> Psychic and social systems have evolved together. At any time the one kind of system is the necessary environment of the other. This necessity is grounded in the evolution that makes these kinds of systems possible. Persons cannot emerge and continue to exist without social systems, nor can social systems without persons. This co-evolution has led to a common achievement, employed by psychic as well as social systems. Both kinds of systems are ordered according to it, and for both it is binding as the indispensable, undeniable form of their complexity and self-reference. (59)

In general, it can therefore be said that the contents of teaching must appear as a problem for students, something they may each be disturbed or affected by, and which they therefore are prompted to deal with consciously.

Conclusions

The discrediting of teacher, which is expressed by advocates for the learning society as part of the slogan about changing the focus from the teacher's teaching to the students' learning, and which regards teaching as a matter for the teacher alone, does not take into account that teaching is a social issue. To proclaim that the teacher should take up less room, adopt a more inconspicuous role as a conversation and collaborative partner for the students so that the students' independent learning processes can instead take up more room is an expression of a preference with regard to method and control, which should not be used to discredit teaching as such. Rather, such a preference should be used to the continuation of the important discussion of what teaching can do in a given historical context and under given historical and social conditions.

To recapitulate, teaching is to be understood as the intended form of communication that is aimed at changing psychic systems. In other words, what is intended is learning which is initiated by the student himself or herself. This means that even though learning is the student's own output, teaching can be planned with the aim of supporting the learning efforts of the student, which in the modern complex society chiefly means that the most important task of teaching is to support the student's handling of complexity through communication.

Notes

1. "Intersubjektivität (ist) überhaupt kein Begriff, sondern eine Verlegenheitsformel, die angibt, dass man das Subjekt nicht mehr aushalten oder nicht mehr bestimmen kann."

2. "steckt dahinter."

3. "wenn etwas der Fall ist, steckt auch etwas dahinter—nämlich die Unterscheidung von dem, was nicht bezeichnet wird, wenn etwas bezeichnet wird."

4. Autopoiesis (from the Greek: autos = self and poiesis = to create) is a concept introduced by the Chilean biologist Humberto Maturana in the beginning of the 1970s together with his student Francisco Varela (1946–2001) in connection with their work on the organization of living systems. According to Maturana, a living system is autonomous by being self-producing or autopoieitic, and he defines an autopoietic system as a system that is organized as a network of processes that produce the components of which the network is comprised. These components participate through their interacting in the realization of the network processes that have produced them and in the continuous generation and realization of the system as a concrete unit in physical space. The system generates both itself and the components that produce the components, the network and the relations between the components it comprises. Everything that functions in the system is produced by the system through a network of its own components (Maturana, 1975, 317f.).

5. The fact that a system refers to itself does not mean that it refers to itself in an ontological sense. Through basal self-reference, a system refers to itself in the form of "an element, for example, an event," which in a psychic system can be a thought, a feeling, or a sensation and in a social system, communication. In the case of processual self-reference, "the self that refers to itself (is) not an aspect of the distinction but a *process* constituted by it." In the case of reflection, "the self (is) the system to which the self-referential operation attributes itself" (Luhmann, 1995b, 443 and following).

6. I use the term joining for those cases in which the second party continues the conversation, while the term accession is applied to those cases in which the second party through his or her contribution declares himself or herself in agreement with the previous communication.

7. "Wenn wir von," "Kommunikationsmedien" sprechen, meinen wir immer die operative Verwendung der *Differenz* von medialem Substrat und Form. Kommunikation ist nur, und das ist unsere Antwort auf das Unwahrscheinlichkeitsproblem, als Prozessieren dieser Differenz möglich.

8. "leisten ein neuartige Verknüpfung von Konditionierung und Motivation."

9. "Verstehen ist Verstehen der Handhabung von Selbstreferenz."

10. I use the term control here exclusively in the sense of the form of control which can be established through communication. This means that the concept of control cannot be attributed to any other form of causality than the one which the communication ensures, and this is highly uncertain, as it includes the selection of understanding of what has been agreed upon by at least two parties, and as the parties must take into account the possibility of pretense in the communication of consent and agreement.

References

Baecker, D. (1999). Wenn etwas der Fall ist, steckt auch etwas dahinter. In *Niklas Luhmann. Wirkungen eines Theoretikers*. Stichweh, R. (Ed.). Bielefeld: Verlag.

Einsiedler, W. (1997). Unterrichtsqualität und Leistungsentwiklung: Litteraturüberblick. In *Entwicklung im Grundschulalter* (pp. 225–40). F. E. Weinert and A. Helmke (Eds.). Hemsbach: Beltz.

Glasersfeld, E. von. (1995). *Radical constructivism: A way of knowing and learning.* London, Washington: Falmer.

Hofstadter, D. (1979). *Gödel, Escher, Bach: An eternal golden braid.* Sussex: Penguin.

Leydesdorff, L. (2002). The communication turn in the theory of social system. *Systems Research and Behavioral Science, 19*: 129–36.

Luhmann, N. (1986). Systeme verstehen Systeme. In *Zwischen Intranparenz und Verstehen,* (pp. 72–117). N. Luhmann and K. E. Schorr (Eds.). Frankfurt am Main: Suhrkamp.

———. (1990). *Essays on self reference.* New York: Columbia University Press.

———. (1993). "Was ist der Fall?" und "Was steckt dahinter?" Die zwei Soziologien und die Gesellschaftstheorie. *Zeitschrift für Soziologie 22*(4): 245–60.

———. (1995a). *Social systems.* J. Bednartz Jr. and D. Baecker (Trans.). Stanford, CA: Stanford University Press.

———. (1995b). Intersubjektivität oder Kommunikation: Unterschiedliche Ausgangspunkte soziologischer Theoriebildung. In *Soziologische Aufklärung* (Vol. 6) (pp. 66–91). N. Luhmann (Ed.). Opladen, Westdeutscher: Verlag.

———. (1995c). Probleme mit operativer Schliessung. In *Soziologische Aufklärung* (Vol. 6) (pp. 12–24) N. Luhmann (Ed.). Opladen, Westdeutscher: Verlag.

———. (1996). *Die neuzeitlichen Wissenschaften und die Phänomenologie.* Wien, Picus: Verlag.

———. (1997). *Die Gesellschaft der Gesellschaft.* Frankfurt am Main: Suhrkamp.

Maturana, H. R. (1975). The organization of the living: A theory of the living organization. *Man-machine studies* (7): 313–32.

Ranson, S. (1994). *Towards the learning society.* London: Cassell.

Rasmussen, J. (1998). Constructivism and phenomenology—what do they have in common, and how can they be told apart. *Cybernetics and systems 29*(6): 553–76.

Schoor, K. E. (1986). Das Verstehensdefizit der Erziehung und die Pädagogik. In *Zwischen Intransparenz und Verstehen.* N. Luhmann and K. E. Schorr (Eds.). Frankfurt am Main: Suhrkamp. (pp. 11–39).

Shannon, C. E., and W. Weaver. (1964). *The mathematical theory of communication.* Urbana: University of Illinois Press.

Spencer-Brown, G. (1969). *Laws of form.* New York: Julian.

Stichweh, R. (2000). Systems theory as an alternative to action theory? The rise of 'communication' as a theoretical option. *Acta Sociologica, 43*(1): 5–13.

Weaver, W. (1948). Science and complexity. *American Scientist, 36*(4): 536–44.

10

On the Critical Paradoxes of Cupid and Curriculum

> When in love, the partners have to put up with the paradoxical nature of intimate communication, indeed, they have to use it expressively.
>
> Niklas Luhmann, *Love as Passion*

In a fascinating study that attempts a selective investigation into fresh differentiation that takes place in a related semantic field or symbolic media of communication[1] prior to the emergence of new ways of acting in social relationships, Niklas Luhmann (1986) has looked at love as a symbolic code of communication using systems theoretical tools to interpret historical data. The primary argument is that symbolic media running through meaning complexes pave the way, as it were, and create successful conditions or otherwise for certain actions to become possible in social relationships. Dipping selectively into some of the literary writings of the past three centuries, Luhmann traces important shifts in the "general symbolic media" that occurred in the semantics of love before social relationships in that domain took a different turn.

Like Michel Foucault, Luhmann works within a posthumanist framework,[2] but unlike Foucault's archaeology that speaks in terms of the power of discourse over bodies, Luhmann's analysis follows the system/environment distinction demonstrating "the non-random character of variations in social relations," entertaining the possibility thereby of looking at the "genesis of particular discourses and their subsequent disappearance" (1986, 4). Luhmann shows that such transformations are not individual or random, but "occur by means of the differentiation of various symbolically generalized media of communication" (5). Methodologically, the issue is treated by Luhmann not within the realms of the sociology of knowledge but as a problem of *observing observations*, or what Heinz von Foerster (1984) has called "second order cybernetics."

Using this methodology, Luhmann treats "society as a social system that consists solely of communications and therefore as a system that can only reproduce communications by means of communications" (1986, 4). Understood in this manner, the tendencies and shifts displayed by societal relations can be seen as a general problem of communication, and love appears not so much as a feeling, "but rather a code of communication," a construct, according to the rules of which one could form, express, and disseminate feelings (20).

The present chapter deals with only a small facet of this larger theoretical effort and will attempt to bring out some of the interesting implications of this research for curriculum deliberation. The part that I am concerned with here is what Luhmann calls the reflexivity or *self-referentiality* of love in modern times. To briefly state the general direction of the study, Luhmann's analysis shows that prior to the seventeenth century love was attributive: it was related to the beauty, grace, virtue, or other characteristics of the beloved, love being justified by and directed toward these qualities. Subsequently, there was a shift toward idealism and love came to be associated with images of the loved one in the lover's mind rather than dependent on any inherent characteristics of the lover. Love was freed from external attributes and driven inward—beauty was in the beholder. And finally, modern times saw yet another major shift, this time toward *self-referentiality* or *reflexion*.[3] Love now was purged of its attributive aspect as well as of idealism, and instead the notion of love for love's sake began to appear in the generalized symbolic media related to *amour*. In other words, "it was possible to justify love by the inexplicable *fact that one loved*" (44).

But this *self-referentiality* was at the same time faced with unique semantic difficulties and involved greater improbabilities for intimacy. Love for love's sake brought in its wake certain inevitable paradoxes of reflexivity and communication.[4] As Luhmann says: "When in love, the partners have to put up with the paradoxical nature of intimate communication" (1986, 56), and what is more, they have to learn to expressly use this paradoxicality to enhance communication and the quality of intimacy. It is in these paradoxes that I am interested here for these can throw light on other fields like education that are strongly dependent on generalized symbolic media and that require close communication. What makes the paradoxes interesting is that they demanded new ways of solving problems, new leaps in action and transformations that were not apparent in the situation itself. The paradoxicality became a guarantee of new worlds-in-action.

These paradoxes, I argue, have a useful bearing on curriculum, and as will be evident on examining them, making a connection across these two domains appears legitimate. While I am not suggesting that the history of curriculum shows parallel evolution with the semantics of love, although certainly there are resonances in that curriculum has gone through behavioristic, psychologistic, and informationally oriented phases, it is enough for our present purposes to allow the case that just as in Luhmann's analysis love is seen as a symbolic mode of communication, we can look at education as nothing other than a system of communication that differentiates at various junctures and generates other communication. That is to say, they may be considered as specific instances of a broader attempt to consider the functioning of generalized symbolic media in order to examine them under systems theoretic constraints. To reiterate, our interest is in the paradoxes that are generated in the communicative process. We will begin by looking at some of the paradoxes that the shift in the general semantics of love produced followed by a discussion on what these might mean for education.

Paradoxes

Paradox of Communication

When love is not directed toward attributes and nor is it a form of romantic idealism, that is, when love is self-conscious expression as in more differentiated circumstances, the situation would imply that communicational interchange becomes central. But interestingly enough there is a paradox in this—sometimes communication itself may hinder rather than enhance love. As Luhmann (1986) says:

> Love is able to enhance communication by largely doing without any communication. It makes use primarily of indirect communication, relies on anticipation and on having already understood. And love can thus be damaged by explicit communication, by questions and answers, because such openness would indicate that something had not been understood as a matter of course . . . In other words, the lover does not need to be tuned in by action, questions or requests on the part of the beloved: the latter's inner experience is supposed to immediately trigger off the lover's actions. (25)

Overt utterances that should have been implicitly understood calls into question the depth of one's love; it suggests that there is an important lack of awareness of the beloved's inner world and therefore a sense of diminished intensity between the pair. To avoid this, therefore, there must often be communication without actually communicating, that is, exchange by other means. The paradox triggers new ways of solving problems of communication.

Paradox of Two Worlds

Among the developments which led up to the modern world, one key transformation was the new meaning given to the notion of individuality. The transition from stratified to functional differentiation[5] of societies brought about greater diversity of individual attributes and led to a sense of enhanced individual differences. "Individuals are all the more provoked," says Luhmann (1986), "into interpreting the difference between themselves and the environment in terms of their own person . . . the ego . . . and the environment loses most of its contours" (15). Individuals now have to find affirmation in the difference between themselves and their environment and "in the manner in which they deal with this difference" (16). Owing to this focus on the self as a measure of difference from the environment, society and the world-at-large tend to appear "much more complex and impenetrable." There arises as a result a greater need for a "close world" that one could make "one's own." That is to say, our individualism forces upon us the need for a private world as the world "out there" appears too distant and remote. But, according to Luhmann (1986):

> A concept of increasing personal individualization does not adequately pinpoint the problems which individuals have to overcome in the modern world, for they cannot simply fall back on their autonomy and the resulting adaptation this entails. What is more, the individual person needs the *difference* between a *close* world and a distant, impersonal one, i.e. the *difference* between only personally valid experiences, assessments and reactions and the anonymous, universally accepted world—in order to be shielded from the immense complexity and contingency of all the things that could be deemed possible. (16)

The increasing individualization must invent a *close* world which paradoxically limits the growth parameters or degrees of freedom for further individualization. This emphasis on personal uniqueness or the *difference* between personal *system* and environment also makes the probability of intimate interchange or communicative love more improbable due to the necessity of internalizing a substantive part of the other person's *close* world, increasing also the chances of incompatibility between different *close* worlds. The interesting proliferation of diverse worlds at one level begins to limit possibilities of further differentiation and leans toward solipsism. This paradox again calls for novel ways of overcoming problems of communication like rearranging feedback patterns, for instance.

Paradox of Non-Observability

This paradox follows from the earlier one. Luhmann (1986) observes that:

> Information is the selective treatment of differences whereby the person experiencing something projects occurrences onto a horizon of other possibilities and sets the limits of his own system by the experience of "this and not something else" or "this and not that." Which, and when further alternatives function as the

comparative matrix for the others, can hardly be assessed from outside the respective system, and yet information is not observable without taking this selective horizon into account. (24)

The implication of this is that one must somehow participate in the other person's self-referential system in order to understand or reconstruct the horizon on which that person projects experience, and yet that horizon is essentially unobservable. That is to say, although we are paying close attention to the loved one, we cannot really see the inner horizon that sets the "biases" of the system nor the selective mappings of experience which are the clues to action. And yet the lover must demonstrate that s/he is on familiar terrain. The only way to make this improbable step possible is by surpassing the observable in some manner. In other words, the way around this is to make some kind of intuitive leaps that can successfully organize action in the area of love. In theoretic terms, the double contingency obtaining under conditions of heightened differentiation makes love probable only in the presence of further differentiation and selection with the possibility that one of those selections will satisfy the expectations of the unseen horizon.

Paradox of Reflexivity

Most social systems become stabilized around repetitive patterns or goals. Theoretically speaking, feedback systems appear giving rise to recurring patterns that may be sustained. For example, in the period of courtly love as well as in the romantic period, love's main objective was to win the hand of the beloved in marriage. In other words, love sought out a homeostasis, an equilibrium as its fulfillment. But with greater differentiation this stage was surpassed. Love as passion has no goal other than love itself. According to Luhmann (1986):

> Once a special semantics has become sufficiently differentiated, the processes ordered by this medium can also become self-referential. Self-referentiality at this level of communicative processes will be termed *reflexivity*. Assuming that this special phenomenon becomes sufficiently isolated, then one can postulate that love is only motivated by love, i.e. love refers to love, seeks love, and grows to the extent that it finds love and can fulfill itself as love. (30)

Having no other goal outside of itself, love becomes reflexive, motivated only by itself. This self-referentiality makes intimacy improbable for it needs endless differentiation within reflexivity to maintain its viability. In terms of theory, positive feedback must occur and yet the system must not collapse.[6]

Paradox of Identity

It is not enough merely to assert love; it must find expression in specific acts. Attitudes such as love require sufficient individualization or differentiation so that those attitudes can be read unambiguously in actions of the lover. In other words, the actions must be such that it becomes possible for the beloved to establish a durable connection or an identity relation between the action and the lover. And yet this identity itself becomes problematic if it appears too fixed:

> One's identity has to be put at risk as a dynamic rather than static guarantor of permanence, i.e. not as "this is the way it always is" but as growing through love. Referring to one's identity initially gives clear contours to one's independence both from extraneous circumstances and from the influence of others. [Subsequently] the semantic properties of such reference have to be erased and/or replaced: by a concept of identity-in-transformation. (37)

While identity may be necessary to provide the security of a stable relation between the lover and her/his actions, paradoxically, this stable contour proves to be harmful to future transactions as it runs the risk of becoming too crystallized and therefore in conflict with the other's world. The semantics of identity must exhibit a certain fluidity so that it is apparent to the beloved that the lover is developing her/his self both through the beloved and through the love of the beloved. This paradoxical code must be maintained in every transaction whereby the contour is visible and yet is in the process of becoming.

Paradox of Fulfillment

Lovers strive to be happy in love. But to be happy and satisfied in love is a contradiction in terms: *"Si la possession est sans trouble, les desires ne sons plus qu'une habitude tiede"* (70–71) [If the possession is without disturbance, the desires are not anymore than a habit].[7] This habit formation or reification kills the passions. Therefore, the moment of fulfillment, paradoxically, spells the end of love. Again this calls for new levels of awareness and response:

> Precisely for this reason one had to hold resistance, detours or obstacles to one's love in high regard, because only through them does love endure . . . Love [exists] as the "not yet"; the moment of happiness and the eternity of suffering mutually determine each other. (71)

Hitting a plateau of stable relations in intimacy is therefore only a step away from indifference. On the other side, the greater the passion, the more tense and circumspect behavior toward each other tends to be. This happens because "both are unsure of the other and experience the situation as asymmetrical." Each thinks that the other may not be as deeply involved or feel as strongly. Each signal is judged for its extent of reciprocity and its "going-beyondness" by both parties. The double contingency makes for a great deal of uncertainty but at the same time a "spiral of enhancement" occurs (62).

These paradoxes must not be understood to imply a need for selection or decision between incompatible alternatives. Rather, they direct our attention to the level or intensity of expectations made in an intimate relationship. They force us to consider new ways of responding in order to make the improbable possible, refusing to allow those involved to settle down into habitual response patterns.

> It is interesting that much of the literature on classroom management itself refers to the importance of establishing routines. Could it be, by "settling down into habitual response patterns," we in fact deaden the potential for novelty, imagination, and creativity in learning?

Curriculum and Paradoxy

Let us next work with the above set of paradoxes to see what pragmatic insights into curriculum they can provide. But why at all must we assume that they should have a bearing on education? In general, paradoxicalization often helps to solve, or rather, *dis*solve structural problems of intimate communication. To put it differently, contradiction forces something to occur which would otherwise be impossible. First, in a paradoxicalized semantics, apparently opposing behaviors or attributes directed at the same thing find their meaningful place simultaneously: a thing might be good *and* bad at the same time in the same ways as both the presence *and* absence of the lover strengthens love. The exclusionary "or" is replaced by the inclusive "and." Second, it allows for a certain flexibility that is outside the code that guides it and serves to complexify the system, drawing out previously unsuspected possibilities of interchange. That is to say, the flexibility deinstitutionalizes systemic responses. Third, paradoxicalization of semantic codes or generalized symbolic media results in a certain amount of instability or disturbance to the system, creating a generative disequilibrium. New patterns of interchange can emerge as a result of this disequilibrium (see Fleener's introduction in this volume). And finally, "paradoxicalization makes possible a new form of distantiation from regulations, techniques and even from received attitudes" (66). In other words, the entry of paradox into semantics brings forth new forms of freedom by breaking free of regulated behavior patterns. These are some of the general advantages of paradoxicalization. Next we will consider the paradoxes discussed individually in the specific context of curriculum and pedagogy.

Let us begin with the first one—the paradox of communication. To recapitulate, this suggests that sometimes explicit communication itself may hinder further communication. Transposing this onto the pedagogic sphere, one upshot of this could be that by paying too much attention to *purposive* curricular communication harm is done to curiosity and the desire to learn. That is to say, the excessive deliberateness with which modernist schooling conducts itself ends up stifling the evolutionary disposition of the organism to learn. What would it mean to act otherwise? The paradoxicalization of curricular semantics would imply that we reverse or at least moderate the deadly sense of "purpose" that grips the generalized symbolic communicative media in education today (see Gregory Bateson, 1991). This sense of purpose instilled in the media semantics attempts to shield the individual from the "structural drift" (Maturana and Varela, 1998) that is a prime condition of all systems and directs effort toward stable goals. But this sealing off fails because education, like love, is too intimate an activity to be isolated from systemic movements that are more in the nature of drift than purposive activity.[8]

Second, we looked at the paradox of two-worlds: the fact that the individual needs the *difference* between a *close* world and a distant, impersonal one. With regard to the construction of symbolic media, this has clear significance for educational semantics. The era of positivism saw the proliferation of scientific/instrumentalist metaphors in curriculum deliberations that established a universally acknowledged world of knowledge whose epistemology was transparent and therefore invisible. But progressives have since moved to a more constructivist approach arguing for "close worlds" constructed both through individual experiences and social participation. Our analysis shows that by themselves each is insufficient. We need both an anonymous world that is beyond our individual horizons as well as a close personal one. It is in the play of differences between the two that we are able to make strategic moves of survival in the world. In other words, we have to acknowledge the system and the environment in order to perceive differences that make a difference. Just as overemphasis on the objectivity of the world destroys the truth of constant interpretation that the organism must undertake, the exclusive stress on constructivism or even social constructionism loses sight of the anonymous and universal features of the systemic environment that all must contend with.

Third, let us recall the paradox of non-observability whereby ego cannot observe alter's horizon and yet must make selections to demonstrate knowledge of the same. Transposing this to the domain of pedagogy, one could take this to imply that the student might be in the teacher's blind spot (just as the reverse might be true). Now, conventionally speaking, that notion immediately triggers alerts in the action spheres of multicultural awareness, multiple representations, student history, and other areas in which efforts might be made to clear up the deficiency. But systems theory shows us that it may not be a simple matter of removing the lack, and here lies an important theoretical issue: *each act of observation must necessarily generate a blind spot* as the observer cannot observe herself/himself observing (see Luhmann, 1989). No matter how hard s/he tries, the observer cannot include the vantage point in the act of observation. This suppression is not a lack, but what Luhmann calls "the guarantee of a world." It implies that all need not be in the glare of the known but instead it is the ability to shift from vantage point to vantage point that may provide for a more dynamic view of things. What this means is that there must be conscious cultivation of *flexibility* on the part of the observer, in this case the teacher and the taught, something not left to mere chance in the curriculum. This flexibility utilizes the blind spots to find new ways of considering things resulting in a much enriched and complex understanding. The paradoxicalization here demands a much enhanced awareness of the ways of approaching things.

Next we have the paradox of reflexivity wherein actions that attain self-referentiality principally do not seek fulfillment outside of themselves. It is in further differentiation that their accomplishment lies. This has important implications for curriculum. Instrumentalist and utilitarian views of education have traditionally emphasized goals and standards that are preset and extraneous to the process itself. Progressives like John Dewey, on the other hand, have challenged those views, arguing that the goals of education must be considered as immanent to the field. Paradoxicalization emphasizes that once a certain level of differentiation has taken place in the symbolic media of education, or the system has become sufficiently complex, the goals of learning can be nothing other than learning itself producing various states of intensity and proliferation of connections.

Fifth, let us recall the paradox of identity which shows that for a situation of close communication to thrive one's identity has to be put at risk as a dynamic rather than a static guarantor of permanence. Situationally speaking, the teacher presents a contour of her/himself that serves as a beneficial anchor for the learner as well as for the teacher. But if this contour or teacher identity becomes reified, or is of settled appearance, it gets in the way of considering things afresh. It results in a diminished sense of teacher-becoming in and through interaction with knowledge, leaving the student with the false impression that knowledge is extraneous to selfhood. Just as the lover may be too caught up in him/herself to have the possibility of co-evolving with the alter, the teacher may project a "fully finished" personality that does not exhibit the possibility of movement in knowledge. And yet, this connection between knowledge and identity is a vital one for learners to make for it establishes the clearest rationale for participating in the symbolic media of learning; it shows unequivocally the importance of the selections we make and the differences we generate. To avoid this schism, identity must be shown to be in a constant process of reconfiguration or fluidity; otherwise the conditions of learning or further differentiation tends to get attenuated.

This leads us to the final bit, to the paradox of fulfillment. The key part is habit formation. Knowledge itself can encourage destructive habits like imagining that everything can be in the known. It is the parallel to the ego's imagining of the final grasp of the semantics of love and the fully realized attention of the alter. The totalizing effect of "fulfillment," or in this case, the sense of having "arrived-in-knowledge" shuts out the ways in which the world continually escapes all description. While it is true that at any moment all we have is a description, but it is also the case that this description is made from somewhere by somebody, making the inherent limitations of the process quite apparent. This problem is also evident in our earlier examination of the blind spots. Therefore, to deny the paradoxicality in the knowing act is tantamount to denying the complexity of observing systems and trivializing the knowing process. Pedagogically, offering an understanding of the arising of knowledge as differences and distinctions within and between systems and between system and environment might be a good way to start weaning away from the seductions of "fulfillment."

Conclusion

Paradoxicalization has a long history. In earlier times it was achieved through irony and humor. It allowed systems to escape from closing in on themselves and jump to newer orbits and newer ways of responding to situations. Subsequently, Platonic idealism and its relentless drive toward representationalism seemed to have withered this process somewhat. All learning, like all communication, in a sense is about the difference between the thing learned and the world; otherwise one would be presented with the world itself in its full impossibility and without distinction. Paradoxy is simply an awareness and acknowledgment of this overwhelming fact. When we are sufficiently overwhelmed, we seek new ways of responding and differentiating.

Notes

1. "Media" here is not used in the sense of the mass media, but in the sense of the "symbolically generalized media of interchange" as described by Talcott Parsons, in Social Systems and the evolution of action theory, New York, Free Press, 1977. Luhmann (1986) further explains: "I think of symbolic media as codes which offer relatively improbable communicative intentions . . . some prospects of success" (6). The media codes increase the "probability of the improbable."

2. Posthumanism appears with the exhaustion of the humanist "exaltation of the subject." It rejects the humanist individual as the indivisible or primary unit of social analysis and instead looks at sub-individual formations and alliances. The systems perspective is particularly suited to carry out posthumanist analyses as it looks at

world construction in terms of differences and distinctions and not in terms of unified entities.

3. A caveat must be registered here. Although historical epochs are being referred to, it must not be assumed that there were clear breaks or caesuras that marked these epochal thresholds. Rather, conditions appeared within the periods themselves which allowed for further differentiation to occur, and once these differences "asserted themselves," it was possible "to give past things a new value and make future things accessible in a new way" (Luhmann, 1986, 42).

4. Luhmann (1986) explains that "codes of generalized symbolic communicative media function to secure an adequate degree of probability for the reception of improbable expectations" (55). It is this basic paradox that enters the semantics of a particular field of relationships and then gives rise to other paradoxes as well as to further differentiation.

5. Stratified differentiation is one which is by class and landownership exhibited by premodern societies, whereas functional differentiation is by social roles like teacher, engineer, farmer, etc.

6. Positive feedback occurs when systemic changes are continually amplified in one direction by the outputs of the system itself. This results in what Gregory Bateson has called "runaway" conditions whereby the system spirals out of control (see *Mind and Nature: A Necessary Unity*, 1979.)

7. Here Luhmann quotes C. Jaulnay, *Questions d'amour*, in the original French. The translation is mine.

8. All difference is immanent within the system, and thus purpose can only be established from outside the system. To take a simple example, it is common to say, "He is shivering from the cold." But systemically speaking, the differences are triggering other differences that produce minor convulsions the net result of which is a rise in body temperature. There is no necessity to imagine an agency directing this process.

References

Bateson, G. (1979). *Mind and nature: A necessary unity.* New York: Dutton.

———. (1991). *A sacred unity: Further steps to an ecology of mind.* New York: Bessie.

Foerster, H. von. (1984). *Observing systems.* Seaside, CA: Intersystems Publications.

Luhmann, N. (1986). *Love as passion.* Cambridge, UK: Polity.

———. (1989). *Ecological communication.* Chicago: University of Chicago Press.

———. (1990). *Essays on self-reference.* New York: Columbia University Press.

Maturana, H., and F. Varela. (1998). *The tree of knowledge: The biological roots of human understanding.* Boston: Shambhala.

11

Classroom Dynamics and Emergent Curriculum

Imagining new realities for schooling is a difficult and complex endeavor that is often met with protest and challenge from outside influences and public opinion. Our best efforts for change are often complicated by our own beliefs and ideas about schooling and perhaps an inability to see beyond traditional ideas about pedagogy and education. Envisioning alternatives for education calls on our ability to question critically not only our own educational experiences but also to question current education practices, constraints, and limitations, and our own ideas about curriculum and learning. Inextricably linked with questioning our own views and those of others must be a desire for change and transformation if we are ever to move beyond the current and traditional approaches to education. William Pinar (2001) states:

> Education is—will we ever learn?—no mechanical affair, and yet, astonishingly, much of the field and the public still seems to proceed upon the assumption that if we only make the appropriate adjustments—in the curriculum, teaching, learning, administration. . . "standards"—then those test scores will soar. (13–14)

Is it possible for us to transform schooling; to see beyond simply attempting to make adjustments in order to raise test scores or better prepare students for the next course in the sequence? How do we envision something different when we are entrenched in a system based on mechanistic notions of order, control, and cause and effect? Can we truly create learning environments with our students that allow them to be engaged in meaningful learning amidst the current constraints of standardized testing and public opinion?

Fleener (2002) suggests that in "exploring the possibilities of and creating curriculum futures, we must address our own boogie man; those ideas, practices, and goals that have constrained our ability to change, adapt or create a new reality for schooling" (12). Is our "boogie man," as Fleener states, "our own fears of change and our own unquestioning acceptance" of the way things are? Or, are these constraints that limit our ability to create alternatives in education imposed from the outside? Are they universally constraining for all educators and readily identifiable or are they more subtle and tacitly accepted? What can be done to foster questioning, challenge our thinking, and create a sense of freedom for educators to envision change and alternatives for schooling and curriculum?

Perhaps in order to envision new realities for schooling, to create dynamic learning environments in which students are invited to participate in meaningful ways, we must consider something qualitatively different for our classrooms. In our efforts to transform school we need to move beyond the rhetoric of reform and the back-and-forth cycles often associated with school reform. We must attempt to "re-create heart" (Fleener, 2002)—"revive schools as places of learning/doing" (Fleener, Adolphson, and Reeder, 2002) and in doing so we must begin to consider ". . . curriculum as the 'complicated conversation' of the participants" (Pinar, 2001, 19). Applebee (1996) describes curricular conversation as comprising the following:

> A series of...discussions taking place over time—weeks or semesters or even years. As they continue to explore the domain, students come to be more effective participants in the larger conversation: Their contributions will grow in scope and complexity; their actions will be surer; their sense of mastery will increase. As they explore new aspects of the domain, their discoveries help them construe and reconstrue the domain as a whole. Engagement with new texts and new issues does not simply expand their knowledge of the tradition, but also casts light on texts and issues that have been discussed before. (44)

As curriculum and pedagogical practices in the classroom give way from linear, lock step approaches to those characterized by the ebb and flow and dynamical interactions of a conversation, as Applebee describes, students can begin to create something whole and meaningful just as a weaver can create a whole beautiful cloth from contrasting threads. Participation in curriculum conversations, which are driven by interaction, relations, and recursion, places students in a rich and complexly dynamic environment in which they can be engaged in meaningful learning. As the complex web of interactions, relationships, and understanding is woven and develops in the classroom, the curriculum emerges as a conversation simultaneously with and as space is created by the teacher and the students.

To offer a context for a curriculum that emerges as "complicated conversation," as a dance of interaction between and among the teacher and the students, I will explore how one middle school mathematics teacher has transformed his way of thinking about curriculum, teaching, and learning. Moving beyond simply making adjustments to his method, now embracing a "global" perspective of curriculum, he creates with and for his students, space for the curriculum to emerge as a conversation as the students in his classes work to solve problems and interact with one another to develop their own relationship with and understanding of mathematics. Students bring to the conversation their own contrasting and varied understandings as they explore mathematics as the study of patterns and relationships and develop their own understanding of and connection with mathematics.

Transformative Change: Moving Beyond Reform

Postmodern thinking promulgates a new paradigm of holism, one imbued with concepts of relationship, self-organization, recursion, order emerging from chaos, and meaning making. This way of thinking values systemic relations and runs in contrast to the control and reductionistic underpinnings of the modern paradigm from which our current education system and our ideas about education have grown and developed.

Postmodern thinking has emerged in response to modernist beliefs as a modification or reconstruction of the basic principles of modernism. These basic principles, based on the belief that there exists universal and natural laws governing both the physical and social worlds, are not considered entirely wrong from a postmodern perspective. Rather they are viewed as becoming idealized to the point that the individual assumptions upon which they were founded are no longer recognized. Postmodernism, then, has been defined as a "rejection," "reconstruction," and/or "framing" of modernist ideas (e.g., Doll, 1993; Fletcher, 2000; Spretnak, 1991). Postmodernism is also considered by some to be a transition between modernism and a new paradigm forthcoming; transitory in the sense that while it attempts to deny and reconstruct the tenets of modernism it needs history and process in order to emerge. William Doll (1993) discusses postmodernism as a "radical change."

> [W]e are in the midst of radical intellectual, social, and political change. We are shifting paradigms (maybe even megaparadigms) from those of a modernist nature to those of a post-modernist nature: post-structural, post-philosophical, post-patriarchal, post-industrial, post-national. In disciplines from architecture to theology, foundations are being shattered. In fact, the concept of foundations, itself, is now challenged. We are entering a new, eclectic, "post" era. In this era, the past will not disappear but will be reframed continually in the light of an ongoing, changing present. (157)

Postmodernism transforms and transcends modernism rather than rejecting it entirely, creating a tension between the past and the present, a strain between rejecting the old for the new and connecting the old with the new. As Doll describes:

> Connecting and transforming modernism with "post" thinking will not be easy. Modernism is so well ensconced in our language and thought that its most basic assumptions seem self-evident. It is only "natural" to talk of imposing order,

connecting effects with causes, transmitting ideas, and finding truth through scientific methodology. (157)

The transformation of education, the connecting and transforming of our modernist notions about schooling will not be easy.

Discussion of reform often includes, with good intentions, ideas about and plans for "improving what we have" and "raising what is expected" or "better preparing students" and, although there is certainly nothing wrong with any of these propositions, it is rare that these discussions embrace the idea of doing something qualitatively different. They tend to simply dance around the periphery of doing things better in some way or another. These discussions shed light on our attempts to address what we view as problems in education from a modern perspective. We

> The word "reform" itself suggests *mere rearranging* of given structures, rather than the kind of transformative changes suggested here. How would transforming a classroom differ from reforming it?

think that a specific change will cause a certain outcome or if there is more order in the curriculum, that if everyone is teaching the same thing using similar methods, then student learning will improve and scores will be better.

The reform movement for school mathematics has been no different. Efforts for change in mathematics education have been persistent and ongoing since the National Council of Teachers of Mathematics (NCTM) was established in 1920. The discussion of issues in mathematics education has fluctuated between the NCTM's stance against the so called "back-to-basics" movement of the 1970s to their current stance against the "mathematically correct" movement of the 1990s to a focus on "students as mathematical problem solvers," and to their notion of students becoming "mathematically empowered" (NCTM, 1989; NCTM, 1991). Despite the longevity of and purpose of the NCTM's efforts, qualitative change has seemingly not been affected for school mathematics (Schmidt, McKnight, and Raizen, 1996). Kilpatrick and Stanic (1995) state that:

> *Reform* may be too strong a word to characterize developments in mathematics education at any point over the past century. Professional and public discussion of issues in mathematics education ebbs and flows. School mathematics continually changes, but it has yet to achieve a form substantially different from that being established in the closing years of the last century. (14)

They further contend that "true reform...may require not doing something better but something different" (15).

The focus of the reform movement in mathematics education has been on making adjustments in the curriculum, changing how mathematics is taught, considering and reconsidering what mathematics is taught, and "raising" the standards rather than a change or transformation in our orientation about curriculum. In order for us to envision and develop curriculum alternatives that are substantially and qualitatively different than our attempts to simply make "things" better we need to question critically and challenge our traditional ideas about curriculum, mathematics, and what it means to know mathematics and we must have a desire for something different even if we cannot yet fully imagine or envision it. We need a desire for transformative change; change that goes beyond the back-and-forth cycles often associated with reform movements in education. If we are ever to embrace curriculum as a conversation, to envision it as an emergent dance of interactions between the teacher and students and their developing mathematical understanding, we need a transformation in our way of seeing and thinking; a change that reflects postmodern thinking, embracing notions of relationship and recursion.

Curricular Conversations

Patterns and Relationships

By considering the classroom dynamics and emergent curriculum of Wesley's middle school mathematics classroom (Reeder, 2002), a picture of how teachers can develop space in their classrooms in which students are invited to be co-creators of and participants in curriculum as conversation may emerge. Wesley's story is one of his own personal transformation as a teacher and the simultaneous transformation of what happens in his classroom. His transition from traditional teaching approaches, to a focus primarily on problem solving—thus, going beyond "teaching as method," and instead, thinking of "teaching as relationships of meaning"—may provide insight for other teachers as they struggle to make similar changes in their own classrooms.

Wesley teaches seventh grade pre-algebra and algebra I in a middle- to upper-class suburban public school on the outskirts of a large city in a Southern plains state. Over the past several years he has won numerous awards and received statewide recognition for his innovative teaching. No longer using a textbook as his curriculum, Wesley engages his students in an ongoing conversation; one driven by his belief that mathematics is the study of patterns and relationships and the presentation of worthwhile mathematical tasks, student interaction, and hermeneutical listening (Davis, 1997).

About ten years ago Wesley attended a professional development summer workshop on problem centered learning (Wheatley, 1991). During this workshop he was asked the question "What is mathematics?" which perturbed his thinking about what mathematics he taught and his pedagogical practices. Wesley reflects:

I think...that question "What is mathematics?"—it started me thinking. Until that point I had never thought about what mathematics was except basically nothing more than addition, subtraction, multiplication, and division of fractions, decimals, and whole numbers for me as a middle school teacher. So I think this is what really started it. That's when perturbation really started for me. That question really caused some disturbance in my world. [Reeder, 2002]

At this workshop a definition of mathematics as the study of patterns and relationships was presented as part of the discussion with articles for the participants to read that supported this idea. Wesley began the following school year with this question and new definition of mathematics on his mind and with the conviction that he would begin to try to implement more problem solving into his teaching and more opportunities for his students to work together interacting in groups. Prior to attending this workshop he had already begun to have students work in groups for certain activities. However, describing his pedagogical practices ten years ago as "traditional" and "teacher centered," Wesley initially viewed these activities as something extra his students could do to explore certain topics on occasion and in addition to his planned curriculum or textbook assignments.

As Wesley began to implement some of the ideas he learned about in the workshop and in his readings, such as more problem solving and allowing the students to work in small groups and then present their findings at the end of class, he began to listen to his students. It was not long before he realized the potential for such activities for students. Wesley's providing the students with more opportunities to talk with one another, interacting to solve problems, provided him with more opportunities to listen to them and converse with them about ideas they were wrestling with and those that made sense. This began a process of change in his classroom. As he listened to his students, Wesley began to realize the importance of listening to his students. In order for him to listen to his students they had to be doing the talking, which meant that he had to ask questions and work to develop an environment that focused on and valued the students' thoughts and ideas rather than his alone. Wesley's role as teacher began to shift from that of "transmitter" of knowledge to that of one who interacts with his students and learns along side them—he began to do less of the talking.

In addition to the initial workshop, Wesley had the opportunity for the next several years to attend similar workshops each summer. Wesley purposively asked questions each year and began immediately to search for "good" problems he could offer his students for them to solve. He began to search for readings and for people he could communicate with that he felt could offer him support and ideas in his desire and quest to transform his pedagogical practices; to ultimately transform his classroom into a place where he and his students are engaged in an ongoing conversation of and about mathematics, patterns, and relations.

Rather than being some final product of his ongoing attempts to change from one pedagogic approach to another, what currently happens in Wesley's classroom is the expression of his beliefs about mathematics teaching and learning wherein a way of communicating with his students about mathematics is the learning environment in his classroom. What Wesley does with his students is more than a model or a set of steps that someone else could follow to create the same thing, it is an orientation about what is mathematics and what it means to teach and learn mathematics, one that views the classroom as a community, the teacher as co-learner, and the curriculum as an ongoing conversation. As stated by Wesley:

> You probably need to be one that is solving problems and enjoys solving and so it can't be done unless you yourself are looking at problems for relationships and for patterns and looking at the richness of activities trying to see those connections that exist in these kinds of tasks we propose. . . . I also...would look at the classroom as a community, not the students interacting, but it is a classroom where there are adults and students interacting and ideas are valued over methods and right answers. . . . I really think that is an issue for some folks who have not taken that step or have not had the opportunity to see what could really be going on with learning. . . . Until you really embrace it . . . it has taken me a really long time to get to where I am at in looking at things from a more global perspective—looking at the bigger picture. [Reeder, 2002]

While Wesley certainly believes he is in a different place in his thinking about mathematics and that his pedagogic practices are entirely different than those a decade ago, he sees himself as still working to make sense of "all of this" as a teacher, a problem solver, and a learner alongside of and with his students.

> I think I continue to look more and continue to appreciate more and I am always looking for the patterns that exist. . . . See, this relationship is something that is new for me, I've had that as part of my vocabulary but I am really now seeing the relationships that exist. Okay mathematics is the study of patterns and I know what patterns are but what of these relationships. I mean I'm evolving in my understanding even 10 years later just seeing those relationships. I learn from the students and their different ways of looking at things and thinking about things continually and that's really exciting. (Reeder, 2002)

This process that began for Wesley and became evident in his pedagogic practices a decade ago is continual and ongoing, propelled, and infused by the contrasting ideas that each student brings to the classroom varying ways of exploring topics and problems, and developing individual relationships with mathematics. As each year begins with new classes of students a newness of experience and the recursion associated with considering some of the same topics and problems in algebra and pre-algebra again creates for Wesley an opportunity to continue to learn and investigate with his students incorporating their ways of making sense and understanding.

Establishing Space for Conversation

Working with students to develop a community of learners each year with each new class and establishing relationships built on trust and respect and the valuing of one another's thinking is something Wesley believes must be deliberately fostered. Attempting to create space for his students to participate in a conversation, at the beginning of each year Wesley strives to establish sociomathematical norms (Cobb, 1995; Yackel and Cobb, 1996) in which students are expected to discuss their thinking. The sociomathematical norms of his classroom reflect that what is valued is their thinking. Wesley deliberately sets out discussing with his students that his mathematics class is "different." Much like the popular automobile advertisement that claims "This is not your mother's Oldsmobile," Wesley says to his students, "This mathematics class is not going to be like others that you've had." Wesley's students come to his class as seventh graders with seven or eight years of school mathematics experiences. They have been involved in mathematics classes where most of their work has been done independently, where practice, drill, and speed have indicated understanding and competency. In the words of one of Wesley's students from a few years ago, "in our other classes 'textbook was king.'" Wesley says:

> When we talk about our class and their other classes I want to be careful that it is not a discussion geared at one way is good and the other is bad. I don't want them to think negatively of their previous teacher but I do want them to realize that what we are going to be doing in this class is different. [Interview data]

Wesley believes that an important part of initially engaging his students in interactions with one another is helping them to question and break through their preconceived notions about how mathematics is taught.

In addition to Wesley's first communications with his students that "This mathematics class will be different than the others you've had," he keeps no secrets from the students regarding his beliefs about mathematics, how those beliefs inform his selection of tasks, and that what he values in his class is their ideas and their thinking. The syllabus for each of Wesley's classes states, "This course will differ from the conventional approach in both method and content." He further explains in the syllabus that students will develop their own methods for solving problems, listen to one another, work together, and participate in whole class discussions. Wesley also emphasizes that while there is a grade scale, he will also consider the students' initiative, attitude, cooperation, participation, and persistence, those things that are not easily measured with exams and assignments when making final determinations regarding grades. In other materials he distributes to his students, Wesley reiterates the expectations in this "different" kind of mathematics class with statements such as "expect to be puzzled or stumped," "expect to work together . . . to negotiate your methods and understanding with others," "expect to explain your thinking to others," "expect a task/problem to require investigation and time," and "expect the possibility of more than one solution or answer." Initially, Wesley continually encourages his students to work with one another and to begin to rely on one another rather than on him. He stresses that each student's thinking and ideas are as important and valued as his with statements such as "If you have a question, ask your teammate. Do not ask your teacher" and "listen carefully" to your teammate.

> These expectations create spaces for open and dynamic mathematical conversations, multiple connections, and relational approaches to learning.

Ebbs and Flows of Classroom Conversations

Discourse, argumentation, and negotiation among the students with their peers and their teacher are hallmarks of Wesley's classroom as students grapple to make sense of the problems they are solving and to devise their own ways of finding solutions as part of their participation in an ongoing conversation. Tasks are selected for students to consider based on the task's potential to provide challenge for the students and creating discussion and questions that will perturb their thinking. Task selection is not random nor are the tasks laid out in some linear or predetermined order that will get the students to a "certain point." Rather, tasks are chosen based on their potential for meaning to the students in their continued and developing understanding and the potential for the task to infuse the ongoing conversation. The following vignette provides an example of students in Wesley's class working together, trying to integrate their previous knowledge of integers in a problem designed to provide an opportunity for students to develop understanding of functions and linear relations.

Wesley provided several "What's my number?" problems for the students to consider as homework for the previous night (similar problems can be found in Wheatley and Reynolds, 1999, and Wheatley and Abshire, 2002). The class spent the entire fifty-minute class period discussing the first problem and sharing their ideas and understandings of integers as they related to this problem (see Figure 11.1).

Wesley: Let's maybe start off looking at a few of our Guess My Number problems from last night. We may not spend too much time here but let's look at number 1 and see what happens. (The page of six problems is displayed using the overhead projector.) Does anyone want to start us off?

Hailey: Well, when I looked at it you add 5. You add 5 to 3 and get 8. You add 5 to 4 and get 9 and so on l you add 5 and get 6. But instead of adding to get to –21 I went higher in the negative by 5 and go –26. (Comes to the board to illustrate as she talks drawing a number line and marking it

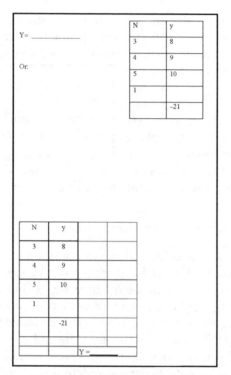

**Figure 11.1 "Guess My Number" Problem. (Inspired by
Wheatley and Reynolds, 1999; Wheatley and Abshire, 2002)**

with 0 and –21). If you are adding 5 then you would have to start somewhere back here in the negatives (she points to the left of –21). So you go
–21, –22, –23, –24, –25, –26, and you get –26.

Several students interject that the rule should be y = n + 5 and the class
agrees. Martha raises her hand.

Martha: I want to say something about what Hailey has up there because
I did it different. I took –21 and then minus 5 (–21 –5) and then you change
it to a positive so you get –21 + –5 = –26. That's the way I was taught last
year.

Wesley: What do you think about Hailey's method?

Martha: I used to do it that way too until my teacher last year showed me
how to change the signs.

Kathy jumps in.

Kathy: I might be completely "whacked out" but I think it is –17.
Because if you are on a number line—we are adding 5 (comes to the board to
demonstrate) I agree with the rule. But if you start at –21 on a number line
and you add 5 you have to go right because if you are at 0 and you add 5 you
have to go right because 0 + 5 = 5.

Then a little later in the conversation:

Tim: Well you're not adding 5 to –21 that's your answer. You are ending up at –21. You are starting at something else and end at –21.

Wesley: We all have to be willing to share what we are thinking. That's how we are going to learn from one another and maybe make sense of some of things.

Jill: Well, Kathy said –17 and Martha and Hailey said –26 but I think it is –16. (Comes to the board.) I've always been taught that when you are on this side (left side) of the zero you go left when you add so you start at –16 and go +5 to the left and land on –21.

Wesley asks Jill to demonstrate 2 + 3 and –2 + 3 on the board using her approach with the number line and she does so.

Jill: No, that's not right (referring to what she had demonstrated on the board). If it's a positive you go right and if it's negative you go left.

Sheila: Why did you start with –16?

Jill: I just started with 16 and added 5 and got 21 so I just changed it to negative and then thought about it on the number line.

Bobby: I don't agree with how you are doing it. I think you are doing the way you do it when you add a negative not a positive.

Many students at this point began to express frustration at the lack of an obvious and certain resolution to the problem they initially felt was simple.

Wesley: You know, that is okay because once we can get to a point that we have some disturbance then we can really get to a place where we can explore some things, listen to each other and maybe make some sense of things.

Several other students shared the ways they thought about the problem and their answer using a number line approach or some way that they had been taught in a previous year by another teacher before Gina interjected her different way of thinking about the problem.

Gina: Everyone has been showing those other ways, like changing signs and the number line but I have been sitting here thinking about it like, if I owed my dad 21 dollars and then I did some babysitting and earned 5 dollars then I would owe him 21 dollars. Right? But for this problem the 21 dollars is what I owe my dad after I pay him the 5 dollars I earn babysitting so maybe I owed him 26 dollars to begin with—I don't know. That's just what I think because I'm not sure about those other ways now. I am kind of confused about those now.

This discussion continued for the remainder of the class period with students interjecting their thoughts and ideas and commenting on what one another said. Wesley did not end class with summing up what he thought the students had discussed or what they were supposed to have learned today, but rather class simply ended with the students' trust and knowing that this conversation would continue the next day or would weave in as part of the ongoing conversation on a later day as they considered a similar problem.

This vignette, taken from Wesley's classroom during the first few weeks of school, captures what is typical in his classroom. Also highlighted is Wesley's working with the students, encouraging them throughout to rely on their own ideas and to discuss and challenge one another's thinking. As each day passes at the

> Part of embracing dynamism is resisting premature closure. It may that there is a tension between the premature closure side of "summing up" and the self-referential, recursive side of "summing up." Learning when and how to emphasize one aspect of an act over another is one of the under explored elements of teaching from a complex perspective.

beginning of the school year in Wesley's class his encouraging and urging the students to work together and trust that he is not looking for "right" answers but rather concerned with what they are thinking gives way to his total participation in the classroom as a learner. As the students begin to fully participate in the conversation, Wesley's role shifts to that of learner as he moves throughout the room while students work together, listening to them and interjecting questions not only to perturb the students' thinking but also for his own understanding (Davis, 1997). The focus in Wesley's classroom is not on what the teacher wants or what is the correct way to approach certain problems but rather on the students developing their own relationship with mathematics.

In the setting of Wesley's classroom, with his "global" perspective of curriculum, tasks are not seen as focusing on distinct concepts and separate from other ideas in mathematics as in traditional textbook-driven classrooms. The task, for example, discussed in the previous vignette is seen by Wesley as part of a much larger and ongoing discussion throughout the year that will involve the students in thinking about linear relations, variables, and functions. Rather than breaking the major ideas in algebra I and pre-algebra into separate bits and pieces to be studied and "mastered" in a linear order, Wesley's viewing the curriculum from a more "global" perspective also helps to create space for his students to explore and understand mathematics in their own way. If the curriculum were driven by the textbook, divided and ordered in a linear fashion, providing opportunities for students to discuss and talk about things would not accomplish the space needed for students to participate in a conversation in the same way they do in Wesley's room. If the direction of the discussion is controlled and driven by the textbook or the teacher rather than the students' interests and needs, then the opportunity for curriculum as a conversation is dampened.

As so beautifully seen in Wesley's classroom it is not only possible to envision new realities for schooling but they can be enacted as well. Through a process of change and transformation Wesley has considered and developed alternatives for his classroom. As he began to provide his students with more opportunities to work together and problem solve he began to listen to them. The shift in his listening to his students from that of "evaluative listening" or "listening for particular responses" (Davis, 1997, 363) to more "hermeneutical listening" which is the "sort of listening [that] is an imaginative participation in the formation and transformation of experience" (369), propelled the transformation process for Wesley placing him as a learner alongside and with his students. His initial perturbation arising from the question "What is mathematics?" proved to be a catalyst for a process of change and transformation in his way of thinking about mathematics and curriculum. Coupled with a desire for change, Wesley's hermeneutically listening to his students (Davis, 1997) supported his belief that students must have space to explore and approach the study of mathematics in their own way. The transformation in Wesley's beliefs about mathematics teaching and learning and the enactment of those beliefs in his classroom are a move beyond reform. The transformation of his classroom and what he does with his students is qualitatively different than what is suggested by most reform movements. He is certainly no longer focused on making adjustments and adaptations in order to raise test scores but rather focused entirely on student learning and understanding.

Through an ongoing conversation students can bring together their varied and contrasting ideas and understandings. The synergistic nature of conversation provides space for students to challenge, validate, and perturb one another's thinking and help one another weave together different ways of approaching and understanding mathematics. Envisioning classroom dynamics and learning "in terms of an ongoing . . . dance" (Davis, Sumara, and Kieren, 1996, 153), wherein "individual and collective meanings are seen to evolve in the course of classroom interactions" (Cobb, Jaworski, and Presmeg, 1996) can help students to create something whole from their contrasting and often conflicting understandings. If teachers can envision and transform their thinking about teaching as helping students to learn "things" to that of working with students to develop their own relationship with what it is they are studying, then they can begin to create spaces for a conversation. Developing space with and for their students to participate in the unfolding of curriculum as a conversation wherein knowledge emerges as meaning transforms the learning environment into a place that is focused on "that which is among them" (Davis et al., 1996, 153); a focus entirely on meaningful learning and the building of relationships.

References

Applebee, Arthur N. (1996). *Curriculum as conversation: Transforming traditions of teaching and learning.* Chicago: The University of Chicago Press.

Cobb, Paul (1995). Mathematics learning and small group interaction: Four case studies. In *The emergence of mathematical meaning: Interaction in classrooms cultures.* Paul Cobb and Heinrich Baursefeld, (Eds.). Hillsdale, NJ: Erlbaum.

Cobb, Paul, Barbara Jaworski, and Norman Presmeg. (1996). Emergent and sociocultural views of mathematical activity. In *Theories of mathematical learning,* (pp. 3–19). Leslie P. Steffe, Pearla Nesher, Paul Cobb, Gerald Goldin, and Brian Greer (Eds.). Mahwah, NJ: Lawrence Erlbaum Associates.

Davis, Brent (1997). Listening for differences: An evolving conception of mathematics teaching. *Journal for Research in Mathematics Education, 28* (3): 355–76.

Davis, Brent, Dennis Sumara, and Tom Kieren. (1996). Cognition, co-emergence, curriculum. *Journal of Curriculum Studies, 28* (2): 151–69.

Doll, William E. Jr. (1993). *A post-modern perspective on curriculum.* New York: Teachers College Press.

Fleener, M. Jayne (2002). *Curriculum dynamics: Recreating heart.* Lang.

Fleener, M. Jayne, Keith Adolphson, and Stacy L. Reeder. (2002). Robotics activities and constructed problem solving: Creating spaces for learning and doing. In *Psychology of Mathematics Education,* Vol. 2 (pp. 361–367). A. D. Cockburn and E. Nardi (Eds.). Norwich: University of East Anglia.

Fletcher, Scott (2000). *Education and emancipation: Theory and practice in a new constellation.* New York: Teachers College Press.

Kilpatrick, Jeremy and George Stanic. (1995). Paths to the present. In *Prospects for school mathematics,* (pp. 3–17). I. M. Carl (Ed.). Reston, VA: National Council of Teachers of Mathematics.

National Council of Teachers of Mathematics (NCTM). (1989). *Curriculum and evaluation standards for school mathematics.* Reston, VA: NCTM.

National Council of Teachers of Mathematics (NCTM). (1991). *Professional standards for teaching mathematics.* Reston, VA: NCTM.

Pinar, William F. (2001). I am a man: The queer politics of race. *Journal of Curriculum Theorizing,* Winter, 11–41.

Reeder, Stacy L. (2002). Emergent mathematics curriculum: A case study of two teachers. (Doctoral dissertation, University of Oklahoma, 2002). *Dissertation abstracts international, 63* (05), 1756.

Schmidt, William, Curtis McKnight, and Senta Raizen. (1996). *A splintered vision: An investigation of U.S. science and mathematics education.* Boston: Kluwer Academic.

Spretnak, Carolyn. (1991). *States of grace: The recovery of meaning in the postmodern age.* San Francisco, CA: Harper Collins.

Wheatley, Grayson H. (1991). Constructivist perspectives on science and mathematics learning. *Science Education, 75* (1): 9–21.

Wheatley, Grayson H. and George Abshire. (2002). *Developing mathematical fluency.* Tallahassee, FL: Mathematics Learning.

Wheatley, Grayson H. and Anne M. Reynolds. (1999). *Coming to know number: A mathematics activity resource for elementary school teachers.* Tallahassee, FL: Mathematics Learning.

Yackel, Erna, and Paul Cobb. (1996). Sociomathematical norms, argumentation, and autonomy in mathematics. *Journal for Research in Mathematics Education, 27* (4): 458–77.

Fourth
Iteration

Aesthetics, Culture, and Learning

 # Patterns That Connect
A Recursive Epistemology

Attention. As a child I learned to find four-leaf clovers as I walked along. A four-leaf clover is a break in pattern, a slight dissonance that can only be seen against an awareness of the orderly configuration in the grass. The same kind of structure attention must have been what allowed my father so often to see a circling hawk or praying mantis or a moth, motionless on the bark of a tree, and point them out. You learn to watch for both harmony and dissonance.

Mary Catherine Bateson, *With a Daughter's Eye*

Introduction

Gregory Bateson spent his career searching for a "simplified and lucid image of our world, one in which neither history, economics, nor politics was given prominent place, but ecological pattern was central" (Heims, 1991, 56). His search for these ecological patterns began as a student at St. John's College of Cambridge University and continued through his study of a variety of fields. Bateson wrote his first book, *Naven*, about the Iatmul tribe in New Guinea. In *Naven*, he identified a pattern of interaction that he called "schizmogenesis." Although the concept was later mostly identified with patterns in schizophrenic families, Bateson understood it as a general pattern of interaction that could be used to describe any situation in which relationships affect each other in a recursive manner. The pattern of interactions, the reactions of each party to the reaction of the other party, is the pattern that Bateson called "schizmogenesis." The patterns interested him because, like other recursive patterns, they could become unstable and escalate, or as in the case of the tribes he studied, the patterns could be maintained in equilibrium.

The patterns that connect and their recursive nature interested Bateson from the beginning and in some ways it could be said that he devoted his career to understanding recursive patterns that connect individuals, families, nations, mind to nature, and the mundane to spiritual. The world he constructed from this quest is one best described by parable and metaphor, which Bateson considered the essence of human thought. Bateson built worlds of ideas in which unity became visible and descriptions of human cognition more closely approximated experience. Contemporary theorists sometimes disagree with Bateson, and with each other; however there is a pattern that connects them. The purpose of this chapter is to describe this connecting pattern and to consider the richness that attends concepts of learning as recursive patterning.

Perceptual Patterns

The pattern that connects traditional models of cognition to one another and distinguishes them from more contemporary models is that the traditional models assume that organisms learn to survive by constructing an internal representation of their environment. The more isomorphic the relationship between environment and representation, the more "true" the representation, and the more useful it is to the survival of the organism. Contemporary theories propose that the way we experience our external environment is misleading. For example, traditional concepts of vision compare it to looking out through a camera lens. Today we know that we construct images from points of light and color. What I see is determined by a number of things, including who I am at that moment. Perception is not a simple matter of taking in the world. It is a complex reconstruction of it.

I read a study long ago (and I long ago lost the reference for it I am sorry to say) in which a surgeon found a way to reverse a type of congenital blindness in adults. The surprising part of the study for me occurred when the bandages were removed. I thought the patients would have the dramatic experience in which the bandages are removed and a woman sees the loved one for the first time and joyously, tearfully cries "Ralph!" Instead, the patients screamed and covered their eyes. They reported that what they experienced was not "Ralph," but many points of light and color. The experience of the unordered points of data was so disorienting that most of them asked for the surgery to be reversed and one committed suicide.

Bateson (1972) says that Warren McCulloch was the first person to demonstrate that what we see is not what is "out there," but what the structure of the seer allows to be seen. McCulloch demonstrated that a frog sees moving objects subtended at only ten degrees to the eye. The frog does not see anything else and, from the frog's perspective, nothing else exists. Bateson's insight was that, like frogs, humans receive only a small portion of the available information from the outside world. Like frogs, anything other than the information that triggers our sense organs does not exist for us. The world we live in is the world we are able to sense.

The essential constraint on human perception is that our sense organs are, Bateson (1991) says, "specially designed to keep the world out," just as the lining of the gut keeps out foreign proteins by only allowing amino acids to pass through (182). Sense organs convert the rich variation of the outside world to a set of digital signals. In this sense, Bateson liked Alfred Korzybski's distinction between the map and the territory. He says that, because of the constraints on our sense organs, we can never know the territory. We have access only to our map of it. The relationship between map and territory, for Bateson, is difference. Bateson notes that "our visual epistemology will only let us receive news of those differences which either already exist as events in time (i.e. what we call 'changes') or which we can convert into events by moving our retina in microstagmus" (226).

Bateson (1979) realized from Adelbert Ames' demonstrations that, while our sense organs *constrain* our perceptions, our sense organs do not wholly *determine* our perceptions. The mind organizes and integrates the shower of impulses from the sense organs to create perceptual experiences. He says that it is as if we know the premises of parallax and create an image accordingly, never letting ourselves know at any conscious level that we applied these rules to the shower of impulses. We perceive the result of this process, but never the process itself.

Our sensory organs determine the parts of the world that get through our filters, but that alone does not determine what we perceive. Clearly there is some correspondence with the world in which we live, because the images we construct are useful. Unlike hallucinations, our perceptions are not generated entirely from internal sources. Bateson (1972) maintains that we are able to learn about the external environment because the communication between person and environment is rich with redundancy. Bateson adopted McCulloch's view that the redundancy of pathways in the brain represents a fail-safe mechanism. The nervous system does not depend upon solitary bits of information, but uses redundancy to check and recheck in an attempt to reduce corruption of information. Our sensory apparatus includes loops and monitoring, actively seeking information, checking and rechecking the information we are receiving.

Further, Bateson says that we use redundancy to make inferences about parts we do not perceive, or relationships between parts and wholes when we have perceived only a part of a sequence or configuration. Our reliance on patterns allows us to infer missing parts and/or relationships. We create meaning by integrating patterns from various sources.

> Such integration, unlike subsumption or synthesis, itself is fractaled.

Autopoiesis

Humberto Maturana and Fransisco Varela (1972), biologists in Santiago, Chile, were studying vision when they realized, like McCulloch and Bateson, that vision is *generated* by the nervous system, not *received* by it. Based on this insight, they proposed that living organisms are defined by what they term "autopoiesis." Autopoetic systems continually change, break down, and build new structures while maintaining their identity. This process of maintaining self-identity is, according to Fritjof Capra (2002), an essential feature of living organisms, extending from the cellular level. Capra describes the cell membrane as " a moving 'conveyor belt' that is continually produced, broken down, and produced again" (8). Self-identity is a dynamic process constrained by attractors, like fractal patterns that represent both change and stability.

Capra says that Ilya Prigogine chose the term "'dissipative structure' to emphasize the close interplay between structure on the one hand and change (or dissipation) on the other" (13). This concept describes the spontaneous emergence of order at critical points of instability, and, according to Capra, "is one of the most important concepts of the new understanding of life" (14). Jean Piaget (1975), who studied children's cognition extensively, noted a similar process that he called "equilibration"; "a process that leads from a state near equilibrium to a qualitatively different state at equilibrium by way of multiple disequilibria and reequilibrations" (3). He notes that reequilibration may be a return to a previous state of equilibrium or it may result in new and better equilibria. For Piaget, "cognitive structures resemble stationary but dynamic states described by Prigogine that are capable of 'constructing and maintaining functional order in an open system'" (3–4). The key to triggering this equilibration process, for Piaget, is perturbation, which may come from an external source or from an internal awareness of gaps, contradictions, and inconsistencies.

Piaget sees cognition as an embodied process of acting on the world. It is the interaction with the world, with each other, and later, with our own thought, that makes cognition a dynamic, changing process. Francisco Varela, Evan Thompson, and Eleanor Rosch (1999) maintain that cognition is for the sole purpose of guiding action and that "cognitive structures emerge from the recurrent sensorimotor patterns that enable action to be perceptually guided" (200). For Maturana and Varela, as for Bateson, "mind" and "cognition" express relationships among living things. Mind is not bounded by skin or limited to organisms with a nervous system.

Maturana and Varela (1987) use the term "structural coupling" to describe a co-evolutionary model of interaction with the environment. In this model, we are not just acting in or on the world, but with it. Maturana and Varela liken it to a person who has always lived in a submarine. From the outside, an observer sees changes in the submarine with respect to reefs, water surface, etc. But "All that exists for the man inside the submarine are indicator readings, their transitions, and ways of obtaining specific relations between them" (137). For Maturana and Varela, like Bateson, changes in state govern behavior, but they add that any change "depend[s] on its structure and this structure depends on its history of structural coupling" (138). Structural coupling, for Maturana and Varela, is "our history of recurrent interactions." It is structural coupling, including linguistic coupling, that makes it possible for us to coordinate actions. In the course of acting out of structurally coupled relationships, our structure and our relationships evolve. In Maturana and Varela's view, we call forth a world through our actions and interactions. For them, "the plastic splendor of the nervous system . . . lies in its continuous transformation in line with transformations in the environment as a result of how each interaction affects it" (170).

Embodied models of thought lead to what Seymour Papert (1994) termed "pilotage," from the metaphor of a captain piloting a ship. Papert says that in real life it is seldom necessary to get it right the first time. What we do in most situations is start out in what appears to

> Like riverboat pilots our course is seldom straight or easily known in advance, yet we seem to expect and communicate to our students that paths to learning are straight and without deviation without detours.

be the right direction, gather feedback continuously, and make adjustments based on that feedback. This is the same kind of tinkering that characterizes all evolutionary processes.

> Unlike the unchanging difference the simple circuit of doorbells creates, however, the self-reflective, recursive nature of cognition adds increasing complexity to the dynamics of thought.

Cognition, for Bateson (1991), is a self-regulating system governed by thresholds that are triggered by "differences, changes, differences between changes" (181). It is not the *state* of the circuit that operates the system, but the *change* in the state of the circuit. Take, for example, an "electric doorbell on the front door. If the circuit is complete, then a magnet is activated which will break the circuit. If the circuit is broken, then the magnet will not be activated, and the circuit will be restored. If the circuit is restored, then the magnet will be activated, and the circuit will be broken, and so on" (181).

Traditional theories imply that learning should be made as easy as possible. It suggests that "acquisition of knowledge" can occur almost mechanically and largely through repetition. That appears to be the way some skills are learned, but much of learning is not about skill. Understanding does not increase as a result of repetition. Bateson's interest in difference and Jean

Piaget's interest in perturbation led me to think about moments of transition in which a currently held point of view begins to seem inadequate, to show inconsistencies and gaps. I began to think about how to teach in ways that make difference salient. In creating spaces for difference I had to learn to listen differently, to respond differently, and to create different kinds of environments. For example, in class discussion I asked students to contribute by adding any way of thinking about the issue that had not already been discussed. This discussion opened up the possibilities instead of collapsing them around a few views with students aligning themselves with one of them. Students found it difficult at first, but once they began there was a sense of the group engaged in a wonderful exploration and, in some cases, an explosion of variety.

I routinely ask students to read different books related to the course content instead of all reading the same book. Depending on the class, we may begin with one book and then branch into different ones, or we may begin reading different books from the beginning. I find that this enriches class discussion and that, as William Doll pointed out (personal communication), students tend to raise issues more than just reporting what the book said.

Recursion

Contrast, the process of detecting difference, is a recursive form of feedback. According to Peter Harries-Jones (1995), Bateson believed that "contrasts emerge when patterns of redundancies learned in one *particular* context are compared to patterns of redundancies discerned in the formation of a whole, and the difference between the two contrasted" (182). This is a self-referencing process in the sense that, in the contrast, whole reenters part. (See Smitherman, this volume).

Recursion, in Bateson's view, is also responsible for "noise eating." He says that, in the endeavor to create patterns of order, difference, even difference in the presence of noise, touches off a process of self-referencing. This process occurs at a higher level of abstraction and, in Korzybskian terms, leads to a construction of maps of maps. Recursive patterns emerge in temporal relations, patterns of betweenness that Bateson refers to as "primarily a dance of interacting parts and only secondarily pegged down by various sorts of physical limits" (188). The recursive synthesis and integration from various sources is what Bateson means by information, meaning, and making sense. He believes that recursiveness generates a special sort of holism.

Much of our curriculum is designed linearly. Classes are organized within disciplines or sub-disciplines. Within a class knowledge is organized according to an assumed structure. To create a curriculum that permits the kind of recursive synthesis and integration from various sources that Bateson describes means rethinking curriculum content and certainly rethinking common notions about "covering material."

Conversation creates a space where together we see what none of us could see alone. My Learning Theories class had been reading Jean Piaget's work. Each of them had read a book of their choosing, resulting in readings of different books by different people for different purposes, written at different times in Piaget's intellectual development. The class had mostly been centered around conversation, and had reached a point where I thought we needed a new view to jump start the conversation in new directions. I gave each of them an envelope of "nodes" (nouns written on small pieces of paper). I asked them to arrange the nodes in a visual representation, connect them however they wished, and label the connections. Then they drew their "maps" on the board and told us about them. We asked questions and sometimes small conversations emerged, but the powerful part was seeing these very different treatments of the same concepts. Students were adding to their maps, changing things, and moving things around. One student moved to another table, disassembled her map and reassembled it. None of this was an imitation or capitulation to the other person's map. They simply saw things in the overlap that they had not seen before. The maps were still just as different as they had been, but they were different than they were at the beginning of class too.

Context: Patterns of Patterns

Traditional representation views of cognition attempt to discover context-independent representations. Varela, Thompson, and Rosch (1999) invert this notion by insisting that the essence of cognition is context-dependent knowledge. Context, for them, is essential. It is not a "residual artifact that can be eliminated by discovery of more sophisticated rules" (148).

Gregory Bateson (1991) says that differences exist not just in signals and patterns of signals, but also in contexts "for, in the whole communicational world, nothing means anything except in the presence of other things" (166). Contexts are maps of maps and, as such, represent a level more abstract than maps.

Bateson suggests that we learn patterns of communication in a variety of contexts and that these patterns, when repeated over time, become expected. There are levels of context and levels of communication within contexts. The student in a science class is not just learning about photosynthesis. The student is also constructing ideas about school, science, and a variety of other contexts. These experiences, when repeated often enough, frame a set of ideas and expectations that the student relies on as a default. The more this is repeated, the deeper the pattern is sunk into the unconscious and the more difficult it is to change. Bateson uses the term "deutero-learning" in his early writing to describe this kind of learning. As learners improve their ability to deal with this type of context, "the subject comes to act more and more as if contexts of this type were expectable in his universe" (1972, 166–67).

Bateson believed that the genesis of some psychological disorders could be explained by what he called the "double bind." This is a bind felt by a child, for example, when a parent says something hurtful but wraps it in non-verbal language that is playful. A woman I know said that her mother used to tell her that she was getting only sticks and coal for Christmas because she was "bad." The mother said it in a playful tone, as if the child should take it as a joke. The child then is in a bind. The child doesn't find the message amusing, but she understands that it was said in a joking context, which means it is supposed to be amusing. If she protests the message, the mother will invoke the context, as in "I am just kidding you." If she accepts the com-municational context, then she has to accept that the idea that she is bad and should get sticks and coal for a gift.

The unintended consequences of teaching can be more powerful than the concepts we think we are teaching. If I teach scientific concepts by asking students to memorize them, they may construct the idea that science is about facts that somehow just "are," even though one of the ideas I have them memorize is the scientific method.

I taught a freshman seminar for several years entitled "Learning, Thinking, Understanding and Inventing." It was a seminar in which we investigated ways to think about our own thinking. In the first three weeks of the class I asked students to read a book a week, of their choice, from a list of novels. They complained and talked about how they couldn't possibly read a book a week. Many of them commented that they "hate reading." I told them that they would not be tested over the book and they would not write a "book report." They were simply to read the book and come to class pre-pared to discuss it with others who read the same book. At the end of the three weeks, I gave them a paper entitled "The Phenomenology of the Novel" and asked them to read it and write about their experience of reading as it related to this paper. The papers were astonishing. Students, almost to a person, wrote about how much they enjoyed the assignment and that they had forgotten how much they used to like to read. They talked about the experience of "going into the book," which was described in the paper. They said that at about fourth grade, the teacher started asking them to remember or take exams over details of the book, and it felt to them like having one foot in the book and one foot out of the book. They said that this was so painful that they did not want to read any more. I doubt that the fourth grade teach-ers got together to try to find a way to make reading painful. I suspect that they wanted students to enjoy reading, but they were also required by the school to have an "objective" basis for grading, so they constructed the exam or report. Messages, for Bateson, occur within a communicational context. The communication depends as much on the relationship of the communicators as on the content or referent of the message. In fact, Bateson thinks that a mark of cognitive growth is when a child learns that not all messages must be believed. Some messages may be doubted or partially accepted, or completely rejected. A message is communicated within a shell of context markers and within a relationship characterized by various shades of preparedness to believe. Meta-communication is communication, often unconscious, about the relationship and/or context. Synthesizing and integrating information from available sources recursively generates all of these processes, from the simplest percept to the most complex, an abstract map of maps of maps. These recursive processes involve the self, beliefs, prior decisions about such contexts, etc.

Nel Noddings said that she asked a number of people to describe their favorite teachers. None of them mentioned method, but all of them told stories about teachers who they thought cared about them. The first adult that I thought believed in me and wanted me to see the beautiful, interesting world she saw was my English teacher. Because of her I studied for the first time in my school life, and because of her I attended college and became intrigued with cognition. Like Nel's informants, I do not remember anything about how she taught, but I remember the way she looked at me and the encouraging, sometimes demanding things she said to me.

I was talking with a teacher once who had just finished a demonstration of an idea she had about teaching. As I watched the demonstration, I saw a teacher whose method was questionable, but whose relationship with the students was so powerful that they were doing what they could to please her. It looked to me as if they were learning in spite of the method and because of the relationship. I asked her afterwards if she often received calls from teachers complaining about the results they achieved with her method. She said she did. I told her my theory and she laughed and said, "So that is what it is." She said that she knew it was not the method, but she didn't know how else to talk about it. Unfortunately, she would probably not have been invited to share with other teachers about relationship building with students, even though that was clearly what made her an effective teacher.

Bateson suggests that communicational contexts are necessary for any knowledge of the "unliving world described by Physics." He calls this unliving world by Carl Jung's term, "Pleroma," which he contrasts with Jung's "Creatura," the world of the "alive." "In distinguishing, creatura distinguishes through the distinctions it draws, and so recursively points to the criteria for distinguishing" (in Harries-Jones, 1995, 97). As Bateson says:

> I can describe a stone, but the stone can describe nothing. I can use the stone as
> a signal—perhaps as a landmark. But it is not the landmark . . . what happens to

the stone and what it does when nobody is around is not part of the mental process of any living thing. For that it must somehow make and receive *news*. (Bateson and Bateson, 1987, 17)

Emergent Patterns

Nonconsciousness plays an important role in cognition in Bateson's view. We are not aware of the constant scanning and monitoring that lies beneath perception. We are not aware of the integration from multiple sources of data that results in our experience of image or sound. We are not aware of the integration of patterns, patterns of patterns, contexts, and beliefs that generates our experiences and governs our relationships. Similarly, Maturana and Varela believe that consciousness is an emergent phenomenon. It cannot be traced directly to its neurological origins because it is not a structure. Instead, Capra (2002) believes, "Mind is not a thing but a process—the process of cognition, which is identified with the process of life. The brain is a specific structure through which this process operates" (37).

Bateson maintains that unconscious thought is qualitatively different from conscious thought. He describes consciousness as linear, partial, and selective. It deals in description, classification, and comparison. Unconscious thought is global. It is the primary means of experiencing relationships between self and others and self and environment. Bateson states that a system of precise, complex mental algorithms co-evolved in people and a world characterized by such redundancy and pattern. Bateson (1991) says that he "distrust[s] consciousness as the prime guide" because it is, by nature, selective and partial (299). The sacred and aesthetic, for Bateson, look for the larger, the whole and give us glimpses of the unity behind the distinctions of consciousness. His last two books, *Angels Fear* and *A Sacred Unity*, connect the ecology of mind with the ecology of nature through the sacred and the aesthetic.

As one of his book titles suggests, Gregory Bateson (1991) ventured "where angels fear to tread," or at least where psychologists seldom tread. He elevated the unconscious and metaphor to an essential form of knowledge. He saw "aesthetic judgment" as "an awareness of criteria of elegance and of the combinations of process that will lead to elegance rather than ugliness" (255). He believed that aesthetic judgment was an essential aspect of cognition. Mary Catherine Bateson (1984) describes aesthetic processes as "one of listening for resonance between the inner and the outer, an echo that brings attention into focus" (201). Aesthetic judgment is critical to the patterns that connect because it "seems to be more intimately concerned with the relationships which obtain within each particular case" (1991, 255).

In *Angels Fear*, posthumously completed by his daughter, Mary Catherine Bateson (1987), her father finished the work he began in *Mind and Nature: A Necessary Unity*. She says that in this book, Gregory "had become aware gradually that the unity of nature he had affirmed in *Mind and Nature* might only be comprehensible through the kind of metaphors familiar from religion; that, in fact, he was approaching the integrative dimension of experience he called the Sacred" (2).

Bateson believed that metaphor is the most fundamental form of human thought because metaphor expresses relationship. He says that "metaphor is not just pretty poetry, it is not either good or bad logic, but is in fact the logic upon which the biological world has been built, the main characteristic and organizing glue of this world of mental process . . ." (30). Metaphor and redundancy provide what Bateson called "double description," where metaphor is meaning derived from the reordering of perspectives and redundancy is meaning derived from pattern. Double description, in this case, is redundancy/metaphor. Elsewhere Bateson discusses "double vision" as the "interleaving of two patterns of redundancy which yields a sense of creativity and beauty" (in Harries-Jones, 1995, 203). He uses the analogy of moiré, a repetitive design on a surface. If two such patterns are laid together, a third pattern is created. Many of us have looked through a stereopticon, like a ViewMaster. By looking through two slides, one with each eye, we "see" a new pattern that is not in either image. Like the moiré, it is the overlapping of the two slightly different slides that create the third image. The image does not exist materially.

In traditional mathematics classes, we teach arithmetic concepts in one time period and geometric concepts in another. My friend Kathleen Martin, teaches the same mathematics concepts from both an arithmetic and geometric perspective. The overlapping perspectives, in Bateson's view, allow students to make sense of the idea in a different way. Double (or multiple) descriptions make a space where something new can emerge.

Mary Catherine suggests (Bateson and Bateson, 1987) that her father viewed knowledge as an artifact of human perceptual processes and actions. For example, she says, "language depends on nouns, which seem to refer to things, while biological communication concerns pattern and relationship" (188). Since language probably emerged from gesture, it is reasonable to believe that "humans, with their manipulative hands, have specialized in describing what they can affect" (189).

This preference for nouns in language leads us to slide contextual frames over sequences of behavior, as a way of creating explanations. Bateson says we make sense of an interchange between two people by using descriptive terms like "dependency" and "domination." These are not descriptive of something *in* a person. They are descriptions of regularities in "contexts of interchange" between persons. Bateson was concerned about such epistemological errors.

Epilogue

Varela, Thompson, and Rosch (1999) also step beyond the usual boundaries of cognitive science to propose that the phenomenological approaches of Merleau Ponty, Edmund Husserl, and the Buddhist traditions are as essential and important as the scientific view in understanding cognition. They believe that we must honor both the lived human experience and the scientific understanding before the two become irreconcilable. They say that "when it is cognition or mind that is being examined, the dismissal of experience becomes untenable, even paradoxical" (13). In this belief, they echo Ulric Neisser who said in 1976 that if psychology doesn't explain everyday human inner experience it is not useful.

There is a good fit between the foundation that Bateson established, Piaget's work with children (especially his later work), and Maturana and Varela's work together and later, separately. While each of these models is different, taken together they point to new and promising directions in Cognition. These new directions include:

- Cognition is constrained but not determined by the characteristics of the sensory end organs and other biological structures.
- Cognition is autopoietic and, thus, can be triggered but not caused.
- Cognition and consciousness are emergent.
- The dynamics of cognition are nonlinear.
- Cognition occurs at points of instability, far from equilibrium.
- Cognition co-evolves and is co-constructed.
- Cognition is best studied at the interface of several perspectives, including at least neurological, phenomenological, cultural, social, aesthetic, and sacred.

Understanding emerges from a variety of descriptive systems, and must include phenomenological, metaphorical, poetic, artistic, and perhaps even the mystical.

Gregory Bateson (1904-1980)

Mary Catherine Bateson (1984) writes of her parents, Gregory Bateson and Margaret Mead, "The minds of both sought patterns of completeness, wholes, and so they thought of worlds entire, whether these worlds were minute images of microscopic life within a drop of water or the planet wreathed in a cloud" (1).

Gregory Bateson thought about human interaction in terms of the "patterns of completeness," the "worlds entire" that his daughter describes. Peter Harries-Jones (1995), who has written an insightful book about Bateson, says, "Bateson believed that relying upon the materialist framework of knowledge dominant in ecological science will deepen errors of interpretation and, in the end, promote eco-crisis. He saw recursive patterns of communication as the basis of order in both natural and human domains" (i).

Bateson published in several fields. He was an anthropologist and did fieldwork in New Guinea, which he first published in the book *Naven* in 1936. He attended the first Macy Conference on feedback mechanisms and circular causal systems in biological and social sciences. His studies of communication began in 1954, when he directed a research project on schizophrenic communication. He later studied animal communication, and it was from these studies of communication that he developed his double bind theory.

He studied epistemology as natural history, and developed his view of an "ecology of mind," published initially in the book *Steps to an Ecology of Mind*, in 1972. He extended his theory to an ecology of mind within an ecological context in subsequent books, *Where Angels Fear to Tread* and *A Sacred Unity*. His daughter published his last book posthumously from his notes and lectures. Bateson was concerned about the consequences of modern thought. He convened a conference (1968) of scholars to discuss the issues and what might be done about it. His daughter, Mary Catherine, attended the conference as an ethnographer and published her description of it in the book *Our Own Metaphor*.

Bateson was criticized for the way he wrote. His stories and metaphors made his points obscure, the critics thought, and yet to do otherwise might betray his belief about the importance of story and metaphor in human thought. Harries-Jones (1995) provides the best summary of Bateson's work, which he characterized as "an ecology of mind in ecological settings—a recursive epistemology" (foreword).

References

Bateson, G. (1958). *Naven: a survey of problems suggested by a composite picture of the culture of a New Guinea tribe drawn from three points of view.* Stanford, CA: Stanford University Press.

———. (1972). *Steps to an ecology of mind.* New York: Ballantine.

———. (1979). *Mind and nature: A necessary unity.* New York: Bantam.

———. (1991). *Sacred unity.* New York: Harper Collins.

Bateson, G., and M. C. Bateson. (1987). *Angels fear: Towards an epistemology of the sacred.* New York: Bantam.

Bateson, M. C. (1984). *With a daughter's eye: A memoir of Margaret Mead and Gregory Bateson.* New York: Harper Collins.

————. (1991). *Our own metaphor*. Washington: Smithsonian.

Capra, Fritjof. (2002). *The hidden connections: Integrating the biological, cognitive, and social dimensions of life into a science of sustainability*. New York: Doubleday.

Harries-Jones, Peter. (1995). *Ecological understanding and Gregory Bateson*. Toronto: University of Toronto Press.

Heims, S. J. (1991). *The cybernetics group*. Cambridge: MIT Press.

Maturana, H. R., and F. J. Varela (1972). *Autopoiesis and cognition*. Boston: Reidel.

————. (1998). *The tree of knowledge: The biological roots of human understanding*. Boston: Shambhala.

Papert, Seymour. (1994). *The children's machine: Rethinking school in the age of the computer*. New York: Basic

Piaget, J. (1975). *The equilibration of cognitive structures: The central problem of intellectual development*. Chicago: University of Chicago.

Varela, F., E. Thompson, and E. Rosch. (1999). *The embodied mind: Cognitive science and human experience*. Cambridge: MIT Press.

Minding Culture

Again we face connectedness at more than one level.
Gregory Bateson, *Mind and Nature*

The term "minding culture" leaps from page to mind, from mind to page. It appeals to me as an ethnographer and as a curriculum theorist. In broad terms, both cultural anthropology and curriculum pay careful attention to mind, culture. As interpretations of culture, both are necessarily involved in the tangled process of cultural representation. In this sense, minding culture means putting minds and words to the ways people make meaning. Such a process always takes place in the context of culture/s, and it often requires that curriculum theorists and ethnographers "enter, in some measure, the conceptual world of another culture" (Bateson and Bateson, 1987, 184). Renato Rosaldo (1989) writes that culture can be seen as a "busy intersection." Such an entrance raises a multiplicity of questions: about relations of self and other; the knowledge that circulates between and among them; and conceptual and social patterns of mind and culture that shape—and are shaped by—intersections and divergences among knowledge, knowing and knowers. In this era, often categorized as postmodern, these sorts of conjunctive, epistemological questions are increasingly central to ethnography and to curriculum.

Such questions also play a central role in the iconoclastic ethnographic work of Gregory Bateson (1904–1980), considered by many scholars to be one of the most important yet misunderstood social scientists of the twentieth century. His intellectual journey took him through zoology, anthropology, psychology, cybernetics, and communication theory, and gave rise to what Stuart Brand (1976) termed "Gregory's unusual sense of theory" (32). Bateson was a "Jack of all disciplines" whose work dips and swings across disciplines to form complex patterns of thought (Wilder-Mott, 1981, 34). He was also a thinker of considerable depth whose theorizing about patterns of mind, culture, and epistemology "was always at the current edge of his own thinking" (Bateson, 1991, x). Often described as visionary, Bateson's work was often on (and sometimes over) the current intellectual edge of his contemporaries. As Stephen Toumlin notes, "those scholars who might most benefit from his thinking are, alas, those most likely to ignore or dismiss it" (in Wilder-Mott, 1981, 33).

It is precisely this deep sense of edginess that makes Bateson's first book so interesting. In *Naven* (written in the early 1930s on work done in the 1920s), Gregory Bateson struggles at the edge of his own thinking, revisits that edge in its first epilogue (1936), and revisits it again in its second (1958). *Naven* is Bateson's *unusual* ethnographic account of his work with the Iatmul people of the middle reaches of the Sepik River in New Guinea. Much like the ethnography of his contemporaries, *Naven* describes significant features of Iatmul culture. Like other anthropologists, Bateson maps moieties, traces kinship, and compares gender roles. He writes about rites of passage, attitudes toward death, and sorcery and vengeance. Yet very little about *Naven* is typical of the ethnography of its day. What makes *Naven* so unusual is the degree to which these typical anthropological topics remain secondary, and are in fact discussed mostly in the service of *Naven's* central concern—the naven ceremony, "in which men dress as women and women dress as men" (Bateson, 1958, 2). English social anthropologist Edmund R. Leach describes the climate of anthropology around the time of *Naven* as "a purely ethnographic field" devoted to "the taking of notes and the collecting of objects" to produce an ethnographic composite of a cultural whole that demonstrates all aspects as functionally linked to ensure survival (in Lipset, 1980, 140). As Leach reminds, the sort of methodology that *Naven* reflects was "very much something that was not done around (here then)" (140).

Rather than providing a comprehensive catalogue of Iatmul cultural facts and a detailed analysis of how the behavior of these primitive people was a "functional response to the imperatives of collective survival," *Naven* focuses on explaining a single constellation of ceremonial transvestite behavior among the Iatmul, and lengthy, sometimes abstract theorizing about the complexities of explanation (Houseman and Severi, 1998, 5). As historians of anthropology have noted, "the entire book is undeniably marked by a lack of balance between the lengthy theoretical discussions [of method, of relationships, of patterns, of epistemology] and the sometimes hasty treatment of ethnographic facts" (3). In *Naven's* glossary Bateson (1958) defines naven as "a set of ceremonial customs of the Iatmul used to illustrate the theoretical analyses in this book" (310). This definition is as telling as it is ironic: *Naven* may have indeed begun as a book about ritual transvestitism (as expressed in a ceremony called naven), but as Bateson himself describes, its purpose soon became "no longer to put forward a theory of Iatmul transvestitism, but to suggest methods of thinking about anthropological problems" (160).

Bateson's ethnographic description and his quite earnest and sometimes less than graceful theoretical wrangling in *Naven*'s epilogues are fascinating on multiple levels. Bateson's book challenges dualities associated with mind and culture while posing questions about the mind of the anthropologist as well as the native mind.

In *Naven*, we find a frustrated Bateson anxiously working the sometimes rigid, sometimes elastic dualities of mind and culture. His struggle for explanations that move beyond binary is palpable, as is his deep desire to frame patterns, which connect. The sort of epistemological questions that Bateson asks in *Naven* are enduring questions central to anthropology. Clifford Geertz (2000) writes, "So far as anthropology is concerned, these ill-framed or elided doubled questions, the mental nature of culture, the cultural nature of mind, have haunted it since its inception" (204). Likewise, these questions are central to curriculum.

Naven is a groundbreaking example of an anthropologist openly grappling with and then recursively revisiting his analysis as part of an ethnographic text. Caught in and simultaneously fleeing a multiplicity of dualisms, it offers a soulful, "pre-linguistic-turn," an inarticulate articulation of the problematics of ethnographic explanation, interpretation and the limits of language. Such discussion predates postmodern angst concerning culture and its representations as addressed by interpretive ethnographers like James Clifford and George Marcus (1986), and Paul Rabinow (1986). As Clifford Geertz (1988) writes about anthropologists and their texts:

> Getting themselves into their text (that is, representationally into their text) may be as hard as getting themselves into the culture (that is, imaginatively into the culture). For some, it may be even more difficult (Gregory Bateson, whose eccentric classic, *Naven*, seems to consist mostly of false starts and second thoughts—preamble upon preamble epilogue upon epilogue—comes to mind. (17)

These false starts—Bateson's recursive expressions of paradoxical scientific faith mixed with skepticism regarding social science and the process of coming to "know" culture—foreshadow his flight from anthropology toward epistemological questions of knowing. This chapter will look at some of these tensions as they manifest themselves ambivalently in *Naven* and epilogues in relation to Bateson's emerging, interpenetrating notions of mind, culture, and epistemology. Both ethnography and curriculum stand to benefit from Bateson's struggles with description and explanation, his illustration of mind and culture as dynamic living patterns, and I think more profoundly, from the way Bateson's epistemology manages to play integration against diversity in order to vitalize both.

I begin with the proposition that the patterns of dualism at work in Bateson's life did much to shape the problems that were at the center of his

thought as they converge in *Naven* (Toulmin, 1981, 358). I continue by situating the epistemological tensions as represented in *Naven* and its epilogues
in relation to notions of mind, culture, and the emerging holistic epistemology that Bateson (1979) suggests might serve as the "pattern which connects" (90). But before beginning, let me stress the complexity of Bateson's
work. *Naven* was often regarded by anthropologists and other scholars as "no
more than an early exotic and confused adumbration of his general theory of
communication" (Houseman, & Severi, 1998, 31). But *Naven* also represents a multilayered pattern of ethnographic description, interpretation, and
reflective reiteration. Reading *Naven* is to "continually face connectedness at
more than one level" (Bateson, 1979, 13). According to Bateson in his 1958
epilogue:

> The book is a weaving of three levels of abstraction. At the most concrete level
> there is ethnographic data. More abstract is the tentative arranging of data to
> give various pictures of the culture, and still more abstract is the tentative arrang-
> ing of data to give various pictures of the culture, and still more abstract is the
> self-conscious discussion of the procedures by which the pieces of the jigsaw
> puzzle are put together. (281)

As Bateson himself notes, this interweaving often makes the book
"clumsy and awkward" (281). Similarly, his analysis is less than graceful. The
interplay between levels of abstraction, and the fact that the coherence of his
epistemological puzzle relies on difference so that its pieces never really
achieve a tight fit, make Bateson's work exhilarating and difficult to write
about coherently. Bateson's own struggle to explain by piecing seemingly
dichotomous abstractions such as mind and culture together and to "use this
explanatory process as an example within which the principles of explanation
could be seen and studied" provides uneasy comfort (281). Bateson (1977)
describes the difficulty of his work:

> From time to time I get complaints that my writing is dense and hard to under-
> stand. It may comfort those who find the matter hard to understand if I tell
> them that I have driven myself, over the years, into a "place" where conventional
> dualistic statements of mind-body relations—the conventional dualisms of
> Darwinism, psychoanalysis and theology—are absolutely unintelligible to me. It
> is becoming as difficult for me to understand dualists as it is for them to under-
> stand me. (236)

Yet in the body of *Naven*, the Iatmul people, Bateson and his readers still
dwell in that deeply conflicted "place" characterized by dualism.

Dueling Dualisms

Bateson describes *Naven* as "a series of experiments, in methods of thinking about anthropological material" (257). Taken out of context, this

description can seem like a deceptively playful alternative to the dogmatic functionalism that dominated much of the thinking in Bateson's anthropological day. But the skepticism toward ethnographic analysis Bateson demonstrates throughout *Naven* is not playful. Though fellow anthropologist and friend Ruth Benedict called anthropology "the healthiest of all skepticism," Bateson's skepticism as demonstrated in *Naven* represents an anxious challenge to the functionalism of his mentors and, more broadly, to the explanatory customs of anthropology (in Babcock, 1995, 105). Such skepticism also interferes with the anthropological aims of his ethnography and complicates (perhaps generatively so) his analysis. Bateson (1958) writes with candor about the depth of this interference:

> As Doll describes (earlier in this volume) there is a culture to method. Disruptions to method are often interpreted as affronts to culture.

> I did not clearly see any reason why I should enquire into one matter rather than another. If an informant told me a tale of sorcery and murder, I did not know what question to ask next—and this not so much from lack of training as from excess of skepticism. (257)

Skepticism toward the best theoretical models of his time interferes with Bateson's ability to gather data as well as to analyze it. Frustration over inadequate theoretical models runs rampant throughout *Naven* and climaxes in its epilogues. *Naven* reveals an anthropologist—a social scientist—who like his natural scientist father, William Bateson, "had something of that burning passion for truth, of that high conception of the calling of the naturalist" (Lipset, 1977, 32). Bateson's edgy quest for a theoretical model drives *Naven*'s tense experiments in thinking.

On *Naven*'s first page Bateson writes that the exposition of culture "may be attempted by either of two methods, by either scientific or artistic means" (1958, 1). The "either" is revealing here. The dichotomy is an old one, but interesting in the conceptual hands of a scholar who later in life would defy it and become regarded by many as a "poetic scientist" (Wilder-Mott, 1981, 37). As his daughter Mary Catherine Bateson (1984) explains, the dualistic "themes of art and science are curiously mixed in all his work" (163). Bateson's anthropological aims in *Naven* reveal the desires of a scientist. As Mary Catherine writes regarding her father's enduring scientific want, "For forty years, Gregory struggled with the question of how to provide anthropology with the clear, taut framework of fundamental ideas that would make it truly a science" (161). Bateson's anthropological work continued to be propelled by the scientific urge to frame the uncertainties involved in trying to understand what it means to know culture, mind and the interaction among them. *Naven* demonstrates that for Bateson this is a complicated, ambivalent desire. Throughout the book, Bateson critiques the scientific urge toward typology and classification. Yet all the while he strives similarly. As he writes in his final epilogue, "I myself hanker for a classification, a typology, of the processes of interaction as it occurs either between persons or between groups" (283).

Despite Bateson's scientific callings, *Naven* was often critiqued by scholars for being too autobiographical and thus not scientific enough. Anthropologist A.R. Radcliffe-Brown dismissed *Naven* as mere "intellectual autobiography" (Houseman and Severi, 1998, 3). According to *Naven* reviewer Kurt H. Wolff, "Bateson's theory . . . includes too many personal elements to be called, without qualification, scientific" (in Lipset, 1980, 146). Ruth Behar (1996) addresses anthropology's long-standing prohibition of the personal: "In anthropology, which historically exists to 'give voice' to others, there is no greater taboo than self-revelation" (26). Similarly, Kamal Visweswaran (1994) demonstrates how the individual experience of ethnographers is marginalized in form as well as content in anthropological texts:

> In traditional ethnographic practice, if the first-person narrative is allowed to creep into the ethnographic text, it is confined to the introduction or the post-script; if a book is devoted to the firsthand experiences of the novice ethnographer, it is after a monograph written in the proper objective manner has been produced. (21)

Naven obeys neither of these disciplinary mandates. *Naven* is Bateson's first book and first-person narrative is interwoven throughout the text. In part because of this *Naven* was dismissed or ignored by anthropologists for many years (Houseman and Severi, 1998). Yet anthropologist Mary Catherine Bateson (1984) describes anthropology as "probably the most personal of all the social sciences" (163). In fact, in a 1925 letter to his father explaining his move from natural science to social science, Bateson describes the change in his professional aspirations in personal terms. As his daughter describes:

> When Gregory decided to shift to anthropology, he described that shift as a shift from "ordinary impersonal science" to "a branch of science which is personal where I should be able to take root a bit," one that would provide the sense of "personal inspiration" he felt he lacked. (M. C. Bateson, 1984, 163)

As his daughter suggests, anthropology for Bateson functioned as a "compromise position" that might "resolve the opposition between science and art"—though in *Naven* this resolution is at best restless (163). Such compromise did not resolve the opposition between anthropology's notion of personal experience as exclusively subjective and the supposed objectivity of science.

Further, the compromise position of anthropology could not resolve the familial tension that Bateson's flight from natural science evoked. This switch from natural science was a sort of rebellion. In embracing social science—or the humanities as his father (William Bateson) classified anthropology—Gregory was rejecting his role as his father's scientific heir. As Gregory tells his biographer David Lipset (1980), "the switch to anthropology was a sort of revolt as far as I was concerned" (116). According to Lipset, "That the last of his sons should, when the search for a scientific heir was in W.B.'s thoughts, take up some sort of humanities, was difficult" (116). Anthropology represented a recursive rebellion against the natural science of his father. As Lipset (1977) reminds, "implicit in rebellion is continuity" (47). Though Bateson's later work is often praised for its "constant integration of concepts derived from one branch of research with problems and concepts derived from another," in *Naven* the tension surrounding the dualities of Bateson the nearly-natural scientist and Bateson the anthropologist is continuously in play (Rieber, 1989, 7).

Similarly, tension involving dualities such as mind/culture, emotion/cognition, aesthetics/science, professional/personal, knower/known, explanation/interpretation and epistemology/anthropology swirl through *Naven*. This tension emerges in different ways throughout the book. It is expressed in Bateson's critiques of functionalism, his descriptions of cultural, emotional (*Ethos*) and cognitive (*Eidos*) phenomena, and in his analysis of his analysis as found in the book's epilogues. More implicitly, the dualisms that haunt Bateson and his book are reflected in his choice of the naven ceremony as the focus of his study—the object of his ethnographic desire.

Leaving English society and heading off to New Guinea for an intensive ethnographic study of the Iatmul people was a complex double journey for Bateson. Not uncommon in Western mythology, it is one in which the hero has to leave home in order to find it. Winding along the Sepik River, Bateson was in some sense leaving his father's home of science in order to find an intellectual home in science, where he might "take root a bit." According to Mary Catherine Bateson (1984), "Gregory's decision to become an anthropologist was both an affirmation of family tradition and a rebellion" (161). As Morris Berman (1981), using Bateson's ideas, explains:

> All social, personal, and biological life has its own "grammar," or code. You can react against your particular code; but you can hardly behave in a way that is totally irrelevant to it. Furthermore, these patterns tend to be bipolar. (212)

Despite his rebellion against natural science, Bateson's work could not entirely escape its grammar. The bipolarity that patterns Bateson's biography is reflected in the subjects of his study. Bateson (1958) describes the Iatmul as:

> A fine, proud head-hunting people who live in big villages. . . . Their social
> organization, kinship and religious systems are developed to an extreme com-
> plexity. The community is subdivided into groups according to two independent
> systems . . . on the one hand there is a division into two totemic moieties . . . on
> the other hand there is a division into two cross-cutting pairs. (4)

Iatmul social life, as observed by Bateson, is characterized by patterns by
bifurcation. Similarly, Bateson found Iatmul patterns of mind (eidos) to be
characterized by "a sense of paradox, a sense of direct dualism—that everything has a sibling—and a sense of diagonal dualism—that everything has a
symmetrical counterpart" (in Lipset, 1980, 141). This strong sense of dualism manifests itself most dramatically in the naven ceremony, which provides
Bateson with an ethnographic springboard from which to theorize about
processes of differentiation, forms of relationship, and the progressive change
he terms *schismogenesis* (Houseman and Severi, 1998, 21).

Bateson (1958) introduces his description of naven by commenting that
the "outstanding feature of the ceremonies is the dressing of men in women's
clothes and of women in the clothes of men" (12). As the reader soon sees,
naven represents a complex pattern of bilateral and symmetrical dualisms,
expressed through transvestivism (7). About this complex pattern,
Houseman (with Severi, 1998) writes that during naven, "Each takes the
place of the other and does so in order to be seen" (ix). Based on Bateson's
description in *Naven*, this ceremonial play of gender duality and reversal
seems to work like this: When a laua (sister's child) achieves some culturally
significant fete for the first time, such as spearing an eel or killing an enemy,
the wau (mother's brother) is responsible for performing a naven ceremony.
It is important to note here that the wau is a classificatory uncle in that he
might be any close male relative related to the laua in a matrilineal way. The
ceremony proceeds with the classificatory wau (mother's brother) putting on
"the most filthy old tousled skirts such as only the ugliest and most decrepit
widows might wear, and like widows they were smeared with ashes"
(Bateson, 1958, 12). Next the wau stumble around the village with exaggerated feebleness looking for their "child" (the laua). Usually the laua have left
the village during the performance to avoid witnessing or being caught up in
the shame of the wau's ritual self degradation. As Bateson describes:

> If the wau can find the boy he will further demean himself by rubbing the cleft
> of his buttocks down the length of his laua's leg, a sort of sexual salute which is
> said to have the effect of causing the laua to make haste to get valuables which he
> may present to his wau to "make him all right." (13)

When women play the role of wau they are acting as classificatory aunts
and dress as men. In contrast to men, their reversal does not find them wear-
ing rags. Rather, the women dress in fashionable male clothes and regalia
associated with highly respected male warriors. Berman (1981) describes the

ritual pantomime of the women (dressed as powerful men) in contrast to that of the men (dressed as feeble women):

> They are referred to by male terminology (father, elder brother, etc.) and affect the bravado commonly associated with male behavior among the Iatmul, while the men act in a self-humiliating manner. The ceremony may also include a pantomime reversal of overt sexual activity. . . . Sometimes the wau will pantomime giving birth to the laua. (203)

In this ceremony the rigidly gendered dualities of everyday Iatmul life are reversed. As Bateson observes, Iatmul women tend to be discrete, gentle, and submissive. The men tend to be self-assertive, competitive, and prideful. In naven, what it means to be an Iatmul man or woman is "tried on," embodied, and exaggerated by the other. As the ritual progresses, the gendered behavior of naven's transvestites becomes increasingly, reciprocally differentiated. The women's (dressed as men) performance of maleness becomes more prideful, ostentatious, and theatrical. The men's (dressed as women) performance of Iatmul womanhood becomes more vulnerable, to the point of utter self-degradation. "Through this confrontation," Houseman (with Severi, 1998) writes, "the antagonism between the sexes erupts into the light of day; the ritual thereby reveals a dangerous intimacy" (ix).

Bateson termed this dangerous intimacy—the vicious circle of accelerated differentiation—schismogenesis, meaning literally "birth of separation" (22). According to Bateson (1958), schismogenesis is "a process of differentiation in the norms of individual behaviour resulting from cumulative interaction between individuals" (175). Bateson uses the terms symmetrical and complementary to differentiate two types of schismogenic relationships. In symmetrical schismogenesis, "progressive differentiation" takes place through competitive, parallel relational responses.

In contrast, complementary schismogenesis is one in which progressive differentiation occurs through the exchange of reciprocal, oppositional relational responses. Bateson (1958) offers this example to help illuminate his notion of complementary schismogenesis:

> If for example, one of the patterns of cultural behaviour, considered appropriate in individual A, is culturally labeled as an assertive pattern, while B is expected to reply to this with what is culturally regarded as submission, it is likely that this submission will encourage a further assertion, and that this assertion will demand still further submission. (176)

Bateson continues by asserting that "unless other factors are present to restrain the excesses of assertive and submissive behaviour, A must necessarily become more assertive, while B will become more and more submissive"

(176). The result is an "escalating spiral" of intensified duality that, left unchecked, might lead to disintegration (Berman, 1981, 21).

As Bateson saw it, this sort of spiral was at work in the relations of Iatmul society. In symmetrical terms, Iatmul men were caught in a vicious gendered cycle of reciprocal aggression and boasting. In complementary terms, Iatmul men and women were caught up in a rapidly escalating pattern of rigid gender opposition. Either pattern left unchecked promised social fissure and a concomitant breakdown of cultural integration. Bateson (1958) suggests that naven interrupts these patterns and thus inhibits the reciprocal escalation of progressive differentiation. According to Berman (1981), the wau-laua relationship "acts as a brake on symmetrical schismogenesis" (210). The wau and laua are in reality brothers-in-law whose separate clan identity is in some part maintained through a symmetrical pattern of boasting. But in the ritual logic of naven, the wau acts as the mother or wife to his laua. Thus, the transvestitism of the naven ceremony rearranges this symmetrical pattern into a complimentary one "that strengthens afinial links and thus softens the harshness of clan opposition" (210).

Similarly, Bateson (1958) proposes (at least in his initial analysis) that the naven ceremony provided a "counterbalance to a burdensome sexual ethos" spiraling through Iatmul society (in Berman, 1981, 209). Somewhat paradoxically, the naven ritual employs the excess of exaggerated duality in service of social integration. As Berman writes:

> Naven also prevents a cultural breakdown along sexual lines by allowing men and women to "become" each other . . . thereby releasing the tension accumulated by progressive personality distortion. Naven thus diffuses the climacteric that builds in both symmetrical and complementary schismogenesis. (210)

Through Bateson's via Berman's eyes, the naven ceremony can be seen as a therapeutic respite that keeps symmetrical schismogenic tension from spiraling out of control, keeping Iatmul people from splintering off and forming their own group. Further, naven can be seen to suspend patterns of gender differentiation, albeit temporarily, so that Iatmul men and women do not grow so far apart that they can no longer "see the other's point of view" (Bateson, 1958, 189). It is important to remember that Bateson's analysis was not as tidy as Berman's. Bateson's analysis is one of tense theoretical fits and starts. At the end of *Naven*, it is clear that "Bateson is also aware that nothing has been settled once and for all" (Houseman and Severi, 1998, 25).

Nonetheless, I want to suggest here that the dualism that structures the naven ceremony gives symbolic voice to the dualism surrounding relations of mind /culture at work throughout Bateson's *Naven*. Further, I want to suggest that one might see *Naven* itself as the ethnographer's metaphor in which the gendered Iatmul dualisms of male and female are used to evoke bipolarities of mind and culture, and a host of other dualisms, that patterned

Bateson's life. In this light, Bateson's initial analysis of *Naven*, in 1936, serves as theoretical or even therapeutic ritual of reconciliation, through which Bateson explores the "dangerous intimacy" of culturally constructed dualisms and how they can be undone through reinterpretation (Houseman and Severi, 1998, ix). In the case of the Iatmul people, reinterpretation is achieved through rituals reliant on exaggerated differentiation, rituals through which radical difference is reconfigured through transvestitism to form a transgressive, symbolic unity. This sort of project is not altogether different from Bateson's own struggles to find epistemological unity through rituals of scientific inquiry bent on uniting the multiplicity of seemingly opposing forces: mind/culture, knower/known, emotion/cognition, aesthetics/science, professional/personal, explanation/interpretation, epistemology/anthropology; Bateson the natural scientist/Bateson the social scientist. In this sense, Bateson's interpretation of the naven ceremony itself reveals the sort of epistemological perplexity with which he directly engages in his epilogues to *Naven*.

Naven, like the Iatmul culture it describes, is a "hot" text, "generating powerful tensions" (Berman, 1981, 209). Yet the powerful tensions at play in *Naven* ultimately are left unreconciled. As William James (1995) asks, "Are not all our theories just remedies and places of escape?" (13). Perhaps seeking remedy or at least relief, Bateson revisits these tensions theoretically in his epilogues. *Again we face connectedness at more than one level . . .*

Epilogical Recursions

Once the ritual drama has ended," writes Berman (1981) regarding naven, "the whole process is ready to begin anew" (210). Likewise, the end of *Naven* is not the end of Bateson's interpretive drama. Instead, Bateson embarks on "a voyage of discovery backward," and begins a two-tiered recursive process via epilogues that spans twenty years (Bateson, 1958, 281). Bateson uses *Naven's* epilogues to reflect on what he had retrospectively come to understand as flawed methods of analysis and particular instances of misunderstanding. This process, however, is of course more than the sum of its parts. For Bateson (1979), whose analysis relies on "connectedness at more than one level," reflection is more than a matter of clearing things up (13). Reflection becomes recursion. It is a process of rethinking more than correcting earlier ideas, and of thinking about the process of thinking about ideas. Bateson uses his particular struggle to construct a picture of Iatmul culture out of scraps of data to explore larger patterns of epistemological perplexity surrounding the unenviable endeavor of "the fitting together of data" (281). These epilogues work together with the body of *Naven* to form an intricate pattern that interweaves the startling particularity of Iatmul life, Bateson's struggle to explain it, and theoretical concerns concerning the complexities of explanation.

Early in his first, 1936, epilogue Bateson (1958) admits, "My whole picture of naven had been wrong" (259). Despite the self-critical tone, there is a sense of ease in *Naven*'s epilogue. Released from the double duty of ethnographic description and theory, Bateson is free to theorize more singularly. But Bateson's epilogue still works on multiple levels. On one level, Bateson uses this first epilogue to revisit fallacies in his analysis—specific ethnographic points where he succumbed to bad habits of thought. On another level, such examples serve more broadly to problematize the process of explanation. His description of the conceptual sloppiness of the categories he used to subdivide Iatmul culture is central to this effort. Bateson (1958) laments:

> I found that I had given no clear criterion for discriminating the elements of culture which I would pigeon-hole as *ethos* from those which I would pigeon-hole as *structure* or *pragmatic function*. I began to doubt the validity of my categories. (261–62)

Rather than rebuilding categories in order to shore up validity, Bateson reshuffles. And he discovers that instead of each bit of culture belonging to one or another category of behavior, categories label perspectives embedded in each bit of culture. Thus the sort of behavioral categories that give form to ethnographic explanation "do not stand too surely as categories of behaviour, but tend to resolve themselves into labels for points of view from which all behaviour may be seen"(262). Fleeing "misplaced concreteness," Bateson comes to understand his previous categories or subdivisions of Iatmul behavior less as solid analytic containers of cultural bits and instead sees them as labels for variable points of view. The point of Bateson's critique is not just to correct his analysis. Rather, Bateson employs his own experience with the fallacy of misplaced concreteness to demonstrate how seemingly concrete categories reflect the perspective of the interpreter, not immutable cultural facts.

Bateson, however, is not suggesting anthropologists abandon the process of categorizing. According to Bateson, conceptual categories such as the ones he used in his analysis of naven "are *really* descriptions of processes of knowing," even if they really only describe processes "adopted by scientists" (281).Thus the Iatmul's descriptions of themselves and the anthropologist's descriptions become inextricably linked in a complex, interrelated epistemological web of patterned description and explanation. As this 1936 epilogue points out, the complementary and symmetrical duality of Iatmul *eidos*

> As mathematics, as descriptions of patterns of regularity, has become the measure of reality during the modern era, so have our educational categories, such as "intelligence" lost their metaphoric sense and become mistaken for actual objects with an independent existence. A. N. Whitehead (1967), a neighbor of the Bateson's when both lived in England, called this independent existence *misplaced concreteness*.

(mind) and its cultural expression (naven) is, at least in part, in the eye of the beholder/s and exceeds the vision that duality as a pattern provides. Both epilogues, 1936 and 1958, suggest that "the experimenters are bound together with those we are experimenting upon in webs far more intricate than we even begin to imagine" (May, 1977, 82).

With more porous categories the interdependent, twin processes of organizing data and explanation and the relationship between knower and known become more fluid in form. Dichotomy becomes more difficult when data can be reshuffled, giving rise to explanations that transcend rigid categories of relevance. Either/or becomes less likely. Patterns become more complex. According to Bateson (1958), the resulting synthesis—recursively reshuffled—"will be all the more complete (though still partial) for having been guided by several types of relevance" (278).

In Bateson's (1958) second epilogue, context replaces category as the main focus. Twenty-one years have passed and Bateson now reexamines *Naven* with new epistemological eyes. As Bateson writes, "In the twenty-one years that have elapsed since the writing of this book, epistemology—that science or philosophy which has for subject matter the phenomena which we called knowledge and explanation—has undergone an almost total change" (280). This epistemological shift merges with the emerging context of a new science: part cybernetics, part communication theory and part mathematical logic, yet still "unnamed and imperfectly envisioned" (280–81). Bateson's intellectual context shifts from anthropology to the emerging field of cybernetics. Concomitantly, the second epilogue sounds a bit different than the first. The context of cybernetics provides a new language; consequently Bateson talks/writes/reexamines *Naven* in new and sometimes less than fluent ways. Much like the first epilogue, the second still leaves the reader reeling with the complexity of interpenetrating classifications and typologies. Bateson's second epilogue continues to demonstrate with force Bateson's idea that "wherever there is learning, knowing, seeing, or sensing, there is classifying. Levels and hierarchies must be understood; patterns of patterns; maps of maps of maps" (Bochner, 1981, 70).

Bateson extends such discussion by proposing that in order to classify it is necessary to consider context. Further, he uses the language of cybernetics to suggest that knowers, knowledge, and the context within which they exist are interdependently linked in interactive circular systems. By expanding the pattern of description to explore systems rather than static categories of data, this epilogue is able to examine (not predict) changes in relationship as well as patterns of relations. Using the language of circular systems, Bateson expands his notion of schismogenesis. The formally dualistic oppositions of Iatmul culture morph into multilayered patterns of self-correction and even learning.

Bateson (1958) articulates a dual purpose for his final epilogue. He wants to relate *Naven* to "these new ways of thought which were only dimly fore-shadowed" in the book's first iterations (282). He also wants to make the naven ceremony relevant to psychiatry. Instead of the tension that surrounds the disciplinary duality in the main body of *Naven*, Bateson now demonstrates "connections, patterns, relations, or more metaphorically, steps, bridges, pathways" between learning and context, among mind and culture (Bochner, 1981, 70). Epistemology serves as a pathway. As Bateson (1958) suggests, "problems of epistemology become crucial for the whole biological field, including within that field both the Iatmul culture and psychiatric diagnosis" (283). In this epilogue Bateson illustrates that the problems of psychiatry (mind) and anthropology (culture) are "shot through with epistemological difficulties" (282).

Fuller explanations—more complete patterns—now become Bateson's *epilogical* aim. In form and content both epilogues implore us "to look for explanations in the ever large units" rather than in microscopic reductions (Bochner, 1981, 75). Bateson's recursive journey back to *Naven* expands the patterns of his own explanation. In reexamining the complex patterns of his own explanatory patterns over time, Bateson layers category and context, meaning upon meanings—striking knower, known, and the context of knowing into relation as interactive parts of a dynamic system. For Bateson such patterns, though they may be more complete than others, are perpetually incomplete. At the end of Bateson's final epilogue there are still elusive questions concerning change—particularly planned change. There are certain mysteries, obscure patterns, that remain "for formal reasons impenetrable." *Again we face connectedness at more than one level . . .*

Cultured Epistemology

A mind is an aggregate of interacting parts.

Bateson, *Mind and Nature*

Culture as a whole appears as a complex fabric in which the various conflicting eidological motifs are twisted and woven together.

Bateson, *Naven*

There is a more conventional definition of epistemology, which simply says that epistemology is the philosophic study of how knowledge is possible. I prefer my definition—how knowing is done.

G. Bateson and M. C. Bateson, *Angels Fear*

In the body of *Naven*, Bateson (1958) expresses the difficulty of integrating dual matters of mind and culture: "The connection between the expression or eidos in the contexts which I have described, and the culture as a whole, is still not perfectly clear" (226). *Naven* is written in the midst of some of anthropology's earliest attempts, arguably led by Ruth Benedict, to "mind culture" through a reconciliation of personality and culture ambivalently based on psychology. Bateson (1991) notes a disciplinary trend in which "more and more" cultural anthropology devotes itself to

> unraveling the very complex problems which arise when we regard as variable not only the whole structure of social groupings, the whole system of behavior, but also, as equally variable, the human individual who exhibits these various forms of behavior. (10)

Many of Bateson's early struggles in *Naven* to explain conceptions of individual Iatmul minds in relationship to culture reveal this hermeneutic problematic. In order to explore the "patterning of standardized thought and the sorts of logic" that might be considered characteristic of Iatmul culture, Bateson (1958) must get into the primitive mind (229). But an understanding of the "cognitive habits" of the individual is impossible without an understanding of the cultural context with which individuals interact. Geertz (2000) points out that anthropologists interested in how people know "have all wrestled with the same angel" in their attempts to bring inner and outer, private and public, personal and social, psychological and historical, and experimental and behavioral into an intelligible relationship through ethnography (204). Bateson's struggles in this regard are evident in *Naven* and its two epilogues.

Cloaked in ambivalent descriptions of the dualism at work in the naven ceremony and laid bare in the epilogue's recursive theoretical strides, the question, "Where does mind stop and the rest of the world begin?" interpenetrates *Naven's* nervous narrative (Geertz, 2000, 204). Likewise, questions about the relationship among the mind of the anthropologist knower, the cultural known, and the knowledge they produce together lurk about its pages.

Quite possibly this tension served as a generative perturbation of sorts that gave rise to, or at least reflected, Bateson's emerging understanding of "mind" as more than individual. Though Bateson rejected psychoanalytic notions of a collective unconscious, as his daughter Mary Catherine Bateson (1984) describes, the concept of mind had collective as well as individual implications: "Thus for him, mind could be recognized in an ecosystem as well as in an organism, in a group as well as in an individual" (189). According to Gregory Bateson:

> The individual mind is immanent but not only in the body. It is immanent also in pathways and messages outside the body; and there is a larger Mind of which the individual mind is only a subsystem. (Bateson and Bateson, 1987, 467)

In *Naven*'s first epilogue, Bateson turns the order of anthropological inquiry on its head to work toward a cognitive picture that transcends the isolated individual mind and instead focuses on relationship. Bateson writes: "In these procedures. . . . we arrive not at pictures of the individual but at pictures of the events in which the individual is involved" (274). Bateson strikes the cognitive particular of the individual and the cognitive whole of culture into relationship so that the knower and his/her world become connected in larger pattern. Thus, his study of the "primitive mind" becomes a more complex cognitive study of the Iatmul "individual in the world" (274). This revisioning of his earlier thoughts on Iatmul *Eidos* allows Bateson to navigate the epistemological tension of deducing individual patterns of thought from larger cultural patterns. *Naven* can be seen as an early articulation of Bateson's desire to explore "ways of thinking" and an expression of his irritation at ways of thinking about thinking that seek to simplify the complexities of interrelated patterns and separate rather than connect.

Bateson (1979) sees an epistemology based on interrelationships of difference as a site of the sort of unity to which his theoretical yearnings in *Naven* seem to point. He defines epistemology as "the science that studies the process of knowing—the interaction of the capacity to respond to differences, on the one hand, with the material world in which those differences somehow originate, on the other" (Bateson and Bateson, 1987, 20). Having spent much of his career as an anthropologist devoted to piecing together scraps of conceptual and social particularities into explanations and representations of cultural collectivities, Bateson understands the fundamental tension embedded in local projects of description: "Most local epistemologies—personal and cultural—continually err, alas in confusing map with territory and assuming that the rules for drawing maps are immanent in the nature of that which is being represented in the map" (21). In "From Anthropology to Epistemology," Bateson (1991) makes a plea to epistemologize particularities of knowing in order to make them part of the same larger conversation of knowledge and culture—to (re)unify mind and matter, mind and culture, and knower and known. Bateson's epistemology, as hearkened in *Naven*'s final epilogue, represents insistence toward a necessary unity born out of frustrated anthropological experiences attempting to link patterns of mind with "configurations of culture"—without the common ground of a science of mind or language (89). For Bateson (with M.C., 1987), epistemology becomes that common language—the pattern that connects but does not confuse map with territory, and knower with known. Such a pattern Bateson sees is contingent upon difference and strikes "integration against diversity to vitalize both" (Babcock, 1995, 118). This notion of relation is a deeply useful understanding of understanding that generatively suspends dilemmas of the relationship between individuals and collectives, or parts and wholes, by relocating knowledge in between, and thereby establishing a functional yet fluid unity among knower and known through the reciprocity of relationship. *Again we face connectedness at more than one level. . . .*

Epilogue

A story is a little knot or complex of that species of connectedness which we call relevance.

Bateson, Mind and Nature

A man's reach should exceed his grasp. Or what's a meta-phor?

Bateson, in Brockman, About Bateson

As Edwin Schlossberg (1977) notes in his essay on the work of Bateson's mindful stories:

> When we make a story or when we make a poem we have the luxury of a context that exists at multiple levels of aggregation although the crossing from one to the other requires an entirely new set of logics and an entirely new way of observing and expressing. (166)

Bateson's *Naven* is such a story. *Naven* is an uneasy story about stories, one of which describes a *strange* transvestite ritual among the proud yet conflicted Iatmul people. But *Naven* also tells multiple interconnected tales: about a poetic young anthropologist/natural scientist/philosopher/communication theorist/mystic (that is another story) trying to find an inter/disciplinary home; about the "dangerous intimacy" of mind/culture, particular/whole, knower/known, emotion/cognition, aesthetics/science, professional/personal, explanation/interpretation, epistemology/anthropology about a thinker tinkering at the edge of his own thinking to find a way to transform dualistic thought into "double habits of mind" that unite "loose and strict thinking" (Bateson, 1991, 75); about interweaving scraps of data and different levels of abstraction in effort to create an ultimately unattainable ethnographic whole; about a theorist working with others on the edge of a new science (cybernetics); about the complexity of describing change, or any process for that matter—including mind and culture. *Naven* is, as Bateson's former wife Margaret Mead (1977) wrote, "a story about thinking" (178). It is a story that explores "ways of thinking about ideas. . . . and ways of thinking about thinking about ideas" and the interaction among these levels of thought (Wilder-Mott, 1981, 39). *Naven's* metacognitive plot pivots on recursion.

And then there is the indeterminate tale of Bateson's emerging epistemology. It is a tale that explores pattern and form, not substance; asks "how knowing is done" instead of what is knowledge; and unites knower and known in complex patterns of interaction (Bateson and Bateson, 1987, 20). Bateson's epistemological framework as suggested in *Naven* is not yet fully formed. There is more to come. Nevertheless, *Naven* provides a sketch that reveals a "reflexively shaped dynamic epistemology wherein discovery moves simultaneously in many directions" (Wilder-Mott, 1981, 40). That reminds me of a story—a story about a system I'll call curriculum.

My story is inspired by Bateson's. The setting, like *Naven*, is an unsettled one. It is a complex curricular context characterized by destructive patterns of dualism and fissure, both *familiar* and *strange*. Picture familiar rites of passage: "programming by bells and buzzers, behavioral objectives, tests and teachers, rows and dittos" (Quinn, 2002, 236). This is a place where strange compensatory rituals of *accountability* obscure the knowledge they purport to reflect, but that for the most part is not there. It is a time when the divisiveness of war and the "misplaced concreteness" of core *knowledge* out-shout the salient murmur of change. Pinar (2004) calls this time and place a nightmare (5).

So mine is a work of speculative fiction whose reach necessarily exceeds its grasp. As Ursula Le Guin (1989), herself an author of speculative fiction, writes defending her form: "Fiction . . . may be seen as an active encounter with the environment by means of posing options and alternatives, and an enlargement of present reality by connecting it to the unverifiable past and the unpredictable future" (44–45). Caught in the midst of overlapping horizons, mine is a selective story of curriculum, necessarily indeterminate, perhaps creative and unifying (Doll and Gough, 2002, 48).

In my story, form and content interweave to create a Bateson-inspired vision of curriculum. This curriculum—much like Stephen Tyler's (1986) description of postmodern ethnography—is "one of cooperative story-making that, in one of its ideal forms, would result in a polyphonic text, none of whose participants would have the final word in the form of a framing story of encompassing synthesis" (126). On one level, curriculum becomes a way of framing (not fencing) a lived epistemology where "academic knowledge, subjectivity, and society are inextricably linked" (Pinar, 2004, 11). Such a framework needs to be "loose" enough so that its relevance moves gracefully among categories and glides smoothly across contexts. On another level it needs to be "strict" enough to give form to fluid relevance. Its course is naturally recursive and relational; questions lead to other questions, and so on; all knowledge falls back upon itself. In such a curriculum "the consequences of past actions" become "the problematic for future ones" (Doll, 1993, 163).

Mine is a tale (like Bateson's *Naven* and its epilogues) of relational cultural meanings that are made and remade in perpetual transaction. Instead of fretting over how to integrate scraps of interaction (multiple perspectives, alternatives, contexts), the tension in this story concerns complex orders, forms, and patterns. Such a curriculum might be one where diverse contexts of interpretation—art and science to name but two—interact, as do mind and culture. Action becomes transaction "which turns both inward to the self and outward to society." Critiques of curriculum in the United States, such as Diana Hoffman (1996), suggest that "discourse, text, and practice in the multicultural domain are imbued with unexamined assumptions concerning such basic concepts as culture, self and individual identity" (204). A curriculum that minds culture examines assumptions about mind and culture and the interaction among them. Culture and mind become reciprocally defined. Curriculum here is a story of a meeting of minds. Where the mind as "a verb, an action verb; an active, seeking verb; an active, seeking, self organizing verb" (Doll, 1993, 131) joins forces with what Bateson (1958) calls the "whole interlocking—almost living nexus" that is culture (2).

In the closing scene of my story we find a curriculum listening carefully "to its own inner voice in the historical and natural world." Listen carefully; you can hear its echo as it whispers:

> Make it all a whole. It, all of it—intellect, emotion, behavior—occurs in and through the physical body. As the body is a concrete whole, so what occurs within and through the body can become a discernable whole, integrated in its meaningfulness. . . . Mind in its place, I conceptualize the present situation. I am placed together. Synthesis. (Pinar, 2004, 37)

Again we face connectedness at more than one level . . .

References

Babcock, B. (1995). Not in the absolute singular: Rereading Ruth Benedict. In *Women writing culture* (pp. 104–30). R. Behar and D. Gordon (Eds.). Berkeley: University of California Press.

Bateson, G. (1958). *Naven: A survey of the problems suggested by a composite picture of the culture of a New Guinea tribe dawn from three points of view.* Stanford, CA: Stanford University Press.

———. (1977). Afterward. In *About Bateson: Essays on Gregory Bateson.* J. Brockman (Ed.). New York: Dutton.

———. (1979). *Mind and nature: A necessary unity.* New York: Dutton

———. (1991). *A sacred unity: Further steps to an ecology of mind.* R. Donaldson (Ed.). New York: HarperCollins.

———. (2000). *Steps to an ecology of mind.* Chicago: University of Chicago Press. (Original publication, 1972).

Bateson, G., and M. C. Bateson (1987). *Angels fear: Toward an epistemology of the sacred.* New York: Macmillan Publishing Company.

Bateson, M.C. (1984). *With a daughter's eye: A memoir of Margaret Mead and Gregory Bateson.* New York: Morrow.

Behar, R. (1996). *The vulnerable observer: Anthropology that breaks your heart.* Boston: Beacon.

Berman, M. (1981). *The reenchantment of the world.* Ithaca, NY: Cornell University Press.

Bochner, A. (1981). Forming warm ideas. In *Rigor and imagination: Essays from the legacy of Gregory Bateson* (pp. 65–81). C. Wilder-Mott and J. Weakland (Eds.). New York: Praeger.

Brand, S. (1976). For God's sake: Conversation with Gregory Bateson and Margaret Mead. *CoEvolutionary Quarterly,* 10: 32–44.

Brockman, J. (1977). Introduction. In *About Bateson: Essays on Gregory Bateson* (pp. 3–28). J. Brockman (Ed.). New York: Dutton.

Clifford, J., and G. Marcus (Eds.). (1986). *Writing culture: The poetics and politics of ethnography.* Berkeley: University of California Press.

Doll, W. E. Jr. (1993). *A post-modern perspective on curriculum.* New York: Teachers College Press.

Doll, W. E. Jr., and N. Gough (Eds.). (2002). *Curriculum visions.* New York: Lang.

Donaldson, R. (1991). Introduction. In *A sacred unity: Further steps to an ecology mind,* (pp. ix–xix), Gregory Bateson. New York: HarperCollins.

Geertz, C. (1988). *Works and lives. The anthropologist as author.* Stanford, CA: Stanford University Press.

———. (2000). *Available light: Anthropological reflections on philosophical topics.* Princeton, NJ: Princeton University Press.

Hoffman, D. (1996). Culture and self in multicultural education: Reflections on discourse, text, as practice. *American Educational Research Journal,* 33: 545–69.

Houseman, M., and C. Severi. (1998). *Naven or the other self: A relational approach to ritual action.* Boston: Brill.

James, W. (1995). *Pragmatism.* New York: Dover. (Original publication, 1907.)

Le Guin, U. (1989). *Dancing at the edge of the world: Thoughts on words, women, places.* New York: Grove.

Lipset, D. (1977). Gregory Bateson: Early biography. In *About Bateson: Essays on Gregory Bateson* (pp. 21–54). J. Brockman (Ed.). New York: Dutton.

———. (1980). Gregory Bateson: *The legacy of a scientist.* Englewood Cliffs, NJ: Prentice Hall.

May, R. (1977). Gregory Bateson and Humanistic Psychology. In *About Bateson: Essays on Gregory Bateson* (pp. 75–99). J. Brockman (Ed.). New York: Dutton.

Mead, M. (1977). End linkage: A tool for cross-cultural analysis. In J. Brockman (Ed.). *About Bateson: Essays on Gregory Bateson* (pp. 171–231). New York: Dutton.

Pinar, W. (2004). *What is curriculum theory?* Mahwah, NJ: Erlbaum.

Quinn, M. (2002). Holy vision, wholly vision-ing: Curriculum and the legacy of the chariot. In *Curriculum visions* (pp. 232–44), W. E. Doll Jr., and N. Gough (Eds.). New York: Lang.

Rabinow, P. (1986). Representation as social facts: Modernity and postmodernity in anthropology. In *Writing culture: The poetics and politics of ethnography* (pp. 234–61). J. Clifford and G. Marcus (Eds.). Berkeley: University of California Press.

Rieber, R. (1989). In search of the impertinent question: an overview of Bateson's theory of communication. In *The individual, communication and society* (pp. 1–28). R. Rieber, K. Oatley, and A. Manstead (Eds.). New York: Cambridge University Press.

Rosaldo, R. (1989). *Culture and truth.* Boston: Beacon.

Schlossberg, E. (1977). For my father. In *Essays about Bateson on Gregory Bateson* (pp. 145–167). J. Brockman (Ed.). New York: Dutton.

Toulmin, S. (1981). The charm of the scout. In *Rigor and imagination: Essays from the legacy of Gregory Bateson* (pp. 357–68). C. Wilder-Mott and J. H. Weakland (Eds.). New York: Praeger.

Tyler, S. (1986). Post Modern Ethnography: From document of the occult to occult document. In *Writing culture: The poetics and politics of ethnography* (pp. 122–40). J. Clifford and G. Marcus (Eds.) Berkeley: University of California Press.

Visweswaran, K. (1994). *Fictions of feminist ethnography.* Minneapolis: University of Minnesota Press.

Wilder-Mott, C. (1981). Rigor and imagination. In *Rigor and imagination: Essays from the legacy of Gregory Bateson* (pp. 6–42). C. Wilder-Mott and J. Weakland (Eds.). New York: Praeger.

Whitehead, A. N. (1967). *Science and the modern world.* New York: The Free Press. (Original publication, 1925.)

 # Chinese Aesthetics, Fractals, and the *Tao* of Curriculum

An inner connection, a bridge, can be made between rational scientific insight and emotional aesthetic appeal; these two modes of cognition of the human species are beginning to concur in their estimation of what constitutes nature.

Gert Eilenberger, in *The Beauty of Fractals*

Art has always been fractal.

John Briggs, *Fractals*

The Chinese aesthetics embodied in the art of garden and fractals are like an odd combination, not only in time and space, but also in history and culture. Such a play with contemporary Western mathematics and the ancient Chinese garden, as strange as it might seem, originated from my recent trip back to China after I was influenced by the insights of fractal eyes. My American guests'[1] enthusiasm over the flow of chaos in gardens inspired me to look at what is familiar as if I were seeing it for the first time: "Every meeting a first encounter" (Bei, 1991, 11). The classic Chinese garden as a way of seeing, a way of re/presenting nature and universe, and fractal as an extraordinary representation of nature in its aliveness, its fracture, and its fluid multiplicity, echo each other and inform each other. Such a calling between the two not only indicates the coming together of aesthetics/art and mathematics/science, but it also initiates cultural conversations to interrupt the neat order implied by the notion of linear historical progression. I certainly have no intention of valorizing the art of the Chinese garden, making it compatible with contemporary breakthroughs in fractal geometry. What I am interested in is initiating interplay between the two. The metaphors of fractals and *Tao*—an underlying principle of Chinese aesthetics and particularly of Chinese gardens—are utilized for rethinking pedagogy, curriculum, and education.

This chapter uses similar threads, yet perhaps with different emphasis, and focuses on both fractals and Chinese gardens to weave a new picture of curriculum. It does not intend to do any comprehensive studies on either fractals or Chinese gardens and its focus is to explore an "impossible meeting," as Jacques Derrida phrases it (in Bernstein, 1992, 27), between Eastern and Western wisdom at the intersection of "curriculum dynamics" (Fleener, 2002).

Harmony in Differences and Fractal Self-Similarity

> *Hills seen from horizon, mounts from side*
> *Forever different, distant or near, high or low*
>   Su Shi, in *A Splintered Mirror*

Fractal self-similarity pervades the bodies of organisms, but it is not the blatant homunculus self-similarity that was imagined by earlier science.
                                      Briggs and Peat, *Turbulent Mirror*

One striking feature of the classical Chinese garden (see Figure 14.1) is the sense of harmony in differences. Not only the layout of the garden but also the concrete design of respective buildings, hills, rockery, water, flowers, and trees all display complicated "poetic symbolism and philosophical allusions" (Siren, 1950) and a cosmic interplay of unity and multiplicity. The patterns of architecture in the overall layout of pavilions, temples, halls, terraces, verandas, towers, gateway arches, or boats in their endless variety, detailed in the designs and shapes of roofs, walls, wall-opening traceries, pavements, and doors, never repeat themselves yet achieve an aesthetically pleasing form of balance.

Harmony achieved by the interaction of *yin* and *yang* is implied in the flowing interplay between seemingly contradictory directions such as connecting and separating, showing and hiding, real and false, open and closed— these are several of the artistic principles of garden design listed by Lifang Chen and Sianglin Yu (1986). Vital relationships are the key to the lively rhythms of harmony. Maggie Keswick (1978) uses the phrase "harmonious vibration" to describe the interconnections within the garden. What makes the landscape of the garden harmonious under the brush of artists and craftsmen is what sets it into movement rather than what makes it uniform or common. To enable such a movement, we must consider the nature of relationships. Keswick is keen to point out that the arrangement of the traditional Chinese house shows a different order of relationships: "formal, decorous, regular and clearly defined" (12). The classical Chinese garden defies such a confining order by building relationships across and within differences in order to mobilize any rigid formal structure. Differences and multiplicity as part of nature's wonder are both connected and separated through an elaborated arrangement to create a garden rich in layers, unexpected in mystery, yet winding and bending throughout a limited space to achieve the ultimate harmony between humanity and universe.

Figure 14.1 Chinese Garden[3]

Harmony is a Chinese notion which is often perceived by Westerners as static and achieved by the suppression of differences. The dynamics in harmony are usually neglected. However, the emergence of fractal language partially called for by the varied scaling of scenic features asks us to re-look at this ancient notion of harmony. The classic Chinese painting and miniature trees and rockery (which are usually part of the garden) have already been acknowledged for their fractal scaling (McGuire, 1991). Garden scenes are also created in different scales to depict what is observed from varied distances. Such a re-creation of nature to show nature in a more lifelike way rather than in a static, "realistic" depiction is echoed in the creation of fractal art, which is based upon self-similarity across different scales. Fractal images are extraordinarily harmonious but at the same time have an infinite variety of patterns. Fractal self-similarity shows a fascinating endless sequence of patterns within patterns that are similar but not identical. Being identical would mean eventual closure but a small difference can keep the dynamics alive. These patterns emerge from the backgrounds of disorder. The harmonious beauty we see from fractal art, as Eilenberger (1986) points out, occurs from the balanced mixture of order and disorder, similar to *Tao*, which balances different forces. This mixture of the two, on the edge between order and disorder, has important curriculum implications, and William Doll (1998) elaborates a new sense of pedagogy through the balanced interplay between stability and instability.

The self-similarity of fractals brings forth a new interplay of whole and part since part and whole are implicated in each other rather than parts accumulating into the whole. Any part of the whole can be a miniature of the whole and the whole can be seen in the parts. Yet at the same time, the interaction between part and whole generates an endless variety of beautiful images. As we go deeply into the boundary area of the Mandelbrot set,[2] we continuously encounter surprises. This is a mathematical embodiment of harmony in differences.

Both fractal self-similarity across different scales and the garden's harmony in differences produce visual beauty and intellectual wonder through playing with fractures and irregularity. Such a blending or blurring between mathematics/science and aesthetics is not surprising and crosses traditional boundaries between disciplines to inspire and generate. The order implicated in fractal geometry and Chinese aesthetics is somehow different, however. Fractals, as chaotic as they may seem, have underlying mathematical equations that intend to "catch" the irregular structures of nature. Benoit Mandelbrot (1982, 1986), Heinz-Otto Peitgen and H. Richter (1986) acknowledge that nature cannot be exhausted by mathematical representation including fractal geometry. The Chinese garden is guided by the aesthetic flow of *Tao* which follows nature as the ultimate guide. The garden is highly naturalistic with necessary artistic elaboration. In simplistic terms, fractals are ordered mathematically and scientifically while a garden is ordered aesthetically and naturalistically. The gap between nature and human, or between aesthetics and science, no matter how much the two become interrelated and intertwined, is still needed to inspire human imagination and creativity. Such inspiration from both realms in their interconnection and separation is what we need in our classroom.

Furthermore, the relationship between part and whole in fractals and gardens has certain different arrangements, too. As Michael McGuire (1991), a photographer who attempts to capture fractal images of nature, and Stephen H. Kellert (1993) point out, fractals particularly, and chaos theory in general, are intensely "holistic." Before delving into the endless details of parts, the first impressions are of the vast interconnections and networks. Different from such an immediately holistic view, the Chinese garden—due to its small size—deliberately conceals the whole in the beginning and makes the whole of the garden visible only after the tour. The spirit of the universe and the mood of humanity, however, always infuse the parts of the garden so that skipping any of the parts may not influence the overall aesthetic experiencing of the whole garden. These somehow different directions of entering into the whole indicate multiple ways of possibly successful pedagogical entrances as long as the intricate relationships between part and whole are taken into consideration.

Such interplay between part and whole challenges our usual way of approaching curriculum. The notion of curriculum as a linear progression of accumulating subtopics to reach the whole can no longer be effective in a fractal world. In traditional mathematics education, we tell young learners that "zero" is meaningless, or "negative numbers" do not exist (always subtract the smaller number from the bigger) because we believe they are not mature enough to deal with complex problems at their ages. Yet (imaginary) complex numbers essential to the birth of fractals start with the square roots of negative numbers. In fact, this fractal way of seeing the world is more in tune with the intuition of the child. By denying the students opportunities for mathematical imagination, we are not protecting them from the shock of encountering the "impossible," but are stifling their self-organizing attunedness to the spirit of the world. Defining any subject in a linear order downplays the students' capacity for understanding and making (fractal) connections. Not only the content of what we teach but also the approaches to how we teach are problematic. If fractal harmony is valued, perhaps our way of knowing the world and teaching/learning about the world needs to be transformed. This transformation raises many questions: What would a fractal curriculum be like? Is it possible to teach through fractal networks rather than along straight paths? How can we create multiple layers of substructures in a subject matter which contain the keys to unlock the whole?

Movement along Irregularity and Nonlinearity

Still mountain moves with water,
Stubborn stone becomes alive with trees.

Chongguang Da, Quoted in Jin

Clouds are not spheres, mountains are not cones, coastlines are not circles, and bark is not smooth, nor does lightning travel in a straight line.
Benoit Mandelbrot, *The Fractal Geometry of Nature*

To use James Gleick's phrase, fractal geometry is "a geometry of the pitted, pocked, and broken up, the twisted, tangled, and intertwined" (1987, 94). The word *fractal* was coined by Benoit Mandelbrot to convey the irregular and fractured quality of this new mathematical concept in its vivid capture of nature's flow. The word "irregular" is ironic since what we see in nature is usually not regular Euclidean mathematical shapes such as straight lines, rectangles, or circles. The fractal shapes that were previously regarded as "monstrous" by mathematicians are actually everywhere in nature. It would be hard to say what is regular and what is irregular if we see through nature's eyes.

Fractals help us adjust our lens to appreciate the beauty of the world in a different way. Nonlinearity can reduce circles to lines through iteration but also can produce complicated images out of iterations of simple mathematical equations with imaginary complex numbers. The video *The Mandelbrot Set and Julia Sets* (1990) vividly demonstrates an elaborated sense of movement out of ruggedness, brokenness, and fragmentation. Boundaries are constantly rearranged and structures are continually destabilized as more and more images emerge as the picture is zoomed at different levels. This new mathematical imagination both fascinates and inspires. Fractals are about dynamics and movement, not about the static.

Regular shapes have been features of classical Western gardens. Chinese garden concepts, in their emphasis on movement out of the irregular, reached Europe in the eighteenth century (Chen and Yu, 1986; Siren, 1950). Until then, "the gardens of the West had been based on straight lines and rectangles" (Keswick, 1978, 9). Irregularity and nonlinearity are no longer new ideas today in the world of garden design, yet the long tradition of the Chinese garden in its artistic sophistication and natural flowing rhythm still has much to offer.

Chinese gardens are composed of "irregular, asymmetric, curved, crooked, undulating lines, planes, and forms derived from nature" (Tsu, 1988, 132). Such an irregularity and curvature is present throughout the garden: ponds, lakes, paths, bridges, stepping stones, mountain trails, roofs, stone plates, pavements, doors, wall openings, wall-opening traceries, rockeries, and waterways. These organic elements within the garden seldom go straight but wind, meander, serpentine, zigzag, undulate, and flow. This movement brings out an extraordinary depth and richness that a linear layout and design cannot reach.

The entrance to the garden is particularly notable in forming a nonlinear flow. The entrance is designed with turns, zigzags, screens, and bends, just as the well-known phrase by an ancient poet Bai Ju-yi states, "A thousand pleas and ten thousand calls brought her [lute player] out, yet her half face was covered by the lute." This nonlinearity contrasts with the entrance to the classical Western garden, where an orderly layout of the garden is present explicitly and clearly. The entrance to the Chinese garden intends to stimulate the imagination and intensify one's interest, initiating the tour of the garden with an appreciation of intricacy rather than simplicity. Thus, a distant landscape is always hidden partially by walls, trees, rocks, buildings, or other clever means of screening, and nonlinearity prevails. The entrance can also be used as a contrast or a preclude to the major scenes of the garden, arousing a sense of surprise and spontaneous enlightenment. There is no sharp sense of ending. There is always more to see, to experience, and to appreciate, as layer upon layer of the scenery constantly unfold.

> This idea of "drama of entrance" is intriguing. How might such dramas in the classroom invite students into the world of ideas?

The sense of ending is also forever suspended in fractals as we can always go into more details yet another time for another adventure. Our entrances into fractals are not straightforward either. The beauty of the whole image at the first sight can fascinate us, but we can also follow the curves of different segments to move into various details. Different entrances bring different paths of wonder, awe, and mystery. "Every foray into the Mandelbrot set," says James Gleick (1987), brings "new surprises" (228).

Such drama of entrance has rich pedagogical implications. The traditional linear way of teaching in its transmissional mode passes knowledge from instructor to student without problematizing the issue at hand in the first place. Without such entrance, such evocation into the delicacy and intricacy of knowledge and beauty, students have become accustomed to ask "what should I do next" or "what are practical applications of whatever you are talking about," refusing to come into a rich and complicated space of knowing and being. Such a space generates and regenerates meanings through participants' lingering to play, to absorb, and to create, much like appreciating (and further making) a garden or a fractal implies. One problem with our current pedagogy is that we assume students can take in knowledge directly. Such an assumption leads to a linear mode of teaching which in turn produces students who do not know how to question, explore, and above all, enjoy the journey of learning. Even many of our graduate students expect to acquire unproblematic knowledge and skills in the class and then implement them practically in their work. The beauty, wonder, and mystery of knowledge are removed and the spirit of life drains away. The crafted intention of the Chinese garden's entrance reminds us of the necessity of starting the tour of knowing with allusion and metaphor rather than direct didactic. William Doll (1996), in his vision of nonlinear teaching, brings forth the notion of throwing out a seed, rich with problematics, to initiate the iterative interaction among teacher, student, and text. This pedagogical seed plays a role more important in propagating zigzags and spirals, an intellectual and spiritual garden, than in providing correct answers. This is a nonlinear flow of multiple layers, as fractals lure us into an extraordinarily complex journey.

Nature is fractal yet harmonious. Fractures, irregularity, and even holes—abundant in nature—form a flowing roughness and untidiness. Both fractals and the Chinese garden have captured the turbulent fluidity of nonlinearity and irregularity in their own ways. The empty spaces in the Mandelbrot set and the Julia sets, as Fleener (2002) reminds us, can be used to trace out "the complexity of interrelated and interconnected influences" (186) and are full of meanings and hidden order. Rockeries, in their deliberate balance of hole and whole—a word play for chaos theory—demonstrate how what is present can be shown in what is absent in an artistic way. Such interplay between full (*yang*) and empty (*yin*) can be traced back to Lao Zi's philosophy:

Putting thirty spokes together to make a wheel,
We find the usefulness in the void.
Molding clay into a vessel,
We find the usefulness in the hollow.
Cutting doors and windows for a house,
We find the usefulness in its empty space.

Lao Zi, *Tao Te Ching,* Chapter 11

To look at these empty spaces with "soft eyes" (Fleener, 2002), we may find more freedom to play with imagination, change, and aesthetic pleasures. This movement out of irregularity, emptiness, and nonlinearity has a temporal dimension to it as the stones have been hollowed by weather and pitted with holes over a long period of time. Such motion is "naturalized" in multiple senses. The spatial and temporal movement of nature challenges us to think about the possibility of organizing curriculum not only with what is present in the textbook, but also with what is absent in the formal structure (Fleener, 2002). What is missing from the picture—those unexpected holes—may take us to surprising realms of imagination and creativity. What has evolved historically as we journey into the unknown is also essential for envisioning our world differently. Empty spaces and silent moments are sometimes necessary for questioning the given. How can new inspirations be generated without first emptying our already filled "mind cups"? Can we nurture pedagogical silence, walk with our students into deep reflection, and arrive yet again, with renewed ways of seeing and understanding? A sense of emptiness may settle in with any provocative teaching, but if we do not run away from it or try to eliminate it as we usually do, but rather cultivate it, to see through screens, new landscapes of knowing may emerge. And, as William Doll (1998) advocates—demonstrates—a new sense of control, different from linear control, can emerge too. Such control evolves with the interactions of all participants, so that the teacher guides the motion, yet is part of the movement (him-) her-self.

Infinity within the Finite and a Pedagogical Journey Beyond

Mysterious structure of famous garden—Compatible with Painting and Zen
The huge universe—Embodied in one seed

Yanting Wang, Quoted in Jin

Each transformation adds a little area to the inside of the curve, but the total area remains finite, not much bigger than the original triangle, in fact. If you drew a circle around the original triangle, the Koch curve would never extend beyond it.

Gleick, *Chaos*

The movement of nonlinearity and irregularity leads to an enlarged visual space which creates infinity within the finite. Within the boundary of a finite area, possibility and variety can be infinite. Such positioning between the infinite and the finite in both Chinese gardens and fractals encourages a pedagogical journey of going beyond what is present into new possibilities.

The underlying conception of the garden-maker is to embody the huge universe within a small but crafted garden. One way to create such a sense of infinity is to utilize zigzags, curves, and bendings in a sophisticated way. The Chinese garden is full of zigzag rooms, crooked alleyways, winding corridors, rugged mountain trails, bending banks, undulating bridges, and meandering paths. Such a winding design serves not only to connect in a surprising way, but also to expand the limited space of the garden. Curves can produce the effect of multiplying visual layers, creating contrasting scenery, leading to an ever-changing kaleidoscope of the universe. What is pregnant along with the curve is unexpected discovery, in-depth appreciation, and endless richness.

The vastness of space visually and experientially presented in a limited environment is also achieved through deliberate ambiguity between "indoors" and "outdoors." Walls and wall openings in various shapes both reveal what can be seen and conceal what can not be seen, which leads tourists to further journey. Even what can be seen shifts when it is seen from another angle. The lure of "moreness" and "beyondness"—to use Dwayne Huebner's (1999) phrase of curriculum as a spiritual journey—is precisely what such a crafted ambiguity intends to do: enter in, to go beyond. It is this lure that will bring our students beyond the present, beyond the taken-for-granted viewpoint, to transcend the confinement of one space into another world, another landscape, and another fascinating journey of intellect, heart, and spirit. Pausing at the threshold, a liminal moment, is important for students to glimpse both worlds, to grasp the previous world, to carry with them in their adventure into the new.

The Chinese garden shows an intricate combination of both density and looseess: "so sparse as to let a horse walk, so dense as not to let a breeze in." Individual objects may also play such a role. Keswick (1978) points out that "even a single rock in a garden may represent a complete range of mountains" (101). Keswick further uses two visuals to show how the rusticness and whole/hole of one rockery simulate the image of a multiple-layered mountain created in classical Chinese painting (102). The imaginative aspect of appreciating rockeries imbues these extra/ordinary stones with an exceptional potential for creating infinity within the confinement of a small garden.

Infinity within the finite is also a striking feature of fractals. As Gleick (1987) points out, the infinite variety within the finite boundary of the Mandelbrot set makes every detail "a universe of its own, diverse and entire" (229). Such a representation of detail and whole is not unlike the relationship between rock and mountain. Fractal images such as the Koch curve have an infinite length but within a finite area. Such a paradoxical relationship between infinity and the finite also mobilizes the interplay between whole and part, which become mutually implicated in each other.

The infinite possibilities generated by the Mandelbrot set are embedded within its bounded patterns and relationships. This interplay between the infinite and the finite is enabled by the combination of contemporary non-linear mathematics and computer simulation to demonstrate the endless variety of nature, which is what the classical Chinese garden intends to do. The function of nonlinear mathematical iterations is essential to showing the whole universe through details and the iteration capacity of the computer expands human possibility in an astonishing way. Fractal art, however, is still different from the Chinese aesthetic embodied in a garden. Briggs (1992) warns us about the possibilities of turning fractals into another dogma and I have deep doubts about the claim that "all questions of pattern, order, and complexity are essentially mathematical" (Capra, 1996, 153). To keep a certain distance between aesthetics and fractal mathematics, I believe, is healthy for approaching the multiplicity of structure and order in nature and human life. The fractal self-similarity embedded in both differences and underlying structure, as near as it is to nature, cannot exactly represent the diverse ways of natural organization. Aesthetic order has its own appeal that cannot be exhausted by fractal order. Aesthetics can be seen through fractal eyes while the understanding of fractals can be enriched and informed by aesthetics—as I am trying to do here. However, whether it is aesthetics or fractals or both, the sense of infinity within the finite has important implications when we think about enlarging pedagogical possibilities within the finite area of any school subject. If we shift the focus of curriculum from linear order to fractal path, can we unfold a creative process of journeying beyond yet not breaking away from the boundary for both teacher and student?

Interconnected Networks and Passages to the Mystery of Knowing

> *Mountains multiply, streams double back—I doubt there's even a road*
> *Willows cluster darkly, blossoms shine—another village ahead!*
> Lu You, in Watson, *Columbia Book of Chinese Poetry*

> In fact, it is by giving substance to the usually vague term *wholeness* that the science of chaos and change is forging a revolution in our perspective.
> Briggs and Peat, *Chaos*

The process of creating infinity out of the finite leads to a complicated network made possible in the Chinese garden by both connecting and separating. Unique design principles such as simultaneously concealing and revealing, opening and closing, creating looseness and density make the experience of touring the garden like the process of unfolding a scroll painting in which independent scenes are linked by flowing water, pervasive mist, or moving clouds. Chen and Yu (1986) point out that tortuous mountain trails and meandering brooks deliberately adopt cut-offs to lure tourists into another view. Such a combination of separation and connection leads to endless joy and excitement as layer upon layer of secret, deep, and serene spaces are opened up. When the path seems at the end or the depth of the garden seems exhausted, with the twist of zigzag movement, another unexpected scene emerges. Such a way of passaging is an interesting metaphor for us in thinking about how to lead students upon the road of the mystery of learning.

Both John Briggs (1992) and Stephen Kellert (1993) point out that fractals are essentially holistic. In such a holism, "everything influences, or potentially influences, everything else—because everything is in some sense constantly interacting with everything else" (Briggs, 1992, 21). Such holism is sensitive to both external influences and internal disturbances. This link between the internal and the external is also reflected in the art of gardens. The inner dynamic harmony within the Chinese garden is expanded into the outside to mingle with bigger spaces. Temples, mountains, or water outside of the garden is deliberately borrowed inside the garden. The gardens within gardens and gardens without gardens, if we use a phrase from self-organization and fractals, are enabled by an inner "dissipative structure" with "strange attractors." In such a network, the center—if there is one—becomes destabilized with a series of scenes that attract, disperse, and redefine boundaries. Since every scene that serves as attractor can be regarded as a miniature embodiment of the garden, just as the garden is the embodiment of the universe, the tourists can capture the message of the garden through immersing themselves in one particular scene. Such a playful interaction between the part and the whole moves with fractal eyes. As Fleener (2002) points out, "the interconnectedness and depth associated with relational meanings and comprehensive explorations" (167) of fractals show us a new sense of depth and richness that can be dug out not by simply working hard but by *playing with* interrelationships and patterns. Such play builds passages to the mystery of knowing which cannot be captured by a step-by-step accumulation of knowledge. One of the paradoxes of fractals is that they are determined by nonlinear mathematical equations but what is present after iterations is unpredictable. There is always an element of randomness built in, yet such an unanticipation must be coupled with interconnections. Such a challenge to

> Play is a most misunderstood concept. As Trueit (this volume) points out, play fills the player with its own spirit—a spirit which animates and enlivens. Hans Georg Gadamer, Martin Heidegger, and Michel Serres all develop the spiritfulness of play and show its relevance for meaningful thought.

the distinction between determinacy and indeterminacy, predictability and unpredictability, randomness and relationships is "revolutionary." The most fascinating area in fractals is at the boundary of the Mandelbrot set whose generative power is endless. This margin between order and surprise is the most complicated, delicate, and creative realm in which both the network and the components can be open to new structures. Relationships are not of static components but of emergent processes. Fractals show an intricate inter-twining relationship between simplicity and complexity, and between the local and the global. The continuous interaction between the whole and the local makes the emergent structure of the global change with the dynamics of local interactions.

Such an understanding of the global and the local also leads to a different perspective on "change." As Doll (1989) points out, *change* from a modern perspective is *handled* in a predictable and incremental way. But in a complex and open system, change *happens* in a spontaneous and transformative way. Emergent properties of the whole as a result of local interactions cannot be predicted in advance. The patterns of the system are seen unfolding only as they unfold. A sense of surprise is always present in the process. Such a trans-formative and creative view of change takes both teacher and student to the wonder of knowing and the surprise of journey.

The *Tao* of Curriculum along Fractal Paths

Tao gives birth to the One,
The One gives birth to the Two,
The Two gives birth to the Three,
The Three gives birth to the myriad things.
The myriad things carry yin and embrace yang,
Through the interplay of energy (ch'i),
Reach harmony.

Lao Zi, *Tao Te Ching*, Chapter 42

Can we develop a creative curriculum that is open to fractal movement? What curricular relationships and networks can we build in order to generate transformations of both teacher and student? What new languages do Chinese gardens and fractals offer us to see curriculum differently? As David Fowler (1996) suggests, Piaget's approach for children's cognitive develop-ment is a process of diminishing the fractal dimension in children's knowing process to "progress" within a Euclidean structure. This notion of progress itself becomes problematic under new eyes and brings up an interesting ques-tion: Are we trying to open up students' potentials through education or does the way we teach our children block their creative expressions? Huebner (1999) phrases this well: "Perhaps it would be more appropriate to ask what prevents creativity than to ask how one learns to be creative" (134).

Traditionally we as educators want to be "certain" that what we teach is passed on to students successfully. This quest for certainty is challenged by nonlinear relationships which make it impossible to predict and control in the usual sense. According to Gregory Cziko (1989), "human cognitive development and behavior, insofar as it is based on creative learning, is by its very nature indeterminate and thus unpredictable" (20). The result of the same instructional intervention upon different students can be dramatically different. This uncertainty calls upon creative pedagogical responses and demands that "teachers must continually Become as they guide their students through the processes of Becoming" (17). This challenge would be too much for any teacher who is afraid that the class is out of control, yet would be exciting for those who dare to take risks.

A fractal curriculum evolving at the edge of order and surprise is imbued with the *Tao* of movement for all participants. As Doll (1993) envisions, a transformative curriculum based upon nonlinearity and complexity "continually regenerates itself and those involved with it" (87). Along the fractal path, curriculum becomes complex, recursive, and creative, and both teacher and student become engaged in their own personal transformation.

Curriculum as a network no longer follows the hierarchy of the traditional curriculum system in which the teacher and the knower are privileged. The teachers' role is no longer to determine what students should do but to exercise influence as part of an ever-changing curriculum web. This shift, however, does not diminish the teacher's important roles in educational processes. On the contrary, in opening to the indeterminate, the unexpected, and the emergent, the teacher must respond to educational situations in a much more creative way. The knower and the known also become intertwined in such a curricular matrix. The knower is no longer a master and objective observer of the known, but both are engaged with each other as participants in the network. In such an interactive framework, knowledge becomes an active construction of transforming and transformative reality composed of interwoven patterns rather than an objective representation of stable reality. As Fleener (1999) suggests, the relationship between students and mathematics should be constructed in such a way that students can know themselves through the process of knowing mathematics. To become engaged with the subject matter—which is not limited to mathematics—students are open to their personal potential for fractal creativity.

David Fowler (1996) proposes a fractal curriculum which not only incorporates fractal concepts in the content of mathematical education but also demonstrates a fractal-like structure in organizing the content and teaching through a globally connected network based on information technology. The fractal curriculum as "a series of thematic connections" (26) around five mathematical themes (dimension, quantity, uncertainty, shape, and change) rather than a linear series of topics organized by objectives is envisioned. For instance, the Sierpinski triangle in which the themes of Shape, Change, and Uncertainty are intertwined becomes an "attractor" of learning. Fowler also proposes to utilize technology and the Internet, or even artificial intelligence systems for "constructing new thematic strands through curricular space" (31). Such an ambitious project, if materialized, would be a heuristic for all subjects.

Teaching along fractal movement requires us to play with ambiguity and contradictions as the *Tao* of creativity emerges from a dynamic interaction between different or even opposite energies. Chinese gardens embody such a moving force through this unique design and layout utilizing the generative power of opposites. A strong sense of play brought forth by nonlinear motion, when introduced into the classroom, can open up infinite pedagogical possibilities. Play leads both teacher and student beyond the limits of conflicts to new realms of life. Ambiguity, like an empty space or a silent moment, is generative, and meaning making through ambiguity is built by connecting differences. The relational nature of both fractals and *Tao* upholds a creative curriculum in which the boundary of what we teach and what we learn cannot be settled but perpetually shifts.

The *Tao* of curriculum along fractal paths moves out of irregularity and nonlinearity, embraces harmony in differences, leads a pedagogical journey through intricate passages to the mystery of knowing. A curriculum envisioned through *Tao* and fractals calls us to journey toward an imaginative realm in which creativity, relationality, and emergence become main themes of education and pedagogy. The contemporary Chinese poet Shu Ting (1991) invites us:

> *In a moment of creation*
> *I will leave shining words*
> *In the pupils of children's eyes*
> *Igniting golden flames.* (92)

To ignite such *golden flames*, let us embrace fractal and Taoist imagination. Calling potentials into existence, let us transform curriculum participants, including ourselves. Shining words flowing out, we create new languages. Let our classrooms be moved with such a moment of creation, vibrant with life, full of the inspiration from the unknown. Such is the *Tao* of curriculum to which we aspire through fractal eyes.

Notes

1. In the Fall of 2000, I accompanied William Doll and Donna Trueit on their visit to China. We toured various gardens in different cities, including the well-known Suzhou gardens. I am grateful to both of them for helping me see my own culture from different angles, and especially to Dr. Doll with his insights about the link

between chaos and complexity theory and Chinese aesthetics. Without their inspirations, this essay would not have been born.

2. The Mandelbrot set is the principal visual symbol for the concept of fractals, and is computer-generated by iterating nonlinear equations. The self-similarity of the fractal leads to patterns within patterns. The boundary area of the Mandelbrot set is particularly generative. Different scales of magnification in that area produce intricate shapes which is continuously self-replicating in patterns, but with a large variety of the overall images. However deeply one goes into the border, more and more shapes are generated. There is no ending point. There is always something more and something new to see.

3. This famous picture is from Patricia Ebrey's website, *A visual source book for Chinese civilization* (http:depts.washington.edu/chinair/home/swangshy.htm). The original source is Guri Pan (Ed.) (1988). *Chinese arts and crafts—architecture art 3: garden architecture*. Beijing: Chinese Architecture and Industry Press. p. 111.

References

Bei, D. (1991). Poem. In *A splintered mirror: Chinese poetry from the democracy movement*. Donald Finkel (Ed.) D. Finkel and C. Kizer (Trans.). San Francisco: North Point.

Bernstein, R. (1992). *The new constellation: The ethical-political horizons of modernity/postmodernity*. Cambridge: MIT Press.

Briggs, J. (1992). *Fractals*. New York: Touchstone.

Briggs, J., and F. D. Peat. (1989). *Turbulent mirror*. New York: Harper and Row.

Capra, F. (1996). *The web of life*. New York: Anchor.

Chen, L., and S. Yu. (1986). *The garden art of China*. Portland, OR: Timber Press.

Cziko, G. A. (1989). Unpredictability and indeterminism in human behavior: Arguments and implications for educational research. *Educational Researcher, 18*(3): 17–25.

Doll, W. E. Jr. (1989). Foundations for a post-modern curriculum. *Journal of Curriculum Studies, 21*(3): 243–53.

———. (1993). *A post-modern perspective on curriculum*. New York: Teachers College Press.

———. (1996). Non-linear teaching. Unpublished manuscript.

———. (1998). Curriculum and control. In *Curriculum: Toward new identities* (295–323). William F. Pinar (Ed.). New York: Garland.

Eilenberger, G. (1986). Freedom, science, and aesthetics. In *The beauty of fractals* (175–80). H. O. Peitgen and H. Richter (Eds.). Berlin: Springer-Verlag.

Finkel, D. (Ed.). (1991). *A splintered mirror: Chinese poetry from the democracy movement*. D. Finkel and C. Kizer (Trans.). San Francisco: North Point.

Fleener, M. J. (1999). Toward a poststructual mathematics curriculum: Expanding discursive possibilities. *Journal of Curriculum Theorizing, 15*(2): 89–105.

———. (2002). *Curriculum dynamics: Recreating heart*. New York: Lang.

Fowler, D. (1996). The fractal curriculum. In *Fractal horizons* (pp. 17–34). Clifford A. Pickover (Ed.). New York: St. Martin's.

Gleick, J. (1987). *Chaos*. New York: Penguin Books.

Huebner, D. (1999). *The lure of the transcendent*. Mahwah, NJ: Erlbaum.

Jin, X. (1999). *Su zhou yuan lin [Suzhou Gardens]*. Suzhou, China: Suzhou University Press.

Kellert, S. H. (1993). *In the wake of chaos.* Chicago: University of Chicago Press.

Keswick, M. (1978). *The Chinese garden.* New York: Rizzoli.

Lao zi. (ancient text n.d.). Changsha, China: Hunan publisher.

Mandelbrot, B. B. (1982). The fractal geometry of nature. New York: Freeman.

———. (1986). Fractals and the rebirth of iteration theory. In *The beauty of fractals* (pp. 151–60). H. O. Peitgen and H. Richter (Eds.). Berlin: Springer-Verlag.

Mandelbrot and Julia sets: Mathematics for lovers. Art Matrix, Ithaca, NY: 1990, videocassette.

McGuire, M. (1991). *An eye for fractals.* Redwood City, CA: Addison-Wesley.

Peitgen, H. O., and H. Richter. (1986). *The beauty of fractals.* Berlin: Springer-Verlag.

Shu, T. (1991). Poem. In *A splintered mirror: Chinese poetry from the democracy movement,* (p. 92). D. Finkel and C. Kizer (Trans.). San Francisco: North Point.

Siren, (1950). *China and gardens of Europe of the Eighteenth Century.* New York: Ronald Press.

Tsu, F. Y. (1988). *Landscape design in Chinese gardens.* New York: McGraw-Hill.

Watson, B. (1994). *The Columbia book of Chinese poetry: From early times to the thirteenth century.* (Trans. and Ed.). New York: Columbia University Press.

Contributors

Brent Davis is Professor and Canada Research Chair in Mathematics Education and the Ecology of Learning in the Department of Secondary Education at the University of Alberta. In his research and teaching, he focuses on the relevance for curriculum and pedagogy of recent developments in the cognitive and complexity sciences. He has thoroughly convinced himself that an imagery rooted in fractal geometry is much better suited to matters of teaching and learning than the deeply entrenched, transparent, Euclidean-based system of images that currently gives shape to so much of the educational endeavor.

William Doll is the V. F. and J. R. Eagles Professor of Curriculum at Louisiana State University. There he co-directs the Curriculum Theory Project and directs the Holmes Elementary Education Program. His books are *A Post-Modern Perspective on Curriculum* (1993), *Curriculum Visions* (with Noel Gough, Lang, 2002) and *Internationalization of Curriculum* (with Donna Trueit, Hongyu Wang, and William Pinar, Lang, 2003). Developing chaotic and complex curricula within a postmodern frame has been a project of his for years.

M. Jayne Fleener is Dean of the College of Education and the E. B. (Ted) Robert Professor of Curriculum at Louisiana State University. Her teaching and research have been in the areas of philosophy, computer science, mathematics, mathematics education, and curriculum theory. Her current research focus is on chaos and complexity sciences as applied to educational contexts. She has over forty national and international publications including the book *Curriculum Dynamics: Recreating Heart* (Lang, 2002) The chapter included in this book includes a problematization of New Science as it relates to postmodern inquiry.

Laura Jewett is a doctoral student at Louisiana State University studying curriculum theory and teaching multicultural education. Why Gregory

Bateson? His iconoclastic and interdisciplinary intellectual lines of flight per-petually frustrate, inspire, and move her thinking, thinking about thinking, and thinking about thinking about learning and teaching. Why *Naven? Naven*, as an early and particularly earnest ethnographic articulation of the epistemological complexity of anthropological fieldwork, challenges us to think and rethink what it means to want to know *culture*.

Robert Kahn works with Orthodox Christian Books in England. He holds a Ph.D. in Education from the University of Missouri-Kansas City, where his dissertation topic was "Exploring Chaos: Can Chaos Theory Inform the Curriculum?" He chose to interview Robert May because he thought that Lord May's interdisciplinary research over a period of some thirty years offered many challenging insights on how to develop patterns of nonlinear education.

Robert May is President of the Royal Society and Professor of Zoology at Oxford University. He was appointed Lord May of Oxford in 2001.

Jens Rasmussen is Professor of Education at the Danish University of Education (formerly the Royal Danish School for Educational Studies). In the autumn of 1999 he was Fulbright Visiting Professor at the University of Georgia, College of Education. His main fields of interest comprise pedagogical-sociological problems in the knowledge society (our complex modern society). Currently he is President of the American Educational Research Association's Special Interest Group, Chaos and Complexity Theories. He became interested in Niklas Luhmann's view of systems episte-mology from work his own work done in the 1980s on the individual learner's sense of selection in the construction of his knowledge.

Stacy Reeder, Assistant Professor of Mathematics Education at the University of Oklahoma, has taught and worked in a variety of mathematics classrooms as a middle school teacher and researcher. She hopes her chapter proffers a vision for new possibilities for mathematics education: a vision wherein doing something different can be realized when educators critically question what is mathematics and what it means to know and learn mathematics.

Sherrie Reynolds is Professor and Director of Graduate Studies in the School of Education at Texas Christian University. Her research has been at the interface of psychology and education. Her research is informed by cog-nitive science and learning theory, cybernetics, systems theory, and artificial intelligence and chaos and complexity theories. Gregory Bateson's work was an early interest and has continued as a friendly companion throughout the years. She has numerous publications, grants and presentations. Her book *Learning Is a Verb* (2000) is in its second edition and she is currently co-authoring a book called *Higher Education Revisited: A Geography of Change* (2005). Her chapter in this book explores the recursive nature of epistemol-ogy and the patterns that connect.

Kaustuv Roy, an assistant professor at Louisiana State University in Baton Rouge, teaches foundations and post-foundations courses in education. In the current political climate that reeks of messianic neoconservative zeal, one way to scramble *telos* is to reach deep into irony and paradox. The powerless can exercise power through a paradoxicalization of their general semantics, thereby subverting the symbolic.

John Shotter is Emeritus Professor of Communication in the Department of Communication, University of New Hampshire, and consultant in KCC International, London. His long-term interest is in the social conditions conducive to people having a voice in the development of participatory democracies and civil societies. He is the author of *Social Accountability and Selfhood* (1984); *Cultural Politics of Everyday Life: Social Constructionism, Rhetoric, and Knowing of the Third Kind* (1993); and *Conversational Realities: The Construction of Life through Language* (1993).

Sarah Smitherman is a doctoral candidate at Louisiana State University, where she teaches mathematics education courses. She explains that, "Nonlinear dynamics has affected every aspect of my life. No longer do I think in terms of linear, cause-and-effect relations. No longer do I perceive relationships as isolated. And no longer do I understand life to have static qualities. Everything is interconnected, rhizomatic, dynamic and recursively changing. Because of my passionate belief that shifting towards a nonlinear viewpoint is significant for perceiving the world as interrelated, I explore chaos theory in mathematics and complexity theory in science as fields of research that describe nonlinear dynamics. These areas of study elucidate how life might be perceived as nonlinear. To move away from predictability and towards emergence is a powerful and rich perspective, one that provides uncountable possibilities for curriculum and education."

Darren Stanley is completing his PhD dissertation in the Faculty of Education at the University of Alberta. His work and thinking are focused on what healthy learning organizations look like and what can be done to create them using complexity-related concepts. His insights have come from conversations with medical practitioners, complexity scholars, and friends. Paying a little attention to traffic jams, birds flocking, the North Shore mountains, children at play, sandy beaches, bees, the Chinese Gardens, birches, and chestnut trees hasn't hurt either.

John St. Julien lives and works in Lafayette, Louisiana where he consults with school districts and businesses on education and technology issues. His academic interests include learning theories, social studies instruction, computer-based instructional design, and complexity theories. He is engaged in designing after-school programs and computer-aided learning models based on the principles animating social connectionist learning and object-structured social play. The chapter included in this book focuses on developing an analytic and logic suitable for a complex age that he hopes will prove especially useful in educational contexts.

Donna Trueit is a doctoral candidate at Louisiana State University, studying curriculum and instruction. Her current project is conceiving curriculum as a *poietic space* for creating "selves," drawing on principles of complexity theory, Gregory Bateson, and Charles S. Peirce. An integral part of this project regards the process, analysis and representation of postmodern inquiry. With others, she edited *The Internationalization of Curriculum* (Trueit, Doll, Wang, and Pinar) (Lang, 2002), and contributed "Speaking of Ghosts . . ." to *Curriculum Visions* (Doll and Gough) (Lang, 2002).

Hongyu Wang is Assistant Professor in Curriculum Studies at Oklahoma State University. She received her PhD in Curriculum Theory and Instruction from Louisiana State University. She published books and articles in both Chinese and English, most recently *The Call from the Stranger on a Journey Home: Curriculum in a Third Space* (Lang, 2004). The poetic aspect of chaos and complexity theory inspires her research interest in curriculum at the intersection of science, aesthetics, and culture.

Index

OMPLICATED

A BOOK SERIES OF CURRICULUM STUDIES

This series employs research completed in various disciplines to construct textbooks that will enable public school teachers to reoccupy a vacated public domain—not simply as "consumers" of knowledge, but as active participants in a "complicated conversation" that they themselves will lead. In drawing promiscuously but critically from various academic disciplines and from popular culture, this series will attempt to create a conceptual montage for the teacher who understands that positionality as aspiring to reconstruct a "public" space. *Complicated Conversation* works to resuscitate the progressive project—an educational project in which self-realization and democratization are inevitably intertwined; its task as the new century begins is nothing less than the intellectual formation of a public sphere in education.

The series editor is:

Dr. William F. Pinar
Department of Curriculum Studies
2125 Main Mall
Faculty of Education
University of British Columbia
Vancouver, British Columbia V6T 1Z4
CANADA

To order other books in this series, please contact our Customer Service Department:

(800) 770-LANG (within the U.S.)
(212) 647-7706 (outside the U.S.)
(212) 647-7707 FAX

Or browse online by series:

www.peterlang.com